SUFIS AND SAINTS' BODIES

Islamic Civilization & Muslim Networks

Carl W. Ernst &

Bruce B. Lawrence,

editors

SCOTT KUGLE

Sufis & Saints' Bodies

Mysticism, Corporeality, & Sacred Power in Islam

THE UNIVERSITY OF
NORTH CAROLINA PRESS
CHAPEL HILL

Manufactured in the United States of America

Designed by Eric M. Brooks
Set in Adobe Jenson Pro by Tseng Information Systems, Inc.

This book was published with the assistance of the Anniversary Endowment Fund of the University of North Carolina Press.

The paper in this book meets the guidelines for permanence and durability of the Committee on Production Guidelines for Book Longevity of the Council on Library Resources.

Library of Congress Cataloging-in-Publication Data
Kugle, Scott Alan, 1969–
Sufis and saints' bodies: mysticism, corporeality, and sacred power in Islam / Scott Kugle.
p. cm. — (Islamic civilization and Muslim networks)
Includes bibliographical references and index.
ISBN-13: 978-0-8078-3081-9 (cloth: alk. paper)
ISBN-13: 978-0-8078-5789-2 (pbk.: alk. paper)
1. Body, Human—Religious aspects—Islam. 2. Body, Human (Philosophy) 3. Sufism—Doctrines. 4. Mysticism—Islam.
I. Title.
BP190.5.B63K84 2007
297.4'12—dc22 2006024970

cloth 11 10 09 08 07 5 4 3 2 1
paper 11 10 09 08 07 5 4 3 2 1

This book is dedicated to my teachers in the Chishtī way, who laugh as they cry, knowing that "God rains misfortune and misery upon the heads of those God loves."

CONTENTS

ILLUSTRATIONS, FIGURES, & MAP

FOREWORD

Sufis and Saints' Bodies: Mysticism, Corporeality, and Sacred Power in Islam is the seventh volume to be published in our series, Islamic Civilization and Muslim Networks.

Why make Islamic civilization and Muslim networks the theme of a new series? The study of Islam and Muslim societies is often marred by an overly fractured approach that frames Islam as the polar opposite of what "Westerners" are supposed to represent and advocate. Islam has been objectified as the obverse of the Euro-American societies that self-identify as "the West." Political and economic trends have reinforced a habit of localizing Islam in the "volatile" Middle Eastern region. Marked as dangerous foreigners, Muslims are also demonized as regressive outsiders who reject modernity. The negative accent in media headlines about Islam creates a common tendency to refer to Islam and Muslims as being somewhere "over there," in another space and another mind-set from the so-called rational, progressive, democratic West.

Ground-level facts tell another story. The social reality of Muslim cultures extends beyond the Middle East. It includes South and Southeast Asia, Africa, and China. It also includes the millennial presence of Islam in Europe and the increasingly significant American Muslim community. In different places and eras, it is Islam that has been the pioneer of reason, Muslims who have been the standard-bearers of progress. Muslims remain integral to "our" world; they are inseparable from the issues and conflicts of transregional, panoptic world history.

By itself, the concept of Islamic civilization serves as a useful counterweight to that of Western civilization, undermining the triumphalist framing of history that was reinforced first by colonial empires and then by the Cold War. Yet when the study of Islamic civilization is combined with that of Muslim networks, their very conjunction breaks the mold of both classical Orientalism and Cold War area studies. The combined rubric allows no discipline to stand by itself; all disciplines converge to make possible a refashioning of the Muslim past and a reimagining of the Muslim future. Islam escapes the timeless warp of textual norms; the additional perspectives of social sciences and modern technology forge a new hermeneutical strategy that marks ruptures as well as continuities, local influences as well as cosmopolitan accents. The twin goals of the publication series in which this volume appears are (1) to locate Islam in multiple pasts across several geo-linguistic, sociocultural frontiers, and (2) to open up a new kind of interaction between humanists and social scientists who engage contemporary Muslim societies. Networking between disciplines and breaking down discredited stereotypes will foster fresh interpretations of Islam that make possible research into uncharted subjects, including discrete regions, issues, and collectivities.

Because Muslim networks have been understudied, they have also been undervalued. Our accent is on the value to the study of Islamic civilization of understanding Muslim networks. Muslim networks inform the span of Islamic civilization, while Islamic civilization provides the frame that makes Muslim networks more than mere ethnic and linguistic subgroups of competing political and commercial empires. Through this broad-gauged book series, we propose to explore the dynamic past, but also to imagine an elusive future, both of them marked by Muslim networks. Muslim networks are like other networks: they count across time and place because they sustain all the mechanisms—economic and social, religious and political—that characterize civilization. Yet insofar as they are Muslim networks, they project and illumine the distinctive nature of Islamic civilization.

We want to make Muslim networks as visible as they are influential for the shaping and reshaping of Islamic civilization.

Carl W. Ernst
Bruce B. Lawrence
Series editors

PREFACE

I have had the good fortune of learning from many profound teachers. Some have been teachers about Sufism in Western universities, while others have been Sufi teachers far from any university. One such sitting was especially memorable though brief, and I never learned the name of this custodian of the Sufi shrine at Bōrabānda, on the outskirts of Hyderābād, India. He is a spiritual guide in the Chishtī way, a middle-aged man with gentle, weary eyes framed by thick black glasses and hair that curled down around his shoulders. He sat on the floor of a bare room that was his office, in a formerly white T-shirt and *lungī*, which was his uniform. The only trappings of power that he had were the yellow shawl draped over his shoulders, whose faded brilliance displayed his allegiance to the Chishti way, and an intangible air of authority born from experience that hung about him like a perfume.

Our conversation meandered through many important topics that afternoon until we began to speak about *khūd-shināsī*, self-recognition. "The only question worth answering," he said to me, "is *who are you*. So who are you?" What began as an observation ended as a question, which hung in the air. I suddenly realized that we were no longer discussing Sufism but rather doing Sufism, whatever that really means. I told him my name. "That is not you, that is your name. You would still be you with a different name." I told him by that I am part of a family, community, and history. "That is not you, that is where you are from. Now who are you?" In a gesture that surprised even me, I pointed to my chest, without saying anything, as if to show that my body, beneath my name and before my history, was somehow the existential ground of my being. "No," he said smiling, "that is not you either." He took my little finger and asked, "Is this you?" And then my hand, "Is this you?" And then my wrist, my arm, my head—"No, no, no, you are other than all this!"

The point seems simple when I write it on paper, but at the time it struck me as profound because I comprehended what he was telling me through gestures even as I did not fully believe it. Yes, the body is not a person's identity, and yet the body is not so easily left behind. Yes, too easy an acceptance of the body and its routines can distract one from deeper tides of the soul, but still, I asked then and still ask now, can we feel the soul's force except with and through the body? The body is a limitation that allows us to move beyond limitations. Our conversation that afternoon created for me greater clarity about the issues I was working on in this book, issues about how the body is imagined in Sufi communities, especially the bodies of holy people known as saints and spiritual guides. Clearly, they are issues that cannot be resolved by reading books (or by writing one!) but only by exploring one's own experience of the body and reflecting on its profound transience with an open heart and clear mind.

So this book is incomplete, and necessarily so. It is an initial exploration into a vast subject. Yet I hope it will also invite the reader to reflect not just about Sufism in times past and places distant but also about things much nearer at hand, such as the breath, bones, belly, eyes, lips, and heart, that link us to people and religious ways of life that may seem, on the surface, remote. From the viewpoint of wisdom, all things that appear remote are actually close at hand, maybe closer than one's own hand. As the Qur'an declares of God, *for we are closer to the human being than the jugular vein* (Qur'an 50:16).

Like the body itself, books are more complex than they appear on the surface. Although this book is published under my name, it contains my own thoughts and reflections along with traces of long conversations with friends, teachers, and colleagues. Without their encouragement, I could never have conceived of these parts as a whole and could never have summoned up the courage to weave them together.

I wrote this book while supported by a fellowship from the International Institute for the Study of Islam in the Modern World at the University of Leiden, the Netherlands. I conducted research for the book while teaching at Swarthmore College, which provided me with unwavering and generous support. Grants from the American Institute of Maghribi Studies, the American Institute of Pakistan Studies, and the American Institute of Indian Studies allowed me to complete the archival manuscript research upon which these chapters are based.

Parts of this study began as lectures, and some were partially published as articles; the audiences and editors who shaped this process deserve my thanks. Portions of Chapter 1 were presented as a Swarthmore College Faculty Lecture entitled "Political Bodies and the Body Politic: Saints, Tombs and Power in a North African Urban Center" and also at the DePaul University Faculty Enrichment Program, in Fes, Morocco, later that year. Some material from Chapter 2 was offered at the Second International Conference on Middle Eastern and North African Popular Culture in Hammamet, Tunisia, organized by Université 7 Novembre á Tunis, the Insitut Supérior du Langues de Tunis, and Oxford University, under the title "Wild Woman or Spiritual Sister?" Portions of Chapter 3 were organized as a lecture entitled "Upwardly Mobile: The Uses and Abuses of Muhammad Ghawth Gwaliori's Ascension," presented at Swarthmore College at the invitation of the Department of Religion and at the Department of South Asian Studies at the University of California at Berkeley. Material from Chapter 4 was presented at the American Academy of Religion Annual Conference as "Shah Hussayn's Sexual-Spiritual Play: Homoerotic Acts and Public Morality in the Mughal Era," and I thank for their helpful comments Kecia Ali, Katherine Kueny, Zayn Kassam, and Khalil Muhammad, fellow members of the panel on "Intimate Acts and Public Consequences: Sex, Gender and Power in Islamic Societies before the Modern Era." Core material from Chapter 5 was presented in a lecture at the American Academy of Religion Annual Conference entitled "The Heart of Ritual Is the Body: The Ritual Manual of an Early-Modern Sufi Master." Part of the concluding chapter was originally presented at the University of North Carolina at Chapel Hill (in February 2002) as "The Body in Ritual: Islam, Sufism and the Greater Jihad at the Emergence of Modernity"; many thanks are due to Carl Ernst and the Department of Religious Studies for the invitation.

For the opportunity to speak on these diverse occasions I am grateful, and to the many voices whose comments and questions helped me to clarify my thoughts and spark new insights I am indebted, especially to Omid Safi, Ahmed Karamustafa, Bruce Lawrence, and Carl Ernst for their advice on revision and Elaine Maisner along with the staff at University of North Carolina Press for their editorial guidance. Special gratitude is owed to my teachers in the Kaleemi-Jeeli Sufi community and all those in the Chishti, Qadiri, and Shadhili paths who have generously shared with me their experience and intuition.

NOTE ON TRANSLITERATION

For simplicity, terms and proper names in Arabic, Persian, and Urdu will be represented with full diacritics the first time they occur in the text but will be represented simply in romanized form after that. The transliteration system used throughout this book to represent the sounds of the Arabic alphabet is as follows: ʾ (hamza), b, t, th, j, ḥ, kh, d, dh, r, z, ṣ, ḍ, ṭ, ẓ, ʿ (ayn), gh, f, q, k, l, m, n, h, w, y. The short vowels are represented as: a (fatha), i (kasra), u (dumma). The long vowels are represented as ā, ī, and ū. Diphthongs are represented as *ay* and *aw*, as in the common words *khayr* and *yawm*. The definite article *al-* is not changed according to pronunciation, for ease of visual recognition; for instance, "the sun" is *al-shams* rather than *ash-shams*. The *ta marbūṭa* is represented as pronounced: as a final *-a*, unless the word is part of an *iḍāfa* phrase, in which case it is represented as *-at*.

Transliterations of words from Persian are spelled in letters derived from the Arabic alphabet and follow the same transliteration system as for Arabic rather than how the words are pronounced. The *iḍāfa* construction in Persian and Urdu is represented by –i or –yi depending upon the sound that precedes it. Additional Urdu sounds are represented by the letters ḋ, ṫ, and ṙ for retroflex sounds and <u>bh</u>, <u>ph</u>, <u>jh</u>, <u>dh</u>, <u>th</u>, <u>ḋh</u>, <u>ṫh</u>, <u>ch</u>, <u>kh</u>, and <u>ṙh</u> for aspirated sounds.

In translations of texts from Arabic, Persian, and Urdu, terms in the original language are given in parentheses for accuracy, while explanations of the translator are given in square brackets for clarity. Quotations from the Qurʾan are represented in italics to set them off as distinct from other kinds of discursive speech.

SUFIS AND SAINTS' BODIES

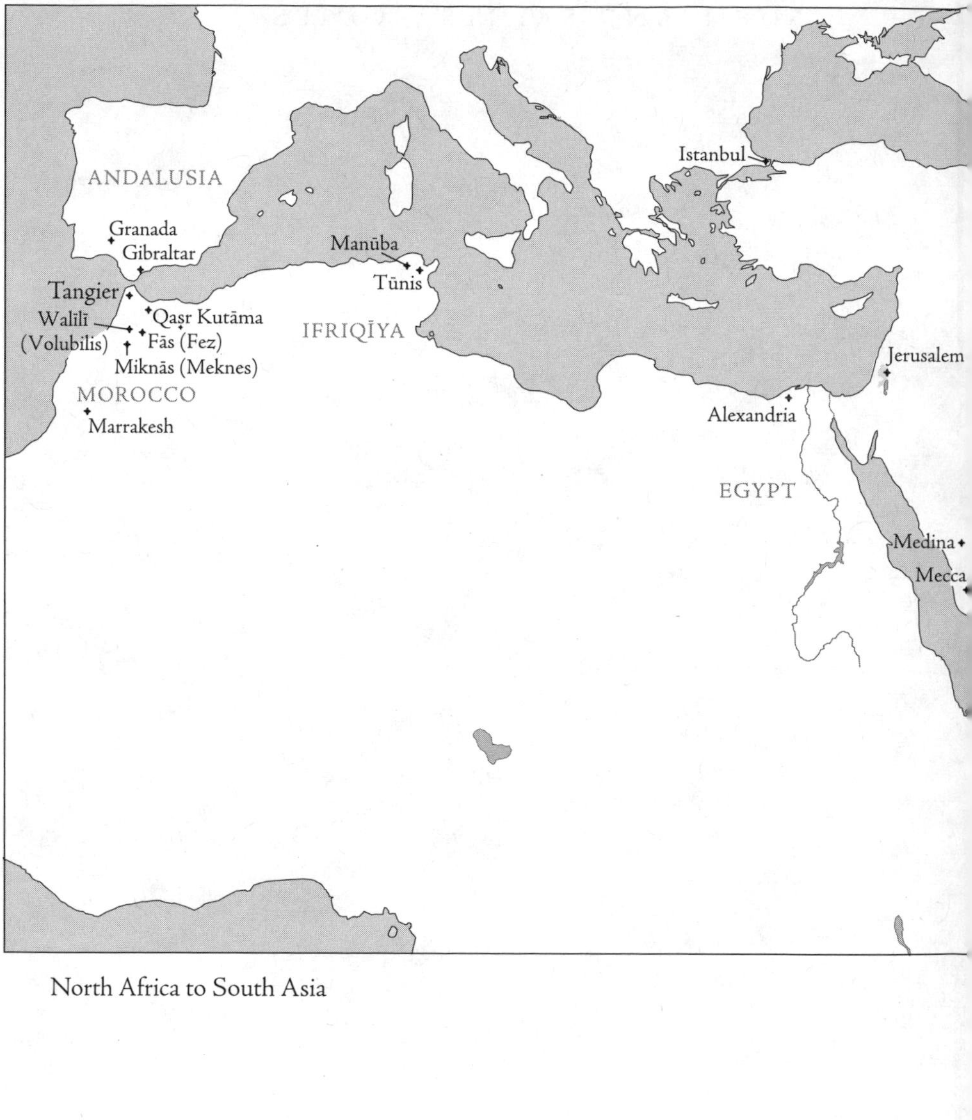

North Africa to South Asia

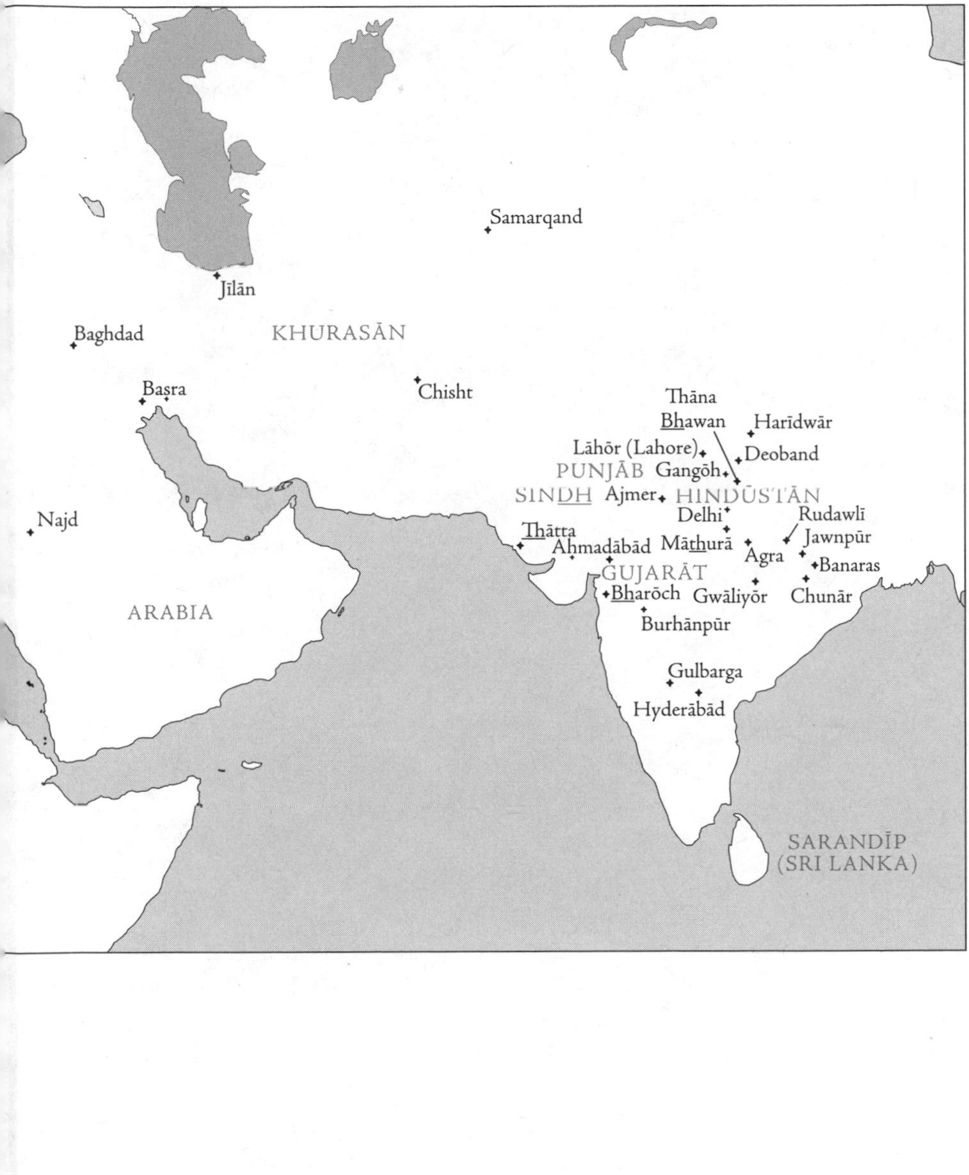
Samarqand
Jīlān
Baghdad
KHURASĀN
Baṣra
Chisht
Thāna
Bhawan
Harīdwār
Lāhōr (Lahore)
Deoband
PUNJĀB
Gangōh
SINDH
Ajmer
HINDŪSTĀN
Najd
Delhi
Rudawlī
Thātta
Jawnpūr
Aḥmadābād
Māthurā
Agra
Banaras
GUJARĀT
Bharōch
Gwāliyōr
Chunār
ARABIA
Burhānpūr
Gulbarga
Hyderābād
SARANDĪP
(SRI LANKA)

INTRODUCTION

You cannot hide
Now that your hearing and your sight
And your skin bears witness against you.
—Qur'an 41:22

This book discusses Islamic images of the human body from the distinct perspective of Sufi understandings of Islam. In particular, it examines the role of saints and their bodies in Sufi communities, stressing that in premodern times saints were figures central to religious life in Islamic societies, in which they often played the role of political leaders and moral exemplars. Before providing an overview of this book's contents and argument, this introduction presents Sufism to an audience that might not be familiar with its tradition. Sufism is Islamic mysticism, comparable to the mystical substreams of other religious traditions but also distinct from them in many ways. It aims not just to understand God, like theological discourse, or to obey God, like legal discourse, but also to love and be loved by God.

Like the Islamic theological and legal discourses, it took some time for the Sufi mystical discourse to emerge from the crucible of the early Islamic community and develop into its mature forms. All three major discourses (theological, legal, and mystical) emerged in roughly the same era. Their advocates interacted intensely, sometimes in cooperation and sometimes in competition, yet all three are authentic human responses to the Prophet Muḥammad's charismatic personality and the scriptural message that he brought, the Qur'an. They also vie with exponents of a fourth discourse, that of philosophy adopted from Hellenism that flourished under the umbrella of Islamic culture.

As an Islamic discourse that centers upon love and intention, both states of the heart, Sufism aims to get beneath the skin of human existence, beneath its routine and rules. Skin, often overlooked as a bodily organ, is the largest organ in the human body, serving as the boundary between self and other, as well as an organ of sensation. The primordial human being, Adam, has a name that derives from the word for earth or dust in Hebrew. However, the same name in Arabic is linked to *adīm*, a skin or surface. The linguistic logic is that dust is the surface of the earth, the skin of the earth, from which Adam was made. Adam's taking his name from the skin of the earth signifies the human materiality that blocks vision and knowledge of what is deeper inside. Sufism, as Islamic mystical discourse, tries to get beneath this skin to a deeper knowledge of human behavior. Our skins, as the children of Adam, both hide and reveal what is inside while giving the body an appearance to the outside world.

It is fitting that God, as represented speaking in the Qur'an, should criticize those who do evil and hide their real intentions by having their skins, which they thought were their safe cover, testify against them on the day of judgment. As in the quotation that heads this chapter, the Qur'an often cites the skin in criticizing those who harbor evil intentions that drive them to commit wrongs in secret and by stealth. Just as the skin conceals the human heart and allows us to express a potential deceitful appearance, on the day of judgment, the skin (along with other parts of the body) will act against our intentions and reveal what has been hidden, as is explained in the Qur'an before the verse cited above. *One day, God's enemies will be ushered toward the fire, distraught and bewildered. As they approach it, their hearing and vision and skin bears witness again them, revealing what they had been doing. They address their skins, "How can you bear witness against us?" They answer, "God has caused us to speak, as God causes all things to speak for God created you in the first instance and you revert inevitably to God!"* (Q 41:19–21). As the skin talks back to its owner, we can hear the Qur'an criticizing the operations of the ego that subvert sincerity, hide our intention, and give an appearance that is false testimony or injustice to others. It is to this ethical urgency and cosmological profundity of the Qur'an that Sufis primarily respond, rather than to its far less frequent legal or governmental directives.

While the Prophet Muhammad was alive, his charismatic presence and ability to speak for God through revelations brought Muslims into a powerfully concentrated unity. Muslims not only memorized the Qur'an and recited it in prayer but also carefully observed the Prophet's ethical behavior and bodily comportment for signs of God's guidance. His wife, ʿĀʾisha, would later reveal the seamless fusion between God's presence through speech and the Prophet's personality by teaching that "Muhammad was the Qur'an walking." Muslims of the early community were so moved by his charismatic presence that they sacrificed their economic well-being, social status, established customs, and often gave their lives in combat in order to join and defend the fledgling community. Under Muhammad's guidance, they formed an Abrahamic monotheistic community that overcame tribal rivalries, family chauvinism, and class inequalities. The early community, after migrating to Medina, even managed to set up a polity that was multireligious and multiethnic by entering into a civil compact with the Jews, who had long lived there as neighbors and rivals of the Arab tribes.

This successful experiment was short lived. The Arab elite aggressively rejected the Muslim experiment, driving the Muslims out of Mecca, attacking them in Medina, and involving some of the Medinan Jews in their strategies. The Muslims responded militarily and against all odds defeated the Meccan Arab elite, absorbing their tribal clients into the now swelling Muslim community. Upon the Prophet Muhammad's death, this Arab elite became nominally Muslim and took over political power. They seized the political force of Muhammad's experiment and fashioned from it an imperial ideology, advocating a morality of entitlement and an ethic of martyrdom. Their project was hugely successful in outward terms, and the Islamic empire toppled surrounding agrarian empires from Spain to India.

The empire's very success bred discontent. Thoughtful and pious Muslims looked back from their material plenty and imperial grandeur to the impoverished times of the early Muslim community. A movement of ascetic renunciation gathered force, which was critical of the Arab elite and preached the awe-filled fear of God's judgment and a return to the example of the Prophet. This ascetic reaction to imperial conquest formed the origin point for all three of the Islamic discourses noted above. Moderates in the ascetic movement reacted to imperial prerogative by creating Islamic legal discourse: they addressed the practical need to regulate all affairs and transactions (ownership, trade, taxation, contracts, marriage, and inheritance) while infusing it with the urge to create a salvific society that embodied ideals of humility, piety, and justice. Radicals in the ascetic movement belittled practical action in the world in favor of other-worldly devotion: they wore only wool; renounced ownership of property, the saving of money, and the establishment of routine family life; and retreated to devotional centers outside urban areas, thereby adopting some practices that resembled ascetic Christianity, which had flourished in areas that became heartlands of the Islamic empire, like Syria, Iraq, and Egypt. Revolutionaries in the ascetic movement revolted politically against the imperial elite, as in the Khārijī and Shiʿī movements.

When ascetic scrupulousness and empire cooperated, they created Islamic law. When ascetic righteous anger and empire clashed, they gave rise to revolt. In between these two extreme reactions was a broad middle ground. Suspicions that the imperial leaders were not acting in good faith produced a rationalist response that endeavored to define faith through discursive theology; this response was represented by the *mutakallimūn*, or theologians, with their many competing schools, from the early Marjiʿī and Muʿtazilī to the later Ashʿarī and Māturidī schools. Such suspicion also produced a response that embraced a nonrational dimension of humanity, calling Muslims to living faith through mystical experience; advocates of this response were the Sufis, who taught a kind of noetic knowledge based on personal experience, inward illumination, and mystical intuition. Their earliest proponents were disciples of the great ascetic theologian Ḥasan al-Baṣrī (died 728), and their movement slowly distinguished itself from the general ascetic reaction over the next three centuries.

Sufis denied the deferral of "the next world" (al-Ākhira) promised by the Qurʾan to some later time. Jurists accepted this gap of deferred time, claiming that it must be bridged by legal rectitude and moral merit. Theologians also accepted this gap as an ontological gulf between the soul trapped in matter and the transcendental immaterial God, to be bridged by rightful belief and eventual resurrection. Sufis, in contrast, were dissatisfied with these stopgap measures. Why try to plug the gap with systems of law or doctrines of belief when one can plunge into the depths of the gap itself? Sufis insisted that "the next world" is immanent in this world. Judgment day is this moment and none other. God's presence is here and not elsewhere. God's presence permeates the world, behind or within or despite its appearance. They argued that anything less than this was admitting that the phenomenal world has an independent autonomy in separation from God, which limits God's nature as "the One real," *al-Ḥaqq*. So Sufis refused to agree with theologians' reliance on rational intellect to apprehend God as purely transcendent. Insisting on God's transcendence to the point of denying immanence is a limitation of God and a denial of God's attributes that are decidedly immanent in the Qurʾan and the Prophet's teachings.

Sufism and the Human Body

It is this affirmation of God's immanence and fascination with God's presence that causes Sufis to value the body in ways fuller and deeper than other Muslim authorities. Their emphasis on loving God as the medium through which people can love each other gave them a special focus on the body and the subtleties of human relations that embodiment entails. They developed the belief that there are special people whose love for God overwhelms, engrosses, and transforms them, taking them far from routine life-ways and beyond routine states of consciousness. These are the saints, the Friends of God (*awliyāʾ allah*), whom God leads through the intuition of selfless love into states of knowledge that are beyond book learning or rational discourse. They teach by inspiration, example, and parable, standing in for the Prophet and extending his charisma into everyday life. Sufi communities that gathered around these saints learned from them by imitating their example and admiring their supranormal acts of generosity and insight (*karamāt*).[1]

It is as if the Sufis saw themselves as the community dedicated to love, which the Qurʾan promised would emerge from the Muslims in their trial. *God will bring forth a community whom God loves and who love God, humble toward those who believe and powerful against those who reject, who struggle in the path of God and fear nobody's reproach* (Q 5:54).[2] The Muslim political elite had lost their ethics and had metaphorically "renounced God's religion" in favor of wealth and power. The juridical elite had lost their insight in exchange for control and authority. The intellectual elite had lost their humility in striving for self-righteousness. Sufis felt that God would give each elite what they hankered after but shift divine bounty to others, to an expansive community of love that would emerge from the hidden recesses of society with no regard to outward status, ethnic pedigree, or rational book learning. The Muslim saints were those given such power through their intimate love (*wilāya*); they became the centers of this community, and their life stories are the proof of divine favor. As one Sufi author, Ḍiyāʾ al-Dīn Nakhshabī, whom we will meet in detail later in this chapter, expressed it: "My dear, whatever has been created in this world or the next has been created by the will of God, but the human being was created by the love of God—*for God will bring forth a community whom God loves and who love God*. . . . O Nakhshabi, love is a characteristic of all human beings / no one can ever be wholly free from its emotion / One who does not suffer from the pangs and distress of love / is not human but a wild beast devoid of devotion."[3]

Sufis formed devotional communities to perpetuate these ideals, communities that gathered around saintly exemplars either living or dead. Such a mystical community became known as a *ṭarīqa*. Western scholars often translate *tariqa* into English as a "Sufi order," each one named after a saintly founder and dedicated to perpetuating his mystical practice. However, this use of "order" is too reminiscent of Catholic monastic orders, from which a Sufi *tariqa* differs in many crucial ways, not least in their approach to the body and sexuality. Literally, the *tariqa* is a "way." In its structure, it is a lineage, representing the transmission of mystical initiation from the Prophet Muhammad through a chain of saints and onward to a community of dedicated followers. In its function, the *tariqa* offers a distinct method of initiation, recitation, and religious exercises designed to bring the dedicated practitioner into a state of holiness compatible with everyday life. Membership in a *tariqa* brings together individuals from many levels of society, including members of the scholarly and juristic class as well as members of craft guilds and mercantile networks. In Sufi communities, therefore, love is not just a personal romantic pursuit or an abstract ideal but rather a "way" of relating to others and therefore of understanding oneself and comprehending God.

The Islamic tradition of spiritual cultivation, Sufism, is the subject of this book. It explores Sufis' engagement with the body through a series of vignettes and shows the persistence and variety of Islamic engagements with saints' bodies from the late medieval through the early modern periods, from North Africa to South Asia.[4] This introduction discusses the congruence of Qurʾanic narratives of the creation of Adam's human body, Sufi understandings of these scriptural images, and modern social theory's conceptualization of the body. Chapter 1 takes us to the late fifteenth century (the beginning of the early modern period) to analyze a tomb shrine built over the long-dead but still-present body of the patron saint of Fās (the city of Fes, or Fez, Morocco). The vignettes then move forward in time toward the nineteenth century to examine not just the architectural presence of dead bodies but also a range of other manifestations: the particular public power of saintly female bodies in Chapter 2, the controversy of bodies in mystical ascension in Chapter 3, the spiritual potential of bodily contact in Chapter 4, and finally the Sufi anatomy of the heart in Chapter 5.

Each vignette centers on a different organ of the body, which gives form to its theoretical inquiry. Each calls upon different intellectual disciplines for the analysis, from architectural studies to gender studies, from the theology of inquisition records to the anthropology of anatomical conceptions. Although a focus on the body may imply a certain intimacy or retreat into the private domain, each analysis focuses on the very public nature of saints' bodies and their importance in political events. That is the advantage of a theory of embodiment, for it connects the intimate spaces of the body to the body-as-metaphor that so dominates public discourses, through which the body can become a marker of communal belonging or a signifier of sacred difference.

One might understandably ask why this study focuses on Sufis and saints. Why not study "the Islamic body" through scriptural interpretation, or legal discourse, or gender relations rather than through mysticism, Sufi communities, and saints? The answer is complex. Sufism invites comparison in ways more open and accessible to contemporary readers than the study of other Islamic discourses. Sufis address those universal values that are most closely shared with other religious traditions; as practical spiritual guides, they engage common concerns of suffering and anxiety, the celebration of joyous rapture, and the terror of confronting death in ways more profound than theologians or jurists. Sufis address these issues with an intellectual sophistication and mythopoetic imagination that make their Islamic narratives accessible and vibrant for others outside the tradition. Finally, Sufism encompasses what might be called "popular Islam" in the period from the eleventh century until the middle of the nineteenth century, when Sufis were increasingly displaced or brazenly assaulted by extremist Wahhabi or literalist Salafi interpretations of Islam, a conflict that features prominently in the concluding chapter of this book. Finally, as mystics, Sufis stress the immediacy of religious experience with, through, and in the body (*dhawq*, or tasting intuitively). Their intense focus on the body, its religious meanings, and its cosmic resonances makes Sufism the ideal place for a study of "the body" in Islamic cultures.

In methodology, this study draws its data from the archives of Sufi literature of many genres. In particular it explores hagiographic texts, a rich and varied genre of great importance to premodern Islamic societies. Hagiographies incorporate fields of saintly biography, family genealogy, manuals of ritual, guides to pilgrimage, accounts of sacred architecture, interpretation of scripture, and assertion of community norms, all amply leavened with poetry. Geographically, the saints whose lives and bodies are documented in these hagiographic accounts span an area from Morocco, in the extreme west of the Old World, where Arab, Berber, and Iberian mix in a distinctive Islamic space, to South Asia, where Persian-speaking Turk and Hindu overlap in a space just as Islamic but differently so.

This geographical span follows my own interests and specialized knowledge, for I lived for several years in Morocco as well as in Pakistan and India, becoming intimately acquainted with Sufi communities in each place and also gaining access to the literary narratives of their saintly ancestors through archival and manuscript records. This approach also has the benefit of generating comparative insights that might illuminate general trends. The choice to bring together in comparison the regions of the far west of the Mediterranean and the wide east of the Indian Ocean echoes Clifford Geertz's aspiration in his popular *Islam Observed*, which did more than any other study to popularize an anthropology of Islamic culture. This study, however, diverges from Geertz's message considerably in its treatment of saints and Sufi mysticism and even in its assessment of modernity. This study makes no grand claims about Muslims and the human body or the historical evolution of Islamic discourses about the body. Its aim is much more modest and tentative (necessarily so, considering the paucity of studies in this field): it explores the hagiographic accounts of six saints, accounts cherished by the Sufi communities that followed them. It analyzes their treatment of the saints' bodies as symbolic resources for generating religious meaning, communal solidarity, and experience of the sacred. In doing so, it refutes the Orientalist assertion that Islam is essentially a rigidly abstract and ascetically rigorous religion, uniquely disengaged from the corporal, without ritual depth, and devoid of spiritual vigor. To do so, this study illustrates the importance of Muslim saints in Islamic societies in premodern times and the centrality of the body to the spirituality and social action of those saints who serve as exemplary models for the Sufi communities that followed them.

The saintly bodies analyzed in this study were selected not only for the vividness with which they illustrate a theme about embodiment but also for their varied life experiences. They include noble and plebian bodies, female and male bodies, living and dead bodies, heterosexual and queer bodies, conventionally clothed and transvestite bodies, and even naked bodies. I have chosen these examples to cover the wide expanse of possibilities for a Muslim's body. Some of these possibilities are far beyond the bounds of what is routinely thought of as "Islamic," either by today's increasingly rigid norms or even by the much more flexible standards of premodern Islamic societies. Each example of a saint highlights certain theoretical problems in a religious studies approach to the body, drawing on resources from the discipline of history of religions, anthropology, and critical studies of gender and sexuality. I focus this somewhat eclectic palette of intellectual theory (scholars of religious studies cannot help but be eclectic, taking into account the complexity of "religion") on a single bodily organ that comes to stand, in a playfully hermeneutic way, for the personality of the saint in question.

This choice of focusing on one organ or body part in each chapter is not to imply that the body is simply the sum of its parts, as it might appear on a dissection table or an anatomical diagram. In fact, the thrust of this book is entirely the opposite: it asserts the holistic nature of the human body as a cultural vehicle that integrates physicality, mentality, and cosmology. The decision to focus on a single body part is purely hermeneutic, to give a point of focus to inquiry into the body that, in its complexity, can quickly become diffused. It is also a decision that follows the discourse of the Qurʾan, which tends to address the body in its parts, allowing parts to stand in for the whole, even to the point of presenting various body parts as having their own voice. The Qurʾan uses this strategy to address humanity with ethical demands and eschatological warnings, as if its message were so profound that addressing human reason and abstract conceptions alone could not convey it and therefore it seeks to embed its message in our very limbs and marrow. This study humbly follows in the footsteps of this scriptural strategy in order to highlight, stylistically as well as analytically, what is distinctively Islamic about Sufi images of the body.

The Body in Religious Studies

It is surprising how little has been written on Islamic conceptions of the body. Islamicists tend to focus on law when dealing with the body, specifically the legal regulations that deal with women's bodies. In a way, there is nothing surprising about this, even if the situation is not satisfactory. Over the past two centuries, Islamic societies have changed dramatically under the impact of European conquest, colonization, and modernity (whether imposed from without or advocated from within). Muslim women's bodies have emerged as the site of contention and the gauge of change, whether as the object of the colonial gaze, the goal of secularist reforms, the concern of traditionalist reaction, or the target of fundamentalist resurgence.

The vast literature on Muslim women's bodies, especially their style of dress, is a symptom of a deeper rift. As political order and social consensus break down under the impact of modernity, bodies take on a heightened importance. This is true whether we focus on Islamic societies or Euro-American ones. In times of political crisis, bodies are no longer accepted as a natural given but rather seen as highly charged with symbolic, social, and ethical significance. The human body is no longer simply appreciated as an organic machine or denigrated as the stable material upon which the autonomous self rides. The body is instead seen as shifting in meaning, as liminal; it can mark communal belonging or signify sacred difference. This insight has fueled recent scholarly interest in the body, specifically an interest in "embodiment" as the human experience of being in and with a body. Though such insights come from Western scholarship, they allow us to circle back to the Qurʾan and its narratives about Adam's breath with new insights, as well as to appreciate the Sufi mystical discourse that is build upon it.

In the past two decades of "postmodern" intellectual debate, the body has emerged as a crucial analytic category. Commensurate with an ideal of human rights and critique of torture, the body emerges as an inalienable dimension of human existence that is powerfully elemental and infinitely malleable. Strathern, one of the more perceptive analysts of this trend in social theory, asks, "When grand theories, paradigms or meta-narratives fail, what can the analyst or ethnographer fall back upon as a starting point or a focus for inquiry? . . . Obviously, our own immediate being, which is most apparent and yet sometimes most hidden to us. . . . Embodiment is, therefore, a new humanism, not exactly soteriological but one that is intended to bring us back to ourselves. It is, put simply, a reaction against disembodiment."[5] Strathern calls the recent theoretical emphasis on embodiment "a muted universalism" in recent anthropology and social theory, which otherwise embrace the relativism of local knowledge and diverse constructions of personhood.

This new perspective on the body in the past two decades has led to an enormous literature focusing on "embodiment." This study delves into this archive in only the briefest way, as many other, more skillful scholars have focused whole books on the issue.[6] They concede that Marcel Mauss and Mary Douglas were the first scholars to have shown us how basic are conceptions of the human body to religious systems of meaning. In his writings in the 1930s, Mauss built upon the sociology of religion of his teacher and father-in-law, Emile Durkheim, but with much closer attention to the human body. Mauss's articles on "body techniques" and on constructions of the human "person" were seminal in this field. He contended that "body techniques" are central not only to becoming fully human in any particular society but also to the religious achievement of communication with God. "I perceive that at the bottom of all our mystical states there are body techniques which we have not studied, but which were studied fully in China and India, even in very remote periods. I think that there are necessarily biological means of entering into 'communion with God.'"[7] Mauss sought to understand the interface between the discrete body of a person and the collective society in which that body moves, acts, and rests. He was not concerned about the use of body imagery in theory or cosmology but rather about the very basic, very physical training of the body: the "arts of using the body." These arts are the most fundamental training, essential to being defined as human within a community; thus Mauss terms them "habitus": Habitus "does not designate those metaphysical habitudes (acquired abilities or faculties) . . . [but rather] the techniques and work of collective and individual practical reason."[8] His basic insight is that there is no natural body. Any person experiences his or her own bodily actions in two dimensions at once: experience of the body in use (what Mauss terms its effective aim) and experience of the body among other bodies (what Mauss terms its religious or symbolic aim). The effective aim of bodily action is instrumental, to achieve an intentional goal, whether for survival or for social purposes. The symbolic aim of bodily action is subtler; Mauss describes it as "the motion of a body among other bodies," meaning that any motion, posture, or action sets up a relationship of continuity and discontinuity with the style of motion of other bodies in the group.

Mauss tried to overcome the Cartesian dualism that had been inscribed into Euro-American modernity. His ideas resonate with ideas from Renaissance and baroque literature, such as the writings of Montaigne, and he recovers concepts of embodiment that were marginalized by the dominance of Cartesian dualism.[9] Following Mauss, Mary Douglas also built on Durkheim's legacy in the sociology of religion. She describes her indebtedness to Mauss as the point from which she takes off. "Marcel Mauss, in his essay on the techniques of the body, boldly asserted that there can be no such thing as natural behavior. Every kind of action carries the imprint of learning, from feeding to washing, from repose to movement and, above all, sex. Nothing is more essentially transmitted by a social process of learning than sexual behavior, and this of course is closely related to morality."[10] In this complementary assessment, she reveals her intention to focus more actively on religion and morality, which in Mauss's essay received only the elliptical but tantalizing phrase about "necessarily biological means of entering into 'communion with God.'" Douglas's first major work on the body, *Purity and Danger,* consequently focused on religious data, Jewish pollution laws, to explore how the human body acts as a metaphor for social order.

In her second major work on the body, *Natural Symbols,* Douglas complements Mauss's insight that the body is "man's first and most natural instrument."[11] She is especially interested in how bodily control expresses social control in order to address Durkheim's central question of how individuals are integrated into a collective entity called society. She concludes that the physical body is not a biological given that is prior to socialization but rather is already understood as a physical body through social categories. She states that the physical experience of the body, always modified by the social categories through which it is known, sustains a particular view of society. There is a continual exchange of meanings between the two kinds of bodily experience: the biological body and the social body, each reinforcing the categories of the other. She acknowledges that society is imagined through metaphors of the body but also that the body adopts forms in movement and repose that express social pressures in manifold ways. Douglas contends that the human body is the central symbolic resource in all religious systems despite their great variety precisely because the body's shape, its divisions, and its privations are universal.[12]

Together, Mauss and Douglas laid the foundation for a theory of the "social body" that is distinct from the physical body. Douglas observed that the social body constrains the way the physical body is perceived. In the 1980s, the sociologist Bryan Turner refined Douglas's perception. In *The Body and Society*, he noted that all societies have to solve four problems in order to exist as societies, and the solutions to these problems affect how the human body is perceived, organized, and conducted. First, continuity over time requires each society to ensure reproduction. Second, continuity in space requires the regulation and control of a population through politics. Third, social life requires the restraint of desire through the elaboration of mores and morality, an issue internal to individual bodies. And fourth, society requires the representation of bodies to each other, facing each other in communication, performance, and recognition, an issue external to individual bodies.

At the prompting of Turner, sociologists and anthropologists have continued to refine such theories in a proliferation of studies of the body in the past two decades. Types of "bodies" have multiplied, with theorists such as John O'Neill differentiating between "the body social," "the body politic," "the medical body," "the consumer body," and the cosmogonic "world body," all of which extend in discursive formations well beyond the physical body.[13] Clearly, social theory centering on the body extends in many directions and addresses varied concerns. In philosophy, studies of social theory critique and overcome the Cartesian dualism between body and mind, which Descartes had adopted from Christian thought and valorized in European philosophy. The work of phenomenologist Maurice Merleau-Ponty has contributed with particular vigor to such debates and provides resources for anthropologists and scholars of religion who seek new perspectives on the experiencing body. In his writing, the mind is not just rooted in and constrained by the body; rather, the body provides a "point of view upon the world" without which thought, reason, and mentality cannot exist.[14] In political theory, such studies address the post-Marxist question of why people obey authority, asked most clearly by Max Weber. They seek to delve beyond materialist explanations to understand how social systems inculcate a sense of order that is not simply ideological but also cultural, disciplinary, and even bodily. The foremost scholar in this line of inquiry is Pierre Bourdieu, who asserts in his research on Algerian Berbers that "the mind is a metaphor of the world of objects."[15] In this way, external space (in the home, the town, the polity) comes together with internal space (thought, consciousness, feeling) to form a person, and the prime mediator between these two fields is the body; he adapts the term "habitus" from Mauss to describe how discipline, training, and memory inscribe social values into the body and how social status and power operations are performed by the body.

Such new directions in social theory have enabled a wide array of provocative studies. Attention to the body as the root metaphor for social values allows scholars to now pay more attention to emotion (as inseparable from thought), to aesthetic performance (as constitutive of political operations of power), and to the senses (as imaginative experience integral to reason). By speaking of the body as an expressive space that allows other expressive spaces to come into existence, new scholarship can portray body's spatiality, as in Merleau-Ponty's words, as "the very condition for the coming into being of a meaningful world."[16] This is what theorists mean by "embodiment." The concept of embodiment asserts that the body is not something residual, like a vehicle upon which the soul rides (in the famous metaphor offered by Plato), or something subsidiary to the mind (as imagined by Descartes). Rather, the body is both the foundation for and the product of the coming into being of a meaningful world, which is human being. By using the abstraction "embodiment," theorists stress that the body is not a thing, as if its materiality made it a simple object. It is instead a concatenation of actions, affecting and affected by culture. It is as much a product of society as it is a precondition for a social person. Strathern, in particular, has emphasized that the human is a "thinking body" in order to overcome the dualism between body and mind that permeates Western culture and philosophy. This offers yet another approach to embodiment, stressing that the body is a means of thinking rather than simply the object of thought.

New social theory about the body is descriptive in that it offers us a more nuanced and refined understanding of how the body is constructed through social images and in turn reinforces social values. However, it is also critical in that it offers activist scholars the means to critique social systems that are judged to be oppressive. In this way, activist scholars in the related fields of gender and sexuality have mobilized new theories about the body to critique patriarchal social order. They have not just mobilized theory but have also actively shaped it. Feminist and queer-liberationist scholars, such as

Michel Foucault and Judith Butler, have been particularly productive, and their ideas have been widely used by others. Their theorizing displays the tension between having to account for the persistence of patriarchy, which fixes gender categories into hierarchical order and limits what sexual expression is deemed moral, and struggling to open a space of acceptance (intellectual, moral, and legal) for "queer" performances and identities that transgress patriarchal boundaries.

In these varied ways, current social theory about the human body has bourgeoned during the accelerating breakdown of philosophy based on "reason." Of course, appeal to the purported supremacy of reason has reinforced the imperialist domination of Europe and America, based on theories of racial superiority, over the Asian and African worlds (which are largely but never totally Islamic). Racial anthropology fell into disuse only because the Nazis applied its ideas and techniques to other European bodies, rather than to "primitive" or "oriental" bodies that were subject to European colonial domination.[17] The breakdown of Euro-American domination has intensified the search for universal values on which to base a politics of civil society after decolonization (in the period after World War II through the 1960s) and more immediately after the dissolution of Cold War ideologies. How have these new theories of the human body affected the story of religion in general and the study of Muslims in particular?

The answer is in an increasing intensity, thanks more to anthropologists than to specialists in the Islamic tradition, who seem stubbornly reticent to embrace advances in social theory that might disturb their philological and textual expertise. However, scholars contributing to the new literature on religion and the body seem to shy away from Islam; worse, many do not recognize that this leaves their writing with serious gaps. It is as if Western scholarship has surrendered Islam to Wahhabi puritans to define as a uniquely "disembodied" religion. This is a very deep problem, one we will explore in the conclusion. For now, let us gauge its depth by considering the example of a French project to bring international scholars together to create a three-volume exploration called *Fragments for a History of the Human Body*. Promisingly and provocatively, the editors aim to address religion up front in the first volume; they ask how we measure the distance and proximity between divinity and the human body "not in order to investigate the presence or absence of anthropomorphism in the conception of divinity. The question to be asked here then is not: given the human body, how does a warrior of ancient Greece or a Christian mystic of the late Middle Ages, a Spanish Kabbalist or a Daoist master, imagine his or her gods? But rather the opposite: what kind of body do these same Greeks, Christians, Jews or Chinese endow themselves with—or attempt to acquire—given the power they attribute to the divine?"[18] The editors then draw together a vivid collection of essays on Greek, Jewish, Hindu, Daoist, Gnostic, Orthodox Christian, Latin Christian, and Japanese Buddhist cultures spanning the classical and medieval ages before following the transformations in Christian Europe through the Renaissance, Reformation, and modern transmutation, all enticingly sprinkled with visual images. This expanse of spatial, cultural, and temporal diversity is impressive, and its scope belies the word "Fragments" in the title. However, there is no mention of Islam. It is as if Islam were unique among other world religions in prohibiting discussion of the body.

Fortunately, some scholars are not content with such a glaring omission. Talal Asad has been particularly acute in forcing anthropology of the body into questions of comparison between Islam and Christianity, focusing on *discipline* as a term that bridges political questions of authority with religious concerns about tradition. His approach is promising, for it forces scholars of Islam to pay more attention to ritual as the performance of power in an approach that includes the theoretical subtleties of Catherine Bell in the study of ritual.[19] Less persuasive is the ethnographic work of Fuad Khuri, which investigates the body by focusing on gestures and postures (kinesis) in Arab culture; this approach is faulty in that Khuri assumes that Arabic culture defines Islamic culture and that contemporary Arabic culture offers a timeless access to what is essentially Islamic.[20] More promising is the work of Marion Katz, who explores the legal regulations that systematize orthodox body practices in classical Islamic culture, combining attention to classical texts with contemporary anthropological attention to body technique.[21] Pnina Werbner and Helene Basu have pushed the limits of past Islamic scholarship with their study of the performance of charisma through body practices. However, while trying to incorporate many different angles of insight from social theory and feminist theory, their study becomes amorphous and abstract. This present work will try to follow their hints while maintaining a more concrete focus on discrete case examples in people known as saints and the hagiographic texts that present them to the public.[22]

This brief overview of recent scholarship in Islamic studies shows the tension within the field over whether and how to adopt recent theoretical advances in the anthropological and philosophical study of the human body. Recent advances in studying embodiment in Islamic culture are due largely to the work of female scholars, who use, sometimes explicitly and sometimes only implicitly, feminist theory and its critique of power relations that are naturalized through gendered social roles. This book contends that extending the study of embodiment into Islamic studies is crucial, not only for women but for men, as feminist insights lead us to more general insights about power and its unequal distribution through forms of social order that are rooted in cultural notions of the human body. If this study achieves nothing more than this, it will have been successful. As scholars try to write an inventory of practices that make up "the Islamic body," it is hoped that this study might also persuade them that the composite picture of such an Islamic body will be complete only with the inclusion of Sufi mystical practices, in addition to gender performance, sexual norms, legal mores, moral exhortations, and political constraints.

Vital Signs of Embodiment

Fortunately, scholars from Islamic backgrounds are integrating social theory about the body with their rich cultural and devotional legacy. Recent scholarship in Arabic addresses the deep tension within Islamic discourses over whether the body can or should be viewed as a holistic entity. In this section, we will try to reintegrate the holistic body by restating the advances in the theory of embodiment presented by Western phenomenology and refining it with keen interventions by a contemporary North African Arab scholar who has contributed to the debate but may not be known to Anglophone readers. Farīd al-Zahī, a Moroccan scholar of Arabic literature and Islamic cultural studies, will be our major interlocutor.

His study, *The Body, Its Image and the Sacred in Islam*, is a major contribution to the field. Al-Zahi translates into Arabic advances in the study of embodiment from French scholars (primarily Merleau-Ponty but also Foucault, Ricoeur, and others), combines them with the comparative study of religion (via Eliade) and psychoanalysis (via Lacan), and applies their insights to the literary, scriptural, and cultural legacy of Arab Islamic society. In doing so, he moves Arabic scholarship far beyond its former limits; before his work, discussion of the body in Arabic scholarship revolved around aesthetic beauty and sexuality. Although such approaches are useful and often beautifully written—for example, Abdelwahhab Bouhdiba's *Sexuality in Islam* or Ibrahim Mahmoud's *Geography of Pleasures*—they give us only partial views of the human body. Al-Zahi takes as his primary dialogue partner Malik Chebel, who contends that Islamic culture addresses the human body only in its parts and never as a holistic entity.[23] In arguing against Chebel's assertion, al-Zahi makes an important intervention in the phenomenological discourse about the body, one rendered possible by terminological subtlety in the Arabic language. He tries to reintegrate the many different "bodies" enumerated in Western theory, seeing them not as different bodies, as the Western terminology suggests, but as different dimensions of what is, frustratingly, a singular body.

In doing so, al-Zahi struggles against the tendency for the body as a whole to dissolve from view, even as its parts are manifest to consciousness. It is as if Western theory confirms our everyday experience that we can never, from the perspective of being embodied, see the body as a whole. Only in a mirror or diagram or another can we see the appearance of a whole body, but then it is only a surface appearance and not one's own body. Therefore, al-Zahi stresses the need for a phenomenological model upon which we can reflect, as in a mirror, our own sense of being in a body. We will restate his argument here, translated into English from the Arabic, and expand upon it wherever possible.

Al-Zahi contends that there are four basic dimensions of bodily experience, all integrated in the singular body. These can be imagined as concentric circles, with the physical body in the center like a core, with progressively more expansive and diffuse circles surrounding it, connecting the physical body to the wider world and defining, in turn, the body that is their core. We will try to represent this as a visual diagram, even though al-Zahi articulates this sense of expanding and diffusing circles through language alone. He builds his system around the Arabic root letters *j-s-d*, which provide the basic structure of the simple word *jasad*, the body. We can render his system into English by finding or inventing equivalent terms that expand upon the term "corps," the body. Each layer of bodily experience will be described in detail in what follows: *jasad*, or corps; *jasadī*, or corporal; *jasadānī*, or corporeal; and *jasadāniyya*, or corporeality. The whole ensemble, all layers taken as holistically, would be the full experience of "embodiment."

The core of the experience of embodiment is the body (*jasad*, or corps). The body, or corps dimension, refers to the material grounding of the human being. As al-Zahi explains, "The body is the first given. It is the locus that forms the foundation of life, motion, action and consciousness. The body is a prior acquisition, before the spirit. In its position as our first criterion for existence, it forms the center of our being and its necessary gauge."[24] Contemplating the skin makes us realize that there is much more to the body than simply matter. The skin is dead matter that the living body sloughs off,

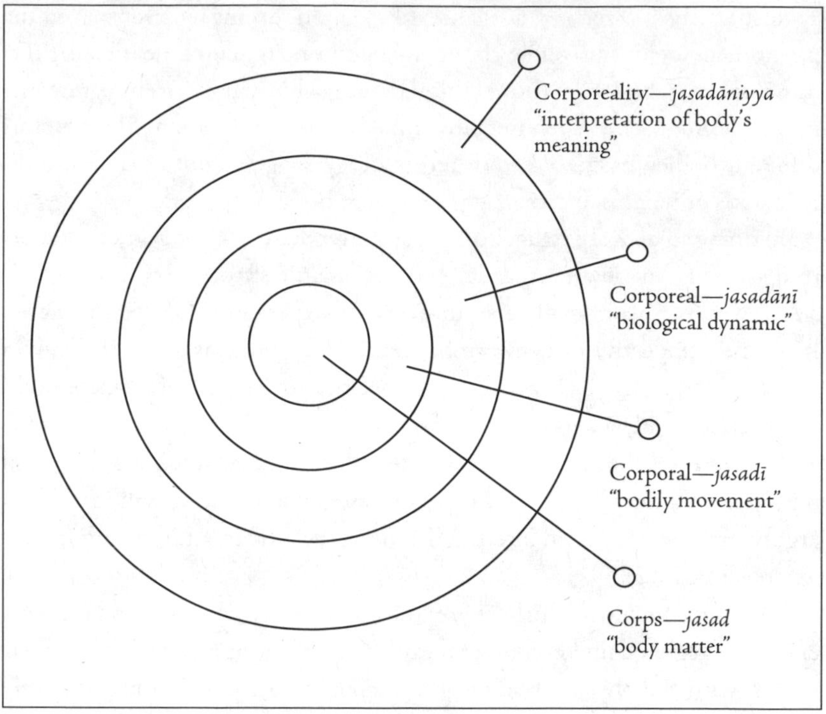

Phenomenological Scheme of Bodily Experience or "Embodiment"

but it is matter animated by motion of the body beneath it: it presents an appearance, a display that is like "clothing" the body with expressive potential.

Actual clothing is easier to manipulate than skin into symbolic meanings and differential status. Its amplification of the skin allows us to identify a further level of embodiment, which al-Zahi calls the bodily dimension (*jasadi,* or corporal). This dimension consists of how the body's material forms an expressive outward appearance and a medium of communication. "The bodily is an expressive dimension. Although the human being is present foremost in the world as embodied, the human exceeds the body itself, in which is latent the ability to express. The body constantly moves itself in theatrical display in many forms. There is the bodily expression of silence, like the appearance of the body itself or expressions of the face alone. There is the bodily movement, like movements of combat or theatrical play or sport. . . . There is the bodily movement of socialization, regulated by custom and made visible in daily life and work. . . . Everybody 'speaks' to achieve any social action. In the bodily dimension, every body appears as a body employed, communicating and connecting socially."[25] This dimension, studied by cultural anthropologists, sociologists, and communication theorists, includes Mauss's "techniques of the body," through which it is socialized and formed in relation to other bodies in society.

If the corporal, bodily dimension is the outward movement of embodied being, then the next dimension al-Zahi identifies, the corporeal (*jasadani*), comprehends its inward currents, drives, and processes. It is the biological dynamic of the material body, which is studied by biologists, chemists, and psychologists. "The corporeal dimension is the biological form of the body's life, which enables the body to act, as if it were the body turned inside out. This corporeal dimension is connected, therefore, to every bodily urge and drive, both male and female, sexual and biological, through which are specified the conditions of sexual and intimate relations . . . including all things not commonly spoken of with others like menstruation, excretion or ejaculation."[26]

Before moving to the fourth and most abstract dimension, corporeality (*jasadaniyya*), al-Zahi offers a concise summary. "The body is the a priori material while the bodily is an almost ethnographic description of the daily postures of the body in its expressions and action. Then the corporeal becomes the personal inner dimension of the former two. Finally corporeality is the higher practices of the body and the appearance of its interpretations. It is a mental superstructure completing a holistic view of the body but is also instrumental in turning attention away from the body in alienation."[27] The dimension of corporeality is an image of the imagination that allows us to conceive of the human being as rooted in the body but not limited to the material body. That is, the physical body is also, always, a social body, social in that it expresses outwardly to others in a continual interplay of signs, and social in that its inner, personal needs and drives find fulfillment only in connection and cooperation with others, whether these needs are nutrition, shelter, hygiene, sex, or emotive affiliation. Our social interactions with and through the body allow the body to participate in and to be shaped by the larger community. They allow a single body to be part of a "corporate body" that is community, society, and polity in which life is not reduced to the biological organism of the body but rather is expanded as life in a network at once more durable and also more diffuse. This reality of bodily life gives rise to thoughts, images, and imaginary schemes by which we think of the human person as greater than the body in which she or he dwells. This is the dimension of embodiment studied by scholars of religion, symbolic anthropologists, and political theorists who are interested in the symbolic meaning of the body that is projected onto wider fields like the polity, the culture, or the cosmos.

The dimension of corporeality gives rise to concepts of the soul, which both enlivens the body and outlives it. However, such conceptions of the soul as a spiritual being existing before the body, beyond the body in this world, and after the body decays in the next world are never finally triumphant. Even as people think and imagine that way, their bodies are constant reminders (through hunger, thirst, exhaustion, sickness, pain, and suffering) of the human body's limitations and eventual reversion to minerals, from which it was compounded in coming into being as a living organism. This reversion is death. So the dimension of "corporeality" is a conception of reality that comprehends our embodiment in a body that dies and also transcends (or struggles to transcend) its inherent limitations. Corporeality is our consciousness of the ultimate reality of our embodied nature, which must answer not only what the body becomes when it is no longer us but what we become (in a moral sense) by being in the body. It has to answer these ultimate questions of meaning: Why are we in bodies? What is the purpose of this embodiment, seeing as how the body inevitably becomes something alien to us and not us? In what way do we, as embodied beings, participate in a greater whole, even as the part that is particular to us, the body, our ground of material being, breaks down from a whole into parts that cease to function?

With respect to the circular diagram of these dimensions of embodiment, some clarification is necessary. The outer layers of these concentric circles are not dispensable or inessential, as might be suggested by the diagram or the term "core." Rather, the outermost edge feeds back into the center; the physical body as a biological organism could not survive without the social, cultural, and symbolic dimensions that surround and permeate it. The whole is not reducible to its parts.

This is the phenomenological scheme of embodiment (or corporeality) that emerges from modern theory when read by a contemporary Arab scholar against the background of Islamic theology and literature. Al-Zahi adopted these four dimensions in order to argue against Chebel's assertion that Islam speaks only about the bodily and corporal dimensions and encourages Muslims to live only in the corporeal dimension; he argues that Islam grants a special importance to body parts and organs but does not comprehend the embodied human being as a holistic entity. Chebel asserts that Muslims find it sufficient to focus on individual body parts: "The vast majority of references to the body in Islam are to the body parts rather than to the whole body. Therefore the Muslim world gives importance only to the heart, or the hand, or the eyes, or the sexual organ."[28] In response, al-Zahi asks whether the matter is really one of the absence of Islamic imagination of the body as a whole: "Does the imagination exhibited by the foundational Islamic texts cancel out the innovative developments opened by the Muslim theologians, philosophers and Sufis? Isn't the matter really about practical transactions with the parts of the body that aim to manifest a practical cultivation of faith on the one hand and try, on the other hand (to which Chebel did not pay enough attention as it deserves) to infuse it, through numerous sacred symbols, into some body parts like the heart?"[29]

This study follows these insightful questions of al-Zahi. It insists, like al-Zahi does, that Islamic discourse focuses on body parts in a limited vision only when Islam is reduced to the Islamic legal discourse, which is all too common among Western analysts and among some Muslims. In contrast to Islamic law, Sufi discourse, which is just as "Islamic" as legal discourse, as it forms an extension and interpretation of the Prophet Muhammad's mission and legacy, is rich with discussions of the body. Islamic law actually needs insights from Sufism to reform its legal structure, especially around issues of human rights, civil equality, and respect for ethical inviolability of individual bodies. This book focuses on Sufism and the body, in part, to foster that necessary dialogue.[30]

The phenomenological scheme described by al-Zahi is very useful. It sums up concisely the insights of contemporary social theorists who struggle to overcome the Cartesian split between mind and body. It emphasizes that human beings are "thinking bodies" and that we think through our bodies rather than despite our bodies. The four levels of bodily existence presented by al-Zahi fuse in each human being, allowing us to live, move, communicate, think, and imagine. "Embodiment" is the abstract term that denotes this state of fusion that gives us our unique being. However, once consciousness arises from an embodied being, it can distinguish itself from the body's materiality. Embodiment is the existential ground upon which consciousness arises, but once it arises, consciousness can assert a dichotomy or disassociation between itself and the materiality of the body that it senses, observes, and conceives. Contemporary phenomenological studies of embodiment can insist that a Cartesian split is an epiphenomenon rather than an ontological reality, but such a split (between mind and body, between thought and sensation, between consciousness and materiality) is a persistent feature of human experience.

Our phenomenological scheme of embodiment must take into account not only the outer dimensions of bodily existence, in physicality, biological drives, social connections, cultural expressions, and religious speculations. It must also address the inner boundary that allows the ego to have different states of consciousness in relation to the body. This study presents four dimensions of bodily consciousness, venturing to supplement and refine al-Zahi's scheme. These four dimensions intersect with the four levels of bodily existence that al-Zahi describes, like four quadrants of the circular diagram. Each dimension describes a basic type of consciousness of the body. Each designates a different mode of relation between the ego and the body, marking different degrees and modes of separateness and control asserted by the ego over the body in its various activities (beyond the basic preservation of the body itself). Three of these states involve waking consciousness in which the ego is aware of itself as distinct from the body, and one involves sleeping consciousness in which the ego is not aware of the body as distinct from itself. The three waking states are restraint, engagement, and enrapture; the fourth is release. Restraint and engagement both stress the ego's distance from and transcendence above the body; in contrast, the states of rapture and release emphasize the ego's intimacy with and immanence in the body. Each kind of consciousness of the body determines certain kinds of bodily comportment in activities as varied as social action, sexual acts, and religious meaning.

The first kind of consciousness through which the ego relates to the body is restraint, or "being against the body." It is most clearly displayed in ascetic control, when consciousness is pitted actively against the body's demands and sensations (beyond what is minimally necessary for the biological continuity of the body). Ascetic control can sometimes threaten to impinge on the body's continuity or even its survival, as in extreme fasting, penitential self-mortification, or other forms of sensory deprivation that actively oppose the body's dominance over consciousness. In far more moderate ways, restraint is the basis of any ritual activity, like prayer or recitation, that focuses awareness away from sensuality of the body. In sexual terms, restraint is the type of consciousness that holds the body in check through celibacy and denial of sexual urges. This type of consciousness is found in less dramatic forms that are nonetheless sexual, such as when people engage in sexual situations to test themselves with temptation or expose themselves to disciplinary pain, or when they engage in sex for pleasure but withhold themselves from orgasm in order to practice restraint and sublimation of sexual urges, as in Tantric ritual. In its furthest extreme in religion, this

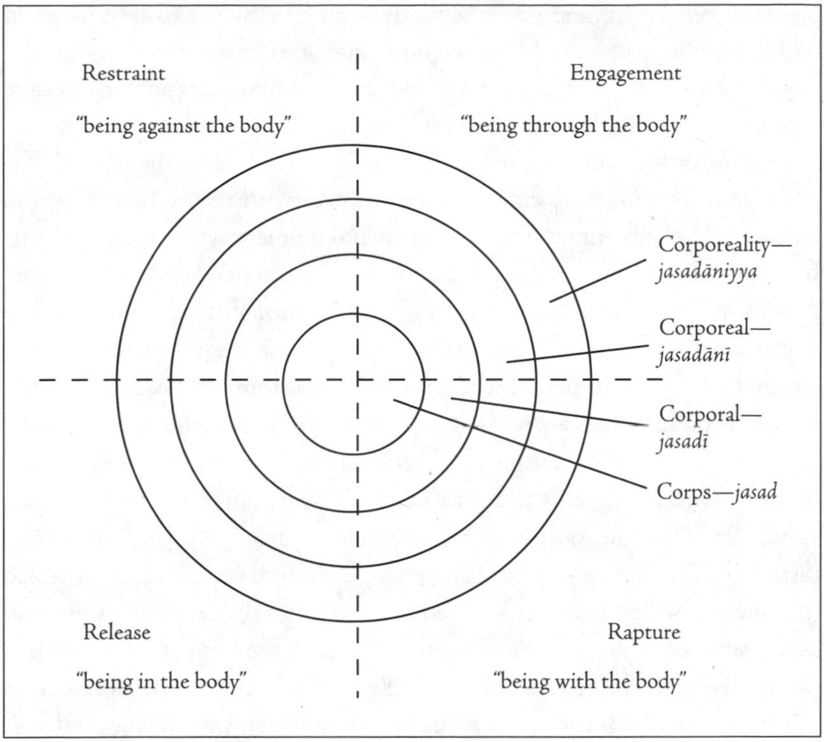

Phenomenological Scheme of States of Consciousness about the Body: The Ego's Posture toward the Experience of Embodiment

takes the form of contemplation in which the body is held totally still and under complete control and intimate surveillance by the ego.

In contrast, a second type of consciousness of the body is engagement, or "being through the body." It is consciousness of the body as instrumental use, as we channel the body to act as a tool to achieve goals beyond the protection, nourishment, and maintenance of the body itself. This type of consciousness characterizes a wide variety of our routine activities in the social world: work for the purpose of social status or material gain beyond what is necessary, building structures, creating works of art, writing texts, engaging in any constructive activity to create structures that will extend the ego beyond its bodily boundaries in space or time. In sexual terms, engagement is when the body is channeled into reproductive acts, not for pleasure alone but for replicating the body and its social identity through progeny and maintaining the intimate ties of family. In its furthest extreme in religion, this type of consciousness takes the form of activities to earn merit, in which the body is focused and extended into acts (ritual or social or artistic) that accrue merit in the next world that will have duration and lasting meaning beyond the decay of the body itself.

A third type of consciousness of the body is rapture, or "being with the body." It is consciousness experiencing intimacy with the body, achieved in a powerful but often tantalizingly ephemeral moment when the ego is suffused into the body's being and movement. This experience leads consciousness to intimate identification with the body through total concentration and absorption into the body's actions. Such experiences are mainly fleeting (in contrast to instrumental use, which is ubiquitous, and ascetic control, which is common) once people reach maturity; often such experiences remind us of childhood. This form of consciousness would include experience of the body in spontaneity and total exertion, such as in play (in pure games, sports, drama, or musical performance) and especially in dance. In sexual terms, this form of consciousness is analogous to orgasmic climax, in which play and sensual pleasure are allowed to build into a rhythm that completely absorbs the ego's consciousness, suffusing it with the body itself. In its furthest extreme in religion, this takes the form of ecstatic experiences, such as possession, in which the ego is so intimately suffused with the body that it temporary loses self-consciousness or self-recognition and is understood to have become united with divinity, possessed by a spirit or divine being.

Finally, the fourth type of consciousness that defines the ego's relationship with the body is release, or "being in the body." It is characterized by equipoise and rest, as when the body is released to follow its own biological processes. When the ego's grip on the body is released, consciousness is allowed to sink in relative tranquility back into the body. This is basically the state of slumber, caused either by the body's tiredness after being directed into activities that tax its resources or by the ego's exhaustion after exerting its control over the body during waking states (or by a happy conjunction of the two). However, such states of consciousness occur not just in nocturnal sleeping; similar, though less explicit, states occur in naps after eating, or in daydreaming during inattention to work, or in a stupor. When the ego is released back into the body, the possibility of dream and fantasy opens, and images from a transpersonal realm can be received (whether called the subconscious, the collective consciousness, or the archetypal realm of spiritual realities). In this state, time and space no longer govern the flow of images, thoughts, and experiences. Upon waking, the ego perceives to have traveled beyond the material confines of the body as it is in the world and to have encountered beings, events, or images from a different and normally inaccessible reality. Being withdrawn into the body, consciousness completely identifies with such imaginary forces that arise from within the body rather than through sensory perception of what is outside the body. Such images and experiences are understood to give insight into the spirit world to which souls are transferred after the death of the body: such is the meaning of the saying that "sleep is the brother of death" or, as a Sufi we will follow throughout this study, Nakhshabi, has said, "sleep is a temporary death and death is a permanent sleep."[31] In sexual terms, this takes the form of the blissful tranquility that often follows orgasm. In its furthest extreme in religion, this takes the form of self-willed death or active surrender to martyrdom, giving up life either for the betterment of the social group (thanatomania) or upon the demand of a divinity (self-sacrifice).[32]

These four states of conscious experience of the body overlap with a fifth state, regeneration, or "being for the body." Regeneration is when the survival urges of the body drive the ego to continue the body's own existence. It is a state that focuses on the core activities that constitute our "animal nature" as embodied beings: to consume nourishment; find protection from danger; maintain the body through excretion, hygiene, and restoration of health; and rest in safety in order to engage in another round of consumption.[33] We often denigrate such activities as relating to animals and not humans, but that is because our cultures often denigrate the body itself. Clearly, these core activities of the body as an animal body blur gradually into the four forms of bodily experiences outlined above. Restraint is necessary to endure hunger, thirst, pain, and distraction while hunting or gathering food and drink. Engagement is necessary for all manner of practical skills in making tools or structures to secure the body's safety. Rapture is part of the body's natural process of digestion and satisfaction. Finally, release is a direct manifestation of the body's need to shut down in order to restore its energy and rejuvenate its processes.

However, the forms of bodily experience should never be reduced to the body as a biological organism, important as that core might be. Rather, our human experiences of the body are rooted in the biological core of body rejuvenation but quickly move into practices that are social-cultural and gestures that are symbolic-religious. Our formation as human beings who conceive through signs (in language as well as conceptual thought) opens up distance between our self-consciousness and our biological ground as an organism. Therefore, the body is not simply reducible to the biological organism that each human being is; rather, the body is a cultural idea and a vessel for religious meanings at the very same time as it is a biological entity. One only has to glance at the literature on medical anthropology to realize how culturally specific and globally varied are human conceptions of what a human body is, how it is composed, why it maintains its life, and to what else in the cosmos it relates as it thrives in its rhythms, frequently suffers, and inevitably fails.

This phenomenological scheme charting embodiment's dimensions offers us a way to understand how the body can be a biological organism, an expressive medium, a source of psychological yearnings, and a symbol for religious coherence. It is all of these together, fused in our human experience of embodiment. No dimension can be elevated as primary without reducing the richness of our human experience, for the human ego projects itself as different from the body through the complex overlap of these dimensions. This enriched understanding of the body helps us to chart the varied states of consciousness that arise as the ego relates to its body. Such states in turn help us understand the variety of religious responses to the body, from ritual engagement to ascetic restraint, from ecstatic rapture to self-abandonment in martyrdom.

Sufi Guide to the Body

We will need the phenomenological tools outlined above as we confront, in the ensuing chapters, the wide variety and imaginative intensity of Sufi conceptions of the human body. We will also need a Sufi guide to the body to lead us through the complexities of the Qur'an's metonymic strategy of singling out parts of the body to signify the whole of the body. One author who can illustrate for us the importance of this mode of imagining the body is the medieval South Asian Sufi Ḍiya' al-Din Nakhshabi (died 1350). He will be our literary and spiritual guide in this whole endeavor, lest it be accused of taking on theoretical imperatives that are outside the Islamic and specifically Sufi tradition. Nakhshabi wrote an astounding work that has not attracted the scholarly or literary attention it deserves. His work, *Juz'iyāt o Kulliyāt*, "The Parts and the Wholes," serves as a prototype and inspiration for the present study. It explores the human body by combining medical knowledge with Sufi insights and literary eloquence.

Nakhshabi was a prolific author of Persian literature in medieval India.[34] In the Chishtī Sufi community, he followed the example of Amīr Khusrō by combining Sufi spirituality with literary eloquence, and he produced charming lyrics in Persian *ghazal* and *mathnawī*. He translated Indian folktales into Persian and Islamic literary idioms through his original poetic compositions. His *Ṭūṭī-Nāma*, or "Tales of a Parrot," transposes into Persian the Sanskrit tale of a parrot telling narratives of love and amorous adventure. Nakhshabi's eloquent praise of music as the best means to reach an understanding of God marks him as an avid Chishti Sufi, and he writes authoritatively on Pythagoras's theory of musical scales and the relation of Persian classical modes to Indian *rāgas*. In his story cycle, a princess asks her parrot a series of questions that arise directly from Chishti ritual gatherings to listen to devotional poetry set to music: "How did the movements of dance originate? How can the state of ecstasy be brought about? What substance is the human made of which is as heavy as lead and yet soft, and how can such an erect figure lose consciousness? How can the body which walks so gracefully become hypnotized by chanting?" To these questions the wise parrot replies, "The soul is like a bird which is nourished by melodious music and is inspired by the playing of musical instruments. Every agreeable melody that reaches its ear is a part of its life, and every pleasing sound that it hears is a rich portion of its spirit. Music is the sustenance of the spirit just as food is the nourishment of the body."[35] His other compositions bridge the expanse between love epic and Sufi spirituality, like his *Ladhdhāt al-Nisā'*, "Sensual Delights of Women," which is a Persian translation of the Sanskrit erotic manual the *Koka Shastra*, a cousin to the more famous *Kama Sutra*. His other compositions were less sensual and more ethical, such as *Silk al-Sulūk*, a collection of mystical sayings of renowned Sufi masters, and *Naṣā'iḥ o Mawā'iẓ*, a prose work of Sufi advice and admonition.

Between these poles of sensual and spiritual lies Nakhshabi's composition that concerns us here, "The Parts and the Wholes." In this work, he describes the human body, through poetry and prose, so that its inward nature's nobility will shine forth from the dense matter of its outward appearance. He tries to amplify the words of God, who said to the angels *I know that which you do not know* when they protested against God's shaping Adam's body and infusing it with divine spirit (Q 2:30). Nakhshabi addresses the reader to explain his intention:

> This lowly servant desires to mention for the readers some of the varied parts of the body, but not all of them. I will discuss them, but not in the style of an anatomical dissection or in the way of a moralist cataloging their sinful characteristics. Rather, I will discuss them in an ingeniously inventive literary way: If I'm incapable of drawing each gleam from this jewel / How should I begin to describe its luminous essence? The goal of this servant's writing about each noble bodily organ and describing each

> majestic part is this: to write in this composition some words that will stir up your desire and some discourse that will immerse you in passion, with amorous expressions and erotic allusion that can be likened to birds let loose from the treasure-house of the tongue.[36]

Lest our erotic passion fly too high, Nakhshabi cautions us that his descriptions will remain within the tether of modest morality.

> I have limited discussion to the noblest body parts, so that mention of these few parts might indicate the flesh of the entire body. This proposed method should be verified by a basic principle. The principle is expressed by Divine Speech [the Qur'an], for God is the most veracious of all speakers. God says, for instance, *their faces submit to the living One, the One everlasting* (Q 20:11). People may ask why God says *faces submit* when the intended meaning is that people submit their souls to God. The answer of the learned sages is that the noble Qur'an was revealed through the rhetorical language of the Arabs. It was the Arab custom to mention distinct parts of the body and thereby indicate the body as a whole entity. . . . By this principle, it suffices for me to mention certain noble bodily organs and some exalted body parts, because when some part is cited the whole body is present in the indication. . . . So this collection is entitled *The Parts and the Wholes*.[37]

We can take Nakhshabi as our literary Sufi guide and follow his example as he explains his own method of evoking the holistic body through its distinct parts. We can also appreciate his justification of this method through analyzing the rhetorical strategy of the Qur'anic discourse, and we will adopt this strategy to guide us in our subsequent explorations.

Nakhshabi divides his composition into forty parts, each dedicated to a body part. Forty is the number of spiritual completion in Islam, and Sufi meditation retreats typically last for forty days.[38] Reading it over a period of forty days, he hints, will incite in one's heart the same intense passion and love that a Sufi retreat might, and the object of contemplation in this spiritual transformation should be one's own body. "O possessor of spiritual vision! If you take a good look at your own spiritual state, you will find nothing better for you than self-recognition (*khūd-shināsī*). Those who do not recognize their own true nature cannot recognize any other truth. Those who do not know the self, that is who they really are, cannot know anything about others."[39] When he makes a profound statement, Nakhshabi usually follows it in poetry, as if he distrusts the ability of prose to express its deepest meaning. Here the couplet reads: "Since he is ignorant of his true self / he ignores the true rights of others."

Of course, one who knows the true self also knows God, and Nakhshabi turns immediately to this mystical principle.

> The sages have said, "Knowledge of one's own self gives evidence for knowledge of the divine creator," but in the way of contrasts, not of equivalence. Those who know their true nature as temporal beings understand their Lord, who is beyond time.[40] Those who understand themselves to be of contingent being recognize their Lord who is the necessary being. Those who understand that they are deserving of humble servitude (*ʿubūdiyya*) know their Lord as worthy of sole mastery (*rubūbiyya*). Recognize your own self in reality / if you wish to know all else in totality. O people who understand the inner meaning! If you wish to arrive at an understanding of the deepest symbolic meaning of your own self, just take a look at your own bodily form (*ṣūra*). Let your gaze alight upon the inner meaning of each part, from the top of your head to your last toe-nail. You will see that your existence is the setting for several thousand precious essences, like jewels, that you call your organs and limbs. It is bedecked with rare gems of universality and possessed of the radiant beauty of comprehensive totality.[41]

Nakhshabi displays an irrepressibly optimistic comprehension of the human body. Such an attitude became increasingly characteristic of the Sufi tradition once it grew in maturity beyond its roots in the ascetic movement of the early Islamic community.

Sufis came to see the body not as the enemy to be opposed by strenuous ascetic effort (though ascetic exercises continued to play a key role in Sufism) but, more subtly, as a sign of the creator, or rather as a whole *constellation* of signs. In its outward dimensions, Sufis praised the human body as the epitome of beauty in the physical world. In its inward dimensions, Sufis maintained that the body is the locus of the manifestation of God's names and attributes—a theophany of the highest order. It is a universal characteristic of religions that the sacred lodges in physical places: in caves or mountains, in temples that imitate the shape of caves or mountains, in stones or springs or statutes that can be approached through ritual, touched through devotion, and through which sacred power can be channeled into more routine social needs.[42] Sufis pushed this logic to an iconoclastic extreme and claimed that the divine fully manifests only in human beauty; in this way they understood the Prophet's teaching that "God created Adam in his image," that is, in God's own image.[43]

Our exploration of Sufi images of the body rightly begins with the Qur'an's description of bodies, especially the primordial prototype of human bodies, that of Adam. *Then your Lord told the angels, "I am making a human being from earth like clay fired and molded. I have formed him and breathed into him of my spirit, so fall before him in prostration"* (Q 15:28). God tells the angels of divine intent to create the primordial human being with a body of irreducible materiality, made from minerals of the earth, in ways that can be compared to the biblical account (in Genesis 2:7). Such usually inert material can be transformed and can take on shapes of astounding complexity and beauty, like soil kneaded into clay, molded with artistry, and fired into firmness.

According to Qur'anic narratives, the human body, like a clay vessel, takes on its shape only by being hollowed from the inside. Into this hollow of the human body God breathes *of my spirit*. This magisterial image of the material body being enlivened with the breath of spirit that blows into it and through it from beyond is the central paradox of the human body from an Islamic point of view. It is material, therefore ephemeral, limited in space, fragile, even brittle; however, it is material infused with spirit and is therefore eternal, unbounded by space, opening into the infinite beyond waking consciousness and participating in durable cosmic being beyond personal weakness. Or, to put it more precisely, the body is matter that acts as the locus for the manifestation of the divine spirit in the world. We are clay infused with light, matter that crackles with the sparks of the energy of life.

The Qur'an, like all scriptures, uses simple images to make profound statements that inspire endless interpretation. The image of God molding the body from earth like clay expresses God's transcendence: God is incomparably lofty and subtle beyond comparison to anything measured by the human body, which is from earth and returns to dust. However, the stark message of transcendence is tempered by the image of God gathering the earth and kneading it to leaven it for forty days between God's two hands, shaping the shell of a human body. The care and attention of this ongoing act of creation and nurture remind us that the transcendent divinity is also a personal one. Finally, the image of God breathing divine spirit into the clay of the human body expresses God's immanence: God must come to our own level, placing lips to the dust, so to speak, in a life-giving connection more intimate than a kiss. In this gesture, the humble body is suffused with

Miniature painting of Adam's body formed of hardened clay, to which the angels prostrate at God's command, except for Iblīs (upper right), who looks on in jealousy from behind a hill. Painted in Shīrāz (Iran) in 1575. From Gazurgāhī, *Majālis al-ʿUshshāq*, ms. (Paris: Bibliothèque nationale de France, Suppl. Persian 776), fol. 11b.

God's own spirit, a transferring of what seems incomparably distant and unreachably beyond our experience into the space within the body. The life engendered within us by this divine immanence impels us, literally kicking and screaming, into the phenomenal world. The circle is completed by the life we lead in and through the body, with its trials, choices, obstacles, and mysterious epiphanies. Do we make of life an opportunity for greater personal awareness, interpersonal responsibility, and transpersonal love? Or do we cringe in fear, gloat in arrogance, and take shelter in defenses that are inevitably stripped from us? Whatever our response to the experience of life, these possibilities are radically shaped by the human body and how it shapes and is shaped by the human personality, which is, at least temporarily, so fused with the body that it is difficult to separate analytically.

As human beings, we are charged with responsibility (*khilāfa*), the trust of responsible custodianship. *We presented the trust to the skies, the earth and the mountains but they refused to bear it and shied away. Rather, the human being bore it, even though the human being was wrong-doing and head-strong* (Q 33:72). This is the challenge to imitate God or, to put it more humbly, to approximate God's care. As Sufis say, we are called to "take on the qualities of God" (*takhallaqū bi-akhlāq illah*). The Qur'an retells the story of Adam's temptation and descent into the world, which provides the basic images for an Islamic understanding of the body, as it does in Judaism and Christianity. As the Qur'an tells the story of Adam, it places the narrative in this moral framework: the human being is enmeshed in a body, given consciousness and free will, and tempted with knowledge solely in order for us to gain awareness of the responsibility entrusted to us.

The angels were upset at the creation of Adam's body, sharing the reaction of Iblīs (Diabolos, or Satan) as he egotistically rears up in defiance. The angels, as beings created of pure light, nonembodied expressions of God's qualities who perform divine will and express divine glory, cried out in protest against the human being with its peculiarly potent body. *They said, "Will you make in the world one that will spread corruption in it and spill blood while we recite your praise and revere you?" God said "I know that which you do not know." . . . Then we said to the angels "Bow down to Adam!" They all fell in prostration, except Iblīs—he refused and puffed up with arrogance and was one who disavowed* (Q 2:30–34). The angels cried out in horror at the destructive potential of the human being. They decried the very elements that mark human beings as inescapably material in their bodies, like corruption and blood. The following chapters deal specifically with blood and corruption (as well as ejaculation, lactation, digestion, and many other bodily processes). Suffice it here to observe how the angels can see only the horror of the human body and not the sublime. Iblis's defiant reaction was fueled more by arrogant jealousy than by horror, as the Qur'an tells us, *God said, "O Iblis, what is wrong with you that you don't join those who prostrate?" Iblis replied, "I'm not one to prostrate to a mere human being you created from earth like clay fired and molded!"* (Q 15:28–33).

Sublimity and horror are always intimately connected. God quickly reveals to the angels the sublime nature of Adam. Not only is Adam's body endowed with reason and knowledge, but also it serves as the locus for the indwelling of God's spirit and the vehicle for inspiration. In this way, *God taught Adam all the names and qualities* (Q 2:31). In the biblical telling of this story, God teaches Adam the names of all the animals, sometimes interpreted as the names of all phenomenal objects in the world. However, the Qur'an is characteristically more abstract, saying that God taught Adam *all the names and qualities* without specifying to whom or to what they belong and whom or what they describe. For this reason, Islamic theologians, and Sufis in particular, understand Adam to have been taught all the names and qualities of God, rather than simply the names and qualities of phenomenal things.[44] Sufis, however, perceive in this revelation to Adam of all God's own qualities an inspired knowledge that is not simply rational but rather intuitional—it is intuitive paradigmatic knowledge that is given through reflection (*ma'rifa*) rather than rational practical knowledge that is learned through observation (*'ilm*). It is intuitive knowledge embedded in human nature and enmeshed in the human body, which comes to the light of awareness only through human experience, specifically the failure of our reliance on egoistic autonomy and our acceptance of our brokenness in humility.

In this way, Sufis understand the teaching of the Prophet Muhammad that "God created Adam in his image" to mean that God created Adam in God's own image. The Chishti Sufi Muhammad Gēsū-Darāz (died 1422 in Gulbarga, India) gives a succinct explanation as he begins his short "Treatise on Love," or *Muḥabbat-Nāma*: "All praise belongs to the One who in the beginning longed to be known, so manifested the essence to the essence, thereby giving appearance to Adam 'in his image,' and made Adam's heart a goldmine of love (*maḥabba*) and trust, and seated Adam upon the throne of responsibility (*khilāfa*) and established him there firmly. Then God placed on his head the crown of intuitive knowledge (*ma'rifa*) and taught Adam all the names (*asmā'*) and qualities (*ṣifāt*) and descriptions (*nu'ūt*), teaching him the names and words by divine care and grace."[45] This "image" is not merely physical but rather refers to the image or form (*ṣūrat*) of God's qualities, God's ninety-nine names. The challenge of the Prophet Muhammad, to "take on the qualities of God," is understood by Sufis to be a process of spiritual refinement, to purify one's consciousness in order to uncover the qualities of God within one's own nature and thereby change one's outward behavior and enliven one's moral conduct. The human body, therefore, is an impediment to this process if one submits to its processes without critical awareness; however, the human body is the only vehicle through which this process takes place, if one can develop an awareness of the body that accepts its limitations while uncovering with wisdom its profound potential. This is achieved through a mode of embodiment in which human action is not dispersed and fragmented throughout the limbs of the body but concentrated in the breath and rooted firmly in the heart.

Sufis, like mystics from other religious traditions, understand this as a process of rebirth, coming to a new understanding of the self-in-body without having physically died. It is like refining metal though intense heat: heat does not actually destroy the metal but rather burns away the impurities to create a substance that is still metal but stronger, more flexible, more useful, and purer. The mineral matter of the human body is like the metaphorical iron of the Qur'an: *We revealed the iron, in which there is intense harm but also profound benefits* (Q 57:25). The story of Adam is crucial to this understanding, not just for its physical portrayal of Adam's body in creation and birth but also for its metaphorical depiction of Adam's consciousness coming to awareness of alienation, separation, and longing for reunion.

The trial of spiritual refinement is not easy. It is complicated by the whisperings of the tempter, Iblis. Who is this Iblis, whose story is intimately woven into the creation of the human body and our struggle to come to awareness through it? He is the being who first said "I" in contradistinction to God! He is the spark of ego run amok. He is the consciousness that says, "I am better than he!" rather than giving thanks for the blessing of being what he is.[46] Thus when the embodied Adam was shaped, Iblis balked, as the Qur'an describes. *God said, "What prevented you from bowing when I commanded you?"* [Iblis answered,] *"I am better than he is—you created me from fire and created him from clay." God said, "Then get down from here! It is not for you to act arrogantly here. So get out, for you are of the lowly ones."* [Iblis] *said, "Give me respite until the day when they are resurrected." God said, "You are among those who have respite." He said, "For your having misled me, I'll ambush them* [human beings] *along your straight path, then I'll assault them from in front and from behind, from their right and from their left—you will not find many of them grateful!"* (Q 7:10–18).

Unlike the angels created from light, Iblis was created from fire. Fire shares in the nature of light, but unlike pure light, fire consumes matter in order to generate its light, giving off heat at the same time. It was the matter of Adam's body to which Iblis clung and that allowed him to burn with jealousy. Reason and intelligence fueled his jealousy—an intelligence that has run wild and leaps into arrogance. His is reason that misrecognizes his own limitations and ascribes to himself autonomy, independence, and authority that is not his. Unlike the other angels who know nothing other than the knowledge God gives, Iblis generates his own knowledge. He observes the body of Adam shaped from clay and observes his own existence rooted in fire, leaping to the conclusion that he is better, since fire can consume and destroy matter. This is the wrong conclusion, based on accurate observation but warped by egotistical reason.

Flickering between the intimacy of the angels and the materiality of Adam's body, Iblis represents egotistical knowledge, which is detached from the body but consumes the body and strives angrily to gain angelic intimacy with God without ever being able to transcend its inherent alienation. Iblis's knowledge is pride, the prime expression of the ego's impossible will to live eternally. The Qur'anic narrative describes how Iblis tempted and tricked Adam and his partner into a false understanding of themselves, saying, "*Your Lord only forbid this tree to you both lest you become angels or become from among those who live eternally* (Q 7:20). Iblis forged his jealousy into vengeance on God by tempting human beings into ruination, by exposing them to the same egoistic flames in which he himself is engulfed. Iblis's strategy of assault is to whisper in the interstices between perception of body and sense of self in which the ego takes shape. He exposes Adam and Eve to their bodies in their carnal nakedness, making them feel shame for the first time: *So he misled them with pride, and when they both tasted of the tree and their nakedness became clearly apparent to them. They sewed together to cover themselves leaves of the garden* (Q 7:22). The nakedness that Iblis causes them to see is not just sexual, in a sense of being prone to get lost in sensual pleasure, but also psychological, in the sense of being vulnerable to finitude and limitation. Iblis sparked in them a fundamental dissociation between self and body, an alienation from the body through which we assert that the self is autonomous, independent, even immortal.[47] In embracing Iblis's whisperings, Adam and Eve could look at their bodies as different from themselves in a denial of the inevitable decay of the body. More than exposing them to the sexuality of the body, Iblis exposed them to the inevitable decay of the body; he did this to tempt them to disobey God's command in order to win immortality. It is a universal mythic theme, that of a primordial human hero venturing to trespass against divine command in order to steal the secret of eternal life, whether in the form of life-giving fire, the elixir of ambrosia or soma, or the water of perpetual youth.

So far in this Qur'anic interpretation, conventional Muslim theologians and Sufis can travel together. However, Sufis diverge from the mainstream by emphasizing the interiority of Iblis. Sufis understand the tempter, Iblis, to operate from within the human body as part of our individual personalities. Sufis therefore oppose the impulse to externalize *shaytan*, or forces of temptation, and take very seriously the Prophet Muhammad's teaching about the greater jihad. Upon returning from a battle against the Muslim's enemies, the Prophet said, "We have returned from the lesser jihad to the greater jihad." When he said this, the Prophet's companions asked him what he meant. He replied, "The lesser jihad is to fight with swords, but the greater jihad is to counter the enemy here," as he held his hands to either side of his own chest.

The Qur'an does personify Iblis as a cosmic being separate from Adam and Eve; however, it also speaks of forces of temptation as *the creeping whisperer who whispers within the people's chests* (Q 114:5). Sufis insist that Iblis, or Satan, is a force internal to human beings, a force that can be avoided only by introspection, thereby resisting the puritan impulse to project his dark light onto the external world in a dynamic of hatred—hatred of despised social groups, religious others, or the human body itself. Sufis countered the socially powerful groups, like jurists and ascetics, who also addressed, with different solutions, the sense that something is disquieting about the human body. Sufis noted the profound irony that Adam's body was both hollow and filled with light. Its outer appearance is one of being hollow, yet the very matter of the body that makes apparent this vulnerable hollowness is clay infused with light. They imagine the primordial light as the presence of the Prophet (the Prophet Muhammad in essence and also all other prophets who are manifestations of his primordial light). In his arrogance, Iblis perceives only the weak outer form of the human being's clay body but fails to understand that the clay is infused with light.

The folk telling of Adam's creation illustrates this tension, as in al-Tha'alabi's version of *The Story of the Prophets*. "The soil was mixed with

Miniature painting of Adam and Eve driven from Eden into the routine embodied world wearing clothing they stitched of leaves. Painted in Tabrēz or Qazwīn (Iran) circa 1550. According to Islamic folk tradition, they rode a serpent and a peacock, animals whose bodily form Iblīs took on in order to gain access to Adam and Eve to tempt them to eat of the forbidden fruit. Iblīs looks on spitefully from the lower left. From Jaʿfar al-Ṣādiq, *Fal-Nāma*, or "Book of Omens," ms. (Washington, D.C.: Arthur M. Sackler Gallery, Smithsonian Institution, Purchase—Smithsonian Unrestricted Funds, Smithsonian Collections Acquisition Program, and Dr. Arthur M. Sackler, S1986.0251a).

water, then combined with the light of the Prophet Muhammad, which was like a luminous pearl, and was kneaded into a pliable clay. The clay was shaped, and the shape left to dry into a hardened form. . . . Iblis passed by him, saw him and said: 'For what purpose were you created?' Then he struck him with his hand and behold! He was hollow. He entered into his mouth and come out of his rear. So he said to his companions among the angels who were with him: 'This is a hollow creature; it is not firm, nor does it hold together.'"[48] Iblis could see only the hollow outer shell of Adam's body. Yet the very hardness of its materiality is due to the prior pliability engendered in it when the elements of soil and water were infused with the pearl-like luminescence of the prophetic light.

This narrative reveals that Iblis, or Satan, is a force internal to human beings, even if he can take forms that seem to be external to them. To illustrate this, a Sufi master from India, Shaykh Niẓām al-Dīn Awliyāʾ, told a parable about Iblis and his little son, Khannāṣ "the creeper." This name is derived from the Qurʾan's description of "the creeping whisperer who whispers inside human chests" and is an excellent example of how Sufis use parables and narratives to offer indirect interpretations of scripture that are all the more powerful for being indirect.

> After Adam—upon whom be peace—descended from heaven into this world, Eve was one day sitting by herself. Iblis came and brought Khannas with him. To Eve he said: "This is my son. Take care of him." Then he left. When Adam returned, he saw Khannas. "Who is this?" he asked Eve. "Iblis brought him," replied Eve. "He told me: 'This is my son; take care of him.'" "Why did you accept him?" rejoined Adam, "This is my enemy." Then Adam—on whom be peace—cut Khannas up into four pieces and cast him upon mountaintops. When Adam—peace be upon him—left, Iblis came back and asked Eve, "Where is Khannas?" "Adam cut him up into four pieces and cast him on the mountaintops," she replied. Hearing this, Iblis shouted: "O Khannas!" Khannas immediately appeared and in his original form! When Iblis departed, Adam—upon whom be peace—came back. He saw Khannas standing there. "What's this?" he asked. Eve told him what had happened. Adam then killed this Khannas and, having burned him, scattered his ashes in a river. Then he left and as soon as he was gone, Iblis returned, enquiring about Khannas. Eve told him what had transpired. Iblis again shouted: "O Khannas!" and again Khannas at once reappeared. Iblis departed just as Adam was retuning. Adam saw Khannas, this time in the form of a sheep. He learned

from Eve what had happened, and resolved to kill Khannas yet again. This time, since he was in the form of a sheep, he cooked and ate him. Soon thereafter Iblis returned and shouted: "O Khannas!" Khannas answered from the heart of Adam, "At your service! At your service!" "Stay there!" commanded Iblis. "That was my design from the beginning."[49]

As this parable illustrates, Sufis assert that the tempter is within us, as a spiritual force integral to our personalities and animate within our bodies. In fact, the very human urge to externalize him and fight against him is the cause of his lodging ever more deeply within our breasts and constricting our hearts. To combat the tempter as an external enemy is only to make him stronger within us, as his laughter echoes through our conscience, "That was my design from the beginning!" Poor Adam continued to be deluded by misrecognizing his true enemy and thinking that the external, lesser jihad was actually the greater, real, internal jihad. He has been duped once again in the lower world just as he had in the upper world of the garden.

The optimistic Sufi assessment of the human body, as the place of manifestation of God's names and qualities, is therefore balanced by a more pessimistic Sufi assessment that the tempter dwells in the human body, through which temptation whispers. Cautious Sufis warned that belief that "God created the Adam in God's image" should never devolve into incarnationism or claiming that God resides in a human body (*hulūl*). Rather, this belief must be properly understood through a subtle spiritual vision that can sift out what is eternal, spiritual, and unchanging from what is created, material, and ephemeral. This criterion is expressed most concisely in the careful intellectually Sufi definition of monotheism of al-Junayd (died 910 C.E. in Baghdad). "Sifting the eternal from the temporal, the essential from the subsidiary, the unchanging from the ephemeral is truly the way to declare the unity of God."

Rather than being theologically careful and intellectually astute like al-Junayd, Nakhshabi is more concerned with arousing erotic passion and transforming it into devotional love. In this Persian composition, he adopts a particularly South Asian poetic genre for religious devotion: the head-to-foot description of the divine body. He calls to mind the genre of Hindu devotional poetry, the *anubhava*, an erotic devotional enjoyment that moves from foot to head, describing the idol of God in sensual detail.[50] With Nakhshabi the motion of the poet's rapt vision is from the top down, known as the Persian poetic genre of *sarāpā*, consisting of a head-to-toe description of the beloved, in a list of rhyming couplets that begin:

If you see the hair as the start of each day's business
    No no, it's the hair that brings each moment to fullness
If you see the head with its mane of perception
    No no, it's the head of a man of distinction
If you think the brain to be possessed by imagined delusion
    No no, it's a brain that possesses wisdom's intuition.

After lingering on each part of the body, the poem culminates with the couplets:

If you think the soul controls the body's action
    No no, the soul moves by the spirit's attraction
If you think loins are for girding with swords and britches
    No no, the loins safeguard the noblest treasure and riches . . .
O fortunate one, to say you are good from head to toe is no vanity
    Even praising each part never exhausts the secret of humanity.[51]

Nakhshabi's intent is not to arouse amorous passion directed toward sensual pleasure but to arouse ethical passion directed to sublimating simple lust to spark spiritual insight. Rather than denying passion in an ascetic move, he is typically Sufi in embracing passion while redirecting it.

Nakhshabi does not realistically describe the body but sees each part as a manifestation of beauty, full of spiritual signs. He sees this as the natural consequence of a hadith attributed to the Prophet Muhammad, "God is beautiful and loves beauty."[52] Nakhshabi urges us to not misjudge the flesh of the body with the jaundiced eye of ascetic distain for gross matter. Rather, sparking love in the heart will kindle subtlety in the eye, and then one can admire and appreciate the flesh of the body in order to arrive at a full estimation of the nobility of the human being, whose locus of existence is the body itself. It is a process of distillation that moves from sensing matter to appreciating the essence that is hidden within and animates the matter. The same approach must be used to understand God's relationship with the universe. "The human body that you may call the fleshy corps has approximately three thousand component parts. . . . All these together make up the body, which is mineral, seminal, dark, dense and subject to change and decay. As for the spirit (*rūḥ*), it is a celestial essence (*jawhar-i samawī*), characterized by living intellect and light. The spirit is ethereal without density, moving without decay or decomposition, and can know and apprehend the form of material things. Imagine the poor body as the form of a dwelling / but know the spirit in it as master of the house."[53]

We follow Nakhshabi's logic about the whole being in the parts, with some parts being simple and others compound, some parts primary and others less important. In this way, he tries to isolate the essential being of the body that is beyond all compounds, and he finally arrives at a concept of the spirit—that evanescent nonmaterial essence that vitalizes the body, giving it life. This study adopts his adventurous sense that logic leads to mystery, but it does not imitate his very Persian sense of honor and shame, for he says, "From these three thousand parts that compose the human body, some are primary parts and some are unimportant parts. . . . On principle, I will abstain from mentioning the lowlier parts of the body, from among those organs that cannot be mentioned with honor. Among them are some whose names cannot, for shame, ever roll off the tongue!"[54] In contrast to Nakhshabi, this study has no shame, coming as it does during the ongoing sexual revolution in the West, and will mention body parts with shameless abandon. As Nakhshabi himself has written in another composition, it is a virtue to flow with the changing times: "Nakhshabi, get up and move with the times / otherwise, you will become a target for the times / The wise men of their day say / He is wise who moves with the times."[55] So in this study, if God created it, we will mention it! High or low, noble or base, public or private, all the body parts are in harmony, and each serves its function to contribute to the holistic totality of the body.

This study accepts Nakhshabi's intention, to praise each body part as a means to apprehend the body whole and admire its creation, even as it breaks with his self-imposed limitations of polite discourse. Such forthrightness is important, for in confronting the body's parts and functions that are obscured by politeness (those that inspire squeamish discomfort, shame, horror, or disgust), we gain real insight into the body's vexing complexity. We will need such boldness as we begin our exploration of Sufi images of the body in earnest, beginning in the next chapter with bones, followed by the belly, eyes, lips, and heart, and concluding with the disintegration or revitalization of the body under threat of death.

I

BODY ENSHRINED

The Bones of Mawlay Idrīs

Look at the bones, how we revive them
And clothe them once more in flesh.
—Qur'an 2:259

The Qur'an insists that there is life after death, announcing the inevitability of resurrection in ways that inspire both awe and dread. In the verses above, an unnamed man passes by a ruined city and cries out in despair, *"How will God bring this to life after its demise?"* God causes him to fall into a deathlike state for a century and then revives him to give him firsthand knowledge of God's power to take life away and give it again. He looks to his donkey, which has turned to bones, and before his eyes God reweaves the flesh upon its frame. Interpreters of the Qur'an have identified this unnamed prophetic figure as Ezra, the Jewish scholar and community leader who returned to Jerusalem after the long exile in Babylon. He found it a ruined city, devoid of the vibrant Jewish community that had once worshiped there. Having expressed despair and survived his trial by God, Ezra mounted his now breathing donkey and set about the task of writing down the Hebrew scriptures anew and reviving Jewish life in the holy city.

Muhammad also tried to revive a holy city, Mecca, which had been hallowed by Abraham's building a shrine, like Jerusalem. Muhammad tried to revive the Abrahamic worship of the singular God at that shrine, the Ka'ba, to revitalize the city's spiritual life, which had become desolate through greed, corruption, and idolatry. His opponents among the Arabs scoffed at the idea that the shrine in the center of their city needed purification, just as they scoffed at the idea that the body could be restored after it had decayed. On the verge of despair, Muhammad conveyed to them the Qur'an's repeated teaching through vivid images, parables, and stories of the prophets. The tribulations of former prophets echoed Muhammad's own trials, and the Qur'an insists that each prophet came with the same message and met the same resistance by the powerful few from the time of Noah until Muhammad: *They retort, "He's nothing special! He's just a man, who eats what you eat and drinks what you drink. If you obey one who is no better than you, then you are surely losers. He warns you, when you have died and become dust and bones that you will emerge once again. What a silly thing you are promised! Life is only this life of ours in the world—we die just as we live and we are never resurrected again to life*" (Q 23:33–37). It is not surprising that bones are the metaphor to which the Qur'an turns insistently to preach the doctrine of resurrection. Bones are a constant reminder of death, for we see them only after the rest of the body has decayed. However, bones are also a constant reminder that we persist and that our personality is durable even beyond the portal of death, since bones remain intact long after other tissues have rotted away.

The Qur'an links the One who firmed up the bones in each gelatinous fetal body in the first instance to the One who will restore life to them after their flesh has putrefied into liquid and drained away. Earlier in the same chapter in which it recalls how the elite of Noah's community rejected his teaching, the Qur'an reminds us of our origin while calling us to bear in mind our inexorable though unobservable fate: *We surely created the human being from an essence of clay. Then we made the clay into a minuscule sperm in a place of safe repose. Then we transformed the sperm into a mucuslike clot. Then we fashioned this clot into a soft fleshy lump. Then we created firm bones within the flesh and clothed the bones with muscle. Then we devised for it another creation* [breathing life into it]. *Blessed be God, the best of creators! Then after your creation you will all surely die, and after death you will all surely be raised on the day of reckoning* (Q 23:12–16). The Qur'an presents God, the best of creators, as both the shaper of the human body and the fashioner of the earth. The two worlds, the human body's inner world and the terrestrial expanse's outer world, are presented in parallel. The bones represent structure and foundation, the framework that allows the whole creation to stand and the firm planting that keeps its motion in order.

This homology between the world and the body is common in ancient mythologies. Often the world is imagined as the body of a cosmic giant, the first primal man, who sacrifices himself and whose divided body constitutes the created world: the dome of the sky is his skull, the earth his flesh, precious minerals his teeth, rivers his blood, and mountains his bones.[1] The bones in the human body are like the mountains of the earth—they give it its characteristic shape while anchoring its surface deep within its structural foundation. One Sufi master taught that "the 360 days of the solar year are equivalent to the 360 bones in the human body which are equivalent to the 360 mountains of the earth."[2]

As a radical monotheism, Islam shies away from this outright anthropomorphism of mythic imagination, for it suggests that God had a body or that a primordial being other than God was responsible for creating the world. However, the Qur'an echoes the ancient fascination with the earth's bones; it replaces the idea of mountains as the cosmic man's bones with the idea of mountains as pegs (*awtād*) driven by God deep into the earth's structure: *Have we not made the earth a smooth resting place? And made the mountains as vertical pegs? . . . And built above you seven mighty heavens? . . . The day of decision is a term appointed! The day the trumpet is sounded—you rise in throngs to come forth like waves* (Q 8:6–18). In this vivid passage, the Qur'an compares the terrestrial and celestial world to the human environment on the scale of the body. The earth is a carpet, the mountains tent pegs sunk deep, and the sky a pavilion's canopies. The universe takes the form of an abode, a habitation, built to the scale of the human body and reflecting its contours. This imagery resembles Daoist cosmologies, for "in China the body is perceived as a replica of the universe. . . . The Daoists were the ones to pursue the most extreme implications of this widely held theory. To them, the body was not merely constructed on the basis of the celestial model and norm, it was the universe, it contained the universe in its totality. The equivalence between microcosm and macrocosm in the *Wufuwu* (Book of the Five Talismans), for instance, is absolute. . . . In the body one discovered not only flora and fauna, but the whole of society and the buildings in which it lives."[3] Al-Zahī notes the same dynamic in Islamic imagery when he asks, "The beauty of the human form . . . acts as a perpetual source of wonder that engenders passionate love and deep contemplation. Isn't human beauty a sign indicating the beautiful goodness of the creation and the harmony of the cosmos? Aren't the human body and the cosmos interchangeable? Since mythological times, it is these two forms through which the being (*al-kā'in*) enters into its body in a relation of intimate adhesion with the cosmic body (*jism al-kawn*) and the universe expansive all around it?"[4] Yet in the midst of this familiarity and comfort comes a warning that it is ephemeral. The body and its abode will pass away and then be recalled on the day of reckoning and decision, when the body will rise again to a world utterly unfamiliar, *when the mountains are moving and disappear like a mirage* (Q 78:20).

The Qur'an's image of mountains as "pegs" that secure the earth's order is very potent in Islamic societies. Sufi communities call saints "pegs" who keep the spiritual order of the earth, specifically by suspending the natural order upon occasion through miracles. Vincent Cornell has shown how certain Muslim saints in the early medieval period in Fes were considered "Pegs of the Earth" and helped to establish a social order with Fes, the imperial capital under the rule of Islamic law. In this chapter, we will explore how the bones of dead saints are pegs that secure the foundation of our human social world, acting as pivot points in time and space that establish a sacred order. As Peter Brown points out, the tombs of saints and other relic shrines create "a privileged suspension of the flat tyranny of distance" in monotheistic societies.[5] The principal architectural feature of Sufi communities consists of shrines built over saints' bones, often with political patronage and popular acclaim. Such shrines also serve as gathering places and ritual sites for Sufis. This chapter explores the posthumous legacy of one body, that of the saint-king of Morocco, Mawlay Idrīs al-Azhar, who founded the city of Fes. His bones are the focus of our inquiry into human obsession with permanence, the urge to build durable structures that will preserve order against that inevitable day when all things pass away. We will follow the Qur'an's hint that bones remain potent even after the death of the body that enrobed them.

Bones, Stones, and the Body Politic

In saints' tombs in Morocco, bones marked powerful epicenters of sacred space and power. However, Muslims do not hold the physical object of bones sacred, as was common in many societies, from Polynesians to Latin Christians.[6] In Morocco and other Islamic regions, the buried body was abstracted as a mark in time and space, much like the Islamic style of art. In the tile work that covers the interior of tomb shrines, shapes that may have origins in living forms become abstracted in their representation. Similarly, the buried body is abstracted, represented by a geographical space in the tomb and a chronological time in the death anniversary celebration. Tombs mark the passage from life to death, giving physical form to the permeable boundary between this world and the next. It is not surprising, therefore, that in all religions, including Islam, tombs become important devotional sites and are defining features of sacred geography. This is especially true of holy people, such as the Prophet himself, his closest companions, his family members and descendants, and saints who are infused with his charisma. The demise of such holy people's bodies marks a sacred time in the calendar and sacred place in geography.

In Islam, tombs are architectural but not sculptural, in great contrast to Christianity. There is no attempt to replicate the shape of the body or the features of the deceased. Even when a raised stone cenotaph is a feature of the tomb (most often for royal or saintly tombs), the stone block provides a three-dimensional form for displaying carved calligraphy (much like the cloth covering of the Kaʿba itself). Rather than re-create the form of the living body, Islamic tombs mark a time and a place, like a threshold object signifying the person's transition from life through death to the life beyond, especially since Islamic custom encourages the dead to be buried on the spot where they died. If the tomb becomes a site of frequent visitation (*ziyāra*), a shrine is built over the tomb by enclosing the tomb in a chamber, covering it with a dome, providing a courtyard for devotional gatherings, and building an attached mosque for formal prayers. The shrine then becomes analogous to a "house" in which the dead body "dwells." By building a house, patrons and visitors emphasize that the person's spirit is still present in this world and therefore providing a conduit to the next world, more concentrated in this spot and most intense at the anniversary of passing.

Just as the body houses a person's soul during life, so the tomb houses a person's spirit after death. It is a powerfully simple analogy. Our Sufi guide to the body, Nakhshabi, recited: "Imagine the poor body as the form of a dwelling, but know the spirit in it as master of the house."[7] Sufis internalized this analogy more systematically and emphatically than other Muslims by stressing the importance of visiting the tombs of holy people. Such visits served many purposes. Shrines provided places for meeting, like community halls. They provided a site for meditation or retreat, a venue for the singing of devotional songs outside the strict norms of ritual prayer, occasion for making vows, offering gifts, repaying debts, and making other kinds of transactions with the sacred realm. Many of these rituals took forms from royal protocol for approaching an inaccessible emperor through his delegated ministers, transposing them into a devotional setting, in which one could approach a transcendent God through immanent mediators who have been granted intimate proximity to the divine. Thus, most important, tombs of saints provided emotional connection with a chain of spiritual masters, some living and some dead, who gave a Sufi disciple a vivid connection back to the Prophet Muhammad and through him to God. So vivid was this chain of authorities that it remained potent even after the personalities who constitute it have passed beyond the life of the body—in fact, it may be more potent through the dead than through living saints.

Many Muslim theologians of a more legalistic orientation were uncomfortable with this ritual use of tombs and the spiritual hierarchal order that they maintained like "pegs of the earth." Long before the Wahhabi ideological challenge to Sufi ritual at tombs, which we will examine in detail in the concluding chapter, Muslim theologians denounced the visitation of tombs, the building of shrines over them, the association of mosques with them, and the mixing of classes and genders that happened around them. However, even when their critique was bitter, these theologians had to admit that the practice of building tombs, visiting them, and considering the dead as present in them was an authentic part of the Prophet Muhammad's teachings.

The issue was not whether one could communicate with the dead or visit their tombs but rather how one communicated and with what intent one made visitation. Of course, in an Islamic environment such arguments returned rhetorically to the specific practices of the Prophet Muhammad and his early community (*sunna*). However, the practice of visiting tombs, based as it is upon a deep-seated analogy between the body and the house, is more universal than its Islamic practice and is embedded deeply in the Abrahamic legacy that Islam inherited and upon which it elaborated.

This analogy is found in Jewish tradition, in controversies around how a building can house the spirit of God, either in the Ark of the Covenant or the Temple. Traces of these controversies are discussed in the Qur'an as it retells the story of Saul, who rose as a ruler over the Tribes of Israel after Moses led them to Canaan and they established a polity there. *Their Prophet said to them, "God has indeed sent Saul (Tālūt) as your ruler." But they replied, "We refuse that he should rule over us for we are more deserving than him to rule and he has not come with sufficient money." He* [the Prophet] *said, "Indeed God has chosen him and increased him expansively in knowledge and in body. Surely God gives ruling power to whomever God wills, for God is the expansive One, the One who knows all things." Their Prophet told them, "The sign of his rule is that he brings you the Ark in which is present the immanence of God (sakīna) by your Lord along with the rest of what the house of Moses and of Aaron left behind. The angels will carry it, so surely in that is a sign for you if you are believers"* (Q 2:247–48). Commentators on this story, in the genre of stories of the prophets, have provided more detail about this episode. The prophet in this era was Samuel, and the Tribes of Israel had asked him to intercede with God on their behalf to raise up a king for them, to lead them against the Philistines with their champion, Goliath. In accord with God's guidance, Samuel indicated that Saul would be their king. However, Saul was a lowborn and poor man (said to be a hide tanner or water carrier). He was from the tribe of Benjamin, not the tribe of priests descended from Levi or the tribe of royalty descended from Judah. So the Tribes rejected him in rebellion against their prophet and the God he represented.

In arguing against the Israelite Tribes, Samuel the prophet insists that it is Saul who will bring to them the Ark of the Covenant. The Ark was a wooden crate (*tābūt*), a term that Arabic speakers also applied to a casket, *in which is present the immanence of God (sakīna) by your Lord, along with the rest of what the house of Moses and of Aaron left behind*. It was a portable prototype of the Temple that had yet to be built and also a "house" that "housed" relics of what the "house of Moses and of Aaron" left behind. The multiple resonance of the term "house" is crucial here. It is a structure that acts a receptacle that gives outward form to indwelling objects or spiritual presences that cannot be seen. These immaterial presences or inaccessible objects represent the continuation of the ancestors' descendants. "House" means tribe but also structure that represents in concrete form the body politic and also the remains of the patriarch after whom the house is named and who gives cohesive social identity to the group.

Muslim commentators gave more information about this strange shrine, the Ark of the Covenant, drawing on Judaic lore. It was neither tomb nor temple but played the function of both. It is the not the "house of God" directly but is rather the dwelling of God's *sakina*, a manifestation of God's spirit in the form of an embodied wind with a feminine nature. If God had a body, the *sakina* would be God's shadow; if God were male, the *sakina* would be God's consort. Like tombs that housed the spirit of the dead or temples whose inner sanctum housed the presence of God, the ark would "speak." It would give guidance from the sacred realm beyond the routine material world. "The Ark would speak to the Children of Israel when they quarrelled and would judge between them. When they were involved in battle, they placed it in front of them, seeking God's assistance through it against their enemy. But when they rebelled and acted corruptly, God gave the Amalekites power over them, and they were victorious over them in spite of the Ark, and they deprived them of it. That was in the day of Eli the priest, who raised Samuel up as a Prophet; and Goliath was young when his people took control of the Ark. In the Ark were remains, said to be the staff of Moses and stone shards of the tablets of the law that he had broken."[8] With this description, the analogy between the ark and a casket is more distinct. The ark houses durable relics, hard objects of wood or stone, which remain long after the body that used them or forged them is decayed and gone. In this sense, they are like bone that "remains" after the other tissues of the body have decayed. The sacred power of the prophet, leader, or ancestor inheres in these durable objects, whether they are bones that had been integral to his body or objects that had been instrumental in his exercise of authority.

Through accepting Saul, the Tribes of Israel will get back their cherished ark. However, at first they reject him as ruler, for he bears no legitimating status, no wealth, and no pedigree. Through their prophet, God argues with them that he is well endowed: he tells them that *indeed God has chosen him and increased him expansively in knowledge and in body*. The Qur'an here pairs two criteria for rule, one outwardly visible in a strong body (*jism*) and the other invisible to physicality but evident through conduct, knowledge (*'ilm*). Their prophet asks the Tribes to abandon their present social order (manifest in their way of judging people's quality by genealogical rank or material wealth) and return to a more egalitarian social order (to judge people by their merits, in strength and knowledge). Ironically, the prophet insists that they do this, even as they request him to appoint for them a ruler, a king like the Canaanite societies around them have! The prophet subverts their expectations even as he answers their petition. Only by accepting the body of Saul as the "head" of their body politic, his body naked of the vestments of ascribed status, can the Tribes reinvigorate their "house." They must accept the conjunction of Saul's body as king, the ark as their tabernacle, and the polity as a salvific corporate group. Only through this powerful conjunction of metaphors can they regain their lost patrimony, the relics of their patriarchal ancestors, and the spiritual presence of God (*sakina*) with them that ensures their military victory and moral salvation.

Eventually, they accept his body as their ruler and solidify the political boundaries of their community as a kingdom. They regain the ark and the relics it houses, the stone and wood fragments that stand in for their ancestor's bones. Through Saul and despite Saul's errors, the kingdom perpetuates itself, defeating the Philistines and establishing a polity. Rule is taken over by David and then Solomon, whom the Qur'an also calls prophets. Solomon roots the power of the ark in a permanent structure, the Temple in Jerusalem, completing the chain of metaphorical objects through which sacred power is channeled into the quotidian world to generate social and political power: the holy body becomes relics, they become a casket, it becomes a shrine, which then becomes a house.

In arguing for Saul's right to rule, the Qur'an draws equivalence between the strong body and moral knowledge. The body politic is strong not when it has the outer trappings of wealth and status but rather when it nurtures within itself right knowledge and moral action; when these qualities are mutually reinforcing, the rowdy and troublesome group or tribe becomes a "house," a corporate group like an abode in which dwells the presence of God. The metaphor of the house is crucial for binding together these different dimensions. The house is a constructed dwelling, built to house the body and its members in the family. The house stands in analogy for the body by metaphorical extension. It mirrors the way the body "houses" the spirit, being the place of indwelling of the spirit and giving it its physical form and manifestation. When the structure of the house is in harmony with the structure of the bodies that inhabit it, it becomes a home—a synthesis we can call an inhabited dwelling. Similarly, when the structure of the body is in harmony with the spirit that inheres in it, it becomes a living organism, an ensouled being. Similarly, when the structure of the temple is in harmony with the God who manifests there (without God being contained by it, for the spatial metaphor is always in tension with the development of Abrahamic monotheism), it becomes a sanctuary, a place kept sacred by interdictions, ritual purity, and deep emotions of awe and dread. Jon Berquist's excellent study of ideologies of the body in ancient Israel, *Controlling Corporeality*, makes these homologies clear and demonstrates their power in ordering a society over many centuries in ways that are durable under cataclysmic changes. He writes that "bodies mediate the creation of culture in every society. . . . Israel's understanding of the body paralleled its understanding of social reality. Society's organization matches the perceived realities of the body. . . . Israel developed an idea of what the whole body was like, and this image changed throughout time as ancient Israel developed a discourse and social practice of the body in parallel with its conception of the larger society. Rituals of the body and rituals of the state are closely intertwined, and both give evidence for the other."[9]

The temple is usually established by a prophet-king, either fused in one personality or acting as a cooperative pair of persons. We could say it is "erected" to highlight the integral connection between the building and the patriarchal male body of the founder. Before the king is formally established, the Tribes of Israel had a prototype of the temple in their ark. It performed the function of a temple but was portable and suitable for nomadic roaming and military maneuvering. While they had a kingdom, the centralized structure of the temple mirrored their polity and reinforced its boundaries. Once the kingdom was destroyed and the polity fragmented, they had decentralized nodes of sacred space in the tombs of holy people.

Although the details of this development differ for Muslims, the process is generally the same. As Arabs, they had the Kaʿba as a relic-structure of Abraham, which they lost through corruption of idolatry. It was restored in function and set as the center of a unified religious polity by a prophet-king, Muhammad. And upon the rapid expansion and inevitable dissolution of the righteous polity, authority also became decentralized and spread over the surface of Muslim societies in sacred places where holy people are buried. Just as a person dwells in a house or the body resides in a tomb, so the soul inheres in the body—and in both the body of a holy person or a shrine-temple resides the indwelling immanence of God.

Building on Bones

Architectural metaphors are integral for conceiving of the relation between body and soul, while actual architectural spaces are integral for enlivening the soul of the body politic. The Torah gives Muslims historical hints about this dynamic in former times, and the Qur᾿an gives Muslims scriptural signs about its continuing significance. We can see this dynamic at play very vividly in the hagiographic story of Mawlay Idris al-Azhar, the founder of the city of Fes, the first Islamic city of Morocco, its occasional political capital, and the center of its religious culture. The recovery of his bones in the center of the old city of Fes led to a revolution that, it can be argued, set the conditions for the emergence of a notion of kingship that continues to hold sway in Morocco. The notion of a divinely appointed kingship, in which a descendant of the Prophet Muhammad rules, dominates Moroccan politics even in the present, despite a period of French colonial "protectorate" and rapid modernization.

Let us begin our investigation of saints' bones, shrines, and the architecture of power in the present and work back into the past. In contemporary Morocco, it often seems that the effects of modernity through French colonization are very shallow, that political order and social networks still operate in great continuity with premodern patterns. While I was living in Fes in the 1990s, I witnessed the yearly procession in honor of the memory of the patron saint of Fes, Mawlay Idris al-Azhar. The procession, on the anniversary of his death, led from the royal palace to his tomb. It is an occasion when the city seems most pulsing with life, when it displays its character most vividly and bears the premodern foundations upon which its life is still based. On this date, the saint is presented with new clothes: an embroidered cloth covering is carried with great ceremony and laid over his tomb. The procession is a bewildering experience of synesthesia: trumpets blare, pipes drone, drums and tambourines beat incessantly, marking the rhythmic repetitions of chanted invocations by various Sufi groups. Brightly colored banners sway overhead, and huge golden braziers of pungent incense are borne on the heads of devotees, filling the alleys of the city with smoke that clouds the vision, tantalizes the nose, and purifies the breath. Animals are driven along with the procession, to be sacrificed at the threshold of the tomb shrine, the scarlet of their blood another purifying element that betokens the expiation of the sins of the community and promises renewal in the year to come.

This yearly procession clearly marks the tomb of Mawlay Idris as the spiritual center of the city of Fes. The procession cuts like an archaeological trench through the spatial-historical layers of this complex city that is both medieval and modern. The government officials who sponsor and officiate over the procession come from the *ville nouvelle*, the modern city and administrative center built by the French Protectorate a little distant beyond a *cordon sanitaire* in order to control the older cities of Fes. The procession begins in earnest at the military garrison courtyard that spreads before the royal palace, the core of the "new city" of Fes (*al-madīna al-bayḍā'*) that was founded in the thirteenth century by the Marinid dynasty to control the old city. The procession gains in intensity as it reaches the gates and squeezes dangerously into the narrow alleys of the old city of Fes (*Fās al-Bālī*) that begin to slope precipitously toward the heart of the city. The old city still has almost two hundred thousand inhabitants living in the densely structured original walled city (making it the largest inhabited walled city of medieval design in the world), roughly according to the urban plan first sketched by Mawlay Idris in 808 C.E. The procession moves downhill and back in time as it reaches the center of the city, where the oldest structures of the city exist. It enters the *ḥurma*, the sanctuary precincts, where wooden beams across the alleys signify the beginning of holy ground, where nobody should ride and only Muslims should enter. The procession finally reaches the mosque of the descendants of the Prophet (*Masjid al-Shurafā'*), which was built next to the house that Mawlay Idris reportedly built for himself and his family. Inside the mosque, with its walls scintillating with intricate tile and carved plaster arabesques, lies the tomb, draped in rich brocade.

When I first encountered the tomb, I tried to comprehend its structure in the terms of religious studies. His tomb and the saintly body it houses would seem like an *axis mundi*, or cosmic axis, that connects the earth with the heavens, around which the life of the city revolves. Though the mosque is in the lowest basin at the center of the city (which is situated in a bowl-shaped valley with the walls around the highest rim), its minaret rises high above the roofs and walls and is one of the most visible landmarks even from outside the walls. As an architectural monument, it is rooted in the earth but rises into the sky. The man buried in the tomb that roots the building in its site was a king, a descendant of the Prophet Muhammad (*sharīf*), the founder of Fes, and is remembered posthumously as a saint. As Mawlay

New cloth covering for the tomb of Mawlay Idrīs al-Azhar, carried on the heads of devotees in the annual pilgrimage to his tomb in the center of Fās. Photograph by Scott Kugle.

Idris first sketched the ground plan of the city and laid its cornerstone, he is recorded to have lifted his hands in prayer, saying, "Almighty God, make of this city a house of knowledge and of legal science, so that in it your holy book may always be read and your laws always respected."

Historical sources actually preserve little information about Mawlay Idris al-Azhar's life as a political ruler. His life is more vividly drawn in premodern hagiographic sources that treat him as a saint. This study draws from one hagiography in particular, entitled *The Precious Pearl and Intimate Light on Our Leader Idris' Virtuous Might*, written in 1686–87. His father, Mawlay Idris I, died with no children born but left a Berber slave, Khanza, seven months pregnant. His faithful servant Rāshid called the elders of the tribes together and declared, "Let us wait patiently until this woman gives birth. And if she gives birth to a male, let us wait until he achieves manhood. If he survives until manhood, then let us declare allegiance (*bayʿa*) to him, to gain the blessing of the Prophet's family and descendants. If she gives birth to a girl, then choose from among yourself whomever you think most suitable to rule."[10] They elected Rashid to rule until the child was born and, if it was a boy, to serve as regent until he reached mature age. A boy was born in 793; when he was displayed to the tribal leaders, they said he was the splitting image of his father, and so he was named Idris the son of Idris and raised as a prince and scholar in Islamic sciences. When the boy turned 11, the regent Rashid led the Berber tribal leaders and representatives of the people to pledge allegiance to him. He then led them to affirm their allegiance five months later, for the leader was still young and the political situation was precarious, as the ascendant Abbasid empire in the east was suspicious of challengers to its power (which extended as far west as Tunisia) and probably considered the nascent Idrisid kingdom in Morocco as Shiʿi upstarts who challenged its own authority. In fact, it was widely rumored in Morocco that Abbasid agents poisoned Mawlay Idris the Elder. The Abbasid empire's closest vassal, Ibrāhīm al-Aghlab, the governor of Tunis, had the faithful regent Rashid killed in 803.

The younger Idris survived this blow, continued to gather the allegiance of Moroccan Berber tribal elders, and even managed to secure the allegiance of some Arab leaders from Ifriqīya (Tunisia and Algeria) and Andalusia (southern Spain). He led the life of a successful provincial ruler, struggling to keep his kingdom independent from the Sunni empires that bordered him and that could not boast sharifian legitimacy, the Umayyad empire of Andalusia and the Abbasid empire, which ruled from Baghdad to Tunisia. Internally, he continued his father's experiment in fusing Berber tribes into a kingdom of Arabic language and Islamic religion. He died in 828 in his early thirties and divided his tenuous Moroccan kingdom among twelve sons. They fell to squabbling and competing, and the kingdom rapidly decentralized until it fell to Berber rule. Thus Mawlay Idris al-Azhar's political life was insignificant in comparison with his symbolic importance as a saint.

Although the author of this hagiography claims to have drawn his information "from every book written, from books of law, biographies, histories and memoirs,"[11] he treats Mawlay Idris al-Azhar more as a saint than as a historical personage or king. It is as if his tomb in the center of Fes were more important than his actual life, since it mirrors his symbolic importance as the center of a believing community and gives the public its main access to God's presence in the city of Fes.

> Nobody arrives at intimacy with God except through him [Mawlay Idris al-Azhar], from him and by his hand, since he is the greatest gatekeeper from among the mediators between creation and the Lord. . . . Imam Idris stands as if in the station of the lower heavens in regard to ascension to the Prophet Muhammad, for he represents the closest access point in the lineage of noble decent from the Prophet. The Prophet can be imagined to serve the function of the divine throne. All who aspire to ascend up to the presence of the throne, the essence of the Prophet Muhammad, start from the lower heaven, the essence of Imam Idris son of Idris. They move up through the essences of his noble ancestors, through seven layers of heaven and seven levels of genealogical descent, until arriving at the Throne of the Muhammadan essence, which is the most precious quintessence.[12]

In this passage the process of spiritual development and refinement (*taraqqī*) is equated with the special and cosmic metaphor of ascension through the heavens to the throne of God (*miʿrāj*).

For Sufis, the ascension is the primary metaphor for mystical experience. In ascension the limited ego is transcended, and the spiritual aspirant tastes an expansive experience of communion with the cosmic vastness and moral elevation of the divine presence. This is expressed through metaphors of physical space, in which the seeker moves upward from the limited, material body through the layers of heaven into proximity with the divine throne, the locus of God's presence. The means of the voyage into the above and beyond is the Prophet Muhammad, whose own ascension through the heavens is the subject of Qur'anic hint, hadith report, and folkloric elaboration. The Sufi experience of ascension is the detailed subject of Chapter 3.

Constructing this allegorical complex is eased by the name of the protagonists, Idris. In Arabic, Idris is equivalent to Enoch in Hebrew. In mystical folklore, he was the first prophet who did not die but was taken up bodily into heaven, to "walk with God" (Genesis 5:24). His rise into intimacy with God is the paradigm for all ascension narratives (both in the Judaic Hekhalot literature and its Kabbala interpretations and in the Sufi genre). The author constructs his allegorical ascension by the number seven, the number of perfection. The Qur'an specifies that there are seven heavens, each more refined from the atmosphere of the earth up to the nonmaterial vastness of the divine throne (Q 2:69). Each of these heavens corresponds, in the hagiographic imagination, to a generation of descendants from the Prophet Muhammad. The author provides the following genealogy of his lineage: (7) Idris al-Azhar, son of Idris, the founder of Fes; (6) Idris I, founder of the Islamic kingdom in Morocco; (5) ʿAbdallah; (4) Ḥasan al-Muthannā; (3) Imam Ḥasan; (2) Imam ʿAlī ibn Abī Ṭālib, husband of Fāṭima, the eldest daughter of the Prophet; and (1) the Prophet Muhammad.

In this mystical allegory, the genealogy of noble lineage reinforces the architecture of sacred space. The author claims that the levels of genealogy from Mawlay Idris al-Azhar until the Prophet are six generations, just as there are six spatial dimensions and as it took six days to create the cosmos.

> From the very beginning, there is a subtle allusion to the fact that Mawlay Idris possesses nobility (*sharaf*) from six directions: the directions of fatherhood [from ʿAli], of marriage [from Fatima], of knowledge, of action, of piety, and prior selection for salvation and elevated status (*sābi-*

> *qiyat al-saʿāda waʾl-sharaf*). . . . Through six days God completed the creation of the cosmos and accordingly through six generations God brought to completion the holy men of this lineage. Just as God completed the creation of the cosmos, in its celestial and terrestrial realms, in six days, so God brought to completion, Mawlay Idris the son of Idris, the perfection of Muhammadan might and the completion of Ahmadic nobility, bringing to fullness the blessing of God's intense intimacy in this world and the next world from his ancestor, the Prophet Muhammad.[13]

Genealogical, cosmological, and architectural spaces add up, in this account, to a whole. It must be remembered that the prototypical Islamic shrine is the Kaʿba, founded by Abraham and Ishmael in Mecca. It is simply a black stone cube, the literal meaning of *kaʿba*.

As an empty cube, the Kaʿba emphasizes not what it encloses but rather that toward which it expands. Its planes face in the six directions: north, south, east, west, upward, and downward. Similarly, all shrines built over the tombs of saints imitate the structure of the Kaʿba. Cubelike, they are rooted in the downward direction by the body of the deceased saint, with faces to the four cardinal directions and with a covering dome bending in the upward direction, as if in yearning, toward the heavens. The author of this hagiography sees Mawlay Idris al-Azhar as the center not only of Fes but also of Morocco as a whole. His tomb shrine stands in for the Kaʿba, and visitation to his tomb is analogous to pilgrimage to Mecca. His proximity bridges the distance to the Prophet Muhammad, and his genealogy brings the Prophet's charisma into the Moroccan locality, making it accessible to the elites, like dynastic rulers who claim legitimacy through his legacy and like commoners who claim blessing through submissive devotion to him. In fact, the shrine features a brass plaque with a hole leading from the alley outside the building directly to the fabric covering the tomb, so that common people (whether workers too busy to enter the building or women, who are prohibited from approaching the tombs directly) can reach through and touch the tomb.

The author of this hagiography, Aḥmad al-Fāsī, saw himself as one of these common people who approach Mawlay Idris as a supplicant and outsider. However, he also claims to have achieved some mystical knowledge and "taste" of divine intimacy through such an attachment. In this passage, he hints at his own inner experience as a Sufi that allows him to describe the outer world (of shrine space, genealogical heritage, and political allegiance) in vivid terms. "When I became inflamed with the passion to spread the aromatic fragrance of remembering the Muhammadan presence and praising the Ahmadic beloved, I threw my passionate loving self in total dependence upon him [Mawlay Idris]. Each delicate breath of my soul stays clinging to his every beauty. I severed connection to all else and secluded my longing soul with him, until with the all-encompassing meanings of its fragrant breath it tasted the sincere desire for loving him alone. Yet, the souls that long for him are not equal to the souls that have tasted of his presence! So I threw myself toward oblivion in him, dedicating myself to praising him, engrossed in witnessing him and gradually becoming one with his existence."[14]

Mystically devoted and erotically charged, the author continues to describe the union between God, the Prophet, and Mawlay Idris. "I saw nothing except that I saw his face (*qubl*). I took witnessing his essence as my orientation in prayer (*qibla*). For haven't you seen the human being in his appearance, created upon the form of his name and attribute? So bear witness to him in each human being that you may see, if you understand the secret of the Qur'an's saying, *Then know that in your midst is the messenger of God* (Q 49:7). As you bear witness to him in every person, acknowledge that the most deserving of your bearing witness are those of the noble elite, who are a piece of him in sharing his attributes, who are his family and share with him in intimate proximity. If you love him then you will love his family and descendants. You will love them in secret and aloud, and love those who love them, for love is not realized just by claiming to love!"[15] He tempers the potentially radical statement that every human being mirrors the essence of the Prophet Muhammad with the specification that the people who most clearly enact this intimacy are the descendants of the Prophet, the imams. We can clearly observe his brand of "sharifian Sufism" that is particular to Morocco, in which the most powerful way to draw close to God is to contemplate the image of the Prophet and the best way to do this is to venerate the Prophet's genealogical descendants as saints and rulers.

The author's life mirrors that of his subject in strange ways and may help to explain why he felt such a spiritual resonance with Mawlay Idris, a resonance so deep that he committed to paper the outer and inner legends of the saintly king that were so much a part of popular practice in his lifetime. Ahmad al-Fasi was born and raised in Aleppo, Syria, but moved to Fes and lived out his days there, just as Mawlay Idris had moved from the Arab east to find refuge in the Moroccan west, urging his son, Mawlay Idris al-Azhar, to establish a capital city there, the city of Fes. The author explains his purpose and method in the introduction:

> I first entered this region, the Maghrib in the year 1080 Hijri [1669 or 1670 C.E.], as if guided by the wondrous phoenix (*al-anqāʾ al-mughrib*). I had happened upon it by destiny and divine intent, and may God make me one of those satisfied by it and content. I struggled through the trial of being a stranger in strange lands and its test, until I entered the city of Fes, the foundation of the Farthest West. I discovered in it benefits whose extent cannot be told, and I adopted it as home and chose it for my abode. Then I became acquainted with these two Imams both noble, known as al-Azhar and Idris, both inimitable, of whose superiority God made all mouths express, spreading their two names like synonyms for might and loftiness. They are Idris the son of ʿAbdullah, possessor of rare virtue and finesse, and his son Abū Qāsim Idris the son of Idris.[16]

The biographer and hagiographer clearly sees his subject through a Sufi lens. Mawlay Idris was not just a limited human ego but a personality that opened a spiritual space for others to inhabit, as if his virtue grew and his character blossomed into a garden. "When I saw their legacy, that their fame was so great and their splendor so radiant, the doves of my thought took flight and through the gardens of their character and virtue flitted with delight."[17] The hagiographer uses a word for garden (*riyāḍ*) that is very pungent: it does not just mean a walled private garden filled with fragrant herbs and fruit trees but also evokes the rhyming term for a tomb (*rawḍ*) and the shrine that encloses it. This makes it into an architectural metaphor for the garden of paradise, a place in which the fragrance of spiritual union and the fruit of virtuous action become manifest.

Mawlay Idris al-Azhar, the king, stands in for the Prophet Muhammad, his ancestor whose light and spiritual radiance suffuses his being. Just as his personality and spiritual secret open upward in transcendence, Mawlay Idris's presence opens outward in immanent accessibility through his tomb. It is a royal court of a saint, open to the public, through which the people reconfirm their allegiance to God, to the Prophet whose message they strive to follow, to the king who rules them, and to each other as citizens of the urban space of Fes. The veneration recorded by the hagiographic text reproduces in words the veneration performed daily by visitors and dramatized yearly by pilgrims in the procession to his tomb. Such veneration, filling with living energy the otherwise inert architectural space of his tomb and the shrine rising over it, affirms that Mawlay Idris is the center of Fes and the *axis mundi* of the Moroccan Maghrib. His tomb and the sacredness that the surrounding society accords to it illustrate Samuel Mills's observations about Sufi shrines and Muslim saints: "Theoretically, the spiritual power which the [saint] possesses is unlimited, in the sense that disciples should not have the impertinence to imagine its limitations. Devotional activity centers power in the [shrine] (space-wise) and reinvigorates it at the annual [commemorative celebration of the death anniversary] (time-wise). The ritual structures which focus the power in exemplary spaces and moments also survive the mortal demise of the [saint] and celebrate his incorporation into the chain of divinely illuminated souls, united with God, through which direct experience of divine blessing can be obtained."[18]

Discovery of Mawlay Idris's Bones

The hagiographic depiction of the saint and his tomb asserts this idealistic centrality. To understand how this ideal picture came to be, we have to take a step further into the past, to the time of the tomb's construction. If we see the tomb as a work in progress rather than a fait accompli, our assessment of Mawlay Idris's body will become more complex: it will affirm the critical connection between bones, blood, and power in the formation of the body politic.

Ahmad al-Fasi hints that all was not as he would like it to be with regard to the legacy of Mawlay Idris. He admits that he composed his hagiography not just out of admiration and devotion but also to engage a conflict over the saint's legacy. "Especially in these times, I've seen some ignorant historians of my day suggest falsehoods about them [Mawlay Idris and his father] in a devious way, against those who rule, and suggest with excessive exaggeration and display. So God, the generous One, gave me this amazing grace, and inspired me to oppose all those lies with a composition, to show clearly what others try to deface, of their noble character and honorable disposition. This is because giving each their due rights is an obligation, while neglecting to honor their rights is the worst kind of rebellion."[19] In addition to expressing his gratitude for finding a home and career in Fes and committing to paper the mystical practices of his community, his more prosaic reason to compose this work was to oppose "some ignorant historians" of his day who suggested falsehoods about Mawlay Idris. This refers to those who impugned the sanctity of the bloodline of those sharifian clans that claimed descent from the Prophet through him. This was a crucial issue because the polity that had only recently established its suzerainty in Morocco when Ahmad al-Fasi lived in Fes, the ʿAlawī dynasty, ruled as descendants of the Prophet; their legitimacy rested not just on the strength of their military or the justice of their administration but, more important, on the sanctity of their genealogy. Their right to rule, we might say, ran in the blood that flowed from the marrow of their bones. It is as Nakhshabi said in his Sufi poem praising each part of the body: "If you think bones are a beggar's ration / No no, in the bones is the scaffold for a great nation."[20]

The ʿAlawi dynasty of Ahmad al-Fasi's day ruled by an ideology of divine right. Its leaders claimed that the kingship of Morocco must rest with the patriarchal head of a sharifian family that claimed patrilinial descent from the Prophet Muhammad through ʿAli. To emphasize this genealogical legitimacy, they claimed not just the practical title "powerful leader" (*sulṭān*) like other Islamic rulers of their day but also "commander of the faithful" (*amīr al-muʿminīn*), which had been granted especially to ʿAli when he was the ruler of the early Islamic community. The sharifian dynasty, therefore, had a special interest in patronizing the shrine of Mawlay Idris and keeping his tomb sacred, for he and his father were the first kings of Morocco and were sharifian descendants of the Prophet. What these rulers and the hagiographer who defended their right to rule conveniently ignore, however, is that this ideology of sharifian right to rule was a rather new invention in late medieval Morocco. If Mawlay Idris al-Azhar had asserted something similar, his ideas died with him.

After his death and during the long medieval centuries in which Fes grew into a cosmopolitan urban center of Islamic civilization, Morocco was ruled by sultans, not by a commander of the faithful. The sultans were Berber chieftains who engineered various ideologies of rule as upholders of Islamic law and theology but never claimed right to rule as Arab descendants of the Prophet. The first two of these dynasties, the Almoravid (al-Murābiṭ) and the Almohad (al-Muwaḥḥid) established Marrakesh as their capital city, while Fes grew into an intellectual, religious, and commercial center. The third of these Berber dynasties, the Marinid (Banū Marīn) moved its political capital to Fes but constructed its palace and garrison outside the walls of the old city, in the adjacent site of "new Fes."

The urban geography of old Fes reflects this political history, for despite the saintly energy of Mawlay Idris's body and the popular devotion to this tomb, his building is not quite the center of Fes. Or rather, we can say that it is a contested question about where the center exactly is and what edifice occupies that priority position. This is because Mawlay Idris's tomb was not always there. It was built in particular historical circumstances, once the body of Idris was miraculously "rediscovered" in 1438, in the waning years of the Marinid dynasty. Its relative newness explains why it stands in strange competition for a central position against the Qarawiyyīn, the grand congregational mosque that was the central place of worship for the city and functioned also as a university and astronomical observatory. The mosque was one of the first public buildings of Fes, built by the property endowment of a noble woman, Fatima al-Fihrī. The Qarawiyyin was always the religious heart of Fes. In medieval times, its centrality was reinforced by the Marinid dynasty's policy of building Islamic colleges (madrassas) closely around it, colleges that brought the devoted, intelligent, and ambitious from all over northern Morocco to Fes to study Islamic theology and law in order to take positions in government-administered courts and schools. The Qarawiyyin mosque served not only as the official site for the sultan's attendance at Friday communal prayers but also as the college's lecture hall. Its central position in the religious life of Fes went unchallenged until the newer tomb of Mawlay Idris was built in the adjacent neighborhood, just across the principal marketplace.

During the long centuries of Marinid rule nobody missed the fact that there was no shrine there and no tomb of Mawlay Idris. Under the Marinids, Fes flourished as the imperial capital and central hub of Islamic colleges. In that era, historians of Fes were apt to count its superiority to almost any other city in the Islamic Oikumeme, the settled lands of Africa, Asia, and the Mediterranean. The author of one such history of Fes, *The Reservoir of Justice*, took the art of counting to great heights: he counted more than one hundred thousand residents in the walled city, living in 89,036 private homes, with 240 places of convenience and purification (public restrooms), 80 public fountains fed from springs, 93 public baths, 136 public bread ovens, 437 hostels for travelers, visiting merchants, and the homeless, 400 government-run paper-making factories, and 1 hospital funded by land granted in perpetuity. Most historians of medieval Fes thought that Mawlay Idris al-Azhar's body was buried next to his father's in the small city of Walīlī (or Volubilis in Latin), for Mawlay Idris I had taken this city as his administrative capital when he first arrived in Morocco, a city established by Roman, Byzantine, and Visigothic rulers. Although Mawlay Idris the son founded Fes as the new capital, the city's construction was hardly finished by the time of his death. To Marinid historians, it seemed perfectly natural that Mawlay Idris the son was buried next to his father. A medieval historian of Fes who was writing before 1341 claims that Mawlay Idris al-Azhar died and was buried in Fes, yet he also notes an older and divergent tradition (recorded by al-Burnūsī) that the saint died in Walili and was buried there next to his father's tomb.[21] Al-Jaznāʾī, a historian of the same age but writing slightly later, glosses over these conflicting traditions and does not document Mawlay Idris's place of burial.[22] The Marinid rulers, Islamic scholars, and medieval historians of Fes did not need his royal and saintly body in Fes. It was only as their rule grew weak and internal dissent gave rise to competitors who challenged their authority that the claim arose that his body was located in Fes.

These historians also noted the centrality of two commercial districts containing 9,082 stores, which were the financial lifeblood of Fes. These commercial districts were known as Qayṣariyya, or Caesar's Place, alluding to the prior Roman commercial and administrative control of North Africa. These commercial centers were hubs in lucrative networks of trade, for Fes connected routes from Spain and West Africa to Egypt and points east. The Qaysariyya was a place of fierce competition between merchants of different communities: sharifian clans of Fes, Jewish merchant families, and recent immigrants from Andalusia. This competition grew more intense as Castillian and Portuguese assaults threatened the last Muslim rulers in Spain, forced Muslim Arabs and Berbers as well as Jews from Iberia, and caused increasing settlement of newcomers in Moroccan urban centers, especially Fes. It was in this context that the bones of Mawlay Idris were "rediscovered" in the center of the major marketplace of Fes.

The Marinid rulers relied on commercial activity to fund their rule and military prowess to enforce it. But they relied on religious elites to legitimate it, since, as Berber strongmen originally from Algeria, they had no claim of legitimacy that inhered in their bloodline or piety (the "body" and "knowledge" alluded to above in the Qur'anic narrative about King Saul). Rather, they claimed the right to rule by upholding Islamic law, sponsoring Islamic scholarship in madrassa institutions, and publicly honoring the Prophet Muhammad. The most important way that they honored the Prophet was by honoring those *shurafa'*, or sharifian clans, that claimed patrilineal descent from the Prophet's son-in-law and cousin, ʿAli.

The Marinid rulers rationalized the status of these clans and engineered an official position for them as a pillar of the state. Marinid rulers recognized a single person as *naqīb al-shurafa'*, "the representative of the descendants of the Prophet," and gave him an official administrative role. In addition, the *shurafa'* took leading roles in many other official rituals and new religious celebrations patronized by the court. Just as the Marinids introduced into Morocco the institution of the madrassa from Egypt and the eastern Islamic world, they also patronized the celebration of the birthday of the Prophet Muhammad.[23] It was the occasion for grand ceremonial processions in which the *shurafa'* played a leading role, raising their social status considerably throughout the period of Marinid rule.[24]

The Marinid ruler invested the leader of the sharifian al-Jūṭī clan with the position of "representative of the descendants of the Prophet." This clan played the leading role in the rising political power of the *shurafa'* through this period. The eminent Islamic historian Ibn Khaldūn describes this clan and their important social position: "The al-Juti branch of the *shurafa'* has the clearest genealogy of all the descendants of the Prophet in the Maghrib, and the most accomplished record in popular leadership. They are the central core of the Idrīsī shurafā' in Fes and the designated leaders of the Prophet's family (*nuqabā' ahl al-bayt*). They continued to inhabit the building [allegedly] built by their ancestor, the king Mawlay Idris. The section of this family that was dominant in Fes in Marinid times was the al-ʿImrānī family."[25] In 1438, the lost tomb of their saintly ancestor, Mawlay Idris, was "rediscovered" in the center of Fes, securing the institutional power of this branch of the al-Juti clan.

The Marinid rulers were quickly enjoined to support the building of a proper shrine, mosque, and tomb for the site. In deference to its holiness, the entire surroundings of the tomb were designated as a "sanctuary" in the care of the sharifian protectors. This area included the Qaysariyya, in which cloth, gold, spices, and other valuable commodities were traded. By a trump of sacred geography, the market was cleared of Jewish merchants and landowners who had grown in power over several generations and was arrogated by the al-ʿImrani family. By this move, the *shurafa'* claimed to embody the axis of Fes, controlling the overlapping arenas of sacred sites, urban space, and economic networks. This new shrine also provided them with a platform from which they would shortly launch their new political role.

The story of the "rediscovery" of the tomb is fascinating and reveals a potent bid for power by the al-Juti *shurafa'*. The cumbersome term "rediscovery" (with all its inherent paradoxes) describes the process by which the tomb came to be a shrine. Although there were rumors that Mawlay Idris's body might be interred in the oldest quarter of Fes, either in the house reputedly built by Idris himself or in the nearby mosque known as Masjid al-Shurafā', those who insisted that Mawlay Idris was present in Fes could not specify the exact place of burial, and therefore there was no cult of pilgrimage and visitation to the site. An anonymous history of the Maghrib tells the story in detail: "Nobody had been able to pinpoint the exact site of the burial, until that moment when Allah willed its appearance, as a sign of compassion and grace to this divinely appointed community of faith. So it was agreed to test the foundation of the *qibla* wall [in the Masjid al-Shurafa'] to the right side [of the *miḥrāb*]. Within the foundation of the wall they found the tomb [*sic*]. But it was impossible to repair or restore the building of the tomb, for almost nothing remained. However, the bones of the deceased [Mawlay Idris] remained there as they were, untouched by earthly decay."[26] This account leaves tantalizing obscurities as to the agency and intent behind this incident. Who was in charge of the "rediscovery" and why were they digging up the foundation of a wall of the mosque? How is it that a tomb was uncovered and needed to be restored when there admittedly was no tomb there in the first place? Answers to these questions point to the critical political importance of this "rediscovery" of a tomb that had never existed before.

The author clearly frames this uncovering of the bones of Mawlay Idris as a miracle, "a sign of compassion and grace to this divinely appointed community of faith." It was certainly a time when a miracle was needed. The Portuguese were assaulting the port of Tangier, and the Marinid sultan appeared unwilling or unable to lead its defense; it was left to various Sufi groups and *shurafa'* to lead troops in the city's defense. The uncovering of the body of their saintly ancestor in the center of Fes seemed to confirm the victory of the defensive jihad against the Iberians led by the *shurafa'*.

The anonymous history also provides some later clues about the agency of those who discovered the saint's body and bones. It seems that the original demolition of the wall's foundation was presided over by the "representative of the descendants of the Prophet," 'Ali al-'Imrani, head of the al-Juti clan in Fes.[27] He identified the bones as those of his ancestor, Mawlay Idris. Because there was no structure that could be identified as a previous tomb, he had a plaque installed, inscribed with the name of the interred saint. "Words were carved into a stone on the wall, certifying that this was the actual tomb. Indeed, the tomb was there, and these words were inscribed so that one could bear eyewitness to the man never forgotten in the traditions told by trustworthy narrators."[28] The leader of the *shurafa'* immediately called upon the chief minister and the prayer leader of the Qarawiyyin mosque.[29] They arrived at the site to authenticate the body. They confirmed that a mortuary building (*ḍarīḥ*) should be erected to commemorate the burial site "and ordered that shoes be taken off around the site so that no misstep might impinge upon his honor."[30] In this way a tomb was "restored" that had never before existed, on the site of a body that had been "rediscovered" where it had been "known" to always be. Some Western scholars have found these circumstances to be so serendipitous as to be unbelievable and have alleged that the sharifian leader, ʿAli al-ʿImrani, staged the miracle by having his ancestor's body exhumed from his father's tomb near Walili and reburied in the center of Fes.[31]

Whether Mawlay Idris al-Azhar's tomb was "discovered" by serendipitous interaction, supernatural intervention, or scheming invention, its new marking as a sacred space proved overwhelmingly popular. It gave Fes a new center, as if a sign of rejuvenation during a military crisis in the north. Indeed, some sources recall that the body of Mawlay Idris was uncovered intact and unchanged since the day of its burial, rather than just suggested by the presence of bones.[32] This suggested to the devoted public not just that the Moroccan polity would persist against the Iberians, like bones persist against the steady moist pressure of decay, but that it would actually overcome them, for the body of its founder and patron never decayed. Ahmad al-Fasi defended the rumor that Mawlay Idris's body was found uncorrupted by decay, even after "six-hundred and thirty-two years, six months and twenty-one days in the ground," even if he had to contradict the explicit words of the plaque that marks his tomb, a plaque that mentions that the saint's "bones" were found.

> Be warned that when the description inscribed on the stone plaque says, "The bones of the deceased remained there as they were, untouched by earthly decay," it does not mean the bone (*ʿaẓm*) in distinction from the flesh (*laḥm*) of the body, as one who is ignorant of Arabic linguistics and grammatical use of words might erroneously imagine. . . . If the author intended to mean bones as opposed to flesh, there would be no purpose to his saying they "remained there as they were," meaning as they were before his death or at the time of his burial. Rather the author emphasized that they remained as they were "untouched by earthly decay." This is a proverbial expression, just as we say, "The earth does not encroach upon the flesh of the prophets (*al-ʿarḍ lā yaʿdū ʿalā luḥūm al-anbiyāʾ*)," upon them be peace. The same is said of religious scholars who practiced righteousness and Sufi sages. Just this year, a jurist in Egypt published a book in which he reported finding the body of saint, when one wall of tomb collapsed, in a pure condition like the day he was buried. If this is true of a common saint, just imagine the state of incorruptibility of one who joins together virtues too numerous to count, like Imam Idris and his father![33]

If this were not proof enough that "the author wrote bones but meant the flesh and the whole body," the hagiographer cites a line of Arabic poetry, sung in mourning for Ṭalḥa al-Ṭalḥāt: "May God be merciful with the bones they buried / in Sijistān, the bones of Talha al-Talhat." He continues:

> It is said of Talha that he was among the most generous of the Arabs. . . . Look closely at the poem as it says, "the bones that they buried." You know by necessity that they did not bury his bones stripped bare of the flesh of his body! Even if it is possible that he was killed in battle, the flesh would not be stripped from his bones upon burial, so that cannot be the intent of the poet. You must realize, then, that the poet spoke the name of a body part to signify the whole of the body . . . for bones are the foundation that support the body (*diʿāmat al-jism*). If one says the bones are together, meaning either gathered together or held together, then one means that the body remains intact, for its foundation (*aṣl*) remains intact. It would be as if one had said body rather than simply bones.[34]

Just as the *shurafaʾ* were leading a war in the north of Morocco to keep the political body from being dismembered or disintegrating, our hagiographer pictures the saint's body as whole, untouched by decomposition and unsullied by the soil that veils it from view.

This cultural obsession with the wholeness of the body as the foundation for moral righteousness and political cohesiveness is common to other cultures. Jewish conceptions of purity offer an enlightening comparison, and Jon Berquist has argued that the whole male body unbroken was the governing image of the pure society in ancient Israel. "What makes a whole body among ancient Israelites? First, a whole body contains all its parts and functions . . . bodies that leak or ooze violate the sense of firm boundaries, and so these bodies are not whole. In particular, whole bodies avoid contact with other bodies that are different: bodies of another gender, bodies of another species, bodies that are not whole, and bodies that are not alive. . . . What was at stake in the wholeness of bodies? For members of the ancient Israelite community, almost everything. The body had two important social functions: it mediated a person's involvement with the rest of society and it symbolically represented social cohesion."[35] These dimensions of the whole male body applied with equal vividness to Islamic societies, and the hagiographer Ahmad al-Fasi extended their importance into the realm of the dead with Mawlay Idris's body, for as a saint he is not really to be considered gone. Rather, his body remains a marker of the potent boundary between this world and the next world, ensuring that the society that centers itself upon him will cohere, remain politically viable, fertile, and strong.

Whether his body was discovered by chance or revealed by stealth, whether what remained were bones or the intact flesh, once Mawlay Idris's burial place was identified and his tomb built, the Marinid rulers and Sufis loyal to their regime were forced to acknowledge sharifian political might. The refurbished tomb shrine gave the *shurafa'* a new architectural symbol of their religious legitimacy as leaders of the people of Fes. The rulers were coerced into giving the *shurafa'* increasing political power as they themselves lost public credibility. As he stood over the site of Mawlay Idris's body to grant money for the reconstruction of a tomb, the minister of state was hailed as "the preserver of love for the *shurafa'*, ever ready to show forth their exalted status and establish their glory, always desiring to revive the example of their glorious ancestor [the Prophet Muhammad]."[36] The same *shurafa'* whom the Marinid officials lauded and graced with a grand tomb shrine would rebel against their rule only twenty-five years later, bringing the Marinid dynasty to an ignoble end and heralding the rise of a new dynastic ideology, the legitimacy of sharifian rulers, which would dominate Moroccan politics until the present.

Bones, Mortar, and Healing Dust

The body of Idris was discovered at a key moment, and his tomb was built suddenly. Its establishment was spectacularly successful, inspired a revolution, and changed the sacred geography of the city entirely. Though its success was without precedent, its design as a tomb shrine did have precedent. Searching Fes for other tombs that evolved more slowly, I found the tomb of another sharifian saint from the Idrisi family, which had evolved slowly into a political pivot point for its custodians and the surrounding community. It gained full prominence in the generation before the discovery of Mawlay Idris al-Azhar. It may have been the success of these *shurafa'* in promoting a tomb as a source of financial clout, religious reputation, and social status that inspired the sharifian leader ʿAli al-ʿImrani to "rediscover" the body of Mawlay Idris al-Azhar in his own neighborhood and construct a tomb shrine around it. Exploring this earlier tomb will help us make sense of the metaphorical extension of the bones through the dust that covers them, the perfumed aroma that arises from them, and the tomb that publicizes their location.

To understand how this alliance between the Sufis and sharifian clans was taking shape in the fifteenth century, we have to examine the Qādirī community of Fes. "Qadiri" refers to people who trace their allegiance back to the great twelfth-century saint of Baghdad, ʿAbd al-Qādir al-Jīlānī. In Fes, Qadiri could refer to those with direct family ties to ʿAbd al-Qadir, which makes them sharifian notables, or it could refer to those with spiritual ties through Sufi initiation leading back to ʿAbd al-Qadir. The pivot of this alliance between Sufi Qadiris and sharifian Qadiris was the tomb of Abū Ghālib.

Because of Castilian aggression around Granada, the Qadiri sharifian clan emigrated from Andalusia to Fes. Led by its patriarchal leader, Abu Muhammad al-Qadiri, this clan carved out for itself devotional niches in the city and gained popular fame in the fifteenth century C.E. Al-Qadiri's descendants settled a neighborhood in Fes in the center of which stood the shrine of a saintly man, whose name was Abu Ghalib (died in 1399).[37] Although Abu Ghalib is not a historically documented personage, his hagiographic story is crucial, for through it the Qadiri *shurafaʾ* allied with Idrisi *shurafaʾ* of Fes and integrated themselves into the city's power structure. As we have seen, the Idrisi *shurafaʾ* were the most powerful clans in Fes, especially the five families of the al-Juti clan. They all trace their decent through Mawlay Idris back to Hasan, the grandson of the Prophet. The Qadiri *shurafaʾ* also trace their lineage through Hasan, through one of his great-grandsons, Mūsā ibn ʿAbdullah al-Kāmil (the Idrisi families, on the other hand, trace their descent through a closely related great-grandson, Idris ibn ʿAbdullah al-Kamil). The Qadiri families would be seen as distant cousins of the Idrisi families, cousins long since separated by geography and culture, with no established status in Morocco. The Qadiris cleverly used the tomb of Abu Ghalib to bridge the apparent gulf in genealogy and status.

Abu Ghalib descended from the Idrisi family of *shurafaʾ*, who descended from Mawlay Idris. A group of these *shurafaʾ* returned to settle in Fes after their long exile from the city. Having been expelled from Fes after losing power, they had found refuge in the town of Ṣirāwa. When political conditions eventually changed in Fes, they returned. The neighborhood they founded in Fes was therefore known as al-Ṣirāwiyyīn, "the quarter of the settlers from Sirawa." A grandson of one of these returned *shurafaʾ*, Abu Ghalib, was a doctor, a surgeon or bloodletter (*ḥajjām*, or in some accounts *ḥakīm*). He developed a reputation (at least posthumously) for pious ecstasy and generosity to the Sufis, who gathered at his home. Eventually, he converted his ancestral home into a Sufi gathering place (*zāwiya*), and when he died, he was buried on the spot.

Abu Ghalib seems to have pursued his profession even after death, for his tomb gained wide renown as a center of healing, especially of open sores or wounds. People sought the dirt of Abu Ghalib's grave or the water from the fountain at the tomb for blessing and cure: so much so that "his miracles as a dead man are more than his miracles while living."[38] The *mawsim* of Abu Ghalib, the celebration of the anniversary of his death, was an occasion for free circumcision of children whose families were too poor to provide the ceremony. The importance of this tomb, however, went beyond free health care. Its popularity as a devotional center provided the *shurafa'* with a platform of power.

The Idrisi *shurafa'* who settled at al-Sirawiyyin were reinforced by another contingent of *shurafa'*, from the al-Ṭālibī clan (a branch of the powerful al-Juti al-ʿImrani family). Marinid rulers had forcibly moved these *shurafa'* from their ancestral stronghold in the center of Fes. In recompense, the Marinids decreed that the financial proceeds from Abu Ghalib's tomb and charitable contributions to its founder would go to the coffers of the al-Talibi *shurafa'*. Through this arrangement, a branch of the sharifian al-Juti clan became the promoters and caretakers of Abu Ghalib's tomb and reinforced the story of his original sharifian genealogy. It may have been the success of these *shurafa'* in promoting a tomb as a source of clout that inspired the sharifian leader ʿAli al-ʿImrani to find the body of Mawlay Idris.

Further, another clan of *shurafa'*, the Qadiris, settled in Fes and became deeply involved in the promotion of the tomb of Abu Ghalib. This clan was descended from the famous scholar and Sufi from Baghdad ʿAbd al-Qadir Jilani. Settling in al-Sirawiyyin, it entered into close relations with the al-Juti al-ʿImrani clan, whose members composed poems lauding the curing power of Abu Ghalib's tomb.

> Abu Ghalib, I call you seeking healing and ease
> for you are a doctor for every disease.
> You answer the one who prays for success
> So sustain me from your loftiness with a fragrant breeze
> Do not seal me out, by your beneficent might
> for I am weak, while your saintly power will amaze.[39]

The arrival of the Qadiris and their alliance with the ʿImrani *shurafa'* was crucial to the success of Abu Ghalib's tomb. They crafted out of the sketchy biography of Abu Ghalib a mythic story in which the saint Abu Ghalib mirrored the personality of their own pious ancestor, ʿAbd al-Qadir al-Jilani. The reputation of ʿAbd al-Qadir as a healer (in the Islamic tradition, second only to Jesus) helped to bolster the local efficacy of Abu Ghalib's earthly remains. As a historian of the Qadiri family later explained, "Jesus was known for reviving the dead and giving them new life. Likewise, ʿAbd al-Qadir was known for having miracles flow through his hands that could revive the dead. Nobody else could compare with them in healing the sick, except for Abu Ghalib, the saintly descendant of Mawlay Idris of Fes. He would heal people with his blessings and cures during his life, and also after his death as people visited him and prayed over his tomb."[40] This is not an unjustified boast from an al-Qadiri descendant, for in the ecstatic poetry ascribed to him, ʿAbd al-Qadir himself boasts of his ability to heal like Jesus. He explicitly ties this miraculous ability to his sharifian genealogical descent in a form of poetry whose outer form is the celebration of wine drinking (*khamriyya*) and whose inner force is the spiritual boast (*shaṭḥiyya*), like this *qaṣīda* attributed to ʿAbd al-Qadir.

> Among God's saints I cast the proof that in my heart reposes
>   they flew into rapture from my inner secret and my outer poses
> My cup intoxicated them, my potent ferment left them rapt
>   wonder-struck drunk by my being and insight that truth discloses
> I read the Gospel and explained it all concisely
>   my brother is none other than ʿImrān's son, named Moses
> I grasp an enigma that Jesus had previously unraveled
>   a Syriac enigma that revives one whom death decomposes
> I plunged into seas of knowledge even before my inebriation
>   I grasped the Hebrew meaning of the Torah's poetries and proses
> Who else among the true men of God has earned my position?
>   pure bloodline of Muhammad, my ancestor, Lordly inspiration transposes
> My family is from Zahrāʾ, the daughter of Muhammad
>   child of God's Messenger, to what nobility my nature predisposes![41]

As the Qadiris lent the miraculous reputation of their ancestor to Abu Ghalib's tomb to undergird the saint's hagiography with echoes of the life of ʿAbd al-Qadir al-Jilani, the crowds poured in. So many people were collecting earth from Abu Ghalib's graveside to use as medicine that the practice sparked a juristic debate on whether it was legal in religious law. The Qadiri clans claimed that the practice was legal, based on traditional reports that early Muslims used earth from the tomb of the Prophet's uncle, Hamza, for

attend with them sessions of devotional music and poetry (*samāʿ*) whenever he had time. Listening, he would sway in a trance and dance in ecstasy. Then he began to practice such sessions at his home, with whoever would follow him there, every Thursday night and into the day on Friday. Those who were wont to listen to such music would gather at his house and keep him company, and he grew famous in Fes for these devotions. His state of ecstasy would flood over into others, and many people would become his pupils. Slowly, his home grew into a *zawiya* where they would live together."[45] What is fascinating about this story is how the uninvited guest, Abu Ghalib, eventually set himself up as the keeper of the *zawiya* and dispenser of hospitality to other Sufis. In this story, we can discern traces of the Qadiri *shurafa'* themselves. They came to Fes uninvited as refugees, but by building alliances with more established Idrisi *shurafa'* they were able to found devotional centers across the city.

Today, the tomb of Abu Ghalib still exists, but it is rarely visited. It no longer functions as the location of a *zawiya*. Abu Ghalib is best known in contemporary Fes not for his tomb, its healing dust, or the raptures that used to happen there but rather for a popular proverb, "Whoever loves the master Abu Ghalib loves him by loving his cats."[46] When cited today, the proverb communicates that one expresses one's love for another by showering love on his or her children, as if the cats at Abu Ghalib's tomb were his children. However, when viewed against the history of his tomb, the proverb takes on another meaning. Whoever wants to love the saint must love his children, so whoever wishes to be close to Mawlay Idris, the ancestor of Abu Ghalib (or the Prophet Muhammad, who was ancestor to them both), must love him through his children, the *shurafa'* who built and patronized his tomb. Yet because the image is of the master's "cats" and not just his children, the proverb is expansive and covers with its canopy of love the Qadiri Sufis as well, who, though not related to the saint by blood, nevertheless claim a powerful spiritual connection to him. At its most abstract level, the proverb teaches that loving a person is most respectfully expressed by loving the objects associated with him or her; at this level, the proverb hints at the contagiousness of sacredness and the love it inspires. Objects close to a person are infused with that person's aura, so a holy person's clothes, artifacts, tomb, and everything found near him or her radiates the holiness of that person, even long after her or his death.

The ability of spiritual value to infuse material objects returns our attention to bones. Throughout this chapter, we have observed how the spiritual potency of people who lived a life of holiness is preserved in their bones. This idea of physical perpetuation of spiritual power is reflected also in the idea of genealogical perpetuation of spiritual power. Just as the holiness of saints inheres in their bones, their holiness can inhere in the children and families they leave behind. This paradoxical relationship between spiritual power and material objects is best reconciled in incense. Incense is usually burning in the shrines over saints' tombs, and its heady fragrance infuses all objects in the vicinity. We earlier observed how incense burners played a dramatic sensory role in the yearly procession to the tomb of Mawlay Idris.[47] Incense is matter, though its sensory presence in its aroma only grows more intense when its solid material form is destroyed. Burning it increases its potency, spreads its effect, and intensifies its durable traces.

By abandoning the limited solidity of its material form, incense "floods over into others" just like the hagiographic record presented above depicts Abu Ghalib's spiritual state flooding over into others when he abandoned himself to rapture. In similar ways, the charismatic presence of the Prophet flows through multiple channels of his descendants' bodies among the *shurafa'* or wells up in distant, diverse springs in the bodies of saints who have Sufi initiations linking them back to the Prophet. All these images reflect and support each other to highlight the interconnection between people in a religious community. The spiritual potency that Sufis insist is most intensely felt at a holy person's tomb is the more general immaterial connection between people that is social, cultural, and religious, a connection that binds people together into a whole, like ligaments bind the bones and the organs that depend on them into a whole body. This image uncovers one of the primary meanings of the word "religion" as derived from *re-ligare*, a binding together again. The lesson we can take from Mawlay Idris and Abu Ghalib is that material props are required to achieve this immaterial effervescence of communal harmony and social unity. Material props must give space a meaningful form through the architecture and urban geography. Time, too, must be shaped into meaningful divisions through the material trappings of ritual and performance of devotion. The tombs of saints in Islamic cultures, reinforced by the mystical practices of Sufi communities, manifest these subtle operations of religion and provide "pegs" to preserve the order of the human cosmos.

Saints' Bodies and the Body Politic

The bodies of people who are accepted by the public as saints are special bodies. They are marked off as sites of sacred power, perhaps while the person is alive and certainly once the person has passed away. Saints are believed to have overcome their selfish egotistical natures, whether through ascetic austerities, ecstatic raptures, or scholarly discipline. Their actions in society, then, contrast with the actions of others. Their actions are seen as the actions of God channeled through them: this is exactly how Muslim authors define miracles, or *karamat*, literally acts of "noble generosity." It is as if the personality of the saint becomes transparent, like glass. When set against the material of the body, which is like metal, the saint can take on the reflective qualities of a mirror. The social public can see its most cherished values and aspirations reflected in a saint. Miracle stories preserve this social role of saints, who are perceived to provide generous sustenance in times of scarcity, water in times of drought, and protection in times of crisis. When saints die, their place of burial retains this sacred quality. It is ultimately unimportant for an outside observer to judge whether miracles happen or not. They are perceived to happen, and miracle stories are told as part of a people's self-understanding. As the mirror of a society's self-understanding, miracles and the saints that channel them have a political potency, especially during times of political instability.

The rediscovery of the body of Idris occurred during a period of intense political instability. The building of the shrine to house his newfound tomb gives evidence of a revolution—a revolution not only in the urban geography of Fes but also in spiritual thought and dynastic politics within the city. It gives architectural evidence of an alliance that was growing in Morocco between Sufi communities and sharifian notables. Only twenty-five years after the rediscovery of Mawlay Idris's body and the building of his tomb, the sharifian clans led a rebellion. Public discontent with the Marinid ruler had reached a climax. The tax burden was increasing. The Portuguese had recently conquered Tangier, and the Spaniards had taken Gibraltar, while the Marinid ruler seemed unconcerned or incapable of military response. In 1465, on the Night of Power (Laylat al-Qadr), the most sacred night in the holy month of Ramaḍān, the people of Fes rose up against the Marinid ruler, spurred on by sharifian notables and Qadiri Sufis. The sultan was executed, and the leader of the *shurafa*ʾ, ʿAli al-ʿImrani, became the leader of Fes. Although this sharifian republic did not last, the rebellion signaled the end of the Marinid dynasty, which reconquered Fes but never regained control of wider Morocco. Within a few generations, it was pushed out by the Saʿdian dynasty, which represented a potent new alliance of a Sufi community, led by a network of living saints, and a sharifian clan from southern Morocco.

The Saʿdian dynasty conquered Fes with great difficulty. The remains of the Marinid dynastic families fought stubbornly, supported by the Ottoman Empire far to the east. In addition, many religious authorities (scholars, jurists, and some Sufis) in Fes were not eager to see the city subjugated once again by rulers based in the rival city of Marrakesh. The Saʿdian leader, Muhammad al-Shaykh, conquered Fes once only to lose control of it shortly thereafter, in 1554 C.E. When his son, ʿAbdullah, finally solidified Saʿdian control over Fes the following year, he was faced with the problem of asserting the legitimacy of his rule over a city that harbored resentment against him. So he turned to the tomb of Mawlay Idris to provide the spiritual authority to rebind the body politic together with himself as its head. "Our Lord ʿAbdullah ibn Muhammad al-Shaykh, when he came to rule over Fes, desired to visit Imam Idris ibn Idris. So his retainers and members of his court said to him, 'How can it be fitting for you to visit Imam Idris when you have constructed nothing in Fes, such as what the Marinid rulers constructed of mosques and madrassas and such beautiful buildings and edifices that remain as testament to them? But look how they covered the resting place of Imam Idris with just a roof low to the ground, no grander than the roof over [the tomb of] the master, Muhammad ibn ʿAbbād! How will you show the loftiness of stature through which those who rule after you [in the sharifian dynasty] will lord over those who ruled before you [the Marinids]?'"[48] Ibn ʿAbbad al-Rundi was a famous Sufi saint of Fes (died 1390). His personality was emblematic of the Marinid dynasty, for he served in its heyday as the head preacher at the congregational mosque of al-Qarawiyyin, was a professor of Islamic law in its official Islamic colleges, and served as a spiritual exemplar in its capital city. Despite his great spiritual stature and popularity, his tomb (located just inside Bāb al-Futūḥ in old Fes) was very humble. The Saʿdian courtiers compared the shrine that the Marinids built over Mawlay Idris with the low-roofed and humble structure they had built over Ibn ʿAbbad in order to encourage the new Saʿdian ruler to outshine them and raise the status of Mawlay Idris as a symbol of their new hold on Fes, far above the archetypically Marinid personality of Ibn ʿAbbad.

Shamed by his courtiers, the ruler of the new Saʿdian dynasty ordered that a new roof be raised over the tomb of Mawlay Idris to enclose three tiled courtyards. "It is said that only after the construction was complete in the most beautiful form and perfect design did he come into the presence of Mawlay Idris with great humility and respect."[49] In this way, the shrine around Mawlay Idris's tomb took the form that it currently has today (despite continuous repairs, enlargements, and elaborations). In contrast, the tomb of Ibn ʿAbbad fell into disrepair and neglect.

Conclusion

In this story of architectural patronage and the devotional intent to embellish and decorate the surface of the tomb, we can observe a more general dynamic. The saint's body acts as a mirror for the religious virtues around which society can adhere and upon which political rulers can establish their authority. Samuel Landell Mills, an astute anthropological observer of Sufi communities, suggests that we understand the importance of the material surface of this mirroring quality, for spirituality is manifested and power only its "material extensions" in physical surfaces that are open to our sensory attachment. Because our attention is focused on saintly tombs as architectural sites, he refers us to the art historian Joanne Waghorne, whose work on South Asian religion and politics, *The Raja's Magic Clothes*, asks us to reassess our Western denunciation of "the surface" as irrelevant.[50] "Waghorne has suggested that the 'vital surfaces' of objects (and of holy persons like South Asian divine kings or Pirs [saints]) have been neglected by religious studies and by anthropology as a result of Victorian bowdlerization of sanctity and the concomitant devaluation of magic. Against the notion that the essence of spirituality is other-worldly and beyond ordinary materiality, perception or intention, Waghorne suggests that 'the spiritual is coterminous with the very outwardness that the nineteenth century scholar assumed must give way to some inner truth.' The very point of the sacred or the divine is its 'suspension in time and space; in other words, its material extensions.'"[51] Waghorne critiques art history in ways parallel to how Asad critiques the anthropology of religion, for both devalued material expression in the name of interpreting essential meaning.

Both Waghorne and Asad remind us that it is through the material surface of the saint, the tomb and shrine that can be built above the bodily remains of his bones, that rulers can forge a social image of the saint for posterity. It is an image that rulers can use or manipulate to reflect their own power, prestige, and authority. While materially dependent on rulers for the vast financial outlay that such building projects require, the tomb shrine is never totally determined by the rulers' intentions. Once built, it is accessible to the public. People can appropriate it for their own needs and extract from it empowerment for their own intentions. It is the ability of the saint, or the bony remains of his or her body, to be something for everyone—he or she can mirror the wishes of those who approach its sacred environment. When a shrine is built around the tomb, it becomes a *mashhad*, "a place that provides a view for witnessing." The tomb becomes a theater or spectacle. It makes evident to the senses (primarily the visual sense but also the senses of smell, taste, touch, and hearing) of what is normally hidden. The building, crowds and rituals make evident the hidden body of the holy person and the life she or he lived. It also makes evident the continuity of life beyond death, amplifying (through architecture, decorative art, devotional music, religious ritual, and social interaction) how the bones themselves mark this continuity. The shrine manifests the miracle-producing permeation of God through the material world—it is a *theophany*, in Eliade's terms, an irruption of the sacred into the profane through a socially created division in space and time.

The building of Mawlay Idris's tomb marked an upsurge of patriotism, religious fervor, and political reorganization that led Moroccans to defend their Atlantic and Mediterranean coasts from assaults by the Portuguese and Spanish. These early modern European powers led the drive to colonize the Islamic world, but they largely failed. They were successful at seizing control of coastal towns and fortifying them as naval bases and trade warehouses. However, Moroccan and wider Islamic resistance pushed the Portuguese and Spanish farther afield: around the southern tip of Africa into the Indian Ocean and, with more devastating consequences, across the Atlantic to the American continents. It took at least three centuries for these European "discoveries" to develop into mercantile networks, colonial empires and nation-states. By the nineteenth century, Islamic polities were being toppled while Muslims increasingly questioned or denounced the building of elaborate tombs for royalty and saints. That tension will occupy our attention in the concluding chapter. However, in the three centuries of the early modern period, Sufi communities continued to cherish the bodies of their saints, during life and after death. The next chapters focus on four saints' bodies that were very much alive through hagiographic stories that captured their vitality.

2

BODY POLITICIZED

The Belly of Sayyida Āmina

To God are the hidden aspects of the heavens and the earth
And the day of reckoning is like a flash of the eye, or even more sudden
For God is capable of all things.
God has brought you forth from the bellies of your mothers
When you knew nothing, and made for you ears and eyes and mouths
That you might give thanks.
—Qurʾan 16:77–78

The Qurʾan speaks of creation in different levels through diverse metaphors. Whether addressing the creation of the expansive universe or a tiny human life, the Qurʾan illustrates the creative dynamic through contrasting pairs: as light from darkness, heaven above earth, water beyond land, spirit within matter, the seen emerges from the unseen. Like each pair in these examples, the Qurʾan depicts human beings in gendered pairs, contrasting female with male. It pictures the process of creation through the union of distinctly gendered bodies and represents them as embodying different elements of the holistic process.

Does the Qurʾan's scriptural bifurcation of the human being into a gendered pair irrevocably inscribe patriarchal values into the core of Islam as a religion? This is a profound question that feminist scholars debate. The stakes in the answer are very high, and the answer is not obvious. As in most questions put to the Qurʾan, the answer is ambiguous. The Qurʾan depicts gendered bodies in different ways at different moments, generating real tensions that authentic interpreters embrace rather than smooth over. As the Qurʾan was revealed in a patriarchal social milieu in Arabia, its images of women's bodies both play into and play off the social norms of its first hearers. It clearly inspired many Arab women to risk all they had (status, wealth, family, and even their bodily safety) to join the new religious community, and it speaks in many places of egalitarian and reciprocal relations between women and men as the ideal norm. However, at other times, the Qurʾan speaks less of ideals and addresses the immediate social needs of a new community in times of crisis, and it appears to reify some aspects of a patriarchal social order. Whether the patriarchal order was a temporary compromise with Arab and Near Eastern cultures or the eternal pillars of a unique religious law is a question with which later Muslims have wrestled, whether they were medieval male jurists or they are contemporary female reformers.

However, as is clear from the verses that headed this chapter, the Qur'an points out women's role in procreation as an integral part of God's continuing, sustaining, and re-creating the human cosmos. The phrasing *God has brought you forth from the bellies of your mothers* stresses the continuity of creative power between God the ultimate fashioner and the mother who is intimately involved in nurturing and shaping that creation with her very body: indeed, the name of God, the merciful One (*raḥmān*), echoes the word for the womb (*raḥim*). It continually reminds us that before we had our own bodies with independent *ears and eyes and mouths*, our bodies were nothing but our mothers' bodies. By associating women with the womb, the Qur'an not only advocates the virtue of caring for others and respecting one's ties to them but also suggests that revering one's mother is the way to understand the compassionate quality of God, for al-Rahman is the most common name for God in the Qur'an after Allah. However, this very association of women with the womb can become the root principle of patriarchal empowering of men over women and misogynistic denigration of women before men.

This chapter explores the belly, especially the belly of women. The belly is an ambiguous region, defined not by a particular organ but by a cultural concatenation of images. Our Sufi guide, Nakhshabi, is of only limited use to us here. He writes, "If you think loins are for girding with swords and britches / no no, the loins safeguard the noblest treasure and riches," meaning the treasure of marital fidelity and the riches of legitimate progeny.[1] His image of swords and britches alerts us to Nakhshabi's very masculine depiction of "loins." He does not even approach describing the belly or loins of women, which are for him "the lowlier parts of the body, from among those organs that cannot be mentioned with honor . . . whose names cannot, for shame, ever roll off the tongue!" In our feminist-informed world, we have to proceed beyond Nakhshabi's politesse, giving him a nod of acknowledgment as we pass him by.

Clearly, the belly of women is the location of the womb and other organs of reproduction, but through a common cultural logic the womb is also connected to organs of nutrition. Thus the womb becomes just one site in a network of connected organs and functions through which women are closely associated with nourishment and sustenance. The anatomical ambiguity of "the belly" represents this network rather than any specific organ. Focus on the belly will give us insights into the life and legacy of a woman saint, Sayyida Āmina bint Aḥmad Ibn al-Qāḍī, who lived in sixteenth-century Fes, in a neighborhood not far from the tomb of Mawlay Idris. Examining her life and contrasting her with other female saints of North Africa will require us to apply concepts from feminist social theory to evidence recorded in hagiographic sources. We will ask how female saints negotiated the patriarchal order of Islamic public space and perhaps reveal something of the limits of that order.

The Children of Eve

In the previous chapter, on the bones of Mawlay Idris al-Azhar and other saints, the protagonists were all male. Although the shrines around their tombs serve as gathering places for women as well as men, the custodians are all men, and men alone are allowed in the inner chamber, where one can touch the tomb's cloth covering. In particular, the political function of the tomb is manifestly patriarchal, serving as it does to justify a monarchy based upon patrilineal genealogy, from a prophet-king, Muhammad, through a saint-king, Idris, to his descendants. We know little of Mawlay Idris while he was alive. He was considered a saint posthumously: the power of his saintly body was fully revealed only long after his death. In this regard, he reveals a general pattern. Most saints' stories (in the genre of hagiography) are recorded after they die and grow embellished after their death with the fortunes of their followers or descendants. We can chart their posthumous career through the object of their tombs, their architectural space and the social relations that are established and renewed through it. In this sense, the tomb is a phenomenon that straddles the binary distinction between "inanimate object" and "animate presence."

However, not all saints are men. Hagiographic collections that record the stories of Muslim saints include stories about women. Their stories are doubly complex, since they present not only how holy women overcome routine limitations to become saints but also how they overcome the routine limitations their society places upon women. Despite the limitations described above, our Sufi guide, Nakhshabi, does record how some women became ascetic renouncers and spiritual exemplars. He tells the story of one such woman whose competing suitors plagued her. Tired from their overweening competitive machismo, she even feigned death, but they revived her in order to continue fighting with each other over who would possess her through marriage. "She said, 'Praise be to God! What kind of families do these men come from? In life they would not leave me in peace, and there was no escape from them even in death. It is best for me not to become involved with a husband.'[2] Then she left her "house of discord" and renounced worldly matters to live in a Sufi hospice, shaving her head and wearing a woolen robe to devote herself to worship in order to cleanse her soul of sensual desires. Nakhshabi interrupts his prose narrative with a poem: "O Nakhshabi, pray for happiness in the life to come / for the good of this world, what brave deeds are you performing? / Blessed are those who today renounce worldly pleasures / and thus achieve eternal bliss in heaven by reforming." When her suitors heard about her actions, they were disappointed and despaired of ever enjoying her company or her conjugal love; releasing her from their claims, each went his way.

Examining in detail the stories of women who became Sufis and even saints is critical to understanding the Islamic patriarchy that defines their horizons of possibility, even as they push against its boundaries and, perhaps, overturn its expected norms. In contrast to Mawlay Idris, some stories of saints reveal more about them as living social persons and illuminate how they came to be regarded as saints while still alive. Sayyida Amina is one of those saints whose story is preserved for us (against great odds) as a woman who was considered saintly in the public spaces of Fes. Her story reveals her individuality as a *majdhūba*, or a mad woman saint whose powers of reason were broken by the divine attraction that pulled her toward God. However, her story also reveals how she broke through the stereotypes that surround women saints as holy people in women's bodies, which patriarchal societies differentiate from male bodies through obsession with the belly.

Patriarchy is a difficult concept to define, for it is used in different ways by authors from different disciplines and varies between being a term of description and one of critique. The sociologist Brian Turner has provided a usefully broad definition of patriarchy that integrates its social, economic, political, and religious dimensions: Patriarchy is "a system of political authority, based upon the household, in which dominant property-owning males control and regulate the lives of subordinate members of the household, regardless of their sex or age. . . . Young males are as much subject to patriarchal authority as women . . . this primitive system of patriarchy

Miniature painting of a woman (lower left) who takes refuge from her husband (top center), who accuses her of infidelity, by fleeing to a graveyard containing the tomb of a Muslim saint. Painted in North India around 1560. From Nakhshabī, *Ṭūṭī-Nāma*, or "Tales of a Parrot," ms. (Cleveland: © The Cleveland Museum of Art, 1997, Gift of Mrs. A. Dean Perry, 1962.279), fol. 10b.

became linked eventually to monarchical power, since there was an obvious parallel between the authority of husbands and that of the monarch over his people. In turn, this husband/monarch system of power was related to divine fatherly rule on the part of a benevolent God."[3] We will see in our conclusion how the Wahhabi movement reinforces patriarchy with ideological force and reformist fervor; in their drive for moral certitude and social control, Wahhabis banish women from the public realm, from positions of independence, and even from vision. The Wahhabis certainly did not invent this regime of puritan patriarchal control, as it was inscribed in Islamic juridical texts and moralistic treatises (in the formative period from the ninth to the twelfth century C.E.). Rather, the Wahhabis interpret these texts more rigidly than other Muslims, apply the norms of gender hierarchy more zealously, and strive to eliminate devotional communities or social spaces in which alternate interpretations are practiced, such as in the Sufi community and at saints' tombs. Feminist scholars often uphold Sufi communities as Islamic spaces in which patriarchal norms are more flexible and women have more scope for independence, expression, and even authority, at least in possibility if not always in practice.[4] Just as Wahhabis did not invent the patriarchy they preach, so also Islamic societies are not unique in their patriarchal norms. Christian and Jewish traditions are also largely patriarchal.

Even in their transition into modernity, European Christians valorized patriarchal ideals. For instance, René Descartes reified notions of mathematical rationality that reinforced the centrality of a dualistic cleavage between mind and body that became deeply entrenched in modern, largely post-Christian societies. In his *Meditations*, Descartes begins his thought experiment to reach intellectual certainty "with a description of his body that is so clinically remote as to suggest that he is speaking in the third person. The body is itemized with such complete detachment that its personal attachment to the speaker comes into doubt: 'In the first place, then, I considered myself as having a face, hands and arms, and all that system of members composed of flesh and bones as seen in a corpse which I designated by the name of a body.'"[5] In this way, Descartes reinscribed in modern culture a patriarchal and highly male-centered view of humanity that he adopted from his Christian background. The patriarchal values of Descartes' quest for intellectual certainty are vividly apparent in his 1864 correspondence with Princess Elizabeth of Sweden, who critiqued his insistence on absolute separation of knowing mind and sensing body that denigrates the body by creating what Judowitz calls "a disembodied reason and the mechanized body."[6]

Princess Elizabeth could plainly see the continuity between Descartes' disembodied reason and Christian ascetic control: despite their different modes of expression and different epistemological frameworks, both systems identified the human body as the site of error, misguidance, and pollution. She could sense, with rare insight from an early modern vantage point, what the novelist Milan Kundera expresses from a postmodern vantage point, namely, that the mind-body split always works against women. In his novel *Laughable Loves*, Kundera allows a female character to try to repeat for herself Descartes' *Meditations*—"She would repeat to herself that at birth each human being received one out of the millions of available bodies, as one would receive an allotted room out of the millions of rooms in an enormous hotel; that consequently the body was fortuitous and impersonal, only a ready-made borrowed thing. She would repeat this to herself in different ways, but she could never manage to feel it. This mind-body dualism was alien to her."[7] Even as this pattern of thought fails to account for the experiences of embodiment shared by both women and men, it is women who suffer most from it. Systems that denigrate the human body and seek perfection or something beyond it always depend on an imbalance of power between genders. Women are more closely associated with the body in patriarchal systems and thus are the victims of family control, social inequality, and moral censure when the body in general is denigrated.

Although modern secular social systems might still enshrine patriarchal values, religious systems of patriarchy based these values on sacred stories, myths, and legends. For Islam, like its Abrahamic cousins Judaism and Christianity, these stories are inscribed in scripture and its interpretation. In particular, judgments about the wholeness of women's bodies and the worth of their personalities depend upon interpreting the creation story, not just of Adam but also of Eve. In one sense, the Qur'an is simpler than the Torah and its appropriation into the Christian Bible, for the Qur'an does not offer two contradictory accounts of creation or insert the twist of Lillith's creation prior to Eve. Yet the Qur'an is highly ambiguous about Eve's status and her mode of creation. The central question for Islamic feminists is whether Eve and Adam were created together or whether Eve was a subsequent creation; a second question depends upon this, whether Eve is considered a "secondary" creation that is "derived" from Adam and therefore ontologically inferior to him. Muslim feminists have stressed the Qur'anic message that both Adam and Eve were created from one single self (*min nafs wāḥida*).

God created the heavens and the earth in truth
And wraps the night around the day and wraps the day around the night
And subjected the sun and the moon, each to its appointed term.
Is not God the lofty One, the One who forgives?
God created you all from one single self then made from it its mate
And brought down for you cattle in eight pairs.
God creates you in the belly of your mothers
Creation after creation through three shades of darkness
That indeed is God, your lord, possessor of dominion
There is no other God, so how then do you turn away? (Q 39:5–6)

Amina Wadud concludes that the key phrase *God created you all from one single self then made from it its mate* could mean two different things. First, it could mean that an original single self was divided into two different beings in differently shaped bodies, giving rise to two differently gendered embodiments, Eve and Adam. Second, it could mean that Adam was created first and Eve was created secondly but from the same process as this "single self" and upon its same pattern. In either case, the interpretive conclusion would be that Eve and Adam are equal in their proximity to God and share the same potential for humane development and moral worth.[8] This, Wadud argues, is the interpretation that accords with the spiritual teaching of the Qur'an, which stresses individual moral responsibility before God regardless of social status and often specifies that the virtues that give moral worth in God's eyes are equally attainable by women as by men.

However, the moments in which the Qur'an speaks to this, what Leila Ahmed calls its "egalitarian voice" that emphasizes women's virtue and value, are often overshadowed by motifs of gender difference that can be interpreted to justify practical hierarchy. For instance, in another chapter, the Qur'an repeats this same phrase, *from one single self*, but then immediately moves to stress gender difference between the beings created. *God it is who created you all from one single self and made from it its mate, that he might live with her in tranquility. And when he came over her she bore a light burden. And when it became heavy, they together called to God, their lord, "If you would give us a wholesome, righteous* [child], *we shall be among the thankfuḷ*" (Q 7:189).

It is very difficult to interpret this key phrase, *from one single self*, or even translate it into English because of the gender ambiguity of Arabic. Self or soul (*nafs*) is a "feminine noun," and mate or partner in a pair (*zawj*) is a "masculine noun." Self or soul has a feminine grammatical gender, regardless of whether the body animated by the soul is male or female with regard to reproductive anatomy or masculine or feminine with regard to social roles. This feminine gender assignment reflects the soul's close association with the mineral body made of clay and earth (*arḍ*), which is also of feminine gender. Body and soul are joined by the spirit (*ruḥ*), which bridges the vast distance between divine nature and human nature, for in the Qur'an God says, *I shaped and breathed into* [the human being] *some of my spirit* (Q 15:29). "Spirit" is one of the few Arabic nouns that can be either masculine or feminine in gender, just as its ambiguous nature partakes of both lofty divinity and corporeal humanity by infusing the body with life and the soul with awareness. Within the delicate interplay of grammatical gender and its metaphorical resonance, it becomes very difficult to assert that the first soul created was a gendered male being, Adam, from whom a gendered female being, Eve, was created in a subsequent, subsidiary, or derivative act of creation.

Michael Sells notes that moments of such ambiguity in grammatical gender are highly creative and evocative in the Qur'an and that inattention to that fact (often fueled by patriarchal presumptions) leads to misleading translations into English and other languages that have a neutral gender for inanimate things or abstract concepts. He cautions that "the language of 'he-God and he-man' is at odds not only with Islamic theology (which denies that God is male or female) but also with the intricate and beautiful gender dynamic that is a fundamental part of the Qur'anic language."[9] In this discussion, Sells refers to a specific moment in the Qur'an when the association of God with the masculine pronoun most clearly reveals itself to be just grammatical convention devoid of deeper significance: *By the night when he covers over and by the day when she shines forth, and by that who created the male and the female, your striving is diverse! One who gives freely and stays wary we shall lead to an easy way. And one who is stingy and complacent and calls a lie the good reward, we shall lead to the hard way* (Q 92:3).

In describing God's acts of creation, the Qur'an persistently uses contrasting pairs: day and night, darkness and light, moon and sun. Its discourse opposes the elements of each pair, one against the other. It does this to display the power of the creator, the One who is neither and has no opposite or matching pair, as in the verse *God created the heavens and the earth in truth and wraps the night around the day and wraps the day around the night*. The opposing parts of the pair are not allowed to stand independently, and neither can claim autonomy or priority, as the One who creates wraps them around each other, each defined by the other in reciprocal mutual dependence. The Qurʾan offers these metaphors through which we can contemplate embodiment in gendered bodies—to contemplate how we define female and male in terms of contrast, their wrapping together in sexual union, and its consequences in procreation—in order to understand that God is not divided by gender. God has no partner or consort, creates without coupling, nurtures without bearing burdens, and sustains without hierarchy or exclusion. In the Qurʾan, God is not a father or a mother and has no relationship to humanity through metaphors of reproductive biology.

That much is clear in Qurʾanic discourse, as well as in the Islamic theological and Sufi mystical writings based upon it. However, classical Islamic theology posits the notion that God empowers men over women, based on some notion of ontological superiority of men (perhaps through physical strength, moral superiority, or the assigning of social roles). Islamic theology has consistently interpreted away the "egalitarian voice" that Muslim feminists seek to recover in the Qurʾan. The theological tradition sometimes even adds details or traditions that warp the Qurʾanic retelling of Eve's creation. As we observed in the stories about Adam's creation, "stories of the prophets" is an Islamic genre that fleshes out the spine of Qurʾanic narratives, drawing on Jewish and Christian tradition, hadith reports attributed to the Prophet, folklore, tribal genealogies, and other sources of local cultural knowledge. The writers in the genre are not as kind to Eve as the Qurʾan is, and they fill in the pregnant ambiguities of its discourse with details that fix Eve's figure in a firmly patriarchal frame.

One writer in this genre describes Eve's creation: "Adam was alone in paradise and did not have a partner from whom he could get tranquility. He slept for some time and when he woke up, he saw a woman whom Allah had created from his rib. So he asked her, 'Who are you?' She replied, 'Woman.' He asked, 'Why have you been created?' She replied, 'So that you could find tranquility in me.' The angels, trying to find out the extent of his knowledge, asked him, 'What is her name, O Adam?' He replied, 'Eve (*Ḥawwāʾ*).' They asked, 'Why was she so named?' He replied, 'Because she was created from something living (*ḥayya*).'"[10] The author, the hadith collector and Qurʾan scholar Ibn Kathīr, was writing in the ninth century C.E., about two centuries after the inception of Islam. He seamlessly interweaves citations of the Qurʾan (such as the detail that Eve was created so that Adam *might live with her in tranquility* [Q 7:189]) with traditions from the early Islamic community (such as the detail about her being created from a rib and her name meaning "created from something living"). Stories in this genre import the detail that Eve was created from Adam's rib (*ḍilaʿ ʿawaj*), as found in Jewish and Christian tradition, as if it were found in the Qurʾan, which it is not. They attribute this detail to a hadith report in which the Prophet Muhammad is reported to have said, "I advise you to be gentle with women for they are created from a rib, and the most crooked portion of the rib is its upper part: if you try to straighten it, it will break, and if you leave it, it will remain crooked. So I urge you to take care of the women."[11] Upon this anatomical detail is built a judgment about Eve's human status: she is derivative from the male, her body is not whole like his, her nature is "bent" like the rib and will "break" if men try to straighten it. Male interpreters in the classical period created a fictive etymology for her name, pretending that that Eve (*hawwaʾ*) is not a Hebrew name transposed into Arabic but rather derives its meaning from an Arabic root, *ḥ-y-w*, relating to "life." Asserting such an Arabic etymology is not itself wrong, though it is certainly fictive; however, the etymology they assert is only one of several possible, and it contains a judgment about Eve's ontological state. They say that the name Eve means "created from something living" to assert that her creation was secondary and derivative from Adam's primary and holistic creation, such that her life comes primarily from Adam while Adam's life comes directly from God. Of course, the similarity of the name Eve (*Ḥawwaʾ*) to the Arabic word for life (*ḥayya*) could give rise to a different etymology that recognizes the power of women rather than their weakness: that Eve rather than Adam is more closely linked to "something living," for she allows other living beings come into existence.

In blatant contradiction to the Qurʾan, many of these exegetical stories place upon Eve responsibility for the temptation and eating of the forbidden tree; her derivative body leads to an unsound reasoning faculty and a susceptibility to temptation and excess. Al-Kisāʾī, for instance, writes that "the serpent spoke to Eve, saying, 'O Eve, you have neglected to eat one wholesome fruit from among the many wholesome things of the garden. Go and eat, and hurry to do this before your mate [Adam], for the one who does it first is better than the other. . . . Then Eve advanced toward that tree . . . and plucked seven fruits from seven branches. One fruit she ate, one fruit she saved, and five other fruits she went and gave to Adam . . . and Adam ate the fruit from her and neglected the covenant that he had taken previously [with God] because of her."[12] In contrast, the Qurʾan always recounts the narrative of their eating of the forbidden tree and its consequences with the dual pronoun, specifying that both acted together. Yet the exegetical stories display the popular understanding of the narrative, in which woman is uniquely susceptible to satanic deception, woman actively subverts the divine order, and woman causes man to forget and fall.

The "stories of the prophets" genre continues to assert that for this crime Eve and her female descendants are "punished" with menstruation, labor pains, and lack of intellect.[13] Fedwa Malti-Douglas has analyzed how these narratives about the first woman are repeated and amplified in Arabic popular literature and fundamentalist Islamic discourse and concludes that "woman's body becomes a pawn between the sinful female and the punitive deity."[14] How far this is from the content and tone of the Qur'anic account of Eve's pregnancy: *And when he came over her she bore a light burden. And when it became heavy, they together called to God, their lord, "If you would give us a wholesome, righteous* [child], *we shall be among the thankful!"* Though it emphasizes Eve's anatomical role as bearer of burden and suggests Adam's psychological role as agent, the two are in the child-producing business together, and their prayer emphasizes reciprocal responsibility and mutual hope rather than the painful punishment of one of the pair. The view of Islamic theology shaped by patriarchy is not necessarily the view of the Qur'an as scripture in critical dialogue with patriarchy.

Although the Qur'an does not explicitly blame Eve, as the prototype of the female body and sexuality, it also does not hold her up as an exemplary woman. That role is reserved for Mary, the mother of Jesus. She stands out from among the many Qur'anic accounts of holy women who play heroic roles in the sacred history of prophethood. Although Islamic theology, as a patriarchal construction, shied away from allowing these women characters to be idealized as prophets or messengers, if any women would be granted that status, it would be Mary. Her purity of being was predicted even before her birth, as her mother, the wife of 'Imran, consecrates to God that which is in her belly: *Once the wife of 'Imran called out, "My Lord, I dedicate to you what is in my belly as a consecrated offering! So accept this from me, for you are the One who hears, the One who knows!" When she gave birth, she said, "I've given birth to a female and God only knows what will come of her, for surely the male is not the same as the female! I name her Mary* [Maryam] *and I implore you to protect her and her progeny from the accursed tempter"* (Q 3:23).

Mary is a holy person whose spiritual connection with God is intimate beyond that of other women, her conscience is inspired, and her conversational interaction with God's angel is as full as that of holy men who are granted the status of prophet. That presents a problem, since *surely the male is not the same as the female*. As a holy person who is a woman, Mary experienced pregnancy, though it was pregnancy without sexual intercourse. It is as if Mary were somehow compensating for the ambiguous origin of Eve's body. Eve was derived from Adam's whole and wholesome body, which was created by God directly without intermediary of a womb. In later times, Jesus is derived from Mary's body, which patriarchal interpreters viewed as defective and degenerate as a woman's body but miraculously made holy, thereby giving birth to Jesus, who is created by God directly without intermediary of semen: *In God's opinion Jesus is like Adam—God created him from dust then pronounced "Be!" and he was* (Q 3:59). In the story of Mary, the Qur'an obliquely confirms the Christian notion that Jesus allowed people return to Adam's original nature. The birth of Jesus revives the problem of Eve but with a twist: Jesus was born through Mary but not of her, while Eve was created of Adam but not through him. The Qur'anic depiction of women and their bodies is surely more ambivalent and subtler than the Islamic exegetical and legal traditions that claim to be scripture's best interpreters.

Breast Milk and Womb Blood

Whether recounting the original adventures of our mother, Eve, or praising the purity of Mary, the Qur'an associates women with fertility, reproduction, and pregnancy. Whether this is descriptive or prescriptive is a judgment that interpreters make. However, Qur'anic discourse clearly reflects (and perhaps reinforces) that patriarchal association of women with their bellies. This anatomical imagination assigns to women the gendered role of being centrally concerned with reproduction and nourishment, tying women's social identity to the womb, to blood and breasts. By metaphorical extension, woman are also tightly associated with digestion and the sociality of eating.

The association between womb blood and breast milk may not be obvious to contemporary readers. However, it was persistent in Hellenic culture and continued in Arab and Islamic anatomical and medical theories. The female belly was imagined as an organ that fused blood and milk, both fluids that flowed beyond the boundaries of her body to sustain and nourish others. As Caroline Walker Bynum writes, physiological theory associated matter, food, and flesh with female. "All medieval biologists thought the mother's blood fed the child in the womb and then, transmuted into breast milk, fed the baby outside the womb as well. For example, a fourteenth-century surgeon wrote that milk is blood 'twice cooked.' One of the Arab texts most frequently used by Western doctors argued: 'Since the infant has just been nourished from menstrual blood [in the womb], it needs nurture whose nature is closest to menstrual blood, and the matter that has this quality is milk, because milk is formed from menstrual blood.'"[15] Some medieval anatomists postulated that the womb and breasts were connected by a blood vessel, making them organs that appear to be distinct from without while integrally connected from within.

This description of the female body as characterized by its fluids is generally benign, even complimentary, for it pictures woman as nurturers and essential links the process of life renewing itself. However, in the Arab-Islamic tradition as well as in the Christian tradition, the association of women with "food and flesh" had less complimentary interpretations. Eating is not just a necessity for continuing life but is also a moral problem. One can eat too much as an embodied sign of wanting too much or wielding too much power; thus, ascetics and moralists despised the belly and its digestive organs as the seat of gluttony and concupiscence. Just as the belly as a site of reproductive organs was intimately linked with organs above it, the mammary glands as sites of nourishment, so the belly was linked with organs below it, the sexual organs as sites of pleasure. Hellenic and Roman moralists often used "the belly" as a metaphor for the genitalia, linking the urge to eat with the urge for sexual pleasure.[16] Both were activities of consumption that threatened the moral order if pursued beyond certain socially defined boundaries, and early Christian communities intensified these preoccupations with sermons against the sinful flesh. "Ancient Greco-Roman moral philosophy mentions the stomach frequently in the context of the discussion on how to master desires and passions. The belly is a key topic of these discussions. It becomes a catchword for a lifestyle controlled by the desires, and is thus to be considered a *topos*. Mastery of the pleasure deriving from the belly is seen as crucial for controlling the passions in general. The pleasures of the belly were excessive eating and drinking which also stirred up sexual appetite. Hence, the three often appear together, and belong together."[17]

Early Christian moralists and ascetics from Paul of Tarsus onward appropriated this anatomical analysis of desire. Their major source to relating Hellenic concerns with the biblical tradition was Philo, the first-century philosophical Jewish interpreter from Alexandria. In Philo's Hellenic-Jewish thought, the belly lurked as such a destructive force that it was given its own agency. He imagined the human personality as driven by three different kinds of soul each seated in a different part of the body: a rational soul in the head, a spiritual soul in the chest, and lustful soul in the belly. There are virtues proper to each part: prudence for the reasoning head, courage for the spiritual and passionate chest, and self-mastery and control for the lustful belly. He associates the belly (the stomach in the abdomen) with "the parts below it," the genitalia in the loins, and groups them together as one.[18] In Philo's allegorical interpretation of the biblical creation story, he makes clear what lies implicit in all patriarchal societies: that the sin of fleshly desire is personified in women's bodies; as he interprets the serpent's temptation of Eve in Genesis 3:14, he links the serpent that crawls on its belly with women who live by the belly, bearing painful childbirth and living in lustful excess.

Philo's interpretive strategy enshrined patriarchal judgments about the corporal nature of women, implying their consequent lack of reason and excess of passion. Such interpretations were to prove central to Christianity as it developed around the Mediterranean and in Europe. Yet Christian Europe witnessed many women martyrs and later, in the early medieval period, many women saints, who rose to social preeminence and religious importance despite these canonical and pervasive judgments about their gendered limitations. Such holy women in Christian Europe are vivid figures and have drawn considerable scholarly attention, giving rise to a large literature on their experiences. Especially since the advent of feminist critical scholarship, this literature documents how holy women's mystical experiences were eminently somatic and corporeal. We can see Philo's allegorical linkage of the serpent with women's bodies in many of these experiences, as they have been recorded in Christian hagiographies, such as the stories of the legendary female saint Margaret.

A thirteenth-century Italian story of Saint Margaret's life illustrates this link between female bodies, sexuality and its renunciation, and the evil serpent. "There appeared before her [Saint Margaret] a great dragon, who was seeking to devour her . . . placing his tongue under her feet, he thus swallowed her. But Margaret, when she perceived that he wanted to swallow her, armed herself with the sign of the cross. Consequently the dragon, by virtue of the cross, burst open, and the virgin issued forth unharmed."[19] The moral of the story is dramatically evident: as a virgin who renounces sexual activity, the chaste woman can burst forth from the belly of the serpent, shedding her bodily nature to attain holiness. The serpent in the form of a dragon approaches her from below, as a manifestation of lowly matter and the evil of embodiment. The serpent does not just swallow her but savors her, licking her feet with his tongue, in a confirmation of the deep connection between the pleasure of eating and sexual pleasure, both of which the virgin holy woman would renounce in order to emerge triumphant from the serpent's belly.

Other holy women in thirteenth-century Italy were molested by satanic serpents, who tried not just to devour these women, like Saint Margaret, but also to crawl into bed with them to caress them. According to Elizabeth Petroff's research, one holy virgin was so threatened by a satanic serpent that accosted her in bed that she "wrapped her clothes around her feet and tied them with a belt, so that the serpent couldn't enter from below, at her feet, and get to her nude body."[20] The serpent threatens her sexual chastity in its intrusive phallic form, but the threat is also her sexuality itself, projected onto another body and personified in a nonhuman form, the better to be grappled with concretely. Often in such hagiographic stories, the saintly women identify the dragon or serpent as lust. Reflecting on these stories, Petroff suggests that female Christian saints from medieval Italy confronted the evil of their own sexual lust, "the dark, obsessive aspect of sexuality," by reading the situation "as a teaching rather than an attack."[21] Such a moral maneuver, she concludes, allowed these women to transform their world and find new creative flexibility in their gendered roles or escape from them altogether.

Such an optimistic interpretation highlights a major challenge to feminist scholarship about holy women, whether in medieval Christendom or in Islamic lands. Feminist scholars ask how women, by becoming known as mystics and saints, moved beyond the gendered limitations imposed upon them by patriarchal society. How could they do this while still preserving, in their internal conception of their own bodies, the patriarchal evaluation of their being particularly fleshy, corporal, and thereby dangerous? Petroff herself notes this apparent contradiction. "Medieval women mystics were public figures. Yet medieval society put women away: in their homes, in convents, even in brothels. In medieval thought, women were bodies (men were characterized as mind or spirit), and bodies were dangerous—dangerous to men and, therefore, dangerous to society as a whole. The physical austerities undergone by women mystics, and that young women often imposed on themselves, underscored society's need to control and purify the female body."[22] In her assessment, the few women who overcame their enclosure in private spaces and gender roles did not break the confines of their sisters; rather, the exceptional few, even while living vivid lives as powerful public figures, reinforced the very circumscribed norm for women in society as a whole.

Other feminist scholars shift the emphasis of such evidence to arrive at a different conclusion. Caroline Walker Bynum acknowledges the particularly "somatic quality" of female mystics and their experiences but sees this as evidence not of the limitations imposed upon women but of important changes in the religious imagination of medieval Christendom. She argues that "female spirituality in the same period [1200 to 1500] was specially somatic—so much so that the emergence of certain bizarre miracles characteristic of women may actually mark a turning point in the history of the body in the West. . . . The spirituality of medieval women owed its intense bodily quality in part to the association of the female with the fleshly made by philosophers and theologians alike. But its somatic quality also derived from the fact that by the thirteenth century the prevalent concept of person was of a psychosomatic unity, the orthodox position in eschatology required resurrection of body as well as soul at the end of time ."[23] Bynum thus sees in women saints' experiences, with their vivid focus on the body, evidence of a considerable step forward in uniting the soul and body in Christianity. It is as if, through these female saints, she sees medieval European society postulating an integral relation between body and soul, one that became orthodox theology even if the women who illustrated it more vividly were never at ease with orthodoxy and its male guardians. This integral unity of body and soul would be sustained until it dissolved under the influence of Descartes.

The miracle that Bynum claims is most indicative of women saints' somatic quality of experience is the bleeding of stigmata, the wounds on hands and feet that were "signs" of empathetic pain with the crucified body of Jesus. Almost all bodily wounds in the form of stigmata are particularly associated with women: "Francis (died 1226) may indeed have been the first case (although even this is uncertain); but stigmata rapidly became a female miracle, and only for women did the stigmatic wounds bleed periodically."[24] The juxtaposition of bleeding wounds and women's bodies dramatically invokes the major difference between men's and women's bodies—the menstrual flow of blood. Upon the menstrual flow is built the whole dichotomy of gender roles in patriarchal societies, and it is a vivid example of how women were pictured as "grotesque bodies." In contrasting the grotesque with the classical, Bakhtin writes: "The grotesque body is not separated from the rest of the world. It is not a closed, completed unity; it is unfinished, outgrows itself, transgresses its own limits. The stress is laid upon those parts of the body that are open to the outside world, that is, the parts through which the world enters the body or emerges from it. . . . The body discloses its essence as a principle of growth which exceeds its own limits only in copulation, pregnancy, childbirth, the throes of death, eating drinking or defecation. This is the ever unfinished, ever creating body, the link in the chain of genetic development, or more correctly speaking, two links shown at the point where they enter into each other."[25] Clearly Bakhtin had in mind more than women's bodies when describing the literary figure of the grotesque: he also included under it clowns, monsters, satyrs, and freaks. However, Petroff is insightful in pointing out how patriarchal societies, by raising the closed and autonomous male body as the ideal human norm, marginalize the contrasting bodies of women as "grotesque." Bakhtin's emphasis on "protuberances" may confuse the issue here, including male features as well as female ones under this rubric. However, his emphasis on "open bodies" that, through their orifices, meet the world and flow into it captures an important contrast particular to women's bodies. Menstruation, pregnancy, childbirth, and lactation are vivid moments when women embody the "ever unfinished, ever creating body, the link in the chain of genetic development," performing functions that men are excluded from, depend on, and consequently fear.

Sayyida Amina and the Edible Body

This scholarship on Christian Europe is very subtle and theoretically astute. In contrast, the scholarship on Muslim women saints is quite limited. This is not for lack of vivid examples and lively personalities. Although it is doubtful that Muslim holy women ever played such a dominant role as Christian holy women did in the high medieval period, Islamic hagiographies contain many stories that are fascinating and have long been ignored by scholars, Muslims as well as Westerners.

Compared with the number of male saints in the annals of hagiography, female saints are comparatively rare, yet they are always present. Often their names are remembered while the details of their lives are forgotten or subsumed into the background of the stories of saints who were men. But some women saints gained public recognition that is perhaps more powerful because of the fact that they are rare. Sayyida Amina's story is relatively obscure in contemporary Morocco, and her name is hardly recognized in her home city of Fes. Therefore, this chapter will begin an archaeology of her personality in a different site, the tomb of a woman saint who is publicly renowned, Sayyida 'A'isha al-Manūbiyya, located on the outskirts of Tunis. We can gain access, conceptually and tactilely, to both kinds of women saints through "inanimate objects" associated with them: not the tomb itself but the edible foodstuff present there.

Let us begin at the tomb of Sayyida ʿA'isha al-Manubiyya (died mid-thirteenth century). She was a famous saint in her time and was considered one of the forty original companions in Tunis of Shaykh Abū al-Ḥasan al-Shādhilī (died 1258), to whom most Sufi orders in all of North Africa owe allegiance. To this day, her tomb is a gathering place for devotees, singers, and common people seeking divine blessing and healing. When I went to Manūba to visit her tomb, I caused quite a bit of tension. The sacred precinct of her tomb is a de facto feminine space through which men may pass but seldom linger. In the small chamber that houses her tomb, three custodians (who were all women) attend the tomb, guide visitors (who are overwhelmingly women as well), and distribute objects that can convey the blessings of the site. They were not so surprised that a non-Arab American would come to the site (after all, Sayyida ʿA'isha is famous), but they were surprised and somewhat troubled that a man would spend time there, praying a little and observing a lot.

Once the strangeness of my presence became routine, one element of the tomb rituals attracted my attention as unusual, something I had not noticed at the tomb of male saints. The women custodians had placed on the actual tomb a variety of foods, including a bowl of raw olive oil in which were soaking red chili peppers and other whole spices. In this way, the woman's tomb became a sort of nourishing dining table. The food objects represented nourishment, good health, and well-being (all cultural meanings of the term *baraka*, or blessing); they were vehicles that could absorb spiritual energy from the tomb and its concealed saintly presence while transmitting it to visitors and pilgrims. The women visitors and pilgrims would dip their fingers in the oil to anoint their forehead or hair, in addition eating candies distributed by the custodians. They would carry away from the tomb candles and small chunks of incense to be burned at home. Like the foodstuffs, these objects are both material and immaterial: they are inanimate and tactile but can be transformed into light, fragrance, taste, and heat—all manifestations of spiritual well-being when absorbed into the body and experienced through the body's sensorium. Olive oil and chili peppers are especially potent in Tunisia as both symbol and substance; they are the basic ingredients of *harissa*, eaten with bread at every meal. As a substance, oil stands in for bread as the basic source of nutritional cuisine. Yet as a substance, oil is far more versatile than bread for ritual symbolism, for it can be poured, drunk, rubbed, or burned. As a liquid, it allows more creative ambiguity between its two states: being an object separate from the body or being incorporated into the person (whether ingested or anointed).

One assertion of this chapter is that nourishment and food are particularly potent symbols through which Islamic culture defines the bodies of women saints. It could be suggested that this is a cultural dynamic common to all patriarchal societies and is not peculiar to Islamic societies; it might also be suggested that this is a cultural dynamic common to all women and not limited to women saints. This chapter explores the limited hypothesis and leaves other researchers to define the horizons of its generality. With this hypothesis in mind, we can turn to Sayyida Amina. Olive oil was just as quotidian and precious in Morocco as it was, and still is, in Tunisia. That lubricant between the realms of sacred and profane served as the medium through which Sayyida Amina initiated her life as a saint in sixteenth-century Fes. We can gain access to her not through her tomb (which is little known and not visited) but through the stories originally told and later recorded about her as a "mad woman saint" (*majdhuba*).

Amina hailed from a prestigious Ibn al-Qadi family of jurists and scholars from Meknes (Miknās), who had branched out and moved to Fes to take up official positions in the Marinid bureaucracy. Her father, Ahmad, was a judge, as his forefathers had been.[26] His daughter, Amina, might have become a female jurist herself, as was possible in Marinid-era Fes.[27] However, she rejected the urban respectability of her juridical family in order to wander the streets, perform miracles, and challenge the conventional morality of her neighbors.

She took this radically unexpected course by becoming an admirer of ʿAlī al-Ṣanhājī, a *majdhūb* in Fes. Who is a *majdhub* or *majdhuba*? *Jadhaba* literally means "to draw out, pull out, or strain." A *majdhub*, as the passive recipient of the action, is one whose spirit has been drawn forcibly to God and whose reason is thus under strain, or completely broken, or expelled from its proper place. The result is social behavior that seems "mad" or "irrational," and we can think of them as "divinely distracted." *Majdhubs* challenged social norms and legal rules, comparable to the "holy fools" of medieval Christendom. They were often exempt from punishments applied to people whose "reason" was intact. A contemporary Tunisian film by Moncef al-Dhoeb, *Sultan al-Madina*, graphically depicts a *majdhub*.

In early modern times, ʿAli al-Sanhaji presents a classic example of a *majdhub*. His public behavior was deliberately aberrant. Although he shocked people by falling into trance states in which his clothing fell off him, revealing his naked body, this did not provoke severe censure.[28] "He acted like a fool and a buffoon, as if a mad love for the divine had dragged his reason out of him. . . . States of possession seized him at all times. . . . He would give reports on unseen matters and tell those who met him about their secret affairs. He paid no attention to either praise or blame from others."[29]

He had no known home and would wander the markets of Fes, gaining the nickname "al-Duwwār," the Turner. He would frequent the market for olive oil and butter, take donations, grease himself and his clothes, and then roll in the dirt to make his appearance repulsive to respectable society. In this state, he would recite poetry to warn people of ethical negligence.[30] The young Amina became an unlikely admirer of this mad "Turner." She would wait for him to wander by in the marketplace, with a bowl full of olive oil to offer him as a token of admiration to soil himself and his clothes in public. Soon, she was devoted to him, as a man and as a saint. Even though she was already married, she began to take care of him full-time. She stepped far outside the role of a respectable lady from a juridical family as she wandered through the markets with a "madman." Amina developed the reputation of being "his servant and his bed companion," though it is not clear whether a sexual relation between them was actual or only perceived by her shocked and angered family.[31] This did cause legal action against him and familial action against her.

Before continuing with her story, let us pause to consider the *majdhub*'s use of edible matter, for it can help us to understand the comportment of these individuals with respect to their bodies. The ritual use of foodstuff is, from a utilitarian or ascetic point of view, a grand waste. If consuming food in the customary manner is one of the basic ways to solidify and replicate social bonds and values, then wasting food is a very visceral way of breaking social conventions. Rather than eating to nourish his body and maintain social ties, ʿAli al-Sanhaji would roll in food to soil himself and break conventional social ties and the hierarchies inherent in them. He smeared his body with oil, butter, and animal fat (the very basic ingredients of Moroccan cuisine, which transforms mere matter into the socially sanctioned category of "food"). Worse, he used their lubricating properties to make himself dirty and polluted, to make of his male body, so valued as the pillar of the patriarchal system, into a grotesque and abject body. Sayyida Amina spent freely of her family's wealth and squandered its pious reputation to allow ʿAli al-Sanhaji to abandon himself to this antinomian practice. Amina turned the "waste" of food into a powerful display of the excesses of sainthood.

As Amina drew closer to ʿAli al-Sanhaji, she had to disobey the regulations of her family and the authority of its men. She disobeyed not only her father but also her husband. She deliberately snubbed them through food, that social substance that bridges the gap between matter and body and around which family draws together and, by eating from a single platter, becomes one social body. "One day her family cooked a chicken and gave her share to her. She gestured to a dog that was there with her at the time, saying 'If this bitch were the dog of my Lord [ʿAli al-Sanhaji], I would give my portion to her!' Then she stretched out her hand and fed the chicken to that dog."[32] In this highly charged action, Amina not only rejected the family ties that the reciprocal sharing of food manifests but also gave the food to a dog, a potent symbol of ritual pollution in the urban Muslim landscape. In this gesture, Amina was embodying a story long beloved by Sufis, the love epic of Majnun, the Madman, and his beloved Layla. Our Sufi guide, Nakhshabi, explains: "Before the lover is united with the beloved . . . there are many demonstrations of loyalty to be manifested and countless amenities to be observed. For example, the least of these occurred when the dog of a beloved was accorded more esteem than any person in the village. You may have heard that when a dog came out of Layla's house, Majnun worshiped the ground it walked on. People said, 'O Majnun, what insanity is this?' He replied, 'You ignorant people, do you realize from whose house this dog is coming?'"[33]

In this single act, Amina made a doubly shocking assertion. The daughter and wife whom her family thought they possessed was actually lowlier than a dog, and the dog, despite appearances and pollution laws, was actually holy if it faithfully served a holy master. Amina's patriarchal society took its revenge on her in the most damning way that it could with a younger woman: she was accused of sexual indiscretion with ʿAli al-Sanhaji. This was, perhaps, the only way her society could rationalize a younger woman repudiating her husband and the marriage that her family had arranged for her. She was known in the streets of Fes not only as ʿAli al-Sanhaji's "servant" but also his "bed companion." These rumors destroyed Amina's honor (that might have been her spiritual goal in the first place) and also threatened the honor of her whole extended family.

Her family acted swiftly to deny her access to ʿAli al-Sanhaji by locking her in her home. But in ways that are stock images in hagiography, routine ploys come to nothing before the sincerity of a saint. "The whole clan of Ibn al-Qadi came from Meknes to try to take her back. [As she resisted,] they ended up locking her in a room and confining her with iron chains. She seemed to take no notice of her confinement. Then suddenly she saw ʿAli al-Sanhaji standing in the middle of the house, calling to her 'O Amina!' He was not stopped by any limits, neither by walls nor by chains. When he called to her she answered, 'Yes, my lord?' He ordered to her leave the room and her chains suddenly fell away from her ankles, and she walked out of the house with him while all her family watched, unable to stop them. Since that day, the people left her to do as she liked."[34] After breaking away from her family's control and dismissing the public approbation against her open companionship with a man, Amina developed a reputation of saintliness for herself.

Female Saints in the Body Politic

Stories of women saints illustrate a double transgression: the woman must overcome her social construction as a woman and then must further overcome the pressures of a routine life to become not just a person but also a saint. Commenting on this double bind, which women saints in any religious tradition face, Petroff writes: "The women saints of the Middle Ages were transgressors, rule-breakers, flouters of boundaries, and yet they were also saints. Of course, in a way, all saints are transgressors, in the sense that a saint lives by excess, lives in a beyond where ordinary measure does not hold; all saints, by their lives, stretch the boundaries of what we have conceived of as human possibility, and their zeal in breaking through conventional limitations can be both attractive and repellent, pointlessly mad and unshakably sane at the same time. Women saints, it seems to me, were doubly transgressors—first, by their nature as saints and, second, by their nature as women."[35] The real transgression of saintly women was not to develop an unconventional personal spiritual practice or experience mystical states; the real transgression was "to go public" and enter the public arena of preaching, teaching, exhorting, and being visible. Only by going public did saintly women break all the cords of the safety net of being "a good woman" in patriarchal society.

Amina's story in hagiographic collections from Fes is not the only one about a woman saint. Her story, though, is an aberration: it is longer and more detailed than others, and it diverges from others in having Amina break patterns of women's domesticity most blatantly. Other women saints in these collections achieve sainthood through domestic duties, not in spite of them. Often they achieve social recognition as saints through connection to a male relative who is a saint, through "devoted service" to a husband, or through caring for others in the generous provision of cooked food. The classic example of this is a certain Sayyida Fatima, who lived a generation earlier than Amina. Fatima was the saintly woman who ministered to Ibrāhīm al-Zawāwī, a male Sufi from Tunis who fell into illness and poverty while traveling to Morocco.[36] She used to fly or teleport from her home in Fes to the middle of the Sahara with fresh food and medicine to care for him. This miraculous ability to fly (along with her more subtle spiritual powers) came from her selfless devotion to her husband: "by undertaking to uphold the duties to Allah that are laid upon me in serving my husband."

In the collection of saints' stories from which these come, the story of Sayyida Fatima is the longest entry for a woman, except for that of Amina. Fatima's story acts as a prototype for other women saints. This is the model of female sainthood that complements official male roles, as saints or scholars, in a patriarchal social order. It is clear that Amina not only diverges from this pattern but openly challenges it. Because of this challenge, one might assume that Amina's story would be unpopular. One might assume that the male hagiographers who recorded these stories would conveniently forget her. The opposite is the case. She was not only popular but was held up along with other *majdhub* characters as prime examples of "popular Islam." The reason for the preservation of her story in popular memory (and later in written texts) is the political potency of her "mad holiness." This notoriety is due to the political force of her body as it became exposed to the public's gaze.

To understand this and her primary miracles, we need to place her in the context of dynastic history in Fes. Amina lived during the last years of the Marinid dynasty's rule. Once the body of Mawlay Idris was rediscovered and his tomb was built, the sharifian clans that claimed genealogical descent from him gained increasing authority. Only twenty-five years later, in 1465, these sharifian nobles led a popular uprising that put the Marinid sultan to death; only after six years of fighting were the Wattasid nobles (related to the Marinids by tribal connections) able to retake the capitol of Fes and establish themselves as "rightful" heirs of the Marinid kingdom. However, their "right" to rule was infirm, and a *majdhub* coalition was a crucial force that pointed out their illegitimacy and undermined their popularity.

In earlier times, ʿAli al-Sanhaji had tacitly acknowledged the right of Marinid and Wattasid aristocracy to rule, even as he encouraged them to distribute their wealth to the poor. However, circumstances at home and in the wider world were rapidly changing. The Portuguese were attacking coastal cities of Morocco as part of their naval colonization and were soon joined by the Spanish. The Wattasid dynasty was unwilling to mount a military defense of the coast, and many Sufi organizations and sharifian families combined forces to wage a defensive jihad. These forces also called for the overthrow of the Wattasid rulers because they could not effectively defend Morocco from European assaults. In these political conditions, ʿAli al-Sanhaji denounced the Wattasid elite. Once again acting as "the Turner," he mounted a central point in the traffic arteries of Fes, a bridge that spans the river and connects the two halves of the city. There he began to turn in a circle, as if invoking the entire city that spun around him. In a state of possession, he began to shout: "Get out, you children of the Banu Marin tribe! By God, we will not let you remain in our land!"[37]

Along with ʿAli al-Sanhaji, Amina graphically displayed her allegiance to those who were fighting the Portuguese. She would wake up in bed covered with miraculous wounds, "as if she had been participating in the jihad."[38] This is a remarkable inversion of the Catholic iconography of the stigmata, those bleeding wounds that Caroline Walker Bynum notes were so important for women saints in European Christendom. In Amina's case, the bleeding of a woman does not embody and display the wounds of Jesus, the incarnate God. Rather, her bleeding becomes a sublime miraculous wound that marks her off as an embodiment of the Moroccan people as a whole, injured in fights with the invading European Catholics. Despite this political opposition and symbolic inversion, on both sides of the Mediterranean, women's bleeding routinely marks off menstruating women as dangerous and impure. Women saints were able to reverse the social dynamic of bleeding: rather than having it be hidden as private, shame-inducing, and a mark of inferiority, they were able to display this holy bleeding as public, pride-invoking, and a mark of their claim to religious leadership.

These persistent miracles of Amina and ʿAli al-Sanhaji display the remarkable ability of these *majdhubs* for inverting the dichotomies of routine ritual, especially in making outward impurity into a marker of internal purity. They also illustrate through bodily symbols their alignment with the ascendant Saʿdian dynasty, which built its reputation for leadership around jihad and armed resistance to European Christian control of Moroccan coasts and port cities. Just as the Saʿdian leaders were asking Moroccans to shed their legal obligation to obey legitimate authority, for many Islamic jurists judged that loyalty to the Marinid and Wattasid leaders was incumbent by law, the *majdhub* coalition was asking Moroccans to shed their trust in rationality. The logic of the *majdhub* is that he or she has lost grasp of the rational faculties, such that his or her body is no longer the locus of a rational person bound by law, responsibility, and social custom. The bodies of such individuals become "empty" of these social meanings and can stand as a symbol of something greater, either the social whole or the workings of divine destiny. The miracles of ʿAli al-Sanhaji and Amina illustrate this logic of the sacred. The actions of their colleague Abū Rawāyin from Meknes also show this logic and even more clearly show how the *majdhub*'s personality came to take on political meaning in the shift of dynastic power.

Like ʿAli al-Sanhaji and other *majdhub* personalities, Abu Rawayin would often depart from accepted custom and even social intelligibility as he would "babble in some nonsense language."[39] Like them, he would acquire great wealth in gifts and then give it all away before nightfall. In addition, he practiced spiritual extortion against the rich or against rulers by saying, "Quickly, buy from me your fortune and you won't come to ruin!" If they paid, he would say, "You are safe." But if they refused, he would pronounce, "You are cut off," or "You are killed," and shortly that would happen.[40] In times of political uncertainty and upheaval, such threats from a "holy madman" gained extra potency. The "emptied" personality of the *majdhub* became a veritable barometer for political and military changes. He was a known proponent of jihad against the Iberians but would confound those who observed him by shouting out one day, "I favor the Portuguese!" and the next day, "I favor the Muslims!" This behavior disturbed the public, who thought that he was, on some days, favoring the enemy and cursing the Muslims' own troops. However, it became apparent that "his favor" reflected who was winning in the wars at that particular time: it did not reflect his rational choice of whom to favor but reflected instead divine destiny that granted either victory or defeat to the Muslims day by day.[41]

Abu Rawayin plays a part in many episodes as power tilted from the Wattasids to the Saʿdians in northern Morocco. His seemingly "irrational" behavior was instrumental in prying loose support for the Marinid-Wattasid regime. In Fes, he convinced al-Miṣbāḥī, a saint who was a staunch loyalist, to "lift his spiritual protection from over the Marinid clan."[42] In another maneuver, very similar to ʿAli al-Sanhaji's mounting the central bridge in Fes, Abu Rawayin went to the town of Qaṣr Kutāma and climbed the minaret of the central mosque, as if to proclaim his body, now cleared of individualist rationality, to be the axis connecting heaven to the social world on earth. From his lofty centrality, he commanded the ruler, ʿAbd al-Wāḥid al-ʿArūsī: "Buy your power from me or you'll be removed from your rule within a year."[43] The al-ʿArusi family that ruled Qasr Kutama hailed from a sharifian clan, yet it wavered between loyalty to the Wattasid regime and independence for itself.[44] Abu Rawayin coerced the family to break away from the

Wattasid camp. When the Saʿdian forces conquered Meknes and turned to assault Fes, Abu Rawayin later went to the Saʿdian leader, Muhammad al-Shaykh al-Mahdī, as he was invading northern Morocco and said, "Purchase Fes [the capital] from me for five hundred dinars!" The Saʿdian commander replied that such behavior was not in conformity with the sharia and that God did not dispose of political power this way. Abu Rawayin pronounced, "Then you won't take Fes this year." Eventually, the commander's son, ʿAbd al-Qadir, intervened and paid Abu Rawayin, who is credited with opening the way for the Saʿdian conquest of Fes in 1549.

It is instructive to contrast the manifestations of "holy madness" in Abu Rawayin and Amina from the point of view of gender. They both exhibited miracles that focused people's attention on the jihad against the Portuguese and Spanish. Abu Rawayin's miracles came through his speech, while Amina's miracles came through her body. Abu Rawayin issued threats, while Amina displayed bleeding wounds. This comparison would seem to support the observation of Elizabeth Robertson that "sanctity is not a gender neutral concept" and that hagiographic accounts "assume a woman's essential, inescapable corporeality" that predetermines that her sanctity must be achieved through her body.[45]

We might interpret Amina's experience as her being confined to feminine stereotypes, just as Bynum analyzed stigmata as confirming the particularly "somatic" quality of women's mystical experiences in conformity with patriarchy's assigning them roles more closely confined to the body. But was Amina silenced by the gendered nature of her body? We could turn the tables and ask, Which type of miracle was more "popular" and effective in supporting the jihad? Abu Rawayin's words gained him access to elites in power and involved him in making and breaking alliances between elites. Amina's wounds did not gain her access to rulers and military leaders, but they did circulate in public. Her wounded body would be a profound statement, more powerful in its emotional force than words. This is especially so because her wounds dramatically invert the ritual and legal codes on women's menstrual bleeding, which is confined to private spaces as the bedrock of social and religious order. To have her wounds, "caused by the jihad," bleeding in public would be a powerful indictment against the Wattasid state, whose détente with the Portuguese and reluctance to commit to defensive jihad were corrupting the moral norms of the Moroccan community of believers. Amina's wounded body acted as a call to arms in the male-dominated public spaces of Fes. Those who could not participate in the jihad along the northern coast could withdraw their allegiance from the Wattasid rulers of Fes. And that is increasingly what happened, with drastic results as the Saʿdian forces pushed north to conquer Fes.

Amina's political involvement in dynastic turmoil, along with that of *majdhub* males in Fes, explains the "popularity" of her story. Her story was not just that of a saintly woman or of an individual madwoman saint; rather, it was included in the wider narrative of the Moroccan defensive jihad against the Iberians and the dynastic change the jihad sparked. This explains why her story persisted in popular memory. But it does not explain how the story was recorded in literary form and included in hagiographic collections. To understand how her story was included in a canonical body of sacred texts, we have to widen the scope of our analysis.

Before we ask how Amina's story came to be written down and included in the body of hagiographic texts that root the city of Fes in sacred time and space, we must compare her story with the stories of other saintly women in such texts. Even as it tells the particular details of her life, the narrative structure of Amina's story confronts a universal problem: to explain how a woman who is manifestly not a "good woman" according to patriarchal social values is nonetheless a "saintly woman." Patriarchal societies are threatened by the "openness" of women's bodies and display a social obsession to enclose them in order to preserve male control. This is a social obsession with family honor and genetic purity that, when enforced, becomes legal imperative, moral injunction, and violent indignation. In contrast to this harsh reality that confined the routine lives of most women in patriarchal societies, Sayyida Amina seems to break out of the walls of domesticity and modesty. She bursts into the public realm through the free flowing of liquids that would normally be confined to the private realm. One such liquid is the edible oil that symbolizes her devotion to ʿAli al-Sanhaji, and another such liquid is the blood that flows in public through her wounds.

Her story's structure is common to women who transgress the limits of their social role to become publicly acknowledged as saints, whether in medieval Europe or in North Africa. However, hagiographic texts apply different themes to different women who break the expectation of patriarchal social roles and become saints. There are three basic themes that rationalize their apparent transgression. First, the women saints could be related to a wider family structure in which a male member is considered a saint (either a father, husband, or son). Second, the woman saint could have a "spiritual marriage" to a divinely blessed figure and the consequent rejection of a routine marriage and the family control that this implies.[46] Third, they could be said to not really be women at all but rather to have become "men" through their spiritual aspiration and fortitude.

A prime example of this third strategy is the judgment hagiographies apply to the most famous female Muslim saint, Rābiʿa al-ʿAdawiyya of Baṣra (died 801). As a slave and the daughter of a slave, she did not have a saintly family to rationalize her own power public claims to sainthood; she also refused marriage proposals by saintly men like Hasan al-Basri and insisted that she achieved intimacy and love for God without any male intermediary. Her major hagiographer, al-Sulamī, therefore concludes that she was spiritually a man in the body of a woman in order to make sense of her outspoken nonconformism and public preaching. In a similar vein, ʿAli al-Sanhaji rubbed salt in the wounds of Amina's family by publicly announcing that "Amina is the greatest member in the whole clan of Ibn al-Qadi—just see how those so-called men came rushing to Fes from Meknes just for her sake!" thereby implying that she was spiritually and virtuously a man able to lead her clan of male judges.

Another way of imagining how a woman with a feminine belly could actually be a spiritual man is through the concept of *jadhb*, or divine distraction. Either a man or a woman could be a *majdhub*, affected so deeply by the forces of *jadhb* that his or her reasoning faculties are persistently or permanently displaced. Strangely, the *majdhub* is allowed to trespass the boundaries of patriarchal gender roles, as if he or she were a "raw" human being who has not yet been "cooked" into social gendered roles. A male *majdhub* is allowed to abandon rational calculation, household control, and aggressive competition, while a female *majdhub* is allowed to abandon household responsibilities, deferential modesty, and domestic confinement. Just as patriarchal interpretations of religion picture women as "deficient" in reason in order justify their social subservience, a *majdhub* who has abandoned reason's constraints can slip out of this patriarchal dichotomy, at least to a certain extent. Therefore, it is not surprising to find strong women saints in a *majdhub* guise. Sayyida Amina is certainly the most prominent female *majdhub* in hagiographic collections from Fes, but she is not the only one. Another woman saint is mentioned in the same collection, Sayyida Amina al-Sāgama (died around 1737). She was "divinely distracted and absent from herself in the alienation caused by the attractive pull of the divine" and would wander the marketplaces with bracelets jangling loudly around her arms and ankles.[47] In Marrakesh, too, one finds stories of saintly *majdhub* women, such as Lālla ʿAwīsh; her story has been analyzed by Mariëtte van Beek, who compares the scant written material about her life with the ample oral stories still told about her by the caretakers of her tomb.[48] Ironically, even as she violates the norms of domesticity, Lalla ʿAwish affirms the intimate relation of women's saintliness with food, as one of her miracles involves passing on mystical knowledge to a man through investing a piece of bread with her saliva and leaving it for him to eat.

The metaphorical extension of women's bellies through food leads us farther from Morocco to a more vivid comparison with the woman saint Sayyida ʿA'isha al-Manubiyya. Her tomb, in Manuba (a town outside Tunis) is converted into a dining room table loaded with food through which her blessing is transmitted to the many women (and few men) who still come to visit her, as mentioned earlier. However, while she was alive, Sayyida ʿA'isha was a very strong and vibrant personality. She has attracted the scholarly attention of social historians interested in the medieval past and sociologists concerned with practices of the present.[49] This chapter supplements these studies by presenting her personality as it is recorded in hagiographic manuscripts archived in Tunis. This allows us to contrast other women's achieving sainthood through domesticity with Sayyida Amina's achieving sainthood through repudiation of domesticity and wasting of food. The primary manuscript source is a hagiography written about her alone, "The Heroic Virtue of the Righteous Woman Saint, the Spiritual Master, Sayyida ʿA'isha al-Manubiyya," by one of the most important early chroniclers of the Shadhili Sufi movement, named Ibn Ṣabbāgh.[50] He also wrote the first biography and collection of teachings and prayers of Abu'l-Hasan al-Shadhili, the founder of the movement, as well as a hagiographic record of Shaykh al-Shadhili's forty close companions in Tunis. Thus Sayyida ʿA'isha's story forms an integral part of the canonical collection of saintly stories from Tunisia that had a profound impact on Sufi communities across North Africa.

Sayyida ʿA'isha's unconventional life began, significantly for the topic of our chapter, when she was still in her mother's belly. While pregnant, her mother was traveling in the wilderness outside Manuba when she confronted a lion; she was terrified until the voice of her unborn girl spoke to her from within her belly. She said, "Don't be frightened, Mother, for you are protected by the preserving power of God! Surely God has loved me and chosen me and purified me and made me beautiful to the world. God has poured out for me a drink and strengthened my hand and made me for the beauty of the saintly Friends of God (*zīnat al-awliyāʾ*)."[51] After birth, she continued to make such bold claims. From even a young age, she persistently and regularly proclaimed herself to be the female axial saint (*quṭbat al-aqtāb*) and mistress of the men of God (*sayyidat al-rijāl*), coining new feminine nouns to be equal to the generally masculine nouns that describe positions of high status among Sufis and saints.

Even as a young girl, she would move through the marketplace, interacting with men as an equal and arguing about religion. This was even more provocative because she had a reputation for being a stunningly beautiful girl. When she was 12, she had a strange experience that would shape her life forever:

> Khiḍr appeared to her in the streets of Manuba when she was a girl twelve years old . . . in the form of a young boy [her own age]. He said, "Get your father to fix your engagement right away or I will take you myself . . . I've been waiting for you for three-thousand years!" She rebuffed him to his face. She went directly home and complained to her father, "O father, a man approached me and said to me such things, and I was afraid of him for he said to me, 'I will take you myself.'" So her father got her quickly engaged to her cousin, the son of her father's elder brother. Her father said, "You know this age is corrupt and by God, I am afraid for her of the obstacles of these times; people are saying many things about her and there are many evil people these days." But she told her cousin, "If you love to take me [in marriage], then you will die, as God wills." Everybody around her laughed. But in the middle of the night, he died.[52]

Thus her first evident miracle, a prognosticative warning, secured her freedom from marriage.

In this way, she began to walk in the footsteps of Rabiʿa of Basra, who remained unmarried throughout her life as a very public saintly woman. Sayyida ʿA'isha told her followers, "I have seen Rabiʿa al-ʿAdawiyya [of Basra] and she said to me, 'I serve you!'"[53] Like Rabiʿa, she became known for bold pronouncements of her own position and special love for God and for ecstatic sayings that sound to others like boasts (*shaṭḥ*). And like Rabiʿa, she was never known as a female *majdhub*, meaning that her sayings and proclamations may have been inspired and audacious but were never attributed to irrationality and holy madness. Instead, Sayyida ʿA'isha seems to have been very deliberate and consistent in her spiritual claims.

Just as she had "seen Rabiʿa," she also saw many other great male saints of the past, and they confirmed her status as the female axis of her age. She saw ʿAbd al-Qadir al-Jilani and Junayd among many others. Importantly, though, Sayyida ʿA'isha never admits to having learned Sufi mysticism from any man or woman, living or long passed away, not even from the mysterious Khidr, whom she met while she was so young. "Junayd rose above the station of other [male] saints (*fawq manāzil al-rijāl*) by three hundred degrees. But I have risen above the station of Junayd by five hundred degrees! And Rabiʿa al-ʿAdawiyya, if she would reach my position, she would rush to serve me and stand at my hand."[54] Rather than learning anything crucial from these human interactions, she took her initiation from God. "I am God's saving power in the earth and heavens. I have not taken this mystical Way as an inheritance from anyone. Rather, I have taken it as a gift directly from my Lord. God has shown me God's self and given me the power to take [spiritual qualities] from Mary. Mary has three special qualities, as revealed in the Qur'an . . . and like Mary I also have these three special qualities. God has nourished me, God has spoken to me and supported me, and God has purified me and kept me clean. I am ʿA'isha of Manuba! Salvation and bliss to those who visit me and stand over my tomb, those who arrive close to me and speak to me!"[55] As discussed earlier in this chapter, Mary is the closest that a woman comes to being a prophet in the Qur'an, so it is no surprise that Sayyida ʿA'isha sees Mary has the archetype through which she is spiritually charged.

Mary had to contend with a patriarchal society that accused her of being a whore after her miraculous pregnancy (Q 19:27–28). Likewise, Sayyida ʿA'isha also had to face the wrath of men who were threatened by the idea of God conferring special spiritual blessing on a woman and exercising divine will through her actions. The hagiographic account records that the religious scholars (*ahl al-ʿilm*) became jealous of her. Once she was reciting from the Qur'an a verse declaring the difference between those who truly believe and suffer for their devotion and those hypocrites who only pretend: *God is well pleased with the early believers who left their homes (muhājirūn) and those who helped them (anṣār) and those who followed them in doing good . . . but some of the Arabs around you are hypocrites (munāfiqūn) and some people of Medina persist in hypocrisy—you do not know them, but we* [God] *know them very well* (Q 9:100–101). In the midst of this devotional act, her reciting was challenged by a jurist, Muhammad ibn ʿAli al-Huwārī, who taught hadith in the congregational mosque and university of al-Zaytūna, the most prestigious institution in Tunis. Unfortunately, the record does not tell us why he challenged her: Did he challenge her style of recitation, did he accuse her of having made an error, or did he contest the right of a woman to recite Qur'an in public? Perhaps it was only because her devotional life, in which she sacrificed the safety of remaining at home, showed up their own hypocrisy. We will never know. But Sayyida ʿA'isha retorted, "My Lord has taught me the Qur'an, not anyone else!" The jurists hid their rancor in the guise of zealously defending the Prophet's legacy (*sunna*). To the sultan of Tunisia, in the Hafsid dynasty, they brought charges "against this girl who mixes freely with men, which is not allowed in the sharia."[56]

While not telling us exactly how she avoided outright persecution, the hagiographic records give us hints. Many of the jurists and scholars who initially attacked her became her devotees and followers. We find their names as narrators of traditions about her sayings and teachings, as preserved by the careful hagiographer Ibn Sabbagh. How could male jurists be drawn to accept a woman as a saint in the public sphere? Sayyida Amina did not challenge the sharia restrictions on women in general but rather challenged the jurists' assessment of her as simply a woman. She coined new locutions to put her ambiguous gender status into language. She claimed to be "the female master of pious men (*sayyidat al-rijāl*)," playing upon the use of "real men" to mean the most pious of saintly people. She also claimed to be "the beauty of the brothers (*zīnat al-ikhwān*)," subverting the inherent patriarchy that defines Sufi communities as a "brotherhood" even when they include women in some roles. In this way, she argued that not all individuals of female gender should be considered ordinary women. It was not her feminine gender that she protested but her ordinariness within that gender category. Just as she reported ʿAbd al-Qadir al-Jilani telling her, "The saints are silver but you are gold. If a saint is silver, nothing can be more beautiful than it except gold!"

In calling herself "gold," as Sayyida ʿA'isha did on many occasions, she makes a subtle reference to one male saint with whom she had an important cooperative relationship. He is Abu'l-Hasan al-Shadhili, who used metallic metaphors frequently in his teachings, saying that people's souls were either of lead, iron, silver, or gold. His followers would hold that al-Shadhili's teachings were the alchemical elixir that, with one touch, could transform base metal of the soul into pure gold. Sayyida ʿA'isha claimed to have seen and spoken with al-Shadhili, and from him she "absorbed his virtues of knowledge and patience."[57] He is the only contemporaneous man to whom she makes deferential reference: "I am a woman of al-Shadhili's community (*anā shādhilīya*) and the female axial saint of the people of Ifriqiya [the North Africa region around Tunisia, Algeria, and Libya], the unique woman saint of my era (*farīda zamānī*), and I beautify all around me and am beautified by none other!"[58]

Shaykh al-Shadhili, the first axial saint of the Shadhili community, hailed from northern Morocco, from a sharifian family that claimed biological descent from the Prophet Muhammad (through his grandson, Imam Hassan) and Mawlay Idris. As Morocco was not immediately receptive to his spiritual teachings, al-Shadhili moved to a small town outside Tunis, called Shādhila. In this region he took on the nickname by which he and his community of followers, including Sayyida ʿAʾisha, would be known until today—"al-Shadhili." Here, he founded his first *zawiya*, or devotional center, in Tunis in 1227. The cave to which he would retreat for devotions (*maqām*) still exists on a mountaintop outside the city. In Tunis, he drew together a large and vibrant body of followers until he had a vision commanding him to move east. He took many close followers to Alexandria, in Egypt, where he built a new devotional center, while leaving other followers to perpetuate the community in Tunis. Shortly before he died in 1258, Shaykh al-Shadhili delegated both his spiritual and communal authority to Shaykh Abuʾl-ʿAbbās al-Mursī, a scholarly visionary who was recognized as the second axial saint (*quṭb*) of the Shadhili lineage. Under his guidance and that of his inheritor, Ibn ʿAṭāʾillah, the Shadhili community in Egypt developed a subtly intellectual mysticism steeped in Islamic law, which spread through Egypt and across North Africa.

However, al-Shadhili's original followers in Tunisia remained active and may have preserved a more charismatic and politically activist style of Sufi devotion close to the spirit of the movement's founder. Certainly, Sayyida ʿAʾisha's boldly charismatic assertions of her authority as a female saint empowered directly by God to preach in public mirror the male claims to sainthood asserted by al-Shadhili himself. Local lore in Tunisia preserves stories of al-Shadhili's "forty friends" who gathered around him upon his arrival there. Devotees of Sayyida ʿAʾisha place her among his "forty friends." However, the hagiographer Ibn Sabbagh does not include her in his collection of biographies of these forty Sufis and instead wrote a separate treatise on her life. Ironically, by treating her separately rather than including her in this group of closest disciples, the hagiographer devotes more pages to her memory than to others.

The ambiguity of Sayyida ʿAʾisha's position is palpable. She claimed to have met Shaykh al-Shadhili to have absorbed from him virtues, and to occupy a feminine counterpart to his position as axial saint of the age. However, other male chroniclers of his community cannot find an easily acceptable place for her bold claims. Although the hagiographic record presents her as ecstatic in her inspired claims and visionary encounters, it never presents her as a mad or irrational saint, a female *majdhub*. She is always conscious of her claims, backs them up with accounts of her visionary experiences or scriptural interpretation, and repeats them persistently and consistently. In this way, she would be even more an explicit challenge to patriarchal norms that treated women as inherently limited or inferior in their public social roles based upon a scriptural and legal interpretation of their different anatomy.

As an ecstatic woman saint who rebelled against the norms of feminine behavior, Sayyida ʿA'isha is probably the strongest prototype for Sayyida Amina bint Ibn al-Qadi. This is true despite the difference noted above and even though the former is not mentioned by name in the latter's hagiography. The search for a prototype is especially compelling because Sayyida Amina does not conform to the other patterns of feminine sainthood preserved in hagiographic collections of Fes. Most of these women saints were presented as relatives in a wider family in which a male member is considered a saint. This pattern plays two functions: it is as if the family relation conferred sainthood on the women that they could not otherwise achieve on their own, and it also made the behavior of women saints conform to patriarchal family structures. Examples of this model of domestic female sainthood are many in Fes, beyond the example of Sayyida Fatima given above, who achieved sainthood through her selfless devotion to her husband. The prodigious hagiographer Muhammad al-Mahdi al-Fasi preserved the record of the mother and daughters of the saint Ahmad ibn ʿAbdullah al-Maʿn al-Andalusī. He considers all four women to be female saints: the mother, ʿA'isha (died 1647 or 1648), and the daughters Raqīya (died 1676), ʿA'isha, and Ṣāfiya.[59] Similarly, al-Kattānī records the life of Fatima (died 1690), the wife of the renowned Sufi Muhammad al-Qadiri, noting that she was a holy woman without giving details of her life or works. He also notes that the male Sufi Shaykh Saʿīd al-Sabʿ, "the Lion," had holy women as a wife and a daughter: Sayyida Fatima al-Arjabiyya (died 1659 or 1660) was the wife, and Sayyida Fatima al-Sabʿiyya (died 1651) was the daughter. Typically, there is little substance to their biographies or record of their miracles; it is enough to highlight their family relationship to a male saint and note their burial within his tomb shrine, for such a position is emblematic of their remaining in the enclosing walls of family propriety. Sayyida Amina does not at all conform to this pattern. In fact, she inverts it! The male members of her family were known as jurists, from whom she manifestly broke, while after her death some members of her family would become prominent Sufis, following upon her lead rather than leading her to follow. In the section below, we will meet one of her later Sufi relatives who did so much to preserve in writing her story and those of other saintly women in Fes.

Finally, hagiographies can present women as saints who enter the public realm through the image of a "spiritual marriage" to a divinely blessed male figure. This is a narrative pattern that justifies their consequent rejection of a routine marriage and family control without totally abandoning patriarchal family norms. We find this pattern prominently in the story of Sayyida Amina. However, to fully understand her "spiritual marriage" we have to delve into the complex relationships she had with men: her spiritual guide, her fellow *majdhub* Sufis, and their followers who both appropriated and perpetuated her reputation. It is through these relationships that Sayyida Amina's story was remembered and later recorded and through which her bold embodied life entered the body of written texts.

The Body of Text

So far, we have considered the story of Sayyida Amina as it has been preserved in written records in hagiographic collections of saints' stories. Clearly the story was told and retold orally and only later written down in literary form. We can ask not only why it was written down in this form but also why it was written down at all! Who recorded her story and how? To understand this, we have to examine who were her companions and admirers and how they built a religious institution in Fes. Examining this process throws into doubt common preconceptions about the dichotomy between "popular Islam" and "official" or "scholarly Islam." Asserting this dichotomy has been a persistent pattern among contemporary scholars in sociology and anthropology, from Alfred Bel through Ernest Gellner and Clifford Geertz, though it has lately come under critique.[60] The pivotal figure in examination is ʿAbd al-Raḥmān, known as "al-Majdhub" (died 1568). He institutionalized a Sufi community during the Saʿdian era and built a legitimizing Sufi lineage around these *majdhub* figures. He was also a popular creator of "colloquial" Sufi sayings in Moroccan dialect that have been fully woven into Moroccan folklore and the genre of song known as *malḥūn*.

ʿAbd al-Rahman grew up near Meknes.[61] After moving to Fes to study, he ran into ʿAli al-Sanhaji, who singled him out and gave him a second "spiritual" birth. This spiritual initiation made Amina his "spiritual sister" through their mutual relationship with ʿAli al-Sanhaji, though Amina's relationship with him was imagined as a "spiritual marriage" rather than a "birth." ʿAbd al-Rahman then began to travel in the countryside to meet other saintly leaders. He met with the politicized *majdhub* Abu Rawayin and then other

Sufi leaders who openly preached the need for jihad and supported the nascent Saʿdian dynasty. Even though ʿAbd al-Rahman claimed that his "spiritual birth" was from his "spiritual father," ʿAli al-Sanhaji, he built his own organized community rather than perpetuate the individualistic idiosyncratic practices of his *majdhub* predecessors.[62] He settled down, married, and attracted many disciples. Before ʿAbd al-Rahman, hagiographic sources had characterized these *majdhub* figures as saints with no explicit lineage or formal system of teaching and passing on mystical intuition. However, they characterized ʿAbd al-Rahman as "one of the axial saints" who began a new powerful lineage for a Sufi community.

ʿAbd al-Rahman recounted how he took on the station of axial saint (*qutb*) in very dramatic terms. ʿAli al-Sanhaji reportedly grabbed him as he was sitting at one of the gates of the mosque the Qarawiyyin and jerked him around. ʿAbd al-Rahman found that he had been ripped from the fabric of routine reality and was standing in a different place. In that irrational state in liminal space, ʿAbd al-Rahman saw ʿAli al-Sanhaji approach his belly, insert his finger in his navel, and lift him up as all the saints gathered around them. ʿAli al-Sanhaji said, "Whoever loves me, accept this [man]!"[63] In this way, ʿAbd al-Rahman transformed a ragtag alliance of *majdhub* characters (with their antinomian and even anarchic practices) into an organized Sufi lineage. Around this lineage he could build an organized institution (*tariqa*). His disciples built the Zawiya Fāsiyya, the Sufi Brotherhood of Fes, which became one of the most prominent and productive Sufi organizations in early modern Fes.

But ʿAbd al-Rahman was caught in a paradox. He was building a bourgeois institution on radical roots. Amina was very important to him personally and spiritually, but she had no place in the patriarchal and authoritative construction of his lineage. In the lineage, he inherits his authority from ʿAli al-Sanhaji directly. However, in the narrative, he admits that Amina had inherited spiritual power (*wirātha*) from ʿAli al-Sanhaji earlier and that he had "shared" this authority with her as her "spiritual brother." Only when Amina died did ʿAbd al-Rahman take on the full share of ʿAli al-Sanhaji's spiritual authority for himself. For this reason, Amina's story complements his own, and his followers told her story and wrote it down, even though she plays no part in the formal lineage.[64]

Despite his reliance upon Amina by sharing with her the spiritual inheritance of their *majdhub* master, ʿAbd al-Rahman's poetry contains many ascetic moments of folk wisdom expressed in patriarchal images that obscure his reliance upon a woman.

The market of womankind is only loss and chance
  Watch out if you enter that way
They'll display a potential profit at first glance
  Then snatch all your money away

O my heart, I set you aflame
  If you hesitate I stoke you
O my heart, you leave me only blame
  You desire one who doesn't want you

This world can be called a she-camel
  In a kind mood she provides milk where she stands
In a moment of rage no skill suffices
  She struggles free right from your hands.[65]

In his poetry, women are unreliable, treacherous, fickle, and dangerous. It expresses the ascetic logic that this world of material goods and desires is like a woman: when you reach out to possess her, she either betrays you or slips from your hand. His poetry clearly expresses ʿAbd al-Rahman's deep ambivalence toward "woman," who, against his will and better judgment, plays such a prominent role in his spiritual inheritance and training. Even though she is left out of the Sufi lineage he constructs, Amina's body with its wounded belly is buried behind the tomb of ʿAli al-Sanhaji; her tomb is an irrepressible material trace that makes it impossible to erase her story even as ʿAbd al-Rahman al-Majdhub tried to neutralize her in the Zawiya Fasiyya that grew over her reputation.

If members of the *tariqa* did not record her name in their lineage, then who first wrote down Amina's story? Amina's story is usually told in conjunction with ʿAli al-Sanhiaji's story. The first to record his story was Ibn ʿAskar, a Sufi and jurist who specialized in collecting the stories of saints who participated in the defensive jihad.[66] However, his early composition, from 1577, makes no mention of Amina and her relationship with ʿAli al-Sanhaji. This is most likely because Ibn ʿAskar was not from Fes and only knew of those whose fame had spread beyond the walls of that city to the northern Moroccan mountains where he lived, whereas we have no evidence that Amina ever stepped outside her native city.

It was not the earliest hagiographers who recorded Amina's story. Rather, it was the hagiographers of the Zayiwa Fasiyya who persistently mention Amina's story as a crucial facet to ʿAli al-Sanhaji's. The first of these was Muhammad al-Mahdi al-Fasi (died 1698), with his collection of saint stories, *Mumti' al-Asmā'*, or "The Delight of Hearing Tales."[67] He devoted a full entry to Amina in addition to the entry on 'Ali al-Sanhaji. His account was quoted and requoted in all later hagiographic collections into the nineteenth century. These authors in the Zawiya Fasiyya were scholars, urban elites trained in Islamic colleges in scriptural interpretation and legal reasoning, yet they were also Sufis. These Sufi scholars built a *zawiya* that was both an architectural site and a social institution. They recorded stories that would root the *zawiya* in the social and religious life of Fes. Amina plays a large role in these stories but does not even appear in the Sufi community's formal lineage. This may make it seem to the modern observer, who is informed by feminism, that Amina has fallen victim to gendered imbalance of power yet again. At the level of institutional records, this is undoubtedly true, for Amina is mentioned only after 'Abd al-Rahman al-Majdhub and is presented as his "servant." It was men who appear in the lineage and men who were the scholars who recorded hagiographic records.

However, we find that members of the Zawiya Fasiyya were uncharacteristically open to the presence of women as powerful spiritual figures. Their hagiographers recorded the names (and sometimes the stories) of many women. These women were mainly singled out because of their family relations (as mothers, wives, and daughters of leaders of the *zawiya*). Yet we know more about them, through these connections, than about women in other Sufi groups. For instance, one 'Abd al-Rahman ibn al-Qadi (died 1671) was raised as part of the household of Abū'l-Maḥāsin al-Fāsī, one of the leaders of the Zawiya Fasiyya.[68] He participated in the scholarly and literary fluorescence led by the *zawiya*'s members in Fes. They became leading historians, genealogists, researchers, and copyists who contributed immensely to Fes's archives, and they included some later members of Sayyida Amina's own Ibn al-Qadi clan. For instance, 'Abd al-Rahman ibn al-Qadi became an expert on hagiographic lore, recording the stories of saints and researching their dates of birth and death and their places of burial. He recorded a large share of the lives of women saints in a text entitled *Ṭarīq al-Sulūk al-Dāriyya* ("The Way of Domestic Spiritual Cultivation"); although it appears that this text no longer exists, its stories have passed into al-Kattani's more modern compilation.[69] Muhammad ibn Ja'far al-Kattani (died 1927) collected these records from written sources and from oral tales that circulated in Fes in a three-volume book, *Solace of Spirits and Discourse of Intellects on the Scholars and Saints Buried in Fes*, in an 1899 lithographic print.[70] Al-Kattani preserved not just the stories of saints but also the location of their tombs during the radical upheavals and changes of the twentieth century. His collection remains the standard reference, even now that scholars in Moroccan universities are editing and publishing earlier hagiographic collections that had remained for centuries in manuscript form.

Conclusion

The story of Sayyida Amina conforms to some norms of patriarchy, such as the more intensely corporeal nature of female saints' bodies; however, she inverted other norms and revolted against them, such as obedience to male relatives, submission to marriage, and obligation to procreate. The story of how her story survived (in oral and later in written form) is also not simple. During her lifetime, Amina opposed "urban doctors" and upholders of legalistic Islam who were her relatives, but her story was recorded, almost a century after her death, by "urban doctors" who were her followers and inheritors of her spiritual authority. It is as if the revolutionary forces of her female holy madness were channeled and preserved by men, fueling the establishment of a thoroughly patriarchal institution. However, the men who claimed social status through this institution, the Zawiya Fasiyya, were the most productive recorders of female saints' stories, through whom these stories have reached us in the present.

This complex interplay of forces reveals the interdependence of male and female religious leaders in Sufism in pre-modern Fes; however this interdependence should not be mistaken as equality or parity of social power. The story of Amina's story also shows the interdependence of "doctors" (scholars and jurists) and figures of "popular religion" as represented by *majdhub* females and males. In the final analysis, one cannot insist on a binary division between "popular religion" and "official religion" in pre-modern Fes and its surrounding countryside (in a pattern that may hold for all North African urban spaces and their surroundings). Any such binary distinction, if asserted in general, will inevitably be found to blur and blend in concrete historical cases. Although oral narratives remain distinct from written chronicles in the stories of saints' lives, scholarly jurists and Sufis did not remain aloof or in open opposition to more populist "holy people" like Amina but rather benefited from a symbiotic relationship with them.

This symbiosis might mean that all saints, women and men, break patriarchal norms, since the goal of sainthood itself is to cultivate an integrated personality that transcends gender divisions. We should pay as much attention to the "effeminacy" of male saints as we do to the "empowerment" of female saints, for it may well be that in each male saint is an inner woman, such that the man who is a *walī* is not a man like other men. Likewise, a woman who is a *walīya* is not a woman like other women. Men become saints by tapping "feminine" qualities that are normally hidden or repressed in men, while women become saints by tapping "masculine" qualities within themselves that ordinary women do not actively manifest. Taking this as an approach to studying gender in sainthood would go beyond the simple search for women examples and role models, an approach of many feminist scholars such as Fatima Mernissi.[71]

Do all saints betray their socialized gender roles in becoming saints beyond the routine? Does sainthood allow men to take on effeminate roles and women to take on emasculate roles? Not all saints cross over the borders that fundamentally order patriarchal societies, but some do, and we will examine this question through queer theory in Chapter 4. From this perspective, the figure of Shaykh Abū Madyan, one of the founders of institutional Sufism in North Africa, takes on a bold new relief. Hagiographies describe him as "al-Ghawth," "the Succor," or manifestation of divine nurture (*ghiyātha*); he "gives birth" to saints from among his followers and "breast-feeds" them with his spiritual training. Similarly, ʿAli al-Sanhaji, Amina's spiritual teacher, took on stereotypically feminine roles by giving "spiritual birth" to his followers, like ʿAbd al-Rahman al-Majdhub, twirling them upon his finger by their navels as if he could play out the function of the umbilical cord.

But is this male appropriation of the metaphor of birth and nurturing really an instance of transcending patriarchal norms and its gendered hierarchy? Is it a respectful acknowledgment of the power of female colleagues? There is reason to doubt this. Sayyida Amina came to an uneasy alliance with ʿAbd al-Rahman al-Majdhub. His followers eventually absorbed her into their very bourgeois and patriarchal institution of the Zawiya Fasiyya. However, by neutralizing her radical challenge to gender norms, they also preserved her story for following generations, and for us as well.

3

BODY REFINED

The Eyes of Muḥammad Ghawth

The heart did not lie in what it saw
Will you then dispute with him his vision? . . .
His gaze did not turn aside nor go too far
He had seen the signs of his lord, great signs.
—Qur'an 53:11–18

It is often argued that vision is the strongest sense that connects us with the world beyond our bodies. Certainly in every human culture, metaphors centered upon the eyes are central to defining the essence of human beings, such as our saying in English, "The eyes are the window on the soul." This reflects the extraordinary power of the physical organ of the eye to express emotional and spiritual states of a person, states that are often hidden or invisible in other bodily media. Just as eyes can reveal what is in the invisible essence of a person, the power of eyes to see can lead the human observer to go beyond the limited physical boundaries of the body. Vision can apprehend what is beyond the body's other senses, like taste (which requires the intimacy of taking an object into the body), touch (which necessitates proximity of contact with the body), or smell (which depends upon an object sharing a confined environment with the body). Like vision, hearing can also lead people to transcend their immediate surroundings and apprehend the existence of beings or forces at a great distance. However vision, when aided by views from a great height and unobstructed vantage point, has clarity and detail that outstrip even hearing in power.

Western culture shares with Islamic culture an *ocularcentrism*. As Anthony Synnott observes, "Sight is equated with understanding and knowledge in much of our vocabulary: insight, idea, illuminate, light, enlighten, visible, reflect, clarity, survey, perspective, point of view, vision, observation, show, overview, farsighted . . . you see?"[1] So central are the eyes to investing the body with its human personality that the first gesture by which others declare a formerly living body a corpse is the gentle closing of the eyes. The eyes often stand in, metaphorically, for the body in its entirety.

Farid al-Zahi has described the phenomenon well in regard to Islamic culture: "In many instances, the face or even just the eyes are used to convey the entire body. At the furthest extent, the body itself is abandoned, concentrated into the face. . . . And beautifying the face creates a new appearance (*ṣūra*) with regard to the body, an appearance that extends through and even beyond many of the functions performed by clothing in all its forms. . . . In this way, the face becomes a second body, giving the biological body its cultural and social existence."[2] By "beautifying the face" al-Zahi refers especially to darkening the rim of the eyes with kohl as the prime way of heightening the features of the face (though his observation applies to other forms of cosmetics or expression). The eyes, not the ears, define the face. Beyond their receptive sensitivity to light, the eyes' movement provides an expressive subtlety in contrast to the ears. Although hearing also connects the body to events at a great distance, vision alone among the senses seems to grow more powerful from great heights. It is little wonder that visionary experiences are so central to religious experience, for vision is central to verifying the truth of external events. Seeing is believing.

In fact, the sense of vision is integral to the founding experiences of the Prophet Muhammad as he received the revelations upon which Islam is based. It must be admitted that the Qurʾan is first and foremost an aural event, a revelation that was heard, then spoken, then recited. It is an inspired speaking, embedded in the sound of Arabic language and performed by a special meditative breath that carries the sound, as illustrated by Michael Sells's inspired essay "Sound, Spirit and Gender in the Qurʾan."[3] Metaphors of hearing are central to the Qurʾan's revelation: the Prophet is reported to have sensed the oncoming of revelation as an intense buzzing or a penetrating resonance like a bell's reverberation and comprehended the precise words as the speech of an angel, Gabriel, who brought messages from God through his ears into his conscience. However, vision was also integral to these experiences. Muhammad saw the angel before hearing the angel's message and reciting it to others: *Recite in the name of your Lord who created* (Q 96:1). Vision also played the dominant role in the miraculous journey that confirmed Muhammad's commission as God's messenger: his ascension into the heavens. The visionary power of the eyes allowed Muslims to imagine the Prophet's bodily ascension with its subtle allusions of transcendent experience.

This chapter explores the power of vision by examining the eyes of Muhammad Ghawth (died 1562 in Gwāliyōr [Gwalior], India), a Sufi who experienced an astounding ascension on the model of the Prophet Muhammad's original experience. This Sufi master of the Shaṭṭārī community became known popularly with the laudatory title of Ghawth. This is the same title given to Abu Madyan in North Africa, whom we encountered in Chapter 2, but it does not bear the same connotation as it did with him. For Muhammad Ghawth, the title does not connote "succor and sustenance" as it did with Abu Madyan but rather connotes "aid from above." In ancient Arabic, *ghawth* meant a cry from the depth of desperation, a plea for aid in distress and a petition for succor in suffering; in addition, *ghawth* was not just the cry but also the transcendent force that answered such a gut-rending cry and was often applied to the rains that fall from above after a great draught. Muhammad Ghawth was given that title by his admirers not because he nourished them but rather because he could direct aid from an unattainable height. He was the axial saint, the pivot of the universe, because he had risen up beyond himself, as he attested in the record of his visionary experience of ascension. This controversial claim hinged on his relationship to his body. Could ascension have happened while he was still embodied, or could he ascend only in visionary experience reducible to dreaming? Before we look into the story of Muhammad Ghawth, let us cast some light on the issue of the eyes, the body's reception of visual stimulus and its crucial importance in religious experience.

Vision, Prophecy, and Transcendence

Vision is the one sense that allows us to experience transcending the body. Vision provides such a detailed mapping of the world around us, the phenomena beyond the body, that we invest its sensory perception with a unique quality of reality. The eyes seem to re-create for us in immediate and powerful ways the world that swirls around us. Under special conditions, the eyes also can reveal for us the world that revolves above us, the divine cosmos of order that lies beyond our ordinary perception. For this reason, the visionary experience of the Prophet Muhammad confirmed and supported his auditory reception of revelation. The Qur'an itself weaves these two capacities of the body's sense perception together in arguing that Muhammad's community should accept his teachings as authentic messages from God. Such acceptance not only should come from the ethical meaning of the revelation or from the moving sound of the message but should also depend on the veracity of the messenger who brings them. That messenger, the Prophet Muhammad, was conveyed beyond the confines of the lower world and was carried into the heavens, where he was shown visions of a cosmic and eschatological reality that is hidden to the eyes of others. The verses that headed this chapter, from the Qur'anic chapter called "The Star," are understood to describe this ascension and its visionary challenge. The Qur'an insists that his vision confirms his veracity as a speaker of the truth and hearer of divinely revealed language. The full series of verses, in the fluent translation of Michael Sells, addresses people with an oath while describing the experience of Muhammad, "your companion":

By the star as it falls
Your companion has not lost his way or is he deluded
He does not speak out of desire
This is a revelation
Taught to him by one of great power
And strength that stretched out over
While on the highest horizon—
Then drew near and came down
Two bows' lengths or nearer
He revealed to his servant what he revealed
The heart did not lie in what it saw
Will you then dispute with him his vision?
He saw it descended another time
At the lote tree of the furthest limit
There was the garden of sanctuary
When something came down over the lote tree, enfolding
His gaze did not turn aside nor go too far
He had seen the signs of his lord, great signs. (Q 53:1–18)

This series of verses describes Muhammad's ascension in elliptical and tantalizing allusions. It complements another series in which Muhammad is described as God's servant *taken on a night journey from the sacred mosque to the further mosque, whose surroundings have been blessed, that we may show him of our greatest signs* (Q 17:1).

This night journey (*isrā'*) from the sacred mosque at Mecca to the farther mosque, the site of the Temple in Jerusalem, is a more physical and geographical analogue to the subsequent spiritual and cosmic ascension (*mi'raj*) from earth into the heavens and up to the divine throne. The two are linked: they are both journeys in which the Prophet witnessed with his eyes *the signs of his lord, great signs*. Like a journey that can take one's body beyond its routine habitat of home, vision can take one's personality, personified by the heart, beyond its routine grounding in the body. This series of verses mentions in close association the heart (*fu'ād*) and the eye or gaze (*baṣar*): *The heart did not lie in what it saw . . . His gaze did not turn aside nor go too far.* Vision becomes a powerful metaphor for transcendent experience, in which the Prophet approached God "face to face."

From the earliest times, Muslim theologians have confronted the vexing question of whether the Prophet's ascension was bodily. Did he travel while still clothed with his bodily form, or did he leave the body in order to travel in spirit? How can such a journey to the farthest horizon beyond the limitations of space and place have taken place through the body? But if it was not an embodied journey, then why does the Qur'an narrate it using the terms "heart" and "eye"? Dogmatic theologians have often insisted that the night journey and ascension were in and with the body in order to heighten their miraculous nature and set them up as a criterion for defining who is a true believer. More philosophically inclined theologians have speculated that the journey was out of body but even more real because of that in order to reconcile religious belief with reasoned observation of the physical universe and conjecture about the transcendent nature of the human soul, which is more refined and durable than the corporeal body.[4] Sufis assert that the ascension was both bodily and spiritual in order to assert that the ascension was not just a miracle granted to the Prophet but also an archetypal experience to be emulated by all believers who follow the Prophet. Sufis love to recount the teaching attributed to the Prophet, "Prayer is the ascension of the believer." The physical movement of lowering the body into prostration toward the ground is the occasion for a spiritual movement of rising into communion with God.

Such conjunction of opposites is, of course, a paradox. Sufis are drawn to paradoxes as skillful means to convey spiritual teachings. Baffling our sense of analytic reason is precisely their power! Without sidestepping our self-centered reasoning, how could we ever taste of the transformational mystery of spiritual experience? In Sufi teachings, mystical experience is a way of integrating the spirit and the body without one overpowering the other and upsetting the balance. The Indian Sufi master Nizam al-Din Awliya' told this parable in one of his teaching sessions, as recorded by his disciple, the poet Amīr Ḥasan Sijzī (1254–1336), to illustrate the miraculous nature of the conjunction of spirit and body:

> It has been reported that once in the presence of Shaykh Abū Saʿīd Abū'l-Khayr—may God have mercy upon him!—a powerful leather maker was beating an animal. Shaykh Abu Saʿid said: "Ah!" with such

Miniature painting of the Prophet Muḥammad ascending from Jerusalem up through the seven heavenly spheres with his winged steed, Buraq, to meet the other prophets and angels of each sphere. Painted in North India in 1808. From Muḥammad Rafī Khā, *Ḥamla-yi Ḥaydarī*, ms. (Paris: Bibliothèque nationale de France, Suppl. Persian 1030), fol. 35b.

> pathos that is seemed as though he had been the one beaten. A skeptic was present. "Such a condition is impossible!" he protested. Shaykh Abu Saʿid disrobed and the signs of that leather belt appeared on his blessed back! One of those listening to the *shaykh* noted that this story implies that a person can feel someone else's condition, but I [Amir Hasan Sijzi] protested that he didn't understand how such empathy works. In response, the shaykh said, "When the spirit becomes powerful and is perfected, it attracts the heart and the heart, too, when it becomes powerful and perfected, attracts the body. Then, due to this union of all three, whatever happens to the heart leaves its outward mark on the body."[5]

At this point Amir Hasan Sijzi (who was writing down the discussion) interjected to ask, "Is it a similar kind of experience that transpired on the Ascent of the Prophet Muhammad—peace be upon him?" "Yes, it was," replied the master."[6] In this way, the Prophet's ascension serves not just as a miracle, belief in which is a criterion for being accepted in the community of believers. For Sufis, it is also an archetype through which to integrate spirit, heart, and body in mystical experience.

For this reason, metaphors of ascension play a crucial role in the teaching of Sufis, who encourage the common believer to have astounding spiritual experiences by not just admiring the Prophet from a distance but rather imitating the Prophet in intimacy. Despite Muslim philosophers' speculations that the Prophet's ascension was not bodily, Sunni orthodoxy eventually settled on the decision that it was bodily to heighten its status as a miracle and set the Prophet apart from others. To avoid appearing to infringe on the superiority of the Prophet, Sufis normally were carefully circumspect, referring to experiences of ascension indirectly through metaphor or poetic innuendo. In this way, they struck a delicate balance, as Sunnis with spiritual insight.

However, talking about the Prophet's ascension could be a dangerous enterprise. When Nizam al-Din Awliyaʾ was asked how the Prophet's ascension happened, he replied that one should not ask the details but should bask in the mystery: "'From Mecca to Jerusalem was the Night Journey, from Jerusalem to the first heaven was the Ascension, and from the first heaven to the place of two bows' length was the Ascent.' Then that dear one elaborated his question, asking: 'Some claim that the Ascension was bodily, others that it was spiritual. How can it be both?' On the blessed tongue of the master—may God remember him with favor—came this verse . . . He came to me, wrapped in the cloak of night / Approaching with steps of caution and fright / Then what happened, happened; to say more fails / Imagine the best, ask not for details."[7] For ordinary believers to intimately experience the ascension in their own devotional lives was a matter of cultivating a certain spiritual taste (*dhawq*) as opposed to developing a rational understanding. Therefore Nizam al-Din Awliya' advises his listeners to refrain from asking about details of the Prophet's ascension, the better to concentrate on laying aside egoistic pretension so that one might possibly experience the spiritual taste of ascension in one's own inner life.

Nizam al-Din Awliya' follows a common pattern for Sufis who adhere to Sunni communal norms. He lapses into poetry to describe the ascension, rather than persisting in prosaic discourse. Most Sunni Sufis resort to poetry to express self-transcendence. This allows them to dissolve the rules of grammar and the confines of prose, letting the poetic resonance of words create the image of transcendence. Poetic metaphors rhyme with the ascension of the Prophet Muhammad but also acknowledge that the mystic's personal experience could not remotely compare with that paradigmatic experience of the Prophet.

Yet the Prophet's experience had also been rendered accessible through narratives. These are mainly hadith reports in which he is reported to have discussed his night journey to Jerusalem and ascension through the heavens to meet various angels and prior prophets until he reached the throne of God, though a few Qur'anic verses are also believed to allude to this experience of the Prophet. Muslim authors normally reserve descriptive prose narratives for describing that paradigmatic original ascension. Although some veered toward folk story telling to recount the Prophet's ascension, most Sufi authors have shied away from crafting too many details to fill out a narrative. Poetic allusions have had greater currency than detailed descriptions. As the early Sufi al-Junayd cautioned, the human craft of language inevitably falls short of accounting for transcendent experience. "On the night of ascension, the Prophet reached a limit for which there is neither expression nor description. By his union in that location with the One and the Singular, by the obscurity of what happened in it, and by the silence of the Prophet, he left off all reports of it."[8] Nizam al-Din Awliya', as a cautious Sufi master, followed the Sunni Sufi patterns based on al-Junayd's teachings and steered clear of provocative descriptions of Sufi ascensions that might infringe on the Prophet's archetypal experience.

In contrast, Muhammad Ghawth was not cautious. He broke with this pattern, as he advocated a new and relatively unknown Sufi order on South Asian soil. Muhammad Ghawth widely popularized the Shattari Sufi community in South Asia. The Shattari community was defined by a series of Sufi teachers, originally of Khurasani origin, who branched out as an independent growth from the Kubrāwī lineage. Shāh ʿAbdullah Shaṭṭār (died 1485) brought this lineage to South Asia from his home in Samarqand after extensive travels in Khurasan. He initiated disciples, including the spiritual masters of Muhammad Ghawth, during a grand tour in Hindūstān, a region whose Sufi communities were otherwise heavily influenced by Chisthi order, whose leading exemplar was Nizam al-Din Awliyaʾ. In contrast with Chishti teachings about common believers' devotional ascent that integrates spirit and body in selfless giving to others, Muhammad Ghawth insists that he ascended bodily, with the permission of the Prophet, and returned to write an eyewitness account. Under Muhammad Ghawth's leadership, the Shattari community became strong during the period of Mughal ascendancy and spread throughout South Asia.[9] In their heyday, the Shattari masters were quite audacious in boasting that their "swift-paced" spiritual method (the literal meaning of *shattar*) was not just distinct from the methods of all other Sufi lineages but effectively superior.

Muhammad Ghawth's narrative strategy renders the ineffable experience of confronting absolute being, or God, in first-person prose. He needs to, since he is ostensibly offering a firsthand account of his personal experience rather than some literary creation, philosophical exposition, or mystical parable. In outward form, Ghawth's narrative presents a passage up through the layers of the astrological cosmos, measured by the orbits, stars, and planets.[10] These cosmic spheres are also layers of a moral and eschatological universe that is inhabited by angels, the souls of saints and sinners, and the spirits of various prophets. However, it becomes apparent as he reaches its climax that this passage is essentially an ascension through the existential levels of his own being, as he dissolves into pure being upon reaching closer and closer to the divine source. Ghawth's narration recounts his rise from his habitual life through the different elements that constitute his materiality (earth, air, water, fire, light).[11] From here he ascended through the various metaphors that make up his moral self (this world and the next world, heaven and hell, hope of reward and fear of punishment), through a renunciation of self-will itself, and up to a consequent eclipse of his self. Even as he eclipses his limited sense of self, Muhammad Ghawth's vision is full, for these cosmic realms and spiritual truths take on the form of bodies, forms and shapes that are intelligible to him and that he can later record for others in literary form. He called this record "a tissue of allusions and metaphors that stand for the ungraspable reality of the experience."

Hagiographic Tissue of Muhammad Ghawth's Body

His calling his record a "tissue" highlights for us the importance of the body in his discourse, for as his physical body in its gross manifestation as material begins to fade, his personality becomes concentrated in the organ of his eyes, and through their vision he is able to transcend not just the body but all limitations of space and time. As the tissues of the body fade in importance (or even in subjective reality as he experiences it), he records his vision in the tissue of allusions, in a body of words woven together with hints and symbols that are clothed in visible forms. His vision, then, makes an ideal way for us to explore the power of the eyes, not only to receive the impress of sensation but also to express. The visual field becomes a realm of communication in which intimacy is more potently expressed than even through spoken words.

The work of Farid al-Zahi can act as our launching point: "The eye is an inexhaustible mine of expressiveness, inasmuch as it creates its own special language. Of course, 'the eye is the gateway to the soul,' as Ibn Ḥazm has said. For these reasons, the eye constitutes a semantic organ of the greatest richness in its ability to hint and allude. Although this language of hints and allusions is limited when compared with the language of spoken discourse . . . the language of the eye says, in communicating allure and intimating seduction, what spoken language cannot say, especially in the context of constraint and prohibition."[12] Beyond the insightful description of the expressive power of the eye that complements its receptive sensitivity, this passage invokes the terms like allusion (*ishāra*) and secrets (*asrār*) that are central to Sufism. One of the goals of Sufi writing is to express in allusions and hints what cannot be expressed directly in prose or discursive speech—not just because the experiences meant to be conveyed are secrets or because of the Islamic environment of hedged-in prohibition and scrutiny by jurists and literalists but also because the nature of the experiences are so fleeting, so intimate, and so personal as to be effectively communicated only in the special "language of the eye," as al-Zahi calls it. In Muhammad Ghawth's case, what he experienced, in all its profundity, happened just in the twinkling of an eye.

In this experience, as Muhammad Ghawth transcends the body's physical limitations, the power of life is concentrated in the eyes. He intensifies the bodily eye's ability to bear witness to what is beyond the body's limits. In this paradox of extraordinary vision, Muhammad Ghawth puts aside the limitation of the individual body and takes on the authority of the body politic. He returns from this visionary ascension as the Ghawth, the axis of the universe through whom is channeled divine aid for human projects. Muhammad Ghawth returned from his ascension to become a kingmaker with the ability to shift the opportunity to rule from one dynastic leader to another. He not only advocated a new literary style and a new Sufi order but also supported a new political dynasty, the Mughal dynasty, that was just beginning its program of conquest and governance in South Asia. Before we can follow the subtleties of his vision, through the question of his eye's relation to his body and into the political ramifications of his teachings, we have to explore Muhammad Ghawth's intriguing personality.

Muhammad Ghawth was a bold and controversial Sufi in sixteenth-century South Asia. Modern scholars of South Asian Islamic history have seen him as an example of "pantheism" or "syncretic" religion. He taught the Sanskrit text *Amrta-Kuṇḍā* ("Pool of the Nectar of Life") on the principles of hatha yoga and may have translated it into Persian and Arabic, about which we will learn in Chapter 5, a fact that might lead this analysis away from the eyes and toward the spine.[13] He also valued the use of music as meditation, and the great singer Tansen was one of his followers, which might lead this analysis toward the diaphragm. Generalizing from these images, many scholars assume that Muhammad Ghawth suffered persecution for crossing the boundaries of religious communalism.[14] However, close examination of his persecution shows that those Muslim scholars and Sufis who opposed him consistently attacked his ascension experience and the uses he put it to in furthering the struggle of the Mughals to control the body politic.

We are fortunate to possess not only Muhammad Ghawth's original writings in Arabic and Persian but also hagiographic sources written about his life and personality. This chapter draws from archival evidence in various genres. These include the literary narrative of the ascension itself, which is presented for the first time in a complete English translation. This translation relied upon the Ascension Narrative as it has been printed in a lithograph print in South India.[15] In addition to the "eyewitness narrative" that Muhammad Ghawth provided of his ascension, this study also relies on a spiritual biography of the Sufi's early life by one of his followers, in a Persian manuscript.[16] Finally, this study supplements these rare sources with the better-known record of political figures who mention Muhammad Ghawth's role in historical events.

Muhammad Ghawth was reportedly born around 1501 in eastern Hindustan. He left home at age 12 to seek religious education at the regional capital, Jawnpūr. The young mystic sought guidance from a Sufi master and set to work carrying wood and working in the kitchen under the care of his master.[17] After a time, the master named Muhammad Ghawth his spiritual successor and sent him to live up in the mountains in isolation "to discover his manhood."[18] His youth displays a marked emphasis on vertical motifs of ascension, and his passage of discipleship under his master was punctuated by a series of vertical connections to higher authorities, symbolized especially by lonely climbs up into the mountains. At about the age of 12 or 13, Muhammad Ghawth stayed in an isolated chamber outside a gate of the mountain fortress of Chunār (near Banaras) for eight years, engaging in rigorous asceticism and intense meditation. He records that he spent up to six months without sleeping at night or being heedless during the day.[19]

He began to gain local renown at this time, and people addressed him with the title "Ghawth."[20] People began to climb the mountain to seek him out and to come up from the settled lands to live with him. He moved farther up the mountain for total immersion in meditation and spiritual exercises, increasing his isolation and rigor while eating little or nothing. At a certain point, Muhammad Ghawth fell unconscious, and in a vision he was taken to Arab lands to meet Shaykh Bāyazīd Bisṭāmī, the first Sufi to have expressed the loss of self-consciousness in imagery of visionary ascension, like a bird in flight. This is just the first of a long series of mystic initiations that were granted to Ghawth by long-dead saints and prophets through visionary experiences that he called spiritual disclosures (*mukāshifāt*).

Muhammad Ghawth crosses vast distances instantaneously, as if space had folded upon itself or had freed him from its bounds completely: he arrives at a destination without having taken a single step. As we have seen above, the experience of vision allows human perception to traverse vast distances. It is as if Muhammad Ghawth's being were being refined into his experience of vision, as might be imagined to happen if his body were to become more like light than matter. He imagines himself to cross the vast distances that we normally assume are only rendered near through the illusion created in our eyes through vision.

Muhammad Ghawth called this traveling within God and recognizing no being that is not divine being. This is a kind of spiritual travel that is really not journeying at all, for being within God is certainly not being within the confines of space. Rather, the mystic is overwhelmed by the transcendent verticality of his direct connection to God, leading him to ascend beyond space as experienced by a materially confined egoself. This was the essential insight that structured the Shattari method of mysticism. This method encouraged disciples to cultivate their own inner identity with God. In their view, the heavens, the universe, and the terrestrial world came into creation through a series of emanations from the primal being, which is God. Further, the human being is the direct reflection of the whole cosmos, containing within him- or herself all the levels and motions that are observed outside in the stars, planets, and heavenly spheres. Therefore, the human being likewise emanated from the divine; the human being subsists through the divine and can return only into the divine. The Shattari disciple does not conceive of spiritual development as passing through a series of arduous stages but rather apprehends that one has descended downward into worldly existence from an initial and fundamental state of nondivergence from the One who creates.

Once the Shattari disciple acknowledges this basic insight and internalizes its profundity, the apparently vast distance that separates the being of the creator from the created beings simply dissolves. Once this distance collapses and the illusion of otherness is eclipsed, the Shattari acts in complete concord with divine commands and personally embodies divine qualities. A major disciple of Muhammad Ghawth explained this method of spiritual training: "Repeating the essential name of God is the most important method of religious discipline. Recitation of the name God should be directed toward your own chest, so that you come to understand that recitation of this divine name is actually addressing your own essential self, that this divine name is actually your own name, and this divine reality is in actually your own soul's ultimate reality."[21] According to this method, the Shattaris claimed to follow religious custom (*sunna*) without paying any attention to custom. In their view, if a person can eradicate the individual ego (which separates the disciple from the divine source, no matter what acts of worship or devotion he or she performs), then whatever words or actions flow from her or him must be in accord with divine commands. "The Shattari way is painless and effective; it requires no arduous struggle and no deference to formalities. . . . Through the Shattari way, Bayazid [Bistami] reached divine realization without becoming trapped in such ascetic struggles and external formalities. . . . Anyone distracted by formalities and external norms will never achieve intimacy with God!"[22] To try to self-consciously follow religious customs would involve self-consciousness and buttress the illusion of an ego, which in the Shattaris' view can only distort the message of the Prophet Muhammad. For this reason, the Shattaris claimed to be an accelerated Sufi community, for "swift or rushing" is the literal translation of their name; in today's nomenclature we might call them "turbo-charged."

By practicing and preaching this method of spiritual discipline, Muhammad Ghawth caused his fame to grow. At just 21 years old, he climbed higher into the mountains to a new, more isolated retreat for another five years. He reports that he completely stopped eating and his body grew so thin that "if the wind was blowing behind him he would go three or four times faster than a normal person, but if the wind was blowing against him, he could hardly take a single step."[23] Even his basic bodily movements were not under his control but governed by the movement of the winds. It was at the end of these potentially deadly ascetic exercises that Muhammad Ghawth experienced, in the year 1526, his ascension up to the throne of God.[24]

By all accounts, Muhammad Ghawth's ascension was an extraordinary vision that expressed his experience of selflessness. The language of his description might even be called hallucinogenic, though that runs the risk of denying its authenticity. Not all Sufis who have such visionary experiences can communicate them or dare to record them. Muhammad Ghawth did record his experience, not only in visual and scriptural images but in the rare form of a firsthand prose account, an "eyewitness report."

Visionary Experience of Ascension

This section offers a full English translation of his account in Persian, interrupted for interpretive commentary. Muhammmad Ghawth begins his account with an abstract introduction, centering on the image of the multiplicity of the material world existing as a mirror that reflects the divine unity of absolute being, which is God.

> The eternal presence raised me up, though I am just the lowest particle of earthly existence. That presence raised me up and made the essence of each particle of existence reflect, as if a mirror, the divine essence. The eternal presence showed me the passage through every level of the cosmos and revealed to me the ultimate reality of the heavenly and earthly realms. Having snatched me away and raised me up to the Beloved, I was engaged in the play of passionate desire until true love was established between us. I was shown plainly the beginning and the end of the cosmos; all was revealed for my eyes to behold, from the time before eternity to the time beyond eternity. Knowing, seeing and conversing seemed to be produced in and of themselves [without my willing].

This introduction leads to a passage in which Muhammad Ghawth situates himself in his biographical context. This frames the fateful day when, during a routine day of ascetic practice in his mountain retreat, he was without warning or preparation pulled out of his daily experience.

> At that time, this lowly servant was living in isolation at a place on a remote mountain called "the retreat." It is located among the mountains that surround the fortress of Chunar. I spent several years there, having chosen to live in isolation. I was in a state perpetual spiritual preoccupation; my body grew lean and mean while my heart was frying and my eyes were crying. But despite this, my breast was full of joy, my vision was full of light, and my heart was full of the holy presence. At one moment, I would be far from myself and filled with the presence of the real One; at another moment, I would feel as if there were nothing to be far from and nothing to fill. I was satisfied with myself, and I needed nothing more. I was present in the being of myself and acutely conscious of the indwelling essence of myself.
>
> In the month of Jumadi al-Awwal, at the time of the afternoon prayers, there suddenly arose from the peak of the mountain a strange roaring, as if a storm wind were hurtling down the mountain. I rushed outside and turned to face the mountain peak. A voiceless voice began to speak, saying "Who are you? What are you? Where are you? Where are you going? What do you have and what do you bring with you? Have no why and no wherefore! Know everything that you may know! Say whatever you may say! Whatever you don't know, I also don't know. Whatever you don't desire, I also don't desire. Offer it up or take it away!"
>
> I cried out, "What can I do?" I fell out of my senses, overwhelmed. When I recovered consciousness again, a voice was reassuring me, saying "I am the very youness of you. I desire you and am searching for you; I have shown you who you really are. Now, who are you and where are you?" As I lifted my head, I saw someone standing over me.

The initiation of his experience was intensely aural: the strange roaring, the rushing of wind, the mysterious voice that both entices and compels. The sounds he heard overwhelm his senses. Regaining consciousness, he raises his head and looks: "I saw a man standing over me." Thus begins the visionary aspect of his experience, which will dominate the narrative.

The man he sees standing over him helps him to his feet. It is Khidr, the semiprophetic figure who represents the constant inspiration that undergirds the Prophet's revelation. Khidr is the muse of all saints and the companion of all prophets; he is associated with the color green, the revival of life through wisdom, and rejuvenation through the water of life. Through Khidr, Muhammad Ghawth would claim that his connection to the divine source was more intense and potent than reliance on the scriptural or legal traces left by the Prophet Muhammad. The visionary figure of Khidr serves as the symbol for continual revelation and direct divine guidance; he acts parallel to prophetic revelation and sometimes surpasses it. He requests Muhammad Ghawth to swear an oath and announces that this night is the night of Muhammad Ghawth's ascension.

> As I lifted my head, I saw someone standing over me. I gave him my hand and went along with him. I took some steps in complete amazement. He appeared as a young man, all clothed in green. He came closer to me and said, "Don't you recognize me?" I answered, "No." He asked, "Don't you know where I've come from?" I answered, "No." Then he said, "Then shall I tell you the answer to these questions?" I said, "Yes, please tell me!" He said, "I won't just tell you straight away; I'll only tell you if you swear an oath with me." I said, "All right, I swear to you, now please tell me." "No, no," he replied, "not like that!" I tried again, "I swear to you by the name of my Shaykh, Ẓuhūr al-Ḥaqq." "No, no!" he exclaimed, "not like that either." I asked, "Exactly what kind of oath do you want?" He answered, "I'll teach it to you and you recite it." I agreed, "Teach me, then, so I can recite it." He specified, "I'll teach you the oath and you memorize it silently and then you can recite it aloud exactly as I've taught." Then he told me the oath, saying "I swear by the appearance of the secret of the One. . . who scatters all the parts of the body, and by the Spirit of Jesus, and by the Witness of Zakaria, and by the Speech of Moses, and by the radiance of the advent of the Light of Muhammad, the beloved of God, and by the Closeness of ʿAli, the friend of God, and by the Beauty of Dhū al-Nūn Miṣrī, and by the Obedience of Junayd Baghdādī, and by the Insight of Bayazid Bistami, and by the Intimacy of Farid al-Din [Ganj-i Shakar] Ajhōdanī, and by the Renunciation of the Mahdi of the end of time. Also I swear that the lineage of sainthood and the lineage of Prophethood are joined as one. Now you say it." I repeated the oath, word for word. He asked, "Do you acknowledge that these two lineages are really one?" I repeated, "Yes, I know it to be true." He asked, "They exist as one?" I answered, "Yes, they exist as one." He said, "Do you attest to this full oath that the Prophets reveal [this lineage's] outer form and the saints embody its inner meaning?" I answered, "Yes, I attest to it and pledge that it is true."

Then the young man said to me, "Tonight will be the night of your ascension. But don't tell a single soul about it until you are carried up and shown all the visions of your ascension. Only when you have returned to your dwelling place can you openly tell of these experiences to both the Sufis and the common people. But do not tell anyone of this until the whole experience has unfolded before you. Don't even say that such and such a man came to me and said all these things and then left. And don't reveal my name to anyone!"

So I returned to my hermitage to wait for the night to fall. I had four companions who were staying with me there; two were intimate friends of mine and two were just acquaintances. However, I didn't speak a word of all these events to anyone and did not describe to anyone the strange events that had overtaken me. I went straight to my corner of the room and stayed engrossed in my habitual devotions. After a while, a state came over me that can't be called sleep but can't be called wakefulness, either. In this state, I passed a part of the night.

As the narrative takes on an expectant and dramatic tone, the senses of hearing and vision become increasingly interwoven. He is woken by a voice and beholds a strange vision, a vision into which he begins to climb, which in its strangeness is more real that routine sight.

In this state, I passed a part of the night. Suddenly I heard a voice calling out, "Come be present for prayer!" In that in-between state, I stood up and was caressed by the hand of bewilderment. I wanted to lay my head down and go to sleep for a little while. I was thinking these vain thoughts when a man came up to me and grasped my hand. He led me away from my hermitage. Then when they had all receded behind me, what did I see?

I saw that all the inanimate objects, all the plants, and all the animals had taken the form of human beings who stood staring up at the sky! When I took another step, they all melted into the shape of one single man, who came forward to me and said, "I dearly desire that you place your blessed foot upon my head, that I may be made noble by your passage." I asked him, "Who are you?" He replied, "I am the earth." So I placed my foot on his head and ascended until I reached the farthest extent of the earthly sphere.

At that point, another human figure appeared before me: clever, quick, and glimmering with brilliant colors. He saluted me and stood before me, and said, "Please place your blessed foot upon my shoulder, that I might accept that honor from you." I asked, "But who are you?" The figure answered, "I am water." So I lifted my foot from the head of earth, and placed it on the shoulder of water, and ascended until I reached the farthest extent of the aqueous sphere.

Then, another figure appeared to me, who looked cheerful and bright, like a true and dependable guide. This figure came up to me, saying "Peace be upon you!" I answered, "And also upon you." The figure responded, "Sir, place your foot upon my shoulder, so that I may prove worthy of carrying you." I objected, "But you appear to be very dignified and noble, so how could I place my foot on your shoulder?" He answered, "There is no way beyond except if you put your foot on my shoulder and step up, for I possess the dwelling place of spirits." So I asked, "Who might you be?" The figure answered, "I am the sphere of air." So I stepped up on the figure's shoulder and ascended, until I reached the farthest extent of the aerial sphere.

At this point, another figure appeared: powerful and brimming with pride, he appeared fierce, wild and crimson colored, with his head bare and a clutch of thunderbolts in his hand. He did not greet me, but just came forward and bowed his head, saying, "Place your foot upon my eyes, so that I may fulfill my pledge." I asked, "Who are you?" The crimson one answered, "I am the sphere of fire." I asked him, "Why do you appear so depressed and sullen?" He explained, "Since the day when Iblis, the mightiest of the people of fire, was repudiated and rejected, I have been worried and anxious; since Iblis was created from my fiery nature, I fear that I might also be punished for his rebellion. So I hope to God that, by your stepping upon me with your noble foot and your graceful presence, my sorrow and worry might dissipate." I stood there for a moment, turning my full attention to God and became aware of a message. I conveyed it to him, saying, "You are the guardian of the inner sanctuary of divine Might, yet there is no guarantee of your safety from punishment." He lowered his head further in sorrow, and I placed my foot upon his eye and ascended, until I came up beneath the heavenly sphere of the moon.

Muhammad Ghawth meets a figure representing each element: earth, then water, then fire. Each invites the mystic to place his foot upon his head and climb up through the elemental spheres. As he uses each figure as a ladder to step up, the figures also render him obeisance as a human being who encompasses, completes and perfects each element, for in Persian, to place another's foot on your head or eyes (*qadam dar sar nihādan*) is to express humility before that person. These are elemental spheres that not only mark the atmospheres between the surface of earth and the seven heavens but also represent the four elements that compose the human body. Therefore ascending upward is also delving inward, through bodily materiality and into the spiritual potency of the human heart.

Confronting the element of fire, Muhammad Ghawth experiences a moment of hesitation: the figure of fire seems threatening and full of pride, in contradiction to the cooperative figures of earth, water, and air. This is because fire is the element from which Iblis was originally created, as a jinn among angels who are created from light, as we saw in Chapter 1. Perceiving in himself the nature of fire was the very means of Iblis's rebellion: *God said, "What prevented you from bowing when I commanded you?" "I am better than he is—you created me from fire and created him from clay"* (Q 7:12). Perhaps Muhammad Ghawth hesitated to confront the figure of fire, fearing that he was Iblis or one of his minions. Or perhaps, in a more subtle insight, he hesitated before confronting the image of his own ego that, like Iblis, can run amok if its fires burn too fiercely, for isn't it egotistic to imagine that one can delve into one's own nature, observing its components with illuminating clarity, comprehending them layer after layer, and transcending them until arriving at one's own refined essence? As we saw earlier in this chapter, this was precisely the goal of the Shattari Sufi method of contemplation, which presumably brought the young Muhammad Ghawth to the threshold of this experience.

Through constant perseverance, he passes this temptation to hesitate. The figure of fire not only cooperates but is also redeemed by bowing low to Muhammad Ghawth, who is becoming refined into the archetypal human being, in a process that is the reverse of the creation of the prototypical human being, Adam. Adam was created from earth that was mixed with water to form a clay, then had spirit breathed into him, and then experienced the kindling of energy in him through motion and consciousness; then he confronted the fiery ego of Iblis, exercised the free will to choose for himself, and descended into the routine world. Muhammad Ghawth was reversing this process. He was ascending above and beyond the routine world, resigning himself from choice and extinguishing the raging of ego; then he experienced himself refined from his compounded elements of earth, water, air, and fire, releasing his essential self and clarifying the vision of his heart.

As he transcends the sphere of fire, he enters the state of those who have transcended egoistic selfishness: in the company of Khidr and the Prophet Muhammad's closest comrades, Muhammad Ghawth passes through the concentric layers of the heavens, meeting various angels, spirits, saints, and prophets. His vision is refined so that he cannot just see but recognize and understand the figure of Khidr, whom Muhammad Ghawth learns he has met before but could not see!

> He [the sphere of fire] lowered his head further in sorrow, and I placed my foot upon his eye and ascended, until I came up beneath the heavenly sphere of the moon.
>
> At this point, there appeared before me one of the people of divine might and one of the spiritual masters of Mount Sinai. He greeted me with peace and I answered with peace. When he came close to me, he shook my hand and said, "I came a few times to your hermitage, but I never found room there." I asked my companion [the figure of fire] who this man could be. He said, "He is the master, Khidr. A voice had whispered in his ear to go to your heritage when you were living along the banks of the Ganges." Khidr said to me, "I met you there several times, but I was never ordered to appear to you in visible form back then." He accompanied me and we ascended up to the upper limit of the heavenly sphere, and it split open. All the stars were blazing brightly.
>
> We entered up into that sphere. Abu Bakr and ʿAli, along with all the other saints, came before us. They greeted us heartily and said, "Welcome, we've been waiting for your arrival!" All the angels of this first heavenly sphere also came before us. With absolute joy they came up singing praises, with the same intensity with which people greet nobles who are returning to their palaces after some great exploit. I can't describe the vision of that joy in writing! The words to express what all I saw can never come to my pen. The nib of the pen has no power to even approximate it, nor can human reason grasp its splendor. Khidr and all the spirits of the saints stood with me, while Abu Bakr and ʿAli accompanied me. We ascended together to the limit of the second heavenly sphere.
>
> The heaven split open, the stars blazed, and we went up inside. All of the spirits of the saints and the jinn who inhabit that heavenly sphere came forward. They turned to greet us, along with the other angels of that realm. They stood politely and called out, "O great Ghawth! It's been

several thousand years since we've been seeing, reflected in the divine omnipotence, that you would be passing by this route. We've been eagerly awaiting the chance to greet you and to kiss your feet!" They all gathered around to greet me. Then with Abu Bakr and ʿAli, I began to ascend up to the limit of the third heaven.

Imam ʿAli, the Prophet's cousin and son-in-law, was his closest follower and the champion of the early Muslim community. The Shiʿa consider him to be the first and only rightful ruler of the Muslim community after the death of the Prophet, though the elders of the community chose Abu Bakr, the Prophet's older friend. The Shiʿa are the "partisans of ʿAli" and recite in their call to prayer the testimony of faith that "ʿAli is the Friend of God." Sufis also admire ʿAli and consider him, as the Friend of God, to be the first of saints, the patron of all saints, and the anchor of all Sufi lineages (except the Naqshbandi lineage with its lineage through Abu Bakr and its anti-Shiʿi stance). The Shattari order in the time of Muhammad Ghawth was in competition with the Naqshbandi order for influence in the new Mughal empire, for the founding Mughal, Bābur, had been affiliated with Naqshbandi masters before coming to South Asia. Therefore, it is of significance that in Ghawth's vision ʿAli and Abu Bakr appear together.

Then with Abu Bakr and ʿAli, I began to ascend up to the limit of the third heaven.

Suddenly, a cry of complaint rang out, "By the sanctity of this mystic, we might be released!" I became very anxious, and asked my companions who was crying out. They answered, "It is just Hārūt and Mārūt [the imprisoned angels]. I asked, "Do they really have no means of getting released?" They said, "No. We must be moving on quickly now, since the Prophet is waiting, so let's go." It came to my mind that my passing my here would have no purpose if I could not be of use solving the problems of others. Then a voice spoke out to me, "Whatever you may desire in this matter, just request it." I answered, "O eternal Lord, you are already well aware of my thoughts." The voice commanded [in answer to my unspoken request], "These two imprisoned angels will suffer suspension no more, nor will they continue to be punished with suffocating smoke; they are released from now until the Day of Judgment. Then they may seek intercession through Imam Ḥussayn on that day to beg forgiveness and liberation. They may then lead Yazīd [who slew Hussayn] to fall down at the feet of the one he killed and beg forgiveness for his sins."

His encounter with Harut and Marut, two fallen angels, is another intriguing twist in Muhammad Ghawth's vision. They are associated with the city of Babylon, where they are credited with having taught people sorcery and black magic, for which Babylon is famous. The Qur'an mentions them only elliptically: *But the forces of temptation (shayāṭīn) disavowed the truth, teaching the people sorcery (siḥr) and what was revealed to the two angels, Harut and Marut, in Babylon* (Q 2:102). They are mentioned in conjunction with the moral degeneration that destroyed the kingdom of Solomon (Sulaymān) after his death. Their names are probably derived from two Zoroastrian archangels, Haurvatāt and Ameretāt. Their story has been fleshed out in folk tales, in the "stories of the prophets" genre. In the Islamic worldview, they are two angels who fell, became embodied in the material world, then accustomed to sensory perception, then enticed by sensual pleasure, then imprisoned in eternal punishment. What seems like a strange diversion in the Ascension Narrative is actually a key element, for the two angels' story helps explain the perils of embodiment and reveals the means for human beings to ascend!

In the time of the Prophet Enoch (Idris), the folk tales say, six generations of Adam's children had passed. Corruption had spread, for Cain (Qābil) had killed Abel (Hābil), and the angels' complaint to God at the time of Adam's creation had come true—"Will you make in the world one that will spread corruption in it and spill blood while we recite your praise and revere you?" Seeing this, the angels again complained to God, and God responded, "If I had sent you down to earth and instilled in you what I have instilled in them, you would have acted as they have."[25] So the angels chose their two most pious fellows, into whom God infused the passionate nature of human beings and sent them down into the world to see what they would do, "commanding them to judge the people justly, and forbidding them idolatry, murder, fornication and the drinking of wine." Not a month had passed before the two angels, Harut and Marut, fell into temptation with a beautiful woman, a queen of Persia. In order to seduce her, they drank wine, then fornicated, then murdered a man who witnessed their acts. As punishment, they hang upside down in a well of raging fire, prisoner to heat and thirst until the day of judgment.

Their story illustrates the power of embodiment in the flesh, which generates an internal heat through consumption and digestion, heat that drives the passions and lustful urges. The angels had allowed embodiment to make them slaves to passion, which led them to commit unjust acts, which in turn led them to become imprisoned. They present an allegory of Gnostic imagination in which the divine spirit is imprisoned in the human flesh. Even imprisoned in the world, such angels are dangerous and wonderful, for their knowledge exceeds that of human beings. For this reason, people seek them out in Babylon to learn sorcery and arcane arts that perpetuate injustice and harm; though the angels give this knowledge to those who persist, they try to dissuade people from seeking it and urge them not to let sorcery lead them to idolatry.

What does their story have to do with Muhammad Ghawth's ascension? Embedded in the story of Harut and Marut is a crucial detail: not only did they teach human beings harmful sorcery, but they also taught them the beneficial "greatest name of God" (*ism allah al-aʿẓam*). The Persian queen whom they seduced refused to make love with them until they told her this arcane but beneficial secret knowledge. "She said, 'You will not have me until you teach me the means by which you ascend to heaven.' They said: 'We ascend by the most powerful name of God.' So she said: 'You will not have me until you teach it to me.' One of them said to his companion: 'Teach her.' But he said: 'I fear God.' The other said: 'But what about God's mercy?' So they taught her the name, and she uttered it and ascended to heaven, and God transformed her into a star."[26] Muhammad Ghawth evidently learned of this greatest name of God during his meditation retreat and ascetic introspection, which fueled his leap of imagination. The angels' descent provided the means for Muhammad Ghawth's ascent, by means of the secret name of God. His rise could free them from the consequences of their fall, fulfilling their hope in God's mercy.

In freeing them, Muhammad Ghawth demonstrates that his sainthood is the fulfillment of the early prophethood of Enoch, who established the archetype of ascension. While ascending, Enoch also heard the voice of the fallen angels, calling to him for deliverance, as recorded in the cosmological treatise "Wonders of Creation" (*ʿAjāʾib al-Makhlūqāt*). "When the era of Enoch's prophethood and responsibility arrived, the two angels went to him and pleaded for him to intercede for them and beg the true One to forgive their sin [that they might reascend into heaven]. Enoch asked them how he should know whether God intends to forgive them or not. They answered that he should request their forgiveness and then turn to discover whether he can see the two of them. If he can see them, this is proof that his petition was accepted, and if not then they will be ruined. So Enoch washed and made two prostrations of prayer, petitioning that they be forgiven. Then he looked in their direction, but they did not appear to his sight. He therefore knew that they were to be imprisoned in punishment, and they were hauled

وازجمله ملائکه آنها اند که موکلند بر کائنات این فرشته چند اند که شان ایشان
اصلاح کائنات است و دفع فساد از کائنات و موکلست بر هر فردی از افراد انسانی
که از ملائکه آنچه حق تعالی خواسته است روایت کرده ابو امامه از رسول صلی الله علیه
که پیغمبر فرموده وکل بالمؤمن مائة وستون ملکا یذبون عنه فذلک بالبصر سبعة
املاک یذبون عنه کما یذب الذباب عن العسل فی الصائف یعنی موکل است
بر هر مومنی صد و شصت ملائکه موکلست که دفع میکنند از و اذیت را از و
همچنانکه باز میدارند مگسان از عسل در صایف اما صد و شصت ملائکه پس آن

off to Babel and held there. God alone knows their real state!"[27] Following on the footsteps of Enoch in ascending, Muhammad Ghawth hears their plea. This explains why he hears them but does not see them, unlike so many of this other encounters with spiritual beings that are intensely visual. The "Wonders of Creation" recounts the amazing tales of heavenly and terrestrial objects and creatures complete with illustrations, beginning from the top with celestial phenomena (*ʿuluwiyāt*) and working its way down, from the throne of God to the pillars of the throne, the angels carrying the pillars, the other archangels, and then terrestrial things (*safaliyāt*), from the rainbow of the air to seas, islands, rivers of the water, to land-locked creatures discovered by explorers to different lands and the different parts of human anatomy. In this hierarchical account of wonders, the story of Harut and Marut plays a special role, for they are celestial beings trapped in the dark fastness underground. They are the reverse image of the rainbow, which bridges the distance from earth to the heavens.

For this reason, it is important for Muhammad Ghawth to tell relate his strange encounter with Harut and Marut. His ascent traces a return to lofty nobility in a motion contrary to the angels' fall. In doing this, he turns the potential energy of Adam's descent into the kinetic energy of becoming the archetypal man, the complete human being (*al-insān al-kāmil*). This process of becoming is analogous to ascension from the earth of imprisonment in its limitations to the heavens of expansive empowerment. Therefore, it is poignant that Muhammad Ghawth meets these angels in midascent; the means for their surprising liberation is precisely their recognition of his becoming the complete human being. This imagery of the human person as the microcosm of the entire macrocosmic universe is very ancient; it is evident in Stoic philosophy as well as the Vedic myth of Purusha. Muslims expressed these images as *al-insan al-kamil*, the complete human being. In Islamic terms, the spiritually realized and completed human is also the paradigm through which the whole world is brought into being and sustained. The Sufi who most clearly wrote about the universe in the shape of the Prophet as the most complete human being was ʿAbd al-Karīm al-Jīlī. A Persian

opposite:
Miniature painting of the fallen angels Hārūt and Mārūt, embodied and suspended upside down in punishment in Babylon. Painted in India, nineteenth century. From Qazwīnī, *ʿAjāʾib-i Makhlūqāt*, ms. (British Library: India Office Islamic Collection, 3243), fol. 106b.

translation of prose by him reveals these images. "Prophets were created from the essential names of God (*asmā' dhātiyya*), while saints were created from the attributive names (*asmā' ṣifātiyya*). The rest of existence was created from the free play of the lower names (*asmā' ḥalliyya*). The leader of the Prophets [Muhammad] was created from the essence of God (*dhāt-i ḥaqq*) and the manifestation of God is in him in his essence (*bi'l-dhāt*)."[28] The multiplicity we see in the created universe is due to the differentiation of God's names and attributes that, like a prism, spray unified light into diverse colors and forms. However, the Prophet Muhammad is not just one among these bewilderingly multiple forms in the universe; rather, he is the very principle through which they emerge. The human being alone has the potential to reflect all God's names and qualities and thereby unify them; however, the Prophet Muhammad alone, as the complete human being, actualizes this potential. Those who follow him among Muslim saints can, in harmony with his primordial example, also fulfill their potential.

Muhammad Ghawth is becoming the complete human being on the model of Imam Hussayn, the heroic martyr who self-consciously chose to die in selfless sacrifice, who was imagined as the complete human being of his age. Muhammad Ghawth acts as the immediate cause of release of the fallen angels, Harut and Marut, while Imam Hussayn can ultimately act as their definitive intercessor in release from punishment. The Prophet Muhammad, for Muslims, is the greatest means of intercession; his essence shares some quality of God's essence. Imam Hussayn (like all the Shiʿi imams) is imagined to extend the essence of Muhammad into the human community through genealogical descent. As a verse in South Asian Sufi devotional singing phrases it, "In the garden of God, Muhammad is the rose, while ʿAli is the redness and Hussayn is the fragrance." The continuity of essences despite the distinctive separation of human bodies is a theme that will return at the climax of the ascension. Muhammad Ghawth plays the role of Hussayn's delegate, through whom the fallen angels might reconnect with God's charismatic deputies and therefore with God.

> We passed by that place, until we reached the limit of the fourth heavenly sphere; the sphere split open; the stars waned like glowing crescents. I passed up into the heaven. The spirits of all the Prophets came forward to greet me. They all shook my hand joyfully, along with the angels of that sphere. They praised me and their faces lit up, saying, "We have been waiting for so long, asking the Lord when you would be passing by this way. On the day that the Prophet Muhammad ascended along this route,

there were with him some saints, and you were one of them. However, at that time, you were in the form of pure spirit. In contrast, this time you are fully attached to your body! This is a completely new and different spectacle." They stood around amazed at my appearance. With ʿAli and Abu Bakr, I ascended until we neared the limit of the fifth heavenly sphere.

At this point, I saw one form with two different inherent essences. Seeing this paradox, I stood bedazzled and confused. Then I suddenly grew joyful when I discovered that both its dimensions were equal. So I asked my companions, "What is the significance of this form with two equal essences?" They explained, "Here the essences of heaven and hell are brought into existence in one single place. On that Day [of Judgment] they will each expand into full form."

This is one of the many surprising moments of Muhammad Ghawth's ascension. In conventional Islamic theology, heaven and hell are clearly and eternally differentiated. One is a place of torment and the other a place of bliss. But here, both exist in the same space, as "one essence with two equal forms." This vision confirms the intuition of many Sufis that both hell and heaven represent states of alienation from God: one is alienation through divine wrath, the other alienation through divine beauty. They appear to be distinct in the discourse of the prophets and their scriptures that warn about one and promise the other, yet in reality this appearance deceives. Muhammad Ghawth continues to get a closer look at the angels who guard hell.

They explained, "Here the essences of heaven and hell are brought into existence in one single place. On that Day [of Judgment] they will each expand into full form." I further inquired, "What does it mean that, when I look through the dimension of heaven, I can see some people beyond it?" They said, "To every person that God Almighty wants to show forgiveness, God makes this heavenly dimension appear before them. From this sphere down to the grave of that person, God bores a hole so that they can each gaze up and catch a glimpse of what heaven will be like."

After witnessing this strange spectacle, we ascended up to the very limit of the fifth heavenly sphere. The heaven split open; the stars glimmered like crescents. I entered up into the sphere. Suddenly, countless animal shapes appeared around me. Their forms were beautiful and their voices were sweet. They came down around me, perching on my hands and settling on my feet. They began to speak. I asked, "You all look like animals, but you speak like human beings! How can this be?" They replied sweetly, "We are the spirits that have descended on our own accord from the realm pure knowledge. We descended to this place and found ourselves clothed in bodies. All the spirits were wondering what it would be like to be embodied. In pure omniscient knowledge, we discovered that Muhammad Ghawth would be passing along this route. We wanted to see you! Now that we have, we hope that the eternal presence will ennoble us by this meeting of ours." I took the opportunity to ask them, "Where are the spirits of those saints that are not enmeshed in any bodies?" They answered, "They are in a place that no angel or spirit has ever entered." I suddenly felt a strong desire to see that place. I asked my companions, ʿAli and Abu Bakr, "Can you show me that place?" They answered, "No." I began to think, how can they carry me up stage by stage through the heavens but leave some of the people of God left unseen? Then a voice from beyond the tissue of unseen certainty called out, "Take him there and show him!"

ʿAli and Abu Bakr took me to that place, and I witnessed the spirits of several hundred thousand saints who were not connected to any bodily form. From among that multitude there were seven saints who were so lofty in their rank that no other saints could ever compare with them. Two of these superior saints desired to benefit from my spiritual emanations, that they might gain the whole expanse of the universe. Having seen this place and admired its wonders, we passed on to the upper limit of the sixth heavenly sphere.

The heaven split open; the stars flared up, blazing brightly. I ascended up into the sixth heavenly sphere. Such wondrous and strange things came into sight while all the angels of that sphere came forward into my presence. They carried in their hands pages, like those of a book. I asked, "What are these pages?" They answered, "These are the registers of Might which will consume the people consigned to the flames. They haven't been displayed yet or made public, but they record all the people's deeds." I asked, "Where are the people of the flames?" They invited me to come this way in order to see. When I came forward, I saw a chamber formed from the purest substance of divine wrath. In it, there were many beings sitting, all in the shape of women. One woman among them was explaining clearly the meaning of divine unity (*tawḥīd*). I asked, "Who is that woman who is teaching so eloquently?" They answered, "That is the mother of all humankind, Eve!"

> I rushed forward to greet her and pay my respects, and asked her, "Why have you, a true Muslim, appeared in the midst of all the people who are overcome by divine wrath?" Eve replied, "We are the most comprehensive, most perfect and most beautiful of all the manifestations of the divine. We are called 'the People of divine Might' who are the manifestation of God's attribute of utter singularity." I requested Eve to explain this to me further; she said, "The authority of God's beauty is delegated to the Prophets, and that authority has already come to its full completion long ago and its delegation is now over. Then the saints were raised up and were given authority. To the saints was delegated the authority of God's beauty mixed with God's might. Now listen, these women whom you see here are the messengers who will be sent to the people punished in hell fire. They are called 'the people of divine might.' They each wish to raise people up from the fires of hell into the realm of pure divine might. The Prophet Muhammad, himself, revealed this from the inner world when he said, 'Women are the emissaries of Satan.'"

This is a supremely surprising twist in the Ascension Narrative. The Prophet Muhammad was reported to have said that when he looked into hell, most of the figures there were women. Accordingly, he is reported to have said, "Women are the emissaries of Satan."[29] Many jurists and ascetics took such reports at face value and claimed that women by nature veered toward rebelliousness and caused social discord. However, Muhammad Ghawth turns that image on its head! In his vision, the women in hell are the disciples of Eve and are manifestations of God's might in the form of wrath. Through these women, men in hell might slowly work through their "punishment" and realize the true worship of God. They do this through divine might, since they missed the boat in the message of the prophets and saints, which manifested divine beauty. In this way, Muhammad Ghawth's vision confirms the intuition of many Sufis, that within the wrath of punishment lays a hidden mercy that will eventually unfold from within it and overwhelm what seems on the surface like wrath; they took very seriously a hadith *qudsī* in which God is reported to say, "My mercy surpasses my wrath." In this vein, Ibn ʿArabī had written, "The state of hell will remain what it is, but Mercy will produce a felicity without the form or the status of the infernal abode being modified, for Mercy is all-powerful and its authority indefeasible forever."[30] Muhammad Ghawth continues his account:

> "The Prophet Muhammad, himself, revealed this from the inner world when he said, 'Women are the emissaries of Satan.'

Everyone sees Satan as the master of miracles and secret knowledge, splendor and power. At first he appears with the attractive power of God's might, but in the end, he behaves with infidelity, betraying the divine power that he at first displays." Then I asked her, "If these are messengers, then who is their angel? Gabriel was the angel who brought messages to all the Prophets, but who is the angel that serves as the intermediary for this group of messengers, 'the People of divine Might?'" Eve answered, "First, the angel Kalkā'īl appears from the essence of divine Might. Then these women whom you see here, under the authority of each one will come several hundred thousand men who have been consigned to the flames. All these men will gain their power from the emanations of authority that radiate from one of these women. You see, the women are empowered by the might of the angel Kalka'il in an interior, hidden exchange of power, while the men are empowered by his emanations in any outward apparent way. These men will then turn to their own people who are in the flames and overpower them and subdue them. They will recognize absolute being only in the limited forms of what they hold dear; they will recognize it and worship it. Through this worship, good and evil will finally become clearly distinguished in their sight. From among these men and women, some will receive emanations of might directly from the angel Kalka'il. They will witness the overwhelming power and might of God directly, without any intermediary, because divine might will blaze forth without any obscuring form to mediate it." Hearing this explanation, I stood there stunned and amazed at my surroundings. I was thinking, "O Lord! These are things that nobody has ever heard of before, yet I've just heard them. I've seen all this with my own eyes! Where could I be?"

With this explanation, the visionary figure of Eve with irony overturns the apparent misogyny of the Prophet Muhammad's observation, as he overlooked the celestial gardens and cosmic flames, "Women are the emissaries of Satan." The pioneering Muslim feminist Riffat Hassan construes this report and others as misogynist, and she endeavors to throw their authenticity into doubt.[31] Muhammad Ghawth did not have to struggle with affirming or denying the outward words of reports like this, for his vision allowed him to grasp their inner meaning, which might be completely contradictory to an outer, literalist reading. Why argue with literalist scholars and hadith experts over the status of Muslim women when he can call upon Eve, the mother of believers?

Hearing this explanation, I stood there stunned and amazed at my surroundings. I was thinking, "O Lord! These are things that nobody has ever heard of before, yet I've just heard them. I've seen all this with my own eyes! Where could I be?"

My companions and I continued on our way, accompanied by Eve, until we reached the highest limit of the sixth heavenly sphere. A fiery figure came lurching forward. I asked who it was. Eve said to me, "I have accompanied you so far from my own place for this very reason, that you might not be terrified upon seeing a person engulfed in the flames of divine might." I asked, "What is this place called?" She told me the name of the place, but forbid me from telling anyone else. Then she said, "Step forward to get a good view of the presence of the divine might." Eve stayed standing in her place while my companions and I went forward and arrived at the seventh heaven.

The heaven split open and we ascended up into it. The essences both lofty and lowly appeared before me. I hesitated there, thinking that, if I don't understand the appearance of these essences, I will have no way to advance beyond this point. I looked to my right, and I saw the archetypes of religious knowledge and intuitive knowledge (*ʿilm-i dīnī o ʿilm-i ladūnī*). My thoughts inclined to find out what religious knowledge really looked like. At that moment, Jesus spoke to me, saying, "Have you ever seen the four Imams [who fashioned the structure of Islamic law]?" I answered, "No." Jesus directed me to look at a certain place in the vastness; there I saw the four Imams standing together, each disputing with the others, saying "No, no, the certain truth is this, not that." I thought to myself, if this is the outer knowledge of religion, then what is the inner knowledge of intuition? The thought simply flashed in my mind, but I didn't say anything to that effect. Just then, all the divine names of God emerged, each in the particular dimension of its knowability, from the realm of the primal archetypes. Each took a distinct shape, giving rise to the whole multitude of perceptible and existent forms. I could see the continuity between the divine names and all the created forms that arose from their various natures. I could see the universe contained within the relation between the divine names that prepared the universe for its worldly existence.

This vision of the divine names as archetypes expresses the cosmology known as *wahdat al-wujud*, or "the unity of being." From a creaturely point of view, God created the world. But from a mystical point of view, there is

و ملایکه آسمان پنجم بر صورت حور العین است و ملکی که موکل است بر ایشان نام او کلکائیلست

و ملایکه آسمان ششم بر صورت ولدانست و ملکی که موکل است بر ایشان نام او انجابلیت

no being except God's being. Creation is really an emanation of pure being, through the archetypes of God's names and qualities, into the realm of conditional being. Here being can take a material form, but each form is actually a manifestation of God's names. In that they reflect God, all phenomena are divine, but in that they are material they pass away into nonbeing. The human being is the most complete manifestation of the divine: in the human being all names of God manifest, and for this reason the human being was selected to be God's vice-regent in the world.

> When I ascended a little further from this place, all the stars that had been blazing in the heavenly spheres suddenly took the form of human beings and all the heavenly beings took on their light. From the distant clot of dust that is the earthly sphere all the way up to the dais of the divine Throne, each and every created being stood as a human figure, each rooted to its particular place and station, each could openly see the others without the thick veil of materiality.
>
> Adam, Moses, Jesus, Abu Bakr and ʿAli said, "Beyond this point, there is no place and no space." ʿAli moved on with me as we left the others behind and ascended higher, beyond the heavens to the farthest beyond. Together, we arrived at the threshold of the divine Throne. Then we passed into its presence. There, I saw the Prophet Muhammad standing before us. When he saw me, he gave thanks to God, the eternal One, saying, "In my community, there are seven people who have arrived to this point beyond all points." Without my own volition or intent, a lofty aspiration arose within me that I might arrive at that place beyond all place.
>
> In one instant, I took off, and arrived in the same instant. The four persons who were with me came along. When we arrived, we saw the form of the angel, Azrāʿīl, who oversees the vastness of divine Might. From the awesome sight of Azraʿil, I was blasted unconscious. After a time, I returned to my senses and saw that some of the saints had arrived and, having witnessed the vastness of divine Might, were bowing down in prostration. What lay before my vision was beyond eyes to see and

opposite:
Miniature painting of angels in human form: angels of the fifth and sixth heavens in the form of pure women and governed from above by the angel Kalkāʾīl. Painted in India, nineteenth century. From Qazwīnī, *ʿAjāʾib-i Makhlūqāt,* ms. (British Library: India Office Islamic Collection, 3243), fols. 100b–101a.

beyond the mind to comprehend. I was lifted up to survey the expanse of vastness. I witnessed the beauty of divine grandeur within the oceanic vastness of divine Might: a grandeur from which rise both the thrones of the Lord of Both Worlds, a grandeur of nonbeing emerging into being, a grandeur that through existence acknowledges nonexistence, a grandeur bringing each thing into its own suchness, from the loftiest vault to the lowliest plane. I saw each and every particle of this calling-into-being, with nothing hidden from my sight.

When each being in that great gathering had come forth in their own proper place and stood arrayed in their integral order, a lofty and captivating voice rang out from beyond the tissue of being, commanding, "You who are Ahmad without the *mīm*, come up to the divine Throne!"

Ahmad is another name for Muhammad, in his intensified spiritual form. It is believed that Ahmad is the name of the Prophet's spiritual essence, distilled from the name of his earthly personality, Muhammad, by removing one letter, *mim*, or *m*. Ahmad, when further refined by removing another *mim*, becomes Ahad, "the singular One," a name of God.[32] With this subtle pun, the divine voice denotes the continuity between a person, the soul, and the divine source. If Muhammad without one *m* is Ahmad, then Ahmad without another *m* is Ahad, hinting at continuity between the Prophet and the name of God, through which the universe was created. In his book "Key to the Treasuries" (*Kalīd al-Makhāzin*), Muhammad Ghawth drew a diagram of concentric circles that graphs how Ahmad emanated from Ahad and how Muhammad then emanated from Ahmad, while through Muhammad the whole universe come into being.[33] The chart illustrates a hadith *qudsi* in which God declares to Muhammad, "If not for you, I would not have created the universe and all that is in it."

As Muhammad marked the path, others can follow and leave individuality behind and realize a cosmic oneness with divine being. The Prophet Muhammad then ascends beyond the threshold of the divine throne and falls into prostration before the presence of God, leaving Muhammad Ghawth bewildered.

When I heard this command call out to Muhammad to rise and ascend, I was confused. I turned to Jesus who was standing beside me and asked, "I thought that this was the night of my ascension, so why should Muhammad be called up now to ascend to the divine Throne?" Jesus answered, "Each saint is a member of the community that was founded by a specific Prophet. The Prophet must ascend first, so that the saint can follow after him up to the appointed place. That way, the structure of prophethood and sainthood can be established in good order." Having heard this explanation from Jesus, my thoughts became tranquil once again. I don't know what happened then. I don't know what became of me or what came over me. When a wave from the outpouring of pure being hits you, you simply become, such that it is now exactly as it was in the beginning.

The Prophet Muhammad gave me the long-awaited signal. I raised my foot to step forward one degree more, suddenly everything that had existed lost its materiality, and everything around me was transformed into pure, subtle light. The angels in union yelled out, "There is a sin incomparable to any other sin that accompanies this young man unawares!" Finally, I was lifted up above all being [beyond even the subtlety of light] and proceeded into the fullness of the verse, *You see them enter into the true relationship with God* (Q 110:2). Not a single particle of human ego and selfish urge remained of me. The deepest meaning of the verse revealed itself to me, *God is with you all wherever you may be* (Q 57:4).

When he arrived at the threshold of the divine Throne, he sat down at the zenith of power beyond cause.

The angels protest that Muhammad Ghawth is achieving this very last stage while his ego is still intact. They protest that he cannot be allowed to remain self-conscious while in God's presence. While teaching his disciples, he had often used this saying, "Your very being is a sin incomparable to any other sin." His followers among the Shattaris were fond of quoting a similar saying, "The very existence of the worshiper is a veil obstructing witness of the One worshiped."[34]

The protest of the angels is immediately followed, the narrative implies, by Ghawth's total immersion in the divine presence that eclipses, effaces, and absorbs his ego. At this point, the narrative signifies selflessness in the eclipse of the first-person subject "I," replaced by the third-person pronoun "he." This is further refined, as the pronoun "he" is not just a cipher for the subject as described from without as a third person. Rather, "he" could stand in a direct reflection of pure being, of divinity itself. In fact, in Persian this pronoun could stand for he or she or it, for there is no difference in the language between these gendered or animate pronouns. "He" could be either figure: the gazer or the reflection of that gaze in the mirror. This deep ambiguity is a special feature of the Persian language and accounts for its poetic force. The "I" drops away, leaving the "naked eye" to see clearly.

The image of the obstructing veil being lifted highlights again the importance of the visual metaphors in his experience, even as it resounds with voices. Sight unobstructed by any veil is a powerful metaphor for intimacy, even sexual union, because of its association with the lifting of veils from a bride in the intimacy of the wedding chamber. As al-Zahi has made clear the importance of the eye in intimacy and seduction: "At its furthest extent, the body is abandoned and is concentrated in the face, to complete its transformation into a means for perpetual seduction. The eye, in this framework, becomes a means of achieving union between inner, hidden desire and its expression through subtle hints and symbolic allusions."[35]

The desire to draw close to the beloved can be achieved through the eyes in ways impossible through words or gestures; at the verge of this state of intimacy beyond any alienation, even the Prophet Muhammad indicated permission to approach closer with a "signal." Then a vision of the beloved fills the eye, subsuming even the seeing "I," and Muhammad Ghawth's narrative can continue only in the third person.

> When he arrived at the threshold of the divine Throne, he sat down at the zenith of power beyond cause. No why or how could possibly penetrate into its uncaused bringing-forth-into-causation. All the other Prophets, saints, angels, and existing worldly beings fell into a profound prostration and were eclipsed, virtually obliterated. The bower and the one bowed-before both remained fixed in their mutual prostration, while there manifested the resonance of the verse, *Everything upon the face of the world is passing away, except the face of your Lord, full of might, full of honor* (Q 55:28).
>
> Suddenly there welled up speech as if between two persons. One began to ask questions while the other responded with answers, recounting matters from beginning to end, giving full knowledge of the essence of all things, making the contrary motion of all things seem harmonious and in accord. From his gazing with love upon his own divine beauty, he clothed all things in their own natures. I don't know how to describe what was happening; at one moment it was as if I were in the midst of the motion of every existing being, and at the next moment it was as if I were in the center of a great void. I witnessed the essence of that being that was prior to any primordial origin, stretching out across the surface of eternity beyond any possible end. I then saw within every form its own origin and its own destiny, interwoven. I descended from the divine Throne.

All things were clothed in the flesh of their own natures by God's loving gaze. For those immersed in the philosophy of the "singleness of being" creation makes sense only as multiplicity emanating from primal and ultimate unity. This "creation" was actually an act of loving desire by the singular One, who loved and longed for intimacy with the other. The motif of the lover gazing in the mirror in order to see his beauty reflected in another is the central metaphor that illustrates how multiplicity could come from absolute unity. Through this motif, Sufis in Persian-speaking lands appropriated the mirror imagery of Ibn ʿArabi and heightened its intensity as a story of loving desire between human beings and their creator. Central to such narratives is the hadith *qudsi* in which God says, "I was a hidden treasure and I loved to be known, so I created all that is created that I might be known." Persian Sufi poets provided the strongest examples of this fusing of love mysticism with existential philosophy, and Persian-speaking Sufis drew their poetic imagery into preaching and didactic prose. Shattari Sufis like Muhammad Ghawth tried to spark divine love in their disciples by invoking these images, as he did in the very introduction of his Ascension Narrative.

Muhammad Ghawth then descends through the various levels of the cosmos. They no longer appear as heavens with angels and stars; they are far more abstract. They are clearly emanations of God, from the rarified source of pure being, through the universal intellect, through the spiritual reality of Muhammad as the primordial human being, then through further emanations of increasing materiality. Muhammad Ghawth came to on the pinnacle of the mountain and in three steps entered his hermitage and collapsed onto his cot.

> I descended from the divine Throne, and reached the level of the primordial emanation and perceived the Holy Spirit. I saw the figure of the chosen Prophet, Muhammad. He said to me, "The first step of the Prophet is the last step of the saint." I came to my senses and descended into the level of the second emanation. I emerged from my pure name and came into my bodily form. I reached the foundation of the Throne as if intoxicated and bereft of self-will. The Prophet said to ʿAli and Abu Bakr, "Now take him back to his own place." ʿAli and Abu Bakr accompanied me, one on each side. When I opened my eyes, I saw before me my former companion [Khidr]. I arrived upon the pinnacle of the mountain. My companions all disappeared from sight, and I found myself alone.
>
> After taking just three steps, I reached the cot in my hermitage, and sat down. I saw that my neighbor, Shaykh Jalāl, was awake, stirring a

pot which sat on the fire. Shaykh Aḥmad Ghāzī was sitting in a corner with his head bowed, deep in meditation. Then he stirred. Without sitting down, Shaykh Jalal asked, "Where did Muhammad Ghawth go?" Shaykh Ahmad answered, "He hasn't gone anywhere—he's just been meditating." Shaykh Jalal said, "No, I saw him go out conversing with some other Darweshes." Shaykh Ahmad told him, "You must have been sleeping and saw that in a dream without understanding the difference. He's been here all along. The most he might have done was get up to wash his hands!"

When I saw that they were really beginning to argue, I said, "You are both imagining things, so why bother with all this chatter?" They both kept quiet. I began to ponder, thinking, "My God, how could this be? I've been away from what seems like years while these two are arguing over whether I have stood up or remained sitting just one moment ago!"

I was pondering this strange situation when I suddenly remembered all the details of my ascension with the Prophet Muhammad. At this, all my vain thoughts were hurled aside. The state that come flooding back to my memory is so astounding that words could never describe it. Nobody but God alone could grasp it fully. I have tried to render it with the pen, to that extent that the experience took a palpable form in my senses and my mind. However, this description is really only a tissue of allusions and metaphors for the ungraspable reality of the experience.

This account was written so that everyone might know that, no matter how far a saint may traverse the spiritual path of perfection, a saint can never pass beyond the rank of the Prophet whom he follows. From the point of view of spiritual training, it seems that the last step of the Prophet is the first step of the saint. Yet in reality, the saint can never pass beyond the rank of the Prophet. I found this to be true after the deepest pondering over my own experience.

May God protect us from confusion and mistakes! I say Amen, O Lord of both worlds, by your mercy, O most merciful of any who show mercy.

With this modest conclusion, Muhammad Ghawth closes off his firsthand narrative of his ascension "rendered with the pen." In an exact inversion, his descent from the heavens, alighting on the mountain, lapsing back into sleep, and then waking into his routine life mirror the process of his ascension.

Bearing Witness and Enduring Cross-Examination

This ascension record purports to be a narrative of selflessness. Muhammad Ghawth's experience of selflessness is framed by the concept of essential congruence between the personal self and the One divine being. The Sufi masters of the Shattari lineage taught that realization of this simple concept was the key to salvation and the secret of heaven, hell, and conventional morality. However, to close the narrative, he reverts to a more conventional Islamic theme: "The first step of the Prophet is the last step of the saint." The saint can experience the path of a prophet, but only by virtue of following that prophet. He means to state that this was a secondhand ascension (and therefore a decent ascension) no matter how fantastic and astounding its eyewitness report may seem to the reader.

However, this modest point is not what really lasts in the minds of those who read this Ascension Narrative or in the ears of those who might have heard of it orally in Ghawth's own time. It is clear that the public dissemination of Ghawth's ascension played a crucial role in his subsequent public role as a popular Sufi leader. For his followers and admirers, his ascension signified that Muhammad Ghawth was truly selfless and thus a conduit for divine will to act in the material and social world. He was therefore a source of blessing and success, whether one's goal was mystical journeying or political conquest.

By the time he was in his early twenties, Ghawth had already written his first and most popular text, *Al-Jawāhar al-Khamsa* ("The Five Precious Essences"). This gave him a reputation for expertise in astronomy and astrology, for the prayers and meditations recorded in this text are calibrated to constellation movements and planetary influences. Muhammad Ghawth gained a reputation for praying to God in concord with astrological alignments in order to influence the course of worldly events. This technique was known as *daʿwat-i asmāʾ wa taskhīr* or "invoking the divine names and subjecting the world to their influences," and both Muhammad Ghawth and his older brother, Shaykh Bahlūl, were experts in this art.[36] This reputed ability to bend the world to his will is most likely the real cause of Ghawth's fame and popularity. However, it is clear that the story of his ascension and his eyewitness observation of the secret reality of the heavens gave credence and justification to his reputation as a saint whose prayers have potent efficacy, since they invoke the names of God through the alignment of the stars and planets.

In these ways, Muhammad Ghawth wove the experience of his ascension into his rituals of initiation and his claims to spiritual potency. His ascension experience was therefore enmeshed in his claim to authority as "Ghawth," "the Spiritual Aid" or axial saint of his age. On this basis, he claimed to be "the voice of the Darweshes" and the leader of those who have renounced the world and self-direction; through them, God's mercy and wrath permeate the world and shift the flow of history. In this role, Muhammad Ghawth staked a claim in issues of social justice and dynastic politics. He refused to endorse reigning sultan of Delhi, the Afghan Ibrahim Lōdhī, and called upon God to remove him from power. Within a year, in 1526, the Turkic Mughals under the leadership of Babur overran the Lodi Afghan's forces and began a new dynasty in South Asia. Muhammad Ghawth's witness to the divine throne beyond the bounds of material existence may have given him a special authority to fill worldly thrones in Delhi. He compared himself, a "selfless mendicant," to the prophet-king Solomon, whose most outstanding feature was his magnificent throne and his supernatural ability to command even the unseen forces of nature. "The Afghans did not lay their heads upon the threshold of the door of the Darwesh, and for that they were made obedient and submissive [by force]. This whole world is [to the Darwesh] like a court under the order of the finger of King Solomon."[37] The Mughal emperor Humāyūn, who ruled from 1530 to 1556, saw in Muhammad Ghawth a political ally and perhaps a spiritual mentor. This is not the place to illustrate how Muhammad Ghawth and his coalition of Shattari Sufis supported the Mughal rise to power, as I have told that fascinating story elsewhere.[38] Mughal rulers hoped that Muhammad Ghawth's popularity and his association with God's throne might give justification to their own claim to the throne at Delhi.

However, so tenuous was Mughal rule that within twelve years of first taking power, the Mughals were faced with a concerted Afghan counteroffensive that drove Humayun into exile in Iran by 1542 C.E..[39] Muhammad Ghawth moved to Gujarāt out of fear of political persecution. Though he arrived in Gujarat as a political exile, the religious notables as a class received him just outside the city, and he quickly attracted socially powerful followers. Muhammad Ghawth predicted that Humayun would return to power, for during his visionary ascension he witnessed how the archetypes of God's names and qualities interweave to give the material world its form and motion. "God nurtures his servant with all of the various divine names, both beautiful and mighty. Some time has passed and you've been nurtured with manifestations of beautiful names; now some hard days have come when your sustenance is through the mighty and wrathful names. Remember that this all comes under the ruling *with each hardship there is ease* (Q 94: 5–6). How quickly the turn of beautiful names will return!"[40]

Not all the Sufis and scholars of the Gujarati capital at Ahmadabad welcomed Muhammad Ghawth. After his arrival, he faced another persecution. This focused more overtly on his mystical writings, especially his ascension vision, though it was not free of political undercurrents. Many in Gujarat did not wish for Humayun to return to power, for the Mughal ruler had invaded Gujarat just five years before, in 1534, wreaking havoc against the Gujarati sultan Bahādur Shāh Ẓafar. Therefore, the Sufis and scholars who were loyal to the independent state of Gujarat had reason to be suspicious of a known partisan of the Mughals like Muhammad Ghawth. Despite these political undercurrents, hagiographic sources specify that it was Ghawth's claims to have experienced a bodily ascension that caused the scholars and Sufis of Ahmadabad to denounce him. The written account of his ascension circulated widely among the learned of the city. In addition, Ghawth orally affirmed that he had this experience, told people details of it, and referred to it in his other written works. Therefore, the scholars gathered together and prepared a declaration (*maḥḍar*) denouncing and refuting Ghawth's ascension story.

In Arabic and Persian, the word for witnessing with one's own eyes (*mushāhada*) is derived from the same root letters as bearing witness to the truth by stating one's belief (*shahāda*). Similarly, in English we have the proverb that "seeing is believing." However, establishing the veracity of one's vision in the eyes of others is another matter, especially when one appears suspicious in the eyes of others. When one approaches the limits of communal consensus or trespasses it, one appears suspicious in the eyes of those community members who patrol that boundary limit. In Muslim communities, this is the role of jurists and theological scholars, who reserve the right to monitor and question the sincerity of Muslims' bearing witness, or *shahada*, which grants them inclusion into the community of believers.

Many saw Muhammad Ghawth as trespassing that boundary, and they questioned the veracity of his vision and the sincerity of his motives. Much of the information that is available about Muhammad Ghawth is due to the persecution campaigns that raged against him. The hagiographic material about the life of Shaykh ʿAlī Muttaqī (1480–1568 C.E.), a Sufi master and hadith scholar from Gujarat, fills out our story as it focuses on Muhammad Ghawth's vision in a critical and denunciatory frame. The details of this story are presented here in detail for several reasons. First, it is says much about vision and its relation to the embodied self: Was it seen in waking consciousness or in dreaming sleep? Second, it shows us Sufis in conflict with one another over the nature of the body, its capacity to misinform the ego, and its relationship to the sharia. Finally, this literature gives us probably the most detailed record in late medieval and early modern times about a Sufi's persecution.

ʿAli Muttaqi presents a personality almost radically opposite that of Muhammad Ghawth. ʿAli Muttaqi spent his lifetime pursuing the exoteric knowledge of hadith reports and scriptural exegesis and saw Sufism as the inner development of spiritual humility that enlivened this exoteric body of communally sanctioned knowledge. In contrast, Muhammad Ghawth finished with scriptural studies in his youth and moved on to probe the depths of his own body for direct access to the divine presence and saw Sufism as an expression of cosmic realities that might be equally accessible by the esoteric teachings of any religion. This basic difference in orientation to the event of revelation, its codification in Islamic law and custom (sharia), and its relationship to the body of Muslim believers set the two on a collision course.

Yet ʿAli Muttaqi also reacted to the same forces of change as Muhammad Ghawth, but in opposite ways. Both were dissatisfied with the Sufi style of devotion that the Chishti order had promoted and that dominated Islamic culture throughout South Asia during the centuries of rule by the Delhi sultanate (1175–1526 C.E.). Muhammad Ghawth advocated a completely new Sufi order in South Asia, the Shattari order, and used his status in this order to bolster the growing central power of the incipient Mughal dynasty. In his youth, ʿAli Muttaqi also became estranged from the Chishtis but settled on a "juridical Sufi" pattern (*taṣawwuf al-uṣūliyyīn*) that eschewed partisanship toward any Sufi order.[41] He became an adviser to the sultan of Gujarat, Bahadur Shah, who came to the throne the same year the Mughals came to power in South Asia, in 1526, and he opposed the growing power in Hindustan of the Mughals, who threatened to invade Gujarat and reduce it to a vassal province. When the Mughals first invaded Gujarat, ʿAli Muttaqi went into exile in Mecca. After the restoration of Gujarati independence under Sultan Maḥmūd III, ʿAli Muttaqi returned to Ahmadabad twice. During the second return (which must have been 1549 C.E. or shortly thereafter), the young sultan named him "Enforcer of the Sharia." From this position, he confronted Muhammad Ghawth and denounced his claim to have seen the celestial realms and their cosmic realities.[42]

ʿAli Muttaqi's personality is memorialized in the collection of saintly biographies by ʿAbd al-Haqq Muḥaddith from Delhi entitled *Zād al-*

Muttaqīn fī Sulūk Tarīq al-Yaqīn ("Provision of the Pious for Traveling the Path of Certain Knowledge").[43] This provides us with a vivid and intimate portrait of his life and teachings. He was born in 1480 C.E. in Burhānpūr, Gujarat, a city that harbored a long tradition of Chishti Sufi activity.[44] ʿAli Muttaqi's father had him initiated into the Chishti order at the age of 7 or 8, and he attended *samāʿ* sessions of poetry, rhythm, and music, which could lead those in attendance into states of ecstasy. ʿAli Muttaqi, however, rejected this musical style of devotion that advocated absorption in meditation, contemplation, or musical ecstasies; instead he urged Sufis to study religious knowledge as the highest form of worship, and he himself became one of the greatest hadith scholars in South Asia. He insisted that Sufis must first study hadith, scripture, and law before being considered qualified to become Sufi disciples and perhaps eventually be recognized as saints. He became critical of Sufis around him who did not follow this ideology, especially other popularly acclaimed saints who enjoyed positions of power.[45] He harshly criticized any Sufi who thought that study and learning were distractions from true spiritual work. "Those who claim to love God and the Prophet but refuse to pursue knowledge are like a person afflicted with passionate love for a sweetheart such that he is helpless without his lover. Imagine that this man is informed that his sweetheart is behind a high wall, and that the only way to reach his love is to climb it. Upon hearing this news, he says 'This wall is a veil, an obstacle between my lover and me, so I'll turn my back on it and reject it!' Hearing this logic, all the people around him will tell him that he is an idiot. He should clearly work to climb the wall to reach his lover, rather than turn his back on the wall altogether. Those who desist from acquiring religious knowledge are all idiots like this man."[46]

ʿAli Muttaqi spearheaded the persecution against Muhammad Ghawth's teaching and presence in Ahmadabad, likely seeing him as one such "idiot." He led the group of scholars who presented a declaration to the sultan of Gujarat charging Muhammad Ghawth with making heretical declarations that placed him outside the bounds of the Sunni community. When ʿAli Muttaqi met him in Ahmadabad, Muhammad Ghawth had already reached a zenith of fame and prestige, and ʿAli Muttaqi's suspicion of his legitimacy developed into open confrontation. By the end of this imbroglio, ʿAli Muttaqi would summon all his resources as a scholar-saint empowered by an official position in the government to denounce Ghawth's spiritual experiences as "nothing but ecstatic boasts and fantastic claims."[47]

The unique manuscript of a rare hagiographic collection, *Mukhbir al-Awliyāʾ*, or "Reporter of Saints," has recorded the details of ʿAli Muttaqi's critique of Muhammad Ghawth through the letters of those most involved in the struggle. Carl Ernst had first explored this episode in an insightful article on persecution and circumspection, declaring it an incident about which one can say very little for sure; however, this precious document now makes this incident one that may be the most detailed account yet of a Sufi persecution.[48] The evidence preserved in it questions the ways this struggle has been distorted and downplayed in the standard hagiographic accounts of all the figures involved.

By the time ʿAli Muttaqi arrived in Ahmadabad, Muhammad Ghawth had been living there for five years and had disciples from the religious elite. His strongest supporter was Wajīh al-Dīn ʿAlawī, who came from an influential family that had produced generations of scholars, jurists, and saints in Gujarat.[49] By the time he met Muhammad Ghawth, Wajih al-Din had founded a madrassa that was to be Ahmadabad's most prestigious educational institution. He combined hadith scholarship with a passion for existential philosophy. Although Wajih al-Din had taken initiation from a variety of spiritual guides in his youth, some vibrancy about Muhammad Ghawth attracted him.[50] At their initial meeting, Muhammad Ghawth insisted on meeting Wajih al-Din later, in private, "to discuss many matters which are secret in nature and not befitting public discussion."[51]

Nobody knows what matters they discussed in private, but Wajih al-Din asked for Ghawth's hand in initiation. Muhammad Ghawth told Wajih al-Din that initiation consisted of four things: taking his hand in commitment, wearing distinctively Shattari clothes, listening avidly to ecstatic music sessions with poetry and dance, and saying his evening prayers late. Wajih al-Din replied that changing his manner of dress was a heavy demand, for he had taken upon himself the dress of the Chishtis when he accepted his youthful initiation from Shaykh Qāżan Chishti; after pausing in meditation, Muhammad Ghawth dropped that obligation. He explained that the reason for saying evening prayers late was to dedicate their efficacy toward releasing the fallen angels, Harut and Marut, whom he had seen in his ascension visions. Muhammad Ghawth did not ask him to give up teaching the religious sciences to which he devoted his life but rather to give up relying on them. He asked him to rely instead on the saint's alchemical touch, which could turn a leaden soul into selfless gold.

Muhammad Ghawth's touch must have worked, for in a short time Wajih al-Din became the Shattari saint's prime disciple and most vocal supporter. Muhammad Ghawth's four sons became students in his madrassa, and the two families began to intermarry.[52] Further, Wajih al-Din began to induct his family members into the fold of Shattari disciples.[53] This growing community of disciples spread Muhammad Ghawth's fame by citing his ascension experience; they may have even disseminated written copies of the narrative of how he ascended bodily up into the heavens, where he met the Prophet Muhammad, who led him into the presence of God. With the financial and political support of these disciples, Ghawth was able to build a house and devotional center (*khānqāh*) in Ahmadabad.[54]

However, enthusiasm for this young, bold, and outspokenly ecstatic Shattari saint was not unanimous in Ahmadabad. By the time ʿAli Muttaqi returned, many Sufis and scholars harbored suspicions about his practices and discontent with his social successes. Many resented his followers for calling him "Ghawth," which they thought signaled Muhammad Ghawth's self-aggrandizing claim to have superseded ʿAbd al-Qadir Jilani (who was regarded by the followers of all lineages as "al-Ghawth al-Aʿẓam," the Greatest Sustainer). A scholar sent his son into the *khanqah* to spy on Muhammad Ghawth and determine the true nature of his teachings.[55] Discontent was brewing.

Dream Visions and Persecution

As more scholars complained to him of Ghawth's reputation for having enjoyed an ascension, ʿAli Muttaqi began to investigate the matter: "When this brief narrative [of Muhammad Ghawth's ascension experience] arrived in the hands of the scholars, they unanimously agreed that they must oppose that saint and denounce him. He had openly confirmed his claim with his own lips and had included it in his books and epistles. The scholars gathered together and prepared a declaration in which they all agreed on refuting and denouncing Muhammad Ghawth."[56] ʿAli Muttaqi went to Muhammad Ghawth for a private interview.[57] He asked Ghawth a number of questions about matters relating to "divine unity and existential realities." The answers reassured him that the problem was not so grave and that a public declaration could quell public speculation about his ascension.[58] He presented the declaration to Sultan Mahmud, calling for Muhammad Ghawth to be judged an infidel and liable for punishment if he did not renounce expressions that signified his bodily union with the divine or seeing the divine in a physical form.

All the respected religious leaders, both Sufi and scholarly, had signed the declaration with the exception of two. Wajih al-Din refused along with another prominent Sufi master of the city, Ghiyāth al-Dīn. The sultan questioned ʿAli Muttaqi about the apparent lack of unanimity, since the signatures of these two notables were lacking. A noble, Afḍal Khān, tried to override his caution, observing: "It is not too difficult to discover the reason for these two leaders to refuse to sign the declaration. In the case of Wajih al-Din, he has already committed himself to the community of Muhammad Ghawth and supports that Shaykh's claims. Anything that reduces his master's status reduces his own status as well, since the fortunes of a follower depend totally on the fortunes of his leader." The noble observed the political and social dimensions behind Sufi initiations and gauged the intensity of loyalties of a Sufi community that puts the saint at its center. Another noble, Wajih al-Mulk, came forward to add, "The saint [Wajih al-Din] has vouched openly that Muhammad Ghawth's claims are sound and true. Therefore, after a little while, Shaykh Ghiyath al-Din opened friendly relations with him, and he began to take forty-day isolation retreats inside the mosque of Muhammad Ghawth's *khanqah*. He had preferred that place for his isolated retreats rather than going anywhere else. This is why he refused to sign his name to the declaration, even though he was not formally connected to the Muhammad Ghawth by initiation."[59] Sultan Mahmud was not fully convinced. He declared that Wajih al-Din was certainly one of the greatest Sufis of Gujarat, and for his sake, the sultan himself would consult him directly.

When the sultan confronted him, Wajih al-Din defended Muhammad Ghawth from accusations of duplicity, ambition, or heresy. He countered:

> I allege that they have extracted just a few words from one of his writings [evidently the Ascension Narrative] and rushed to declare him an absolute infidel. I have never heard from Muhammad Ghawth's own lips the kind of expressions with which they are slandering him. . . . They accuse a Muslim of being an infidel, but there is no visible trace of infidelity in his actions: he says his five prayers each day in congregation, and otherwise stays engrossed in his meditation. He firmly adheres to the beliefs of the common majority (*ahl-i sunna o jamāʿa*). [Jurists] have decided that if a man is examined and has ninety-nine signs of being deceitful, yet exhibits just one sign of being sincere, which is Islam, then you must always give him the benefit of the doubt . . . but if he's not sincere, then still it is not up to others to punish him. If they accuse this young man [Muhammad Ghawth] of ecstatic boasts and fantastic claims, then this should be compared with people whose reason is overcome by their spiritual state and those who are intoxicated with ecstasy, and should be regarded as one of them [who are not legally responsible for their words].[60]

Sultan Mahmud returned to the scholars and expressed his reservations about punishing the *shaykh*. With "no visible trace" of heretical action, how could they judge him a heretic, for jurists judge people by their outer actions observed by reliable witnesses. The sultan urged them to find another way to solve the conflict. The religious leaders then asked Ghiyath al-Din to facilitate a visit to Muhammad Ghawth and to persuade him to repent from his errors, beg forgiveness of God, and repudiate his heresies so that all threats of punishment might be withdrawn and the climate of tension might dissipate. If not, they threatened to press their demands on the sultan. Ghiyath al-Din agreed and led a group of religious notables to the *khanqah* of Muhammad Ghawth. He met Ghawth and told him that he had brought these notables so that he could beg forgiveness of God before them and show his repentance for all that had transpired.

Muhammad Ghawth would have taken this option to avoid further persecution if not for the intervention of Wajih al-Din, an intervention that relied on another dimension of the intimate eye—duplicity. The nobleman Afdal Khan had tried to prevent Wajih al-Din from entering the *khanqah*, but he surreptitiously entered by a small rear door. After greeting the group of scholars and Sufis, Wajih al-Din approached Muhammad Ghawth and placed both hands on his knees as if in greeting. In this moment of intimacy, he gave his *shaykh* a signal (*ishara*) to be wary and refute the allegations of infidelity lodged against him. He communicated through the corner of his eye a secret message that could not be spoken and that even contradicted his speech at the same moment!

Then Wajih al-Din rose, faced the others, and said, "My Shaykh, why don't you tell us what you saw in your vision of the Prophet?" Muhammad Ghawth recounted what he had seen in his ascension, until he finally said, "I saw nothing more after that—my eyes opened and I found myself awake." Wajih al-Din then asked whether they were "visions seen in sleep (*ru'iya o wāqiʿa*)" or something of a different ontological status. At this prompting, Muhammad Ghawth answered, "Very well, they were all things that I saw as visions opened to me in my sleep." Upon hearing this, the religious notables and courtiers accused Wajih al-Din of having taken advantage of the opportunity of greeting his master to give him secret instructions to answer in such a way. They denounced his defensive intervention as treachery for which he would be answerable on the Day of Judgment, and the meeting broke up in anger.[61] Under the pressure of persecution, Muhammad Ghawth appears to contradict his own written account, in which the angels told him, "On the day that the Prophet Muhammad ascended along this route, there were with him some saints, and you were one of them. However, at that time, you were in the form of pure spirit. In contrast, this time you are fully attached to your body!"

Since this informal adjudication failed, the conflict returned to the court. Scholars had Muhammad Ghawth brought before the "Enforcer of the Sharia" (*ḥākim-i sharʿ*), who was none other than ʿAli Muttaqi. At the instigation of the objecting scholars, he wrote an affirmation and personally requested Ghawth to sign it for the benefit of public piety and his reputation. The affirmation read like this: "My fellow Muslims, I declare myself innocent of any relations with those who hold doctrines of the incarnation of God or union with God, or those who compare God to worldly objects or claim that God takes material form, or those who hold that God's existence and worldly existence are in continuum (*waḥdat al-wujūd*) or who cleave to anything else that is against the religious custom of our Prophet Muhammad. I declare myself innocent of any of my writings that may contain expressions based on these false doctrines. If any writing of mine be found to contain these doctrines, then I will wash the paper clean of ink or allow my brothers in faith to do likewise."[62] ʿAli Muttaqi and the scholars whose complaints he represented showed this affirmation to Muhammad Ghawth in the presence of his followers, who forbade Muhammad Ghawth to sign the affirmation. The opposing scholars, who would have been content with this affirmation, became angry when they saw that he had no sincere intent to sign it, and they withdrew any offer of reconciliation.

Later, Wajih al-Din came to ʿAli Muttaqi, offering to write a slightly different affirmation that would be acceptable to both sides that Muhammad Ghawth would surely sign. ʿAli Muttaqi agreed in good faith, "not knowing at the time of the many deceitful deeds of this man." Wajih al-Din wrote out a revised affirmation: "My fellow Muslims, from the time I came to maturity until now, I have been innocent of any relation with those who hold doctrines of incarnation or union or comparing God to worldly objects, or any other doctrine that goes against the religious custom of Muhammad, our Prophet. Further, I grew up with the doctrine of the Sunni majority (*ahl-i sunna o jamāʿa*), and there does not exist any expression in my writings that bears traces of these doctrines that cannot be explained metaphorically. If any such traces be found, then erase them and may God reward you for your good deed."[63] ʿAli Muttaqi took the affirmation from Wajih al-Din and told him that he would show it to the objecting scholars; if they were satisfied with it, then he, too, would accept it.

However, the scholars did not accept it and accused Wajih al-Din of subtly changing the content with the addition of an escape clause, specifying heretical doctrines "that cannot be explained metaphorically." They also suspected deceit in his purposefully eliding the doctrine of those who "claim that God takes material form, or those who hold that God's existence and worldly existence are in continuum," the two clearest charges against Muhammad Ghawth. They told ʿAli Muttaqi that he had allowed himself to be duped by trusting Wajih al-Din. Most hagiographic literature portrays Wajih al-Din as a mediator who tried to calm the angry ʿAli Muttaqi. However, in his own letters, ʿAli Muttaqi presents himself as the official mediator to both sides of the conflict, while Wajih al-Din comes across as a partisan willing to cheat by saying one thing with his lips while signaling something else with his eyes.[64]

ʿAli Muttaqi combed through Ghawth's texts for expressions that contradicted the Qurʾān and hadith, especially the Ascension Narrative and its related work, *Kalīd al-Makhāzin*, "The Keys to the Treasuries." In this text, Ghawth gave a systematic explication of the levels of the cosmos, asserting that each level had emanated from the divine and they will be reabsorbed into the divine by the end of time. He had witnessed the essence of this cosmic structure during his ascension, although he didn't write it all down in that narrative.

The scholars called Muhammad Ghawth before ʿAli Muttaqi to answer detailed questions about some of the passages that occurred in his writings and also in his beliefs and doctrines. He answered evasively. At this, ʿAli Muttaqi began to send extracts of Ghawth's texts to Sultan Mahmud to force him to attend a final inquisition. ʿAli Muttaqi explained the organization of a public hearing. "I acquired his writings, like *The Keys to the Treasuries* and the *Ascension Narrative*. I read them over and found that, sure enough, they contradict the Qurʾan and the Prophet's example. I thought to myself, if I confront him [Muhammad Ghawth] alone and he washes the ink off the pages in my home, then nobody else will know of it—what good would that be? But if he has to wash it off in front of all the Muslims and publicly swears not to teach books about such speculative claims to supposed cosmic realities, then he will be fully reconciled with all the scholars and common Muslims and the matter can be put to rest."[65] With "written proof" of heresy in his hand, ʿAli Muttaqi organized a final public meeting in the presence of the sultan between the objecting scholars and Sufis on the one hand and Muhammad Ghawth on the other.

The day before the examination, Sultan Mahmud happened to meet with a "holy man" named Sīdī Wajdī, an obscure figure who does not appear

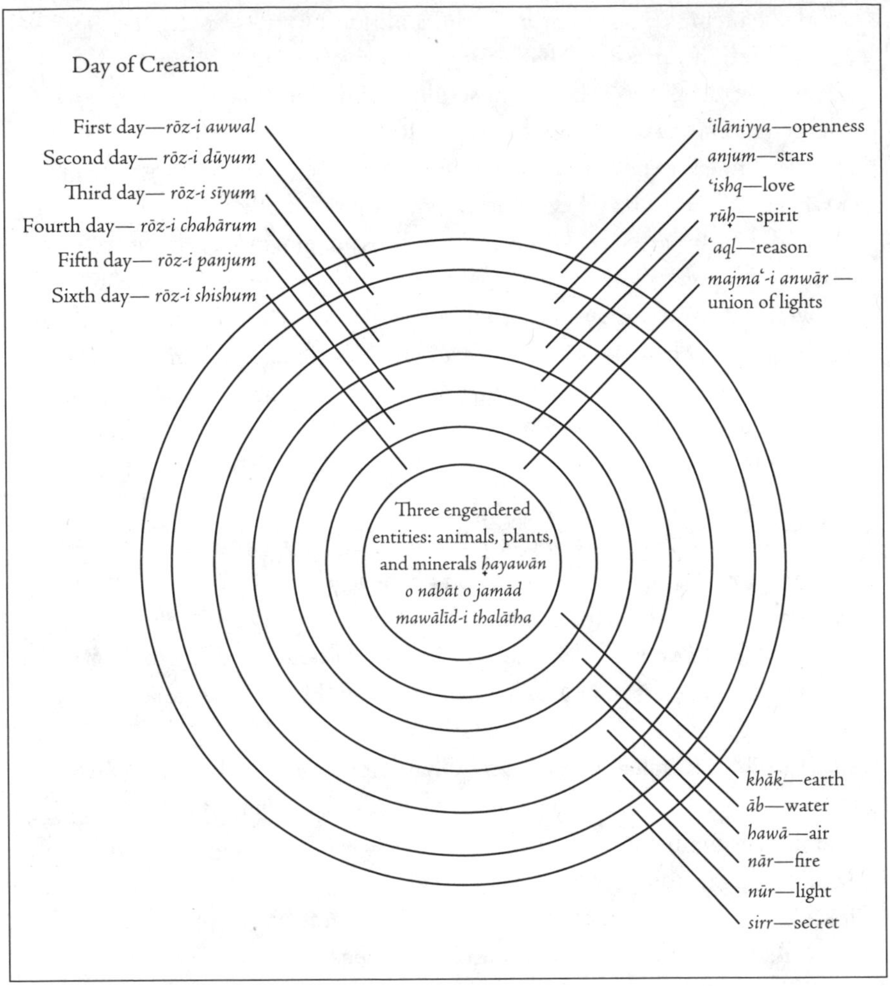

Layers of the Cosmos

Source: Adapted from Muḥammad Ghawth Gwāliyōrī, *Kalīd al-Makhāzin*, ms. (Patna: Khudabakhsh Library, 1376 Farsi Tasawwuf), fol. 31.

in other hagiographic accounts of ʿAli Muttaqi, Muhammad Ghawth, or Wajih al-Din. However, Sidi Wajdi appears to have been sympathetic to Muhammad Ghawth and was perhaps a Shattari disciple. Speaking with the sultan on the day before the scheduled public inquisition, Sidi Wajdi suggested that he go on a hunt, moving the whole court with him from Ahmadabad to Maḥmūdābād. Then he turned to the prime minister, Āṣif Khān, and suggested that perhaps Muhammad Ghawth might find shelter outside the city with his loyal followers if by some carelessness the city gates were left unguarded late at night. Sultan Mahmud accepted the suggestion and left for the hunt. After midnight, the minister Asif Khan informed Sidi Wajdi that Muhammad Ghawth and some followers like Wajih al-Din had disappeared from the city, heading toward Bharōch.[66]

Upon hearing news of the Shattari saint's flight, ʿAli Muttaqi sent a letter to Bharoch, addressed to Muʾayyad Khan, a noble of that city whom he trusted. He requested the noble to detain him and send him back to Ahmadabad in chains and accused his vision of being a distortion. The letter reads, "I am well, thanks to God. I am only distressed over the soundness of religious faith in the kingdom and the confusions caused by those advocating inauthentic religious practices. It should be known that Shaykh Muhammad the Liar, the Cheater, the Distorter (otherwise known as 'the Ghawth') has fled surreptitiously from this place and should be captured, imprisoned, and brought back. He had been brought before me many times, as you yourself witnessed. Under questioning he declared, 'My spiritual states and my religious beliefs are in full accord with the Qurʾan and the example of the Prophet. I absolve myself of any of my writings which may be shown to contradict the Qurʾan and the example; I give permission for any such writings to be washed clean.'"[67] ʿAli Muttaqi then explains his reaction to this declaration. "I trusted his words, and in front of everyone I held him to be innocent and willing to reform. So much so that I went personally to see the minister Afdal Khan [who was eager to punish Ghawth] and pleaded his innocence and his willingness to sincerely repent. . . . But on the very day that we all decided to schedule a final gathering to conclude this matter to the benefit of everyone, that very night, Muhammad Ghawth fled the city. Therefore, if that Liar and Fraud comes to Bharoch claiming anything that contradicts the facts in this letter, don't you believe him. For I have personally tested him and know from experience [that he is a liar]."[68] ʿAli Muttaqi appended to this letter a copy of the conclusion of Ghawth's "Keys to the Treasuries," so that the reader could judge for himself the extent of Muhammad Ghawth's "heresy."[69]

An ally of ʿAli Muttaqi's, Muhammad Māh Chishtī, also wrote a letter, addressed directly to Muhammad Ghawth, warning him to come back to the capital and face his accusers eye to eye. He criticized the Shattari saint's views and beliefs, especially "those written in a certain set of papers with vain and fanciful words that provoke evil and mischief and are not supported by true religious certainty," meaning his Ascension Narrative.[70] He accused him of selfish manipulation of miraculous happenings to boost his ego (*istidrāj*) and called his Ascension Narrative "a vast expanse of infidelity as wide as the ocean of hell." He referred to Muhammad Ghawth's words in the inquisition as "completely inappropriate" and his actions during the trial as "deceitful and cheap." He further stated that, despite Muhammad Ghawth's dissimulation, "I know full well what you are; you are a *muwaḥḥid*, and you speak the language of a *muwaḥḥid* [one who believes in *waḥdat al-wujud*, that God is in unity with the created world]. If you contest that my opinion is wrong, how can you claim that all the scholars of Ahmadabad are wrong?" Finally, he challenged Ghawth about his title, claiming that it is the sole right of ʿAbd al-Qadir Jilani to be called "Ghawth al-Thaqalayn" (the "Sustainer of Both Worlds"), and anyone abrogating this name for himself is a counterfeit. Further, he suggested that it would be more fitting to be entitled "Rawth al-Baqarayn" (the "Shit of Two Cows").

The unique and detailed record of this persecution ends here. No other letters by ʿAli Muttaqi and his allies exist to reveal how the high tensions were resolved. It is unclear how long Muhammad Ghawth spent in hiding in Bharoch or why the nobles of that city did not act on ʿAli Muttaqi's letter to force Ghawth to return to the capital. Wajih al-Din left his madrassa to stay in Bharoch for some time and then later returned to Ahmadabad and resumed his teaching. Hagiographic sources mention nothing more of the danger of persecution. Eventually, Ghawth also returned to Ahmadabad, where he was able to live peacefully, training disciples and building a communal mosque in the city.[71] When the Mughal ruler, Humayun, reinvaded Hindustan in 1555 C.E., he was able to firmly establish centralized Mughal rule. Muhammad Ghawth then safely returned to his home at Gwalior, near the Mughal capital at Agra, by which time the young emperor Akbar had risen to the throne. Although Akbar had a magnificent shrine built over his tomb, Muhammad Ghawth never achieved the level of popularity and political influence that he enjoyed during the reign of Humayan, Akbar's father.

Veridical Vision or Satanic Delusion?

Although these accounts richly document the course of a Sufi persecution, they do not specify to what ʿAli Muttaqi and other Sufi scholars took exception. Nevertheless, based upon the full translation of his Ascension Narrative, we can conjecture that the persecutors saw that Muhammad Ghawth's vision of the cosmos coming into being through emanations from the divine conflicted with the Qurʾanic imagery of creation from nothingness. They might have been angered by Ghawth's insistence that hell and heaven were part of this emanation and would both be reabsorbed up into

The tomb of Muḥammad Ghawth in Gwāliyōr, India, which was built around 1565 during the reign of the Mughal emperor Akbar. Photograph by Scott Kugle.

divine being, so that even those in hell would not suffer eternally. This story implies that such absolute alienation from God, who is the ground of all being, was impossible. ʿAli Muttaqi may have perceived an event in this ascension as belittling the sharia itself. When Muhammad Ghawth witnessed the essence of "outer religious knowledge," he saw the four great jurists arguing among themselves like schoolchildren. In his vision, totality and comprehensiveness came from "the inner religious knowledge," while the outer religious knowledge could lead only to dissension, partisanship, and contradictions. This might have been the substance of ʿAli Muttaqi's accusation that the Ascension Narrative was against the Qurʾan and the example of the Prophet Muhammad, the two scriptural sources for the edifice of outer religious knowledge.

Beneath all these narrative details, ʿAli Muttaqi opposed Muhammad Ghawth because of a structural issue: he claimed religious legitimacy through a "transcendental connection" to God that threatened the historically validated forms of Islamic legitimacy.[72] Muhammad Ghawth's spiritual authority rested on a unique intimacy with God that competed with the kerygmatic role of the Prophet Muhammad. Further, he achieved this special intimacy through personal experience, ascension to the throne of God and direct vision of God, rather than through religious learning or socially legitimized channels of authority.

Muhammad Ghawth claimed that scriptural traces, left by the Prophet Muhammad, alluded to their experience and rhymed with it, granting them special spiritual dispensation. In ʿAli Muttaqi's view, scriptural sources did not allude to the ecstatic and visionary experiences but rather precluded them entirely. ʿAli Muttaqi held that any transcendent vertical connection to God is immanent in the horizontal connection to the Prophet; it is immanent there and should always be only implicit. He held that Muhammad Ghawth led his followers to relegate the hadith-based pattern of the Prophet to the dustbin of irrelevant data. At its sharpest, ʿAli Muttaqi's critique inverted the Shattari metaphor of ascension: he claimed that Ghawth had only "climbed up to the throne of the Tempter" rather than having met with the Prophet at the foot of God's throne. In the wake of Ghawth's public claims to have ascended, ʿAli Muttaqi circulated a hadith reporting words ascribed to the Prophet Muhammad. He was reported to have said, "Satan has a throne placed between the heavens and the earth; if he wants to afflict someone with being the cause of social discord (*fitna*) then he reveals to that person his throne."[73]

Citing this report about Satan having a throne between heaven and earth, to tempt those who imagine that they might ascend, ʿAli Muttaqi also made oblique reference to the Qurʾan's discussion of political authority, moral conduct, and the throne. The report quotes indirectly the story of Solomon, who, when he grew arrogant as the king of Israel, was tried and tested: *We tried Solomon and cast upon his throne a body (jasad) that was not his, and then he repented. He said, "O Lord, forgive me and give me a kingdom such that none may ever desire in later times, for you are the One who gives." So we subjected the winds to him to obey his command and conform to his every wish, as well as supernatural forces (shayāṭīn) skilled at building and searching, and others shackled in fetters, saying, "This is our bountiful gift, so entrust it* [to others] *or keep it* [for yourself] *as you see fit." He had a relation of intimacy with us and a fair recourse* (Q 38:34–40). When Solomon was tempted by arrogance in his royal authority, God cast on this throne another body, which some interpreters imagine was a dead body. This was a stark reminder that he ruled only by God's will and as long has he stayed without the bounds of outward justice and inward conscientiousness. Otherwise, either his heart would be dead within his living body or another's body would take his place as king.

Citing this Qurʾanic invocation of Solomon was an apt counter to Muhammad Ghawth's claim that God had subjected the world and its unseen forces to his command because he was a selfless mendicant: "The word of the Darwesh is a command from God and the world is under the power of his choice . . . like a court under the order of the finger of King Solomon." In particular, Muhammad Ghawth claimed that the power of *taskhīr*, of having divine will bend the world to conform to his command, just as God had *subjected the winds to him* (*sakhkharna la-hu al-rīḥ*). With this subtle citation, ʿAli Muttaqi countered him, reminding him that such power was granted to Solomon only after a dangerous test; Solomon was tempted to arrogance until he saw with his own eyes the foreign body of an imposter, a rival or a corpse on the throne he had arrogated for himself. Likewise, ʿAli Muttaqi charged that Muhammad Ghawth suffered the same temptation and failed; in his arrogance of claiming to have seen cosmic realities in his ascension, he in fact saw only a false body on a pretend throne—Satan's throne that is only partway "between the heavens and the earth," which makes the one who gazes upon it "the cause of social discord (*fitna*)." Not all visions are veridical and truthful, he charges. Muhammad Ghawth's vision was not simply hallucination or dreaming; it was the delusion of arrogance.

In this way, ʿAli Muttaqi challenged Muhammad Ghawth's faculty of vision and the spiritual insight that infused it. By publicizing this little-known hadith, ʿAli Muttaqi denounced all heavenly ascensions except the original ascension of the Prophet Muhammad, asserting that any claim to have risen beyond the earth into the heavens and reached the divine throne is really the product of satanic delusions that cause social turmoil and discord. In contradistinction, he asserted that truth is found in a body of legal and ritual norms and is not found in eccentric visions that transcend the body. This body of legal and ritual norms is the Prophet's legacy, based on what his followers heard him recite and what they observed him do. What the Prophet did in daily actions with his body and practical guidance in his community was more sacred that what the Prophet might be imagined to have done or experienced in any heavenly ascension.

ʿAli Muttaqi also asserted that it is the scholars (and especially Sufis who are scholars and jurists by training, loyalty, and social role) who uphold the law, and it is the law that establishes the right to rule. Nobody should act as kingmaker by claiming sainthood by ineffable experiences like ascension to God or union with God. He himself became the adviser to kings only by urging them to limit their bodily action and moral attitude to the example of the Prophet. Before trying to persuade the young Sultan Mahmud of Gujarat to persecute Muhammad Ghawth, ʿAli Muttaqi had acted as his spiritual preceptor, demonstrating to him a very different approach to the human body. The body is not made sacred and powerful by being left behind, outstripped by speculative vision. Rather, it is made sacred and powerful by being disciplined and constrained by practical actions that imitate the exemplary pattern of the Prophet (*sunna*).

When the sultan was just coming to power, ʿAli Muttaqi endeavored to support his rule indirectly, through the body of ritual and law that constitutes the sharia, by teaching him how to wash the body in ritual ablutions, as one hagiographic source illustrates: "ʿAli Muttaqi paid special attention to the psychological needs of the sultan. Once he was present with the sultan during prayer times, and he observed the sultan at his ablutions. The young sultan was taking so much time washing that he used a huge amount of water, which would have sufficed others for a full bath with some left over!"[74] ʿAli Muttaqi knew what his weakness was, but he kept silent until the sultan finished praying; then he asked Mahmud directly about his doubts and misgivings, and the young man confided in him and complained of his many anxieties and fears. ʿAli Muttaqi told him that if God wills, all these will pass away, and he stayed with him until the next prayer time came. "When the sultan went to make his ablutions again, ʿAli Muttaqi took from his hand the pitcher and poured the water for him, showing him how to make his ablutions according to the Prophet's practice [which uses very little water]. The sultan accepted his direction with politeness even though it was very difficult for him to carry out his ablutions with only a minimum of water; still, he forced himself to have patience at the hand of the *shaykh* and obeyed his advice. ʿAli Muttaqi would say to him, 'If you prefer the Prophet's method, then you can wash like this. . . . If you adopt this method, then God may help ease your mind from all the doubts that burden you.'"[75] The Sufi scholar would pour water for the sultan and help him keep his ablutions within the Prophet's pattern for a number of days, until his blessings were thereby concentrated upon the young sultan, who was soon taking a full bath with the amount of water that would have barely sufficed him before for washing his face and hands.

What strange doubts and misgivings could lead the young sultan to hand washing of Macbethian proportions the historical chronicles do not specify. Yet set against the backdrop of Sultan Mahmud's struggles to come to power, it becomes clear that his waste of water relates to the blood he spilled in coming to power. His washing (which might be termed obsessive-compulsive today) was the outward manifestation of inward anxieties that hindered him from exerting mature political power. In this incident of pre-modern psychoanalysis, ʿAli Muttaqi addressed the obsessive symptom and uncovered the underlying anxieties that drove it. The seemingly innocuous problem of washing with less water is actually a highly charged symbolic event.

From ʿAli Muttaqi's perspective, any one part of the Prophet's pattern of behavior (even something as routine as ritual ablutions) was imbued with the spiritual significance of the whole sharia.[76] By inviting the young sultan to change his method of washing (from one that reinforced his own fears to one that expressed devotion to the Prophet), ʿAli Muttaqi freed him from his personal limitations so he could grow into a strong ruler. The reformist saint did not try to release Mahmud from his anxieties through a display of miraculous power or prayers but rather deferred a dramatic display of personal potency in favor of adhering to the legal and ritual norms of the sharia.

Conclusion

Muhammad Ghawth cleverly avoided persecution by allowing that his miraculous spiritual journey might have been simply a dream. However, rather than being merely the record of a dream vision, his Ascension Narrative offers us an exquisite allegory of the power of vision. Whether or not we concur that his experience was an eyewitness account of cosmic realities, we can perceive in Muhammad Ghawth's account an acute witness to the eye.

To Muhammad Ghawth, the eye represented the personality's power of extending beyond the body's spatial confines. When one's vision is turned inward through contemplation, one is riveted to one's own navel to discover there, like a lustrous pearl hidden in a lowly oyster, the secret of God's greatest name. Invoking this name with ascetic rigor unleashes, for Muhammad Ghawth, the latent potential of the divine that infuses all being and comes to its fullest manifestation in the human being. This explosive spiritual combustion propelled him from his routine habit, through the layers of his material being, into the celestial realms of his ascension. Once turned inward, in a way almost analogous to the Yogic teachings that he helped to translated and spread, his vision could act as the key to unlock the hidden potential of the human body; such a refined vision could then turn upward, unconfined by bodily eyes and the density of space, and act as the conduit for the human spirit to revel in its nondual union with God.

For Muhammad Ghawth, leaving the body behind and following one's vision into the heavens was not just solipsistic introversion. Rather, it was an empowering experience, granting him both spiritual insight and worldly might. However, other Muslim saints of a more cautious spiritual demeanor and a more legalistic concern for social order begged to differ. Like 'Ali Muttaqi, they saw in Muhammad Ghawth's experience a brash claim to political power based on delusion, not on vision. They cautioned that the eyes, goaded by arrogance, could deceive. The eye could become merely a mirror for the "I," the ego, the vision of oneself as whole and worthy of admiration. Such visions were moral trails that should remind us to lower our gaze and see only our own faults, limitations, and inevitably mortality. One should lower the horizon of one's gaze rather than raise one's gaze toward the highest horizon. One should simply struggle to wash one's body the exact way the Prophet did, rather than trying to soar on speculation to follow the Prophet's path of ascension. In this way, ʿAli Muttaqi emphasized that humility was the goal of God's gift of vision to Adam. "As soon as God breathed the soul into Adam, it entered his brain and wandered for a period of two hundred years, when it settled in his eyes. The wisdom of this was that God wished to show Adam the beginning of his creation and his origin, so that when tokens of God's respect for him would be bestowed on his successors, pride would not enter him or self-love."[77]

4

BODY ENRAPTURED
The Lips of Shāh Ḥussayn

We have created the human being in the throes of loss.
Does he think that none have power over him?
He says, "I have lost masses of wealth!"
Does he think that none is watching over him?
Haven't we made for him two eyes, a tongue and two lips?
And guided him to two places of safety in distress?
—Qur'an 90:4–10

The Qur'an chides the human being for falling into despair in situations of apparent danger, material loss, or emotional distress. Why do we spin so quickly into despair? Don't we realize that the One who created us still watches over us? The sensory organs through which we grasp at the world and cling to its pleasures lock us into a prison of false perception. *We have created the human being in the throes of loss.* This seemingly simple statement of the Qur'an makes a subtle word play on words, for "at loss" (*kabad*) draws from the same root letters as "the gut" (*kabid*). The gut usually signifies the liver, which in Islamic notions of anatomy is the seat of passionate emotion, much like the heart. We experience loss because we do not understand our own gut; we feel our security in the world depends on external situations, like controlling wealth, wielding power, and existing autonomously, rather than actually depending on sincerity of heart and purity of passion. The Qur'an counters our perceptions by asking: Aren't the very sensory organs bodily signs of our noble creator's presence with us? Hasn't the creator made for human beings *two eyes, a tongue and two lips?*

This chapter investigates the lips, as invoked by this Qur'anic passage. It does so by exploring the body of Shāh Hussayn, a Sufi of the Qadiri community and a Punjabi poet (1539–99 C.E.). We follow his bodily gestures of sexual intimacy, social rebellion, and doctrinal heresy as he defied convention in the Mughal regional capital of Lāhōr (Lahore in contemporary Pakistan). Through his example, we will come to better understand the lips as the gateway to taste and the locus of a kiss. We will find that the lips reveal the spiritual secrets of saliva, which represents an intimacy that boldly breaks all routine social and even legal boundaries. In other words, the lips play a much more complex role than being merely physical guardians of the oral entrance to the body or only the final articulators of speech. They transport into visible, audile, and tactile space what is essential, invisible, and burning in the gut within the body. Their touch conveys something of the soul in a position of utmost intimacy. As Nakhshabi has said: "If you see the lip as truthful testimony told / No no, the lip is a ruby like sacred blood shed. . . . If you see the mouth as always occupied in haste / No no, the mouth is master of drawing in each breath."[1]

In the previous chapter on the eyes, we observed that ʿAli Muttaqi's persecution of Muhammad Ghawth did not succeed directly. The latter was not forced to recant; nor was he physically punished. He was not forced to materially erase his experience by washing the ink of his books from their pages. However, the persecution did work indirectly. Muhammad Ghawth was forced to give up his claim to have ascended bodily and publicly declared that his experience was only visionary. People could dismiss it as hallucination, or dream, or satanic delusion. The persecution also compelled Ghawth's followers to publicly ascribe to the sharia and take shelter in the orthodoxy of the madrassa setting.[2] As a result, Muhammad Ghawth's followers in the Shattari community walked a fine line between outer conformity to orthodox Sunni norms and inwardly radical contemplative practices.

However, not all Mughal-era Sufis walked such a fine line. Some ventured boldly into the public with antinomian teachings, even to the point of flaunting gender and sexuality norms that were perceived to be the foundation of the sharia as social order. Shah Hussayn was one of these recklessly bold Sufis known by the label "Qalandar," whom we know as antinomian (*be-sharʿ*) for their flagrant and deliberation transgression against legal norms. His bodily comportment had great theological significance, for he saw the body in all its postures as spiritually vivid, and through sensual pleasures he crafted a very rebellious notion of morality as "spiritual play."

Imagine this scene of pandemonium: a large public square stretches out before the high walls of the Red Fort in Lahore, into which crowds surge, eager to witness the public execution of criminals. One by one, criminals are brought out into the square and killed: rebels against the Mughal emperor, highway robbers, and tax evaders. Suddenly, a very different sort of man is brought forward in chains. His body is marked off as distinctive from others, both the common criminals and the audience that watches him. He wears ragged scarlet clothes. His head is shaved, and his beard is shaved clean. He walks into the public square, laughing without fear.

The man is Shah Hussayn, a Sufi who will become one of Lahore's patron saints. As the police drag him into the square, the chains keep falling off his wrists and ankles. This is very frustrating for the chief of police, who had been looking forward to personally administering the punishment. Perhaps the crowd draws back as the chains keep falling to the ground; perhaps the crowd begins to laugh at the chief of police. In frustration, the police chief, Kotwāl Mālik ʿAlī, begins to verbally attack the vulnerable Sufi and threaten him with corporal punishment. This is the scene depicted by a biographical poem on the Sufi's life, which reports the police chief as saying: "As a rebuke and punishment, yours will be a disgraceful death, driven through with a spike: a spike that will go into you from behind so that your soul will leave you from behind, such a long spike I will use to impale you that it will go in from behind and come out your side. On this very day I'll do it, not a day later, I'll sit you on a spike that opens the seam of your side!"[3] The police chief threatens the Sufi with impaling him up the backside, in a gruesome pantomime of anal rape. What did Shah Hussayn do to provoke such a threat, and why did it come in the unusual form of impaling?

This chapter tries to explicate the complexities of this dramatic scene, with its many elements involving Shah Hussayn's lips and body, their countercultural deployment in homoerotic situations, and the potential sanctity (or possible heresy) of this deployment in the field of public power. First, we must find out who this unusual character in Lahore, Shah Hussayn, really was. Then we can ask about his alleged crimes and the threatened punishment—and what the status of corporal punishment and impaling is in Islamic law (as practiced in Mughal South Asia) and how Shah Hussayn's Sufi practice contravened law or the public moral order. We will apply recent insights from gender and queer theory to illumine Shah Hussayn's unconventional life through his own Punjabi poetry and untouched sources from the archives of Sufi hagiographies in Persian and Urdu.

In Chapter 2, we applied feminist theories from gender studies to understand the body of Sayyida Amina. In this chapter, we will add to this repertoire theories from queer studies to address the question of his sexual orientation, or nonnormative sexual interactions with other men. Queer studies sounds strangely modern and theoretically complex, but it is really simple. If feminism is the radical notion that women are human beings, then queer theory is the radical notion that heterosexuality is not normal. In other words, heterosexuality (the concept that sex only happens, only can happen, uld happen between persons of opposite genders) is not com- inevitable. If one looks at history, religion, and law through this orld is suddenly transformed. Heterosexuality, rather than being ; assumed to be "natural," becomes something asserted, enforced, and policed; meanwhile, other possibilities are marginalized with rt, silenced, criminalized, described as pathological or as an affront to morality. In other words, gender and sexuality are inherently plural. They are sites of discord and conflict, creativity and argument. Heterosexuality, which asserts that genders are polar binaries and come together only in sexual acts that reinforce this polarity, is only one option among many, one that persists through argument, conflict, and force. Other possibilities include phenomena that we label today as celibacy, hermaphrodism, gender-transforming behavior, gay or lesbian homosexuality, or bisexuality.

Queer theory asserts not only that such phenomena exist but also that they are important in their own right to study. It goes further to assert that social norms (heterosexuality and the patriarchy built upon it) can be really understood only by taking stock of the phenomena that lie outside, beneath, or beyond these norms. Up to this point, queer theory has hardly interacted with Islamic studies. This chapter is one small step in that direction, inspired by the idea that Islamic studies would be much more interesting if we take seriously the concepts of gender and sexuality and try to realistically assess the complex and multiple ways that they intersect in Islamic societies of the past. Islamic legal discussions of marriage, Qur'anic exegesis about sex acts, and rituals of bodily purity suddenly take on new vividness if we see them not just as discursive norms but norms that were questioned, challenged, or even flaunted.

Shah Hussayn's lively personality is the perfect experimental starting point for such an inquiry. He was a theologian turned Sufi, a Sufi turned social rebel. He was a great poet in Punjabi and one of the most vivid Sufi personalities during the reign of the Mughal emperor Akbar. In addition, Shah Hussayn was more open about his sex life than most premodern historical personages and appears to have been gay (if we can apply that term to premodern, non-European figures—but that is another debate altogether).[4] At least we can say, in more clinical detachment, that he never married, never raised children, never was the patriarchal leader of a household, and had a primary erotic attachment to another man who also never married. He also displayed behavior that called into question the "naturalness" of gender and the social power inherent in inverting gender expectations.

We know this much about him because hagiographers made a detailed record of his life. The Mughal prince Salīm (who matured to become Emperor Jahāngīr) ordered one of his courtiers, Bahār Khān, to attend to Shah Hussayn daily and write down his teachings and doings to preserve for posterity.[5] This work is now lost, but bits of it have been preserved in later hagiographies, including a long poem, a *mathnawī* in Persian (written by a devoted follower one generation after Shah Hussayn's death), entitled *Ḥaqīqat al-Fuqarā'* ("The Truth of Those Impoverished by Love").[6] This source brings up many interesting events that force us to rethink the relation of sainthood to sexuality and the relation of Islamic law to social order, for the intimate acts of sexual play were not just personal for Shah Hussayn but were integral to his whole approach to Sufi spiritual cultivation and were on very public display in the streets of sixteenth-century Lahore. Further, his public assertion of sexual-spiritual play brought him into conflict with the police, judges, and government, conflicts in which he ultimately prevailed.

From Smile to Seduction to Initiation

In order to give a sense of Shah Hussayn's life story, we will turn to portions of this *mathnawi* translated here into English. He was born around 1539 C.E. and pursued religious studies in his youth. This consisted of memorizing the Qur'an, learning Arabic, and studying scriptural and legal interpretation. He also joined the Qadiri Sufi lineage at a young age, in which he learned the value of poetic eloquence and ascetic rigor.[7] For the first half of his life, he lived as a mendicant student, wandering in the empty lands outside the city walls by day and returning at night to stay in the shrine of Lahore's patron saint, ʿAlī Hujwīrī (known as Dātā Ganj Bakhsh).

Despite these ascetic rigors, Shah Hussayn continued to study scripture with a well-known religious guide, Saʿdullah. It was at the age of 36 that he experienced a dramatic spiritual opening. While Hussayn was studying an interpretation of the Qur'an, his teacher recited the verse *The life of the world is nothing but play and pleasurable distraction* (Q 6:32, echoed in 29:64 and 47:36). This verse suddenly struck Hussayn as profoundly true, and he resolved then and there that the only way to live a life of sincerity was to throw off constraints of ascetic piety, legal rectitude, and rational seriousness; he would instead lead his life as a child at play, abandoning all pretense, hypocrisy, and ambition as well as fear of social blame. The hagiographic poem records him as declaring;

Isn't it better to dance through the marketplace
than to study knowledge without putting it to practice?
This verse has opened wide the eyes of my understanding
that I make myself into the living interpretation of its words
The life of this world is such a burden—
escape complaining by abandoning yourself to play!

While his teacher argued with him that this verse should not be taken literally and out of context, Hussayn's flash of insight had already moved him to cast out all seriousness and inhibition from his life. He proceeded to immerse himself outwardly in pleasure and play in order to retain an inward sense of pure devotion to God.

The playful spirituality that he advocated was not totally innocent. Like the Qalandars before him, Shah Hussayn's playful practice took the form of actively contradicting Islamic legal norms and social customs. He took to drinking wine. Our Sufi guide, Nakhshabi, illustrates the multiple valences of wine in Islamic communities, with its potential for aesthetic beauty, erotic arousal, medicinal wisdom, and transgressive criminality. "Although wine is prohibited by our religion and has been the subject of many proclamations by the leaders, the physicians know that it has many benefits and innumerable physical advantages for the human body. It is a tonic which changes a sallow complexion into a rosy hue; it is a salve which brings a rosy tint to saffron-colored cheeks; it cleanses the mirror of the heart from the shadow of grief; it removes the impediment of stammering from the tongue-tied; it brightens the natural vivacity; it brings an abnormal temperature into equilibrium; it restores darkened blood to purity; it washes away impurities in the veins . . . it reduces desire for excessive eating and relieves agonizing pain. O Nakhshabi, what a miraculous substance is wine / It will banish excessive anxieties from the heart / Although it is considered by religion as evil / This rejected drink much happiness does often impart."[8] In addition to drinking wine in public, Shah Hussayn took to singing and playing musical instruments while dancing in the streets with his band of devoted friends and followers. Apparently, his excessive anxieties were banished from the heart, in a way that went deeper than temporary inebriation through sipping with the lips.

An apocryphal story can help illustrate how his contemporaries regarded his childlike abandon. One of Shah Hussayn's contemporaries was a saint named Ḥassu Tēlī, "the Oil Seller." He was also a Qadiri Sufi of Lahore and was a disciple of Shāh Jamāl (whose tomb is still a popular pilgrimage place). Shah Hussayn used to stop in front of his oil shop to dance and raise havoc. Shaykh Hassu teased him by saying, "O Hussayn, why this dancing and shouting? You have no cause for such ecstasy, for I have never seen you in the court of the Prophet [Muhammad]!" But on the following day, when Muhammad held his court in the spirit world, with all the prophets and saints in attendance including Shaykh Hassu, a child appeared. The child first sat in the lap of the Prophet, then passed to each member of the assembly, before finally coming up to Shaykh Hassu. While playing on his knee, the child reach up and naughtily plucked some hairs from Shaykh Hassu's beard. When he next chided Shah Hussayn for his public misbehavior and alleged that he was not worthy to sit in the court of the Prophet, Shah Hussayn silently produced before him a hair from his very own beard. At first greatly disturbed, Shaykh Hassu finally said, "So it was you, was it? Ah well, it was as a child that you got the better of me."[9] Though Shah Hussayn earned himself disrepute among the Muslim notables of Lahore, who saw him as a dissolute drunk, his lips were skilled in more than just emptying goblets of wine. He began to earn the love and admiration of the common people as a saintly poet who was aloof from accruing worldly power through social status or religious reputation. This is one symbolic meaning of his "plucking the hairs" of Shaykh Hassu's beard, for the beard is an outward sign of piety for Muslim men and a way of signifying one's reputation, whether justly deserved or hypocritically displayed.

In this state, a second dramatic event took place that shaped Hussayn's subsequent life. He met a Brahmin youth named Ma<u>dh</u>ō and fell passionately in love with him. This event provides us with a deeper symbolic meaning to his plucking out the beard hairs from conventional Muslim male saints, for this act was a way of questioning their manhood and was often used as a form of criminal punishment and public shame against adult men of high social status. Because it calls into question assumptions about manhood, gender, and sexuality, the relationship that developed between these two men, a renegade Muslim saint of forty-odd years and a Brahmin teenager, has caused modern writers to be equivocal and evasive, a concern to which we turn later in this chapter.

Hussayn's first meeting with Madho was unpromising. The older man was smitten, and his love was a deeper step into self-abandonment and rapture, a dynamic readily recognized by our Sufi guide to the body: "O Nakhshabi, romance is a delightful recreation / Fair play is never a serious consideration / Whenever one becomes enraptured with a love idol / He will not have time for any other occupation."[10] Persian poetry uses the language of "idolatry" to describe the enchanting effect of youthful beauty, teasing grace, and arrogant pride. Consistent with these themes, Shah Hussayn's hagiography in Persian poetry presents the Brahmin Madho as a pagan idol.

> Madho was wondrous in his beauty and his grace
>   A young man refined, noble Brahmin by descent
> Tender and delicate, from the liquor of this youth's wink
>   the worshiper of grace would fall down flat drunk
> Raised as a Hindu, his faith was pure haughty infidelity
>   stone-hearted, he flaunted beauty to oppress those ensnared
> Madho went out one day to steal hearts for sport
>   riding through the streets with alluring arrogance and captivating pride
> On that same street Hussayn was reeling
>   drunk with wine, surrounded by his loving companions
> In that state of ecstasy, he saw Madho's glowing face
>   and his heart wailed with a cry of delicious pain
> My friends, he cried out, look over there
>   that young man has just stolen away my heart!
> He lifted everything I had from me with a glance
>   he snatched my heart from my soul, swiped my soul from my body
> I'm dazzled with passion for this youth
>   my friends, what should I do, I'm helpless in his grasp
> I'm a captive to the sorrow of being separated from him
>   I can't bear the burning fever of not seeing him for an instant!
> When his companions heard him reveal this secret
>   they replied by revealing another secret
> Oh God, our friend Hussayn doesn't even know
>   who this boy is who is playing with his heart.
> I know, insisted Hussayn, that my heart's curse
>   is a young infidel, who will raze the house of my faith to the ground
> With the graceful curls of his hair, this bare-chested idol
>   has tied up my heart, hung it from his shoulder thread.[11]

He soon began to follow Madho wherever he would go and to spend the night upon his doorstep. But the two were separated by age, class, and religion, and Madho looked askance at Hussayn as a social inferior, a source of caste impurity, and a general threat. The poet interprets these social barriers as the intrinsic quality of Madho as a classic "beloved" in the Persian-Urdu poetic tradition: he is beautiful but cruel, graceful but unsympathetic, luring his desperate lover only to further humiliate him.

From longing to glimpse his beloved
  Hussayn would stand weeping before Madho's door
Crying with passion he would remain immobile
  standing day and night in Madho's alleyway
Even when he tears ran dry Hussayn stayed restless
  without sleep, without patience, without sense, without peace
Since he dropped the reins of self control
  this open passion ruined his reputation throughout Lahore
Vitality vacated his soul, tranquility slipped his mind
  he writhed in the searing flames of passion
Burning day and night in the fire of yearning
  his heart fevered in the heat of longing
He wandered restless with this incendiary love
  yet Madho never even glanced his way once.[12]

The language of the gaze emphasizes their separation. As we saw in the previous chapter, vision through the eyes is a way for the body to transcend distances, yet it deals only with illusions that cannot firmly grasp the reality of the other. Erotic longing can be sparked by sight but never satisfied with it. Shah Hussayn's "incendiary love" began to transform his eyes from organs of clear sight into organs of gesturing expression: he weeps. As passion mounts, the eyes fill with tears, blurring vision in order to express something more profound—not mastery through discernment but vulnerability through weeping. In weeping, the eyes lose their visual acuity and take on the character of the lips. They run with tears just as the lips slobber uncontrollably to express emotion more profound than speech can express.

Their separation was temporarily eased in the spring celebration of Basant, which gave the two a chance to interact personally. This holiday of frolic and play was perhaps the only time that two such different people could meet and speak. All conventions can be broken, all hierarchies can be overturned, and all restraints can be flouted. People of all classes can mingle, and separation between men and women is temporarily suspended as people celebrate Hōlī by throwing colored power or dye over each other's heads, playing pranks, and running amok in celebration of the spirit of bucolic love that flowed between the Hindu god Krishna and the cow maids who danced with him. This spring festival is the classic example of a liminal state through carnival, as described in the symbolic anthropology of Victor Turner.[13] As the poetic biography relates:

Basant arrived, the day the world is flooded with joy
  Hindus play Holi colors: music and wine, flirting and teasing
Everyone gathers together that day without a care
  the honorable mingle freely with the shameless
Drinking wine surrounded by cup-bearers with bodies like silver
  Drinking with vigor, at a lively pace, engrossed in beauty
Dancing limbs, plucking strings, wine, tales, melodies
  luscious forms finely arrayed, color and fragrance mingled
Everyone on the street takes up the intoxicated play
  joy struts stately and seductive in each alleyway
Finally, on that day Madho stooped to show
  sincere kindness and a courteous face to Hussayn
For the buoyancy of spring had arrived
  the season that sparkles like dusky wine in crystal pitchers
In that season all energies become restful
  Indians lay aside their concerns, relax and play
So Madho, too, was playing Holi on Basant
  handsome and graceful, winsome and coy
Playing with everyone, immersing himself in frolic
  teasing everyone and dallying seductively
He strode up to Hussayn very shyly
  and threw colors over his head and his shoulders
And as he poured colors over his hair and clothes
  he sang and his body arched in a dance before him
Hussayn, in his longing, took on a lively air
  his feet suddenly nimble, his steps answered Madho's dance
To his haughty grace Hussayn's every gesture implored
  and Madho himself became Hussayn's game of Basant
His friends gathered around in support
  playing and clapping around them in concert
From that joyous day onward Hussayn devoted
  himself to play as if each day were Basant.[14]

The ice of social convention finally broken, the two became intimate, and Hussayn slowly persuaded Madho to trust him, first as a friend and then as a spiritual guide. Madho's Brahmin parents and his extended family did not accept this dangerous intimacy. They tried to hinder their meetings and to assassinate Hussayn. It is not clear how the two managed to overcome this conflict with Madho's family and the Brahmins of Lahore. However, the two continued to meet and grew closer. At one point, Madho's family planned a pilgrimage to the Ganges source at Harīdwār, to take Madho away from Hussayn and urge him to forget his love. Madho defied them and stayed back in Lahore, but Hussayn, in a miracle, took him from Lahore to Haridwar in one step.[15] This miracle may contain hints at reconciliation between Hussayn and Madho's family. If he was willing to help Madho take a pilgrimage to Haridwar, he was not adverse to Madho's Brahmin religious obligations; nor was he trying to threaten the religious status of his family.

Eventually, Madho was convinced of the sincerity of Hussayn's love for him. Hussayn offered to "initiate" him into his own personal brand of sensual mysticism, through his lips. The action of drinking wine "in intimacy" from the same cup was both actual and metaphorical. Drinking in the spirit referred to both the intoxication of wine and the rapture of erotic kiss. He invited Madho to spend a day or two with him in private in a hut in the village of Bābūpūr, far from Lahore. Madho understood from the outset the sexual nature of this offer and resisted it out of fear for his reputation.

One day Hussayn said to Madho
  "My head reels with desire to take you to Babupur
We will travel together, just you and me
  We will drink in intimacy the wine of our heart's desire
What I truly long for is the pure delight
  of sitting alone with you and sipping your wine
We could be alone together there for an ample time
  and drink, laying in each others embrace."
Madho asked, "Tell me what's your obsession
  with drinking wine in my intimate company?"
"Since your liquor is the very spirit of my life
  you are my livelihood and you alone are my joy
My dear friend, at that moment I'll drink from your hands
  and gaze at you in ecstasy in my arms."
"Speak the truth now," Madho contested
  "and to hell with what will come of all your obsessions
Who am I to you? Why am I the object of all your desires
  that I should let you ruin my good name

What if, as we stay together in intimacy,
someone should spy me laying upon your breast?
Tell me yourself, where would I end up
when people across the world begin to insult me?
They will inflict merciless blame upon me
and toss my honor and reputation to the winds.
Enough, you arrogant man, for God's sake
don't ruin me with these inclinations of yours!"
Hussayn coaxed him, "You're playing hard to get
how I'll weep upon the blade of your teasing
When you sit with me alone in intimacy
who will be brave enough
That they could stand up to denounce me
or stain my clothes with their accusations?
Nobody has the boldness to face me
or soil your reputation on account of me."
Madho at this time didn't know
that Hussayn had a secret way to lead him to God
Madho didn't understand Hussayn's real intent
that these seductions were for his own salvation
He didn't know that Hussayn really desired
to raise his star up to the zenith of salvific bliss
He couldn't have known Hussayn's secret
how brightly he would kindle his star
He knew nothing of those who are united with God
how they can convey to others such rapture.
For this reason Madho remained so anxious
and worried since his heart was not yet ripe.[16]

Although this account is clearly hagiographic, leaving no doubt that Shah Hussayn is a saint and will prevail, it describes this seduction in delightfully realistic tones. Madho is anxious and refuses, while Shah Hussayn is forced to cajole and argue, using his lips not only for speech but also for unspoken gesture. As our Sufi guide has said: "O Nakhshabi, a person will always seek his own kind / the lips of the drinker will join the lips of the pitcher / Do not be surprised nor grieved to discover selfishness / Yet you will find the perfect one to make your life richer."[17] Shah Hussayn tries to reassure Madho, "When you sit with me alone in intimacy, who will be brave enough that they could stand up to denounce me or stain my clothes with their accusations?" He denies that others can stain him with the dirt of their accusations, but he employs an image of stained clothes that is highly ambivalent and potent, resonating deeply with Persian mystical and erotic poetry.

The ecstatic Sufi who has renounced all concern for social convention already wears stained clothes, so who can sully him with accusations of immorality? In Persian Sufi poetry, the Sufi's clothes are stained with wine or perhaps with tears. This ambivalence sets up a tension between the weeping eyes and the imbibing lips, a tension that we saw earlier in Shah Hussayn's poetic biography. Khwājā Mīr Dard, a Sufi poet from Delhi, defined the chaste register of the tear-stained cloth of the lover who persists through eternal separation: "The candle as it burns down and out / lets tears rolls to its foot / With wet eyes we came into the world / Now rapt in wet cloth we go out." However, an earlier Sufi poet, Ḥāfiẓ Shīrāzī, epitomized the ecstatic register of the wine-stained cloth of the lover who abandons self-control in an intimate moment: "The neighborhood of good repute I'm not allowed to enter / If you're not pleased, feel free to change my fate / O pure clothed master, Hafiz could not don / this wine-stained cloak by his own hand in any state!"[18]

Eventually, Madho agreed to meet Hussayn in private at this secluded house, though he insisted on traveling separately in order to avoid suspicion and interference. In private intimacy for the first time, the two entered into a spiritual communion that was also a sexual union.

Hussayn and Madho sat together in one room
    together they laid aside the sorrows of separation
Hussayn was kneeling in respect
    his eyes and his heart focused only on Madho
Madho took from his hand a glass of deep-hued wine
    he drank from it, and Hussayn kissed his wine-sweet lips
Then Madho gave him a glass filled to the brim
    and kissed Hussayn in answer on his reddened lips
He took a sip from the goblet and gave one to Hussayn
    he accepted a kiss and gave one to Hussayn
Hussayn rose again to give of himself more generously
    and Madho graciously accepted his advances
In this way, the lovers engaged in a play of passions
    demanding and acceding, teasing and refusing
Each enticed the other, stirring his desire

mingling wine and kisses like sugar dissolved in milk
In this duet of beseeching and tenderly replying
the two friends made love with each other
Both of them in each act are captivated by the other
loving each other with the kindest intimacy
One kisses the other with an ecstatic breath
moving from his wrist to his hand, his strong arm, his shoulder
Then he kisses his forehead and then his cheek
gently kisses both his eyelids and then his brows
Then with sweet affection he kisses his lips
with love he kisses the smooth skin beneath his chin.[19]

After this erotic initiation, Madho began to live with Hussayn at Bāghabānpūr on the outskirts of Lahore (the neighborhood is now within the expanding city just next to the Shalimar gardens). The sexual nature of their relationship was widely known, for the poet notes that some of Hussayn's followers observed their sexual play through the keyhole and were troubled for a time by doubts about its propriety. The poet defends their sexual play as a "spiritual initiation" in which Hussayn passed on to Madho the spark of divine love through touch, which conveyed to him mystical knowledge more holistically and powerfully than words possibly could.

Many Sufis held that a kiss on the lips between men was the vehicle for transmission of sacred power, rather than a routine expression of sexual desire.[20] Islamic scripture envisions the kiss as the most intimate bestowal of grace and compassion, as in God breathing life into Adam or Jesus bestowing life to the dead through the breath, whose closest physical embodiment is in the lips (Q 3:49 and 5:110). Mawlana Rumi, the renowned Persian poet and Sufi master (whose homoerotic themes will interest us later in this chapter), explains why an ardent monotheist would engage in the ritual of kissing the black stone of the Ka'ba: "The pilgrim kisses the black stone from his innermost heart, because he feels the lips of his beloved in it."[21]

The kiss as a bestowal of grace or spiritual power is common trope in Sufism, but Shah Hussayn took it very literally. He asserted that sexual play is the best path toward spiritual cultivation. In the gesture of the kiss, empowered with erotic attraction and refined with spiritual care, he found the intimate mingling of souls; the kiss was a gesture of self-abnegation and spiritual renewal. The poet-biographer goes on to try to explain how such erotic play could actually be a spiritual initiation.

When you look at these two true men embracing
don't think that you are witnessing a sin
Their play of kisses are ripples from the ocean of guidance
not from selfish lust—their aim is greater than that
When Hussayn takes Madho's lips in his own
he transmits his blessing in the most intimate way
When Madho answers his lips with shy delicacy
he coaxes from each blessing many more blessings
Hussayn is training Madho from the depth of his soul
how to pass along the mystic path to truth
He wants to burnish within Madho the passion for God
he plays this love off against that love, intensifying each
When Hussayn sips from Madho's goblet of wine
he burns with the longing passion for Madho's beauty
In this burning, his soul rises from its place
he can kiss then directly from his heart
Madho kisses Hussayn's lips until his breath like a cool breeze
ripples over the heart of Madho, stirring his passion.[22]

However, it is clear that despite this rhetorical defense of Hussayn, his initiation of Madho was far more sensual and more fully erotic than a mere conventional drop of saliva. The poet narrates this sexual scene only in relation to their "initiation," implying that it was a one-time instance of ritual union. However, their relation was erotically charged and physically emotive from their first meeting during that fateful Basant celebration.

Sexuality's Queer Connection to Spirituality

It is a persistent theme in the Islamic tradition that mystical insight can be passed on through bodily contact, especially through a shared drink or saliva. Initiatic dreams or visions often contain the image of a spiritual master passing a bit of his saliva to a follower's mouth with his finger or through a kiss. Shah Hussayn himself is reported to have met the perennial spiritual guide Khidr in his boyhood. Khidr poured out some water from his jug into his own palm, and Hussayn drank from his hand.[23] This transmission of spiritual blessing allowed him to finish memorizing the Qur'an with ease and eventually pushed him toward sainthood in his adult life.

There is no reason to believe that Madho and Shah Hussayn's bold sexual play at "initiation" was a singular occurrence, especially since the two lived together in complete intimacy. So inseparable were they that Hussayn himself became known by the name of his lover, as "Madho Lal Hussayn."[24] Further, there is no evidence to suggest that Hussayn "initiated" any of his other followers with such erotic overtures, though he did initiate many companions in his playful brand of mystical devotion. Hussayn's relationship with Madho, then, resembles a man's love, emotionally and sensually, for another man, rather than any missionary endeavor or tantric rite. It forces us to acknowledge that Shah Hussayn's sexual orientation was queer: if using the modern term "gay" to describe him seems anachronistic for a premodern and non-Western personality, "queer" is a more open label for his deliberate unconventionality.

Most modern scholarship has shown a deliberate misrecognition of the queer erotic dimension of Shah Hussayn's relationship, even though the Sufi mystical tradition among the Muslims of South Asia is rife with stories of saintly persons "falling in love" with young men. Although the followers and chroniclers of these saints use vivid emotional terms to describe such intimate friendships, they normally remain silent about whether such friendships actually had a sexual dimension. Incidental evidence suggests that erotic desire was the basis of such relationships, whether the desire was fulfilled or not. These loves usually transgressed the boundaries of age, class, ethnicity, and even religious persuasion. They were friendships with no basis in the social structure and often earned both the mystic and his beloved social censure and blame.

It is logical to conclude that the only basis for such socially unlikely pairings is erotic. Despite this, most modern writers equivocate on the issue of erotic friendship or openly sexual relations between the mystic and his beloved. They either fail to mention the possibility or apologetically assert that such love was surely "platonic." Sometimes they even translate the gender of the beloved surreptitiously, transforming a young man into a young woman to better fit their own conception of what love should look like.[25] The personality of Shah Hussayn is unique in offering vivid evidence that this Sufi's love affair with a younger man was not only erotic and openly sexual but to a large extent accepted as such by his contemporaries.

In stark contrast to the explicitly erotic terms used in this medieval biography, modern writers seem to be at best uncomfortable and at worst shallowly moralistic when confronted with the life of Shah Hussayn. These two men became friends, then master and disciple, then lifelong companions; still, most writers do not want to admit they were lovers, even though they lived together and Hussayn never married.[26] This scholarly silence is all the more surprising because Hussayn's biography is preserved largely in one poetic source that vividly describes their meeting in sensual terms and illustrates their initiation in explicitly sexual terms. Although later Muslim biographers cite this poem as their primary source for the biography of Hussayn, they suppress the sexual dimension of the relationship between them. Most modern Indian authors, whether Muslim, Sikh, Hindu, or Christian, rely on these intermediary sources, rather than returning to the unpublished original manuscript at Punjab University in Lahore.[27] They are unwilling to admit the sexual nature of Hussayn and Madho's relationship because they have been unable to access the records that display it.

The modern writer Lajwanti Ramakrishna has written the definitive book on Shah Hussayn and his poetry. She refers to the possibility of a homoerotic relation between the two men as a rumor, writing that "many people had become suspicious of the un-natural relationship."[28] She further reveals her misunderstanding of their relationship when she writes that "Hussayn tried for sixteen years to possess the lad," even though the biographical sources show that Hussayn was not interesting in possessing Madho but only in loving him. Ramakrishna further deviates from the biographical sources in speculating that Madho moved in with Hussayn not for love but only for shelter, since he had been "excommunicated" by his parents and the Brahmin community after having eaten with Hussayn and his companions. Finally Ramakrishna tries to back up these baseless analyses with an equally baseless theory, claiming that a Sufi's falling in love with a young man is a practice of "foreign origin" from Persia that has nothing Indian about it. She writes that a man loving a youth "is opposed to the Indian concept of Divine Love." By excluding homoerotic love (with which she is obviously uncomfortable) from the Indian tradition she tries to de-emphasize its importance in the life of Hussayn. However, Ramakrishna cannot explain why a very Indian Sufi like Hussayn would opt for a "foreign" practice like loving a young man, especially when his poetic output is so clearly Punjabi and draws so intensely from local Indian folklore and Hindu myth, as we will see. His family had joined Islam only a few generations before without claiming any Persian ancestry or educational ties. Further, she never clarifies whether "the Indian concept of Divine Love" excludes the erotic love between two people or only the erotic love between two men. Ramakrishna's whole biography of Shah Hussayn and Madho is an exercise in bad faith, in regard to both the biographical sources and the personality of Shah Hussayn.[29]

Another modern Indian scholar, Shuja Alhaq, is more frank in his assessment when he writes, "Hussayn became enamored of his [Madho's] beauty at the first sight of him. From then onward he could not rest without seeing him. He had to live in separation from him for some time until the youth also began to be attracted to him." However, Alhaq posits that this event of male attraction was "probably in the later years" of Hussayn's life, thereby erasing the element of eroticism and mutual commitment between the two. His subsequent analysis focuses on Hussayn's philosophy and poetry, with no mention of how sexuality may have shaped both of these dimensions.[30] However, it is clear that their relationship was not a passing phase or a private element of Shah Hussayn's life but rather made a deep impact on his religious activities and public persona.

Madho stayed with Hussayn and his companions for a few years and then asked permission to join the military service. He left Lahore in the service of Raja Man Singh for a three-year stint in the army, fighting in Bengal and the Dekkan, but returned to live with Hussayn until the saint's death in 1599 C.E. at the age of about 60. Hussayn had prepared his own grave next to their home. Madho slipped into a deep depression at the loss of his lover. He was inconsolable and grew weak with mourning, wishing to die in order to be reunited with Hussayn.[31] After some time, he recovered and joined the army again, journeying for twelve years throughout Hindustan. Finally, he returned to Lahore to live at the tomb of Hussayn for thirty-five more years. He lived in isolation (and was not known to have married). He become the spiritual successor of Hussayn's saintly authority, and upon his death, Madho was buried directly beside Hussayn.

Later biographers claim that Madho converted to Islam at the hand of Hussayn. If this were true, it is doubtful that he would continue to be known by his given, Hindu name (which is inscribed upon his tombstone today). Rather, this story is another manifestation of the "missionary position" that later writers used to dilute the passionate and sexual nature of their relationship. In the view of later followers who may not have known them personally, the only explanation of why a Sufi became so close to a Brahmin was in order to "convert" him rather than to love him. Surely Madho's own Brahmin community would have seen the situation in those terms. However, what we know of Hussayn's free-spirited philosophy and irreverent nature makes it clear that he accepted Madho as a "Muslim" in the broadest sense as one who submits to God in dedication and service, rather than insisting on some ritualistic or legalistic "conversion" as popularly understood.

If modern scholars from South Asia have been so loath to recognize the erotic and frankly sexual dimension of Shah Hussayn's playful approach to spirituality, what alternate intellectual approaches can we find to make sense of it? The first thing we must do is reject moralistic approaches, such as the prudishly Victorian outlook of Lajwanti Ramakrishna or the defensive posture of Shuja Alhaq. I have written elsewhere about how Victorian morality forced its way into the scholarship on poetry in South Asia.[32] Some contemporary Western scholars, mainly literary experts, have moved beyond moralism and see Shah Hussayn's sexuality as part of his literary talent; among these scholars are Anna Suvorova and Christopher Shackle.[33] The advent of gay and lesbian journals (in India and among Indians abroad) has contributed to such new honesty and deeper analysis. In one such journal, a younger Indian scholar, Yogi Sikand, has reclaimed Shah Hussayn as a gay Sufi whose sexuality was an important part of his spirituality and poetic work. He writes, "It is possible and indeed very likely that Hussayn's greatly unconventional involvement with Madho had a deep impact on his own thinking, his mystical poetry and most all his religious life."[34] There is certainly merit in delving into the archives of the Islamic past for figures who might have new importance in the identity politics of the present. However, it must be stressed here that although Shah Hussayn may have been gay (as we currently define terms of sexual orientation), as he was a Qalander, his personality was also drawing on popular currents of religious devotion.

The Qalandars were radical Sufis who stormed across Islamic boundaries of social etiquette and legal rectitude in an attempt to rescue ritual from the demands of order and restore it to its primordial status as "play." Sufi leaders railed against this competing group of radical Sufis, whom Ahmed Karamustafa calls "deviant renunciants" in his perceptive study of their movement, which thrived across Central Asia, Turkistan, and into South Asia throughout the later medieval period. As "renunciants" the Qalandars shared an affinity with Sufis; however, as "deviant" they rejected not only routine states of consciousness but also the boundaries of social order. Rather, they claimed to embody a state of holiness by breaking social norms, ritual boundaries, and legal rules and thereby saw themselves as real Sufis who criticized the leaders of Sufi communities who adhered to social norms and Islamic law. So threatened were Sufi leaders by Qalandars that they urged political leaders to suppress them by force. "They are the excess of the earth," explained one leader to the invading Mongols who inquired about the Qalandars, as he urged them to execute the "deviant renunciants."[35] Shah Hussayn's red clothes and his face shaved of facial hair marked him as a Qalandar.

By the early modern period, Sufi communities had become the powerful organized forces that were fully integrated into Islamic societies, despite the protracted and flamboyant critique of Qalandars. Yet Qalandars remained on the scene, exercising their militant form of bliss and offering an alternative, not just to routine life in a patriarchal society but also to the moderate asceticism of Sufi communal life. Katherine Ewing, for instance, calls them "the abject" created by the ideological formation of the Sunni-Sufi world order: "by operating as an inverted mirror that challenges the background understandings of daily life, the qalandar potentially exposes to scrutiny basic issues of subjective experience for the ordinary person . . . [yet paradoxically] functions as a foundation on which the lawful Muslim subject rests. . . . The qalandar is 'not-Me.'"[36] Skillfully using Julia Kristeva's theoretical term "abject," she documents the Qalandars' persistent critique of Islamic moralism into the present, in Pakistan as elsewhere in South Asia.

The fundamental root of the conflict between Qalandars and conventional Sufis is over the importance of "play." Conventional Sufis usually maintain a fairly serious demeanor; after all, rejecting attachment to the world is hard work. We can see this attitude in the portrait of Shah Hussayn as an ascetic Sufi before his flash of insight. He used to stand up to his waist in the Ravi River, lips blue from cold, while reciting the Qur'an all day. In contrast, the moment of spiritual insight that led him to toss aside all restraint was the realization that work earned one nothing because it only reinforced egoistic self-righteousness. The Qur'anic verse *The life of the world is nothing but play and pleasurable distraction* could have two contradictory meanings: it may criticize worldly life as a distraction from moral work, but it could convey the inverse, criticizing work as having no moral worth. Qalandars embody this intense reaction against bourgeois notions of work, countering them with "holy waste." They renounce productive work, refuse reproduction of the family, and resist the labor it takes to conform to religious custom and law. Those who oppose Qalandars see their lives as waste—wasting their time, living as parasites off productive society, and squandering the opportunity to earn religious merit through conventional morality.

Shah Hussayn was not as nihilistic as to celebrate waste for its own sake. Rather, he believed that what others thought of as waste, that is, simple play, was really of ultimate value. Whether the play was dress up, make believe, dance and song, or seductive love play, Shah Hussayn saw it as the only way to live sincerely in the world without giving the world value it did not have in God's sight. Play prevented people from grasping after the world with greed or angrily rejecting it with ascetic rigor. His poems (*kāfīyān*) that rolled off his lips in Punjabi give the clearest view of his religious vision.

Sound asleep at night you are
And wandering throughout the day
So full of frolic and fun
Oh small self of mine

Get up now and repeat
The Name—this stay is so short
And today arrives the Groom

Don't indulge in deep ponderings
This is your only trip
To this world, says Hussain.[37]

He advocates waking up and repeating the names of God, like conventional Sufis. However, his mode of reciting the names of God is to wander all day in frolic and fun while sleeping soundly at night, precisely the opposite of Sufi advice to work hard in the day and stay awake part of the night in devotional vigils. Even "deep ponderings" are a waste of precious time when there are so many ways to play.

In this poetry, we can hear Shah Hussayn's words, but they emerge through the lips of a woman. In his poetry, he often spoke in the voice of a woman, specifically a young woman just reaching the age of betrothal. In this way, he not only breaks conventions about sexuality but also transgresses the boundaries of gender roles.

In the grip of the Lover am I
Who holds me by the wrist
How could I say let go?

Only those know of love
Who feel it in their bones
The rest just dig shallow wells
In waste and dreary lands
Some sow their tiny seeds
In dry and billowing sands

Why spend yourself
On affairs so worldly wise

Which you will one day leave?
Lock eyes with eyes!
So says Hussain,
The mendicant of the Lord.[38]

He dramatized his rebellion against routine and calculation through the metaphor of a woman's work. She is faced with a choice, to spin and weave dutifully in the hope of finding a husband or to abandon the bounded courtyard of respectability and search for the passionate embrace of the lover, the groom. She knows that time is fleeting because her groom is about to arrive, and her excited heartbeat registers the imminence of his arrival. How can someone work, performing ritual acts by the book as if sowing tiny seeds, when the beloved groom is about to appear? The gendered imagery intensifies as the female speaker calls her body "a burning oven." This is a common metaphor for women's sexual desire, as revealed by our Sufi guide, Nakhshabi; he has his female protagonist complain of longing for her illicit beloved by saying, "The enticement of temptation and the anguish of separation have kindled a flame in the furnace of my heart; the torture of pain and the agony of desire have made a forge of my garments."[39]

A burning oven is my body
Ever full of flames, hot signs
My heart pines and burns
When I make for the bed
So enamored of him am I

A body alone could know
The plight of a body in anguish
A heart alone could measure
The longings of a heart
An intimate alone
Could read my inner thoughts.

Oh people of the world
Why entangle and ensnare me
On false pretexts in vain?
So asks Hussain, the Faqir.[40]

Of course, a young woman who refuses to work has given up all hope of having her family arrange a marriage for her. She needs to earn the marriage, for her family will need to pay the dower to a groom. Shah Hussayn's poetic imagery of forgoing labor in order to break out of the domestic courtyard and race to the beloved's bed is therefore very dangerous.

A thousand taunts for me
Numberless abuses
But I would still cling
To the hem of my Groom

My head may leave my body
But the secret I won't reveal
My plight I would narrate
To none by him, my Lord
Whose talk falls on my heart
Like a soothing caressing balm.
To die before death
That is what we desire
So says Hussain, the Faqir.[41]

The stakes are very high when one chooses to defy familial and social norms. Taunts would be the least punishment, with execution more probable. Sufis may idealize a state of selflessness that is "to die before death," but one who follows Shah Hussayn's path may not be far from actual death. However, one rapt in love and longing perceives that fear is only the shadow of pride.

Laugher and play
The Lord ordained for me
Some are left behind in tears
While others have carried the day
With laughter loud and cheery
Discard this pride of yours
And be ever humble
What will pride achieve?
May he leave this world
Sated and in safety
So says Hussain, the Faqir.[42]

With such moments of dramatized fear woven into his optimistic prediction of leaving the world "sated and in safety," Shah Hussayn pursued his spirituality of play. It was through his lips that these inner states bubbled to the surface in audible and visible signs, as the oral tradition of his poetry that was originally sung before being written down and as laughter in the face of distress through which he confronted the police chief and other critics. Our Sufi guide to the human body has noted the importance of the lips in this regard: "Wise men have said that laughter is the sign of gladness and a smile is the symbol of sorrow's absence. When joy becomes excessive in the human mind and happiness becomes boundless in the human heart, therefore, it permeates all the veins, joints, limbs and organs so that the body becomes relaxed. Joy overflows and must find an outlet so it is by compulsion forced to come out of the mouth. If the amusement is little, it will turn to a smile; if moderate it will induce a grin; and if overpowering, it will end in hearty laughter. O Nakhshabi, how can a person in distress be gay? / Alas, can laughter find a place with desolate grief? / Merriment is a characteristic of happiness / A heart burdened with care cannot laugh with cheerful relief."[43]

Playing between Sufi and Bhakti Love Mysticism

The transgression of gender roles in his poetry is just one facet of Shah Hussayn's assertion that "laugher and play the Lord ordained for me." At its deepest, he asserts that religion and morality should be embodied in playfulness, even if most religions, including Islam, have evolved in a deeply pathological pattern of self-righteous seriousness. Working backward to find the evolutionary origin of religion, the theorist Johan Huizinga has argued that cult and ritual are best understood as "sacred play." He further speculated that ritual evolved from play in the more basic sense. The gist of his theory is that the religious person (*homo religioso* in Eliade's terms) is actually *homo ludens*, the human being at play. Huizinga defined play through five formal elements:

1. Play has a primal, irreducible nature—it is completely voluntary and is an end in and of itself.
2. Play is superfluous and nonutilitarian, a complete "waste of time."
3. Play takes place outside ordinary time—though it absorbs the player's complete attention, it is not serious.
4. Play proceeds with orderly rules within its own limits of time and space.
5. Since play surrounds itself with secrecy and otherness from ordinary life, it can give rise to cohesive social groups.

These five elements, he argues, allow us to argue that ritual activity is based upon the prior activity of play.[44] "In the form and function of play, itself an independent entity which is senseless and irrational, man's consciousness that he is embedded in a sacred order of things finds its first, highest, and holiest expression. Gradually the significance of a sacred act permeates the playing. Ritual grafts itself upon it; but the primary thing is and remains play."[45] Huizinga does not just assert an evolutionary relationship between play and ritual, with play being prior to and forming the necessary basis for later formalization of ritual. He also suggests that the best way to approach ritual is as play.

Although Huizinga makes a descriptive argument and limits his discourse to an intellectual understanding of the "origin of religion," it is clear that Shah Hussayn perceived these same connections between play and ritual in a prescriptive pronouncement. He preached that we should abandon ritual formality and its hope of earning merit in order to embrace play like a child, a musician, or a lover. Although not widely engaged by later scholars in religious studies, Huizinga's theory contains much that makes sense of Shah Hussayn. Most important, it offers us a framework through which to understand his erotic playfulness as a form of spiritual cultivation, rather than just an individual expression of sexual orientation (which it also most likely was).

In contrast to its general neglect, Huizinga's theory that religion is essential play has struck some scholars of Hinduism as profound. In particular, David Kinsley, in his book *The Divine Player*, analyzes Krishna devotion as an example of religion imagined and practiced most vividly as play. In bhakti forms of Hindu love mysticism the image of Krishna becomes central. Devotees eschewed Krishna's more martial and dutiful incarnation as Arjuna's charioteer (as he is depicted in the *B͟hagawad-Gīta*) in favor of a more youthful Krishna: the beguiling dark youth who engages his female devotees in erotic play, or *rās-līlā*. The sound of his flute extends the power of his lips to play over the senses of those both far and near.

The fact that Shah Hussayn fell in love during Holi, which is not just a spring season festival but is also closely associated with Krishna, alerts us to the complexity of his situation. It is only with this background on Krishna devotion that we can understand Shah Hussayn's poetry, in which the speaker often takes on a female voice. It is the same voice of female longing that speaks through the character of the Gopis, the milkmaids seduced by Krishna's amorous play. Shah Hussayn is a Muslim but in a very Hindu context, and his form of sexual-spiritual play draws on both religious contexts. Holi is the festival of springtime (Basant) most intensely identified with Krishna's frolic. During Holi, all forms of routine-breaking and hierarchy-inverting play are identified as expressions of joy, love, and bliss. The *Bhagawad-Purāna* has Krishna say: "Whoever, desirous of liberation, is fond of the acquisition of knowledge and is regardless of liberation, should become my devotee by renouncing all Asramas [formal devotional retreats] having characteristic signs and should wander about independent of regulations. Although senseless, he should sport like a boy. Although skilled, he should behave like a stupid person. Although learned, he should talk like a maniac. Although regarding the Vedas, he should act like a cow disregarding all rules."[46] This description of the medieval Krishna cult applies very well to the joyous ranting of Shah Hussayn and his boyish followers.

However, in its mature flowering, advocates of the Krishna cult took this advice even further. They ceased to identify as boys at all and instead took on the identity of the Gopis, the girls who abandoned everything to draw close to Krishna's passionate touch. The Vallabhāchārya sect of Krishna devotees, founded in the fifteenth century and very active in Gujarat and Rajasthan, were the most vivid exponent of this daring spiritual transformation. They identified with Rādha, the chief milkmaid, in trying through play to gain the love of God in the form of Krishna. Male devotees would not just mentally identify with the female Gopis but would dress in women's clothes and adopt women's dialect, sometimes only in ritual spaces but sometimes for life.[47]

So powerful was this movement that some Muslims were attracted to join. The most famous was Rās Khān, who serves as an apt comparison to Shah Hussayn. Ras Khan was a Muslim noble of Afghan descent who fell in love with a younger man and ended up throwing away his social respectability to follow his lover in complete abandon. However, he eventually sublimated this queer same-sex attraction. Some Vallabhacarya devotees challenged him, claiming that the painted image of their lord, Krishna, was more beautiful and alluring than his male beloved. Upon gazing at their image of Krishna, the dark-skinned beautiful cowherd with his flute raised provocatively to his pursed lips, Ras Khan was immediately and profoundly converted.[48] He shifted his erotic attraction to Krishna and sublimated his same-sex sexual attraction to the spiritual love play of Krishna. Ras Khan's ardent poems in Braj Bhāsha, a vernacular dialect of Hindi particular to the locale of Vridavan (the region associated with Krishna as a youth, near the city of Māthurā), are comparable to those of Shah Hussayn in Punjabi. Although Muslim hagiographers do not mention Ras Khan personally (we know of his life and poems from Hindu bhakti hagiographies), some Sufi texts do acknowledge the presence of Muslim worshipers of Krishna during the early Mughal era. One of the disciples of ʿAli Muttaqi, whom we encountered in Chapter 3, criticizes Sufis who make pilgrimages to Mathura, the site of numerous temples to Krishna and the center of Vallabhacarya activities.[49]

Viewing Shah Hussayn against the background of the Vallabhacarya cult allows us to make sense of his gender-bending in his literary production. Though he never directly cites the name of Krishna's lover, Radha, he does use the name of the female heroine, Hīr. He often cited the love epic of the Punjabi folk heroes Hir and her lover Rānjhā, placing himself in the persona of the woman, Hir.[50] Punjabi poets and their eager audiences poured into Hir and Ranjha the same erotic emotion that was invested in Radha and Krishna in regions closer to the Ganges. The story of Hir and Ranjha became a favorite Sufi device for conveying the value of erotic passion in spiritual life. Shah Hussayn's poetic outpourings in Punjabi continued to explore the theme of divine love manifested in the passion between two people, in terms Islamic, Hindu, and indigenous Punjabi.[51]

In this commitment to the spirituality of play, Shah Hussayn found a Qur'anic equivalent to the bhakti practice of *ras-lila*, the sensuous and amorous play of Krishna among his loving devotees. Such a synthesis of Hindu and Islamic ideas was even more meaningful because Hussayn belonged to a community of weavers, who had as a caste converted to Islam only a few generations before.[52] Such "New Muslims" found support and patronage from Rajput noble families, who themselves provided military and political support to the growing Mughal empire in the sixteenth century. Mughal royalty provided religious justification for their rule through forms of synthesis of Islamic Sufi and Indic bhakti devotion, in court life, literature, music, and dance as well as in devotional communities. In this social and political environment, it would be natural for Shah Hussayn to find equivalence and convergence between Islamic and Hindu devotion, rather than only irreconcilable differences. His sexual spirituality of play blurred the distinction between religions, just as he blurred the distinction between religiously marked bodies in loving Madho. We will see later how Mughal authorities received his street antics.

Even as we acknowledge the deep affinity between Shah Hussayn and the Hindu mystics devoted to Krishna, we must be careful. Shah Hussayn was not merely a bhakta in Islamic disguise, therefore easily ejected from the community of Muslims. Rather, he draws upon persistent themes in the Islamic Sufi environment, a fact that should not be obscured by this comparison to Hindu bhakti mysticism. Though his story is unique in that his bodily rebellion was so bold, Shah Hussayn represents a long tradition in Sufism of Qalandar rebelliousness and homoerotic sensuality. By exploring these countercultural currents in the Sufi tradition, we can better understand how Shah Hussayn's personality is a point of contact between Iranian and Indic, between Islamic and Hindu, between Sufi and bhakti.

A point of social theory can help us understand the commonalities between bhakti and Sufi practice. Anthropologists have often described how the inversion of social norms is a form of supplication or a way of requesting closeness to a source of power. As one approached the emperor in the Mughal court (as well as in most other courts of agrarian empires), one approached in prostration: one's habitual bodily comportment was radically altered. Abdellah Hammoudi has very adroitly shown how such inversion of norms in deference to royal authority was even more complexly applied in Sufi communities in Morocco: one approached a powerful saint by suspending or abdicating one's routine comportment as a patriarchal male.[53] A male disciple could approach a male spiritual guide only in one of two ways: as seducer in a homoerotic social role that inverts sexual norms, or as a subservient effeminate in a feminine social role that inverts gender norms.

The relationship of gender transgression and sainthood presented here consists of two intermeshed but distinct arguments. First, in order to express personal sanctity, Sufi Muslims often cross the socially defined boundary of gender. Here "sanctity" connotes perceptible markers of self-surrender, abandoning worldly ambition, devotion and love of God, and "gender crossing" signifies that a man takes up the social markers of a woman: to wear women's clothing; to adopt women's speech, song, gesture; to take on a woman's role in erotic interactions or even a woman's role in sexual interactions. Second, as a sign of surrender, male Sufis may shed many of the signs of social status, including the patriarchal status of masculinity (wearing red clothes, wearing no clothes, shaving the beard and mustache, leaving family and ascribed status, inviting condemnation and blame), without performing these signs of surrender into the outer form of "feminine" gender. Rather, they are refocused into an assertion of male passion for another man, a re-creation of the subject into a passionate lover, in which love transgresses social-religious boundaries as a metaphor for transcending them. In this way, transgender behavior and homoerotic behavior are closely linked but are not reducible to each other. Sufis in South Asia inverted gender roles or cultivated homoerotic attraction in order to show supplication. In situations of deference to the authority of a Sufi master, and to render the self open and vulnerable to receive mystical insight, men's bodies were placed in positions that contradicted patriarchal norms. We can observe this in action in the hagiographic stories about Amir Khusro (died 1325 C.E.), who dressed in women's clothes once to dance before his Sufi master Nizam al-Din Awliya', and Mūsā Sadā Sohāg (died 1449 C.E.), who did the same only to end up wearing women's clothes and bangles for the rest of his life.

Musa Sada Sohag's story is fascinating, and I tell it fully elsewhere.[54] In a claim of Muslim sainthood, he fully renounced not only the patriarchal prerogatives of maleness but also his actual maleness. He took on women's clothes and behaviors in a permanent transgression of gender norms and was perceived as a saint with special affinity for the Hijras, or men who become women in South Asia. In contrast, Shah Hussayn did not consistently invert gender roles but rather inverted sexuality roles through same-sex eroticism. He exhibits with great vividness a whole range of "homoerotic" phenomena in which the male gaze eroticizes the beauty of a masculine figure. In this case, desire is transgressive because it does not conform to the expected gender of the object of desire. In this case what is queer is the sexual orientation of the subject in relation to the object of desire, which is not oppositely gendered according to patriarchal norms.

In Sufi hagiography, there are many examples of this dynamic, of male Sufis who look upon other men with erotic desire. Often these are Muslim males who look with erotic desire upon men of a distinctly different class: either younger men or non-Muslim men. Such a practice is called, in Persian and Urdu, *shāhid-bāzī*, or "playing the witness game." It has a long history in Persianate Sufism as a sign of surrender and renunciation, as well as an active pursuit of beauty and devotion to the ideal of comradely intimacy. The Sufi practice of playing the witness game was worshiping the beauty of God as it might manifest in any created form. Most medieval Persianate Sufis found manifestations of divine beauty most clearly and consistently in the form of young men. Such homoerotic gazing contemplation (whether combined with actual romantic attachment, physical intimacy, or sexual desire or left "chaste") was an important though controversial feature of both Iranian and South Asian Sufism. Hagiographic and poetic evidence attests to its presence in the lives of eminent mystics.[55]

What is "queer" about Sufi poets who wrote love poetry directed toward male beloveds, whether they were younger men or esteemed spiritual guides, and who serves as prototypes for Shah Hussayn? Their metaphors of same-sex love extended even to God, whose divinity was not just transcendently other but also fascinatingly present in beauty, no matter where it might be found. Their poetry is completely informed by *wahdat al-wujud*, the "oneness of being." This Sufi concept, which elevated all loves to act as pathways toward love of God, was popularized in South Asia through *sama*ʿ, or listening to love poetry in a devotional setting that might erupt into ecstatic gesture or rapturous dance; such ritual and the attitude behind it were clearly in harmony with the bhakti movement, which extolled Krishna's dance of bewildering love, the *ras-lila*. Playing the witness game was so popular in South Asia by the sixteenth century that a vocal minority of cautious and juridical Sufis began to write against it. Controversy seems to have raged in particular around Burhanpur, from where the Sufi master, Muhammad ibn Faḍlullah, hailed. He wrote a treatise against the practice of *shahid-bazi* and warned Sufis not to keep company with beautiful young men. ʿAli Muttaqi, who also was raised in Burhanpur, wrote in his short treatise "Warning to Lovers on the Signs of Sincere Passion" that love of God is never reflected in love of a woman or a young man.[56]

In the end we must ask whether either of these patterns, homoerotic desire and gender transgressive desire, are protests against patriarchy in South Asian Muslim society. Potentially yes, but more routinely no. Most of these cases are individual and do not lead to social movements that might permanently alter the fabric of patriarchal norms. As individual cases, they are forced to conform to some pattern by which society can recognize and understand them. Male Sufis with masculine beloveds fall into a pattern of social co-optation in which they ultimately "convert" the beloved from non-Muslim to Muslim. While upholding the poetic conviction that beauty lies in contrast (dark Hindu, light Turk), this glosses over the male-to-male transgression of sexual desire by painting it over with the missionary motif of Islamic devotion. Though Madho often suffers this fate in modern accounts, Shah Hussayn stands out from the background of Persianate Sufism, for he explicitly challenges patriarchal norms. For this reason, he suffered persecution and threats of corporal punishment. We can now turn to analyzing these threats against him and the status of corporal punishment in Islamic law to understand how his surrounding society viewed his particularly potent lips.

Paying Lip Service to Islam

Shah Hussayn's erotic acts were not mere poetic metaphors or ritual gestures. They were linked to a widely known romance with another man, and he combined them with public forms of abandon: singing, drumming, dancing, wine drinking, shaving off all facial hair, trespassing divisions of social class, voluntary poverty. He displayed these practices in public to draw out from others their hypocrisy. Those who blame others are not introspecting to find and repair their own faults. He saw his behavior, however, not as instrumental but as integral to his own spiritual state, which was free as a child's, unburdened by responsibility or convention. Mughal elites were willing to see Shah Hussayn's difference as marking him off as sacred rather than ejecting him as perverse or rejecting him as criminal. The erotic nature of his gestures of abandon only confirmed for them that his ultimate passion was for God. The erotic and the divine were not separate or opposing attractions, according to the conceptual framework of *ʿishq-i majāzī*, or metaphorical love, in which any form of love is a rung on the ladder of ascension toward the love of God. Love in its sensual, sexual, and romantic aspects differ only in degree from love in its devotional, aesthetic, or spiritual aspects: Without the lower rungs, how can anyone aspire to climb the ladder of being, through the metaphors of materiality to the reality of spirituality? Through this conceptual framework Shah Hussayn explained his sexual-spiritual play, and through it the public understood, elevated, and cherished Shah Hussayn's provocative behavior. They saw his behavior as metaphorically Islamic, that is, comprehensible in an Islamic worldview, even if not literally Islamic in conformity with religious proscriptions.

However, not all state and religious authorities were as accepting as the general public. Shah Hussayn had courted resistance from some religious authorities in Lahore. His teacher, Saʿdullah, argued with him not to take literally the Qurʾanic verse *The life of the world is nothing but play and pleasurable distraction.* To take it as prescriptive and live in pleasant abandon would lead him to ruin! Even to take it simply as descriptive, that life's labor in the end amounts to nothing serious, is a misinterpretation that would be folly. No, Saʿdullah insisted that the Qurʾan's tone of voice in this verse is sarcastic, as if saying "You act as though the life of the world is nothing but play, but wait and see what's really coming!" It is a warning of judgment, a sarcastic parental threat of calling to account.

On hearing of Shah Hussayn's playful rebellion, his first Sufi master, Shaykh Bahlūl, rushed to Lahore, ready to join Saʿdullah in urging him to return to "the straight path." But when he saw Hussayn in ripped red clothes, dancing and drinking wine, he realized that this was his personal path to religious sincerity. The Shaykh blessed him and returned to his home. These two diametrically opposed reactions, initial rejection followed by considered acknowledgment and respect, would set the pattern for Hussayn's reception in the wider society.

Hussayn's reputation as a libertine (*laund*) and a drunk (*rind*) was widely known. "He wears red clothes, drinks wine openly, sings and plays music, and is surrounded by smooth-faced young men as beautiful as the moon. He dances with them in the street in front of his home. He shaves his beard off but lets his mustache grow long."[57] These actions inevitably brought Shah Hussayn in conflict with the authorities of Lahore: the police chief, the chief judge, and finally the emperor himself. We must keep in mind that Lahore was a seasonal capital city and home of the Mughal court during its perennial rotation. The police chief of Lahore, Kotwal Malik ʿAli, was requested to keep a watch out for Hussayn's misdeeds. One day, the chief was administering public punishment of a criminal in the market while Hussayn was present by the side of the road, indulging in some flirtatious eye contact with a handsome young man, who happened to be the police chief's own son. When told that this amorous man was Shah Hussayn, the police chief arrested him and had him chained up, charging him with being a heretical innovator in religious matters (*mubtadiʿ*).

Most important for our study of the body, the police chief threatened to have Shah Hussayn impaled as punishment for his "crimes." He threatened impaling with a stake (*mekh*) "from behind" that would pierce the Sufi's liver until the stake came to his throat, a mimetic punishment that stands for anal rape.

When Hussayn saw that he was to be chained like a criminal
  he addressed the police chief, laughing like a woman
"For what reason do you treat me like this
  what sin have I committed, you stupid ass?"
He said, "Look closely at your self and think it through
  admitting your own crime is better than such insults
You commit debauchery (*fisq*) and drink wine
  and always stare at beautiful young people
With the beat of a kettle drum and your wild song
  you smash the mirror of religious law against a stone
What kind of sainthood is this? What kind of holiness?
  Why are you so blind to your own obvious faults?"
Hussayn assured him, "Yes sir, you speak the absolute truth
  but tell me, why bother with such an inquisition
I may be a sinner in respect to the religious law
  but how have I injured you or the king who sent you?
If my actions are a sin, then I sin against God
  but I commit no crime against anyone, you or your king!"

He said with a groan, "As a rebuke and punishment
    yours will be a disgraceful death, driven through with a spike
A spike that will go into you from behind
    so that your soul will leave you from behind
Such a long spike I will use to impale you
    that it will go in from behind and come out your side
On this very day I'll do it, not a day later
    I'll sit you on a spike that opens the seam of your side!"[58]

The police chief's violent imagination turned to this unconventional execution in reaction to Shah Hussayn's flirtatious glances at his own son as retribution for bringing the homoerotic potential of his son to the surface. The perverse logic of patriarchy asserts that heterosexual order must be maintained by violence and rape: it is the absolute inverse of Shah Hussayn's playful, open and consensual practice.

This inversion links Shah Hussayn's lips to his anus in a pattern of patriarchal logic. Of course, lips are often associated with the female vulva in a pattern of patriarchal logic that leads many Muslim jurists to mandate a woman to cover her mouth with cloth in public just as she would cover her sexual organs. Although Shah Hussayn is portrayed kissing his beloved Madho, the texts never portray him as penetrating him anally or being penetrated, and the reasons for this lack of disclosure are not hard to understand—it would subject them to social stigma and possibly legal punishment. To be a man anally penetrated would reduce one to a status of less-than-man. The anxiety of men, that the anus may become a site of penetration like the vulva of women, is one readily evident in Islamic legal literature. It is very clear from their quarrel that the police chief assumes, rightly or wrongly, that Shah Hussayn is less than a real man and also engages in anal sex. Associating homosexuality with anal sex is a persistent feature of Islamic legal and moral writing, as immediate and condemning as it is unproved and unprovable.[59] This is a pattern not just in Islamic patriarchy but in modern Euro-American patriarchies as well. Through the nineteenth century, medical doctors produced forensic handbooks that documented not only physiological changes that, they claimed, were produced by "pederasty" but also physiological features that were congenital with homosexual orientation. Such signs linked the face to the genitalia in a strange code: they include voice timbre and lip contour, flabby buttocks, corkscrew-shaped penises, and "infundibular" anuses with a characteristic funnel shape.[60] As doctors increasingly took over from police the job of regulating sexual behavior, such manuals proliferated and continued to be reprinted Europe and America into the mid-twentieth century.

This patriarchal logic is imposed upon Shah Hussayn as the police chief leaps on the threat to turn the alleged site of penetration for pleasure into a site of penetration for pain, to the point of torture and death. The hagiographic source portrays Shah Hussayn's response to this threat in a startling way: "He addressed the police chief, laughing like a woman, 'For what reason are you treating me like this? What sin have I committed, you stupid ass (*kūdan*)?'" This is the only moment in the hagiographic literature when Hussayn's behavior is compared to that of a woman (as opposed to his own poems, in which he speaks in the voice of a woman). The comparison "laughing like a woman" may express Hussayn's frivolous and haughty way of laughing at the supposed moral seriousness of the police chief, rather than depicting literally an effeminate gesture or high pitch. However, suddenly taking on the tone of a woman's voice might be a satirical acknowledgment of the police chief's imposition of patriarchal limitations of manliness upon him, limitations that Shah Hussayn clearly will not abide by, rendering him vulnerable to sadistic punishment. It is a sick irony well known to those thrown in prison for being accused of homosexuality: the one reviled for enjoying anal penetration is punished through anal rape by those who supposedly reject anal intercourse.

The police chief certainly imagines that, as an empowered male and enforcer of social order, he upholds "Islamic values" in meting out such punishment. Since he responded to the mockery of Shah Hussayn's lips with a threat against his anus, let us follow his logic and focus on the issue of impaling (anal or otherwise). For clarification, we must turn to legal texts. The most famous medieval collection of legal decisions in South Asia was the *Fatāwa-yi Tātār-Khāniyya*, compiled in the fourteenth century.[61] The author, ʿAlīm ibn al-ʿAlāʾ Indrāpatī, attempted to make a comprehensive book of Hanafi legal judgment, including all previous authoritative judgments and replacing the separate books. This collection of fatwas gives us concise definitions of crimes and punishments according to Hanafi practice.

Crimes of a sexual nature are found in "Kitāb al-Ḥudūd" (" Chapter on Exemplary Punishments"). It is there that we must begin to find out if impaling was considered an Islamic punishment related to same-sex sexual intercourse, either *ḥadd* (exemplary punishment of a fixed form dictated by scripture) or *taʿzīr* (discretionary punishment of a flexible form determined by the will of authorities), in the Hanafi legal school as practiced in South Asia. The text gives the following definition of fornication (*zinā*): "Fornication that necessitates the *hadd* punishment is penetrative vaginal intercourse (*waṭaʿ fī qubl al-marʾa*) between a human male and human female who do not share a contract [of marriage or ownership] or anything resembling a contract, in which both participants are actively desiring intercourse."[62] The *hadd* punishment for fornication is lashing or stoning: lashing for an unmarried person or stoning for a married person (but never lashing and then stoning, as argued by other legal methods). Continuing in this passage, the author adds, "We have made this definition of 'fornication that necessitates the *hadd* punishment' contingent on the penetrative act being vaginal. If a man penetrates a woman anally or a man penetrates another man anally, this is not punishable with the *hadd* punishment, according to Abū Ḥanīfa. Rather, it falls under 'discretionary punishments' or *taʿzir*, such as imprisonment until repentance. This is so despite other legal schools saying that the *hadd* should be applied in the case of male penetrative anal intercourse."

As a responsible jurist, Indrapati notes difference of opinion. Jurists from the Mālikī and Shāfiʿī legal schools insist that anal sex between men is a *hadd* crime punishable by death (if the perpetrator is already married). Both interpret anal sex between men as a *hadd* crime, equivalent to *zina*, or fornication between a man and a woman.[63] In contrast, Indrapati adheres to the Hanafi position that although same-sex anal intercourse is an immoral act and is forbidden, it does not qualify as a *hadd* crime, for the Qur'an literally specifies a punishment only for fornication between a man and a woman. Hanafis insist that there should be no capital punishment but rather that government authorities are free to punish the act as they see fit.

Hadd penalties are by definition those penalties described explicitly by the Qur'an itself. Jurists are not supposed to exercise legal reasoning and analogy in cases of *hadd* penalties. Hanafi jurists were keenly aware of this problem and argued that anal intercourse between men could not justifiably be considered a *hadd* crime. "The punishment for fornication (*zina*) is known [from the Qur'an explicitly]. Since this act is known to be different [in nature] from fornication between a man and a woman, it should not be treated as a *hadd* crime equivalent to fornication. . . . This act [anal intercourse] is a kind of sexual intercourse in a bodily opening that has no relation to legal marriage and does not necessitate giving a dowry or determining parentage. Therefore it has no relation to the *hadd* punishment for fornication between a man and a woman (*zina*)."[64] The Hanafi jurists mounted a strong case against the Malikis, Shafiʿis, and Hanbalis and accused them of applying a *hadd* penalty for an act that was not defined in the Qur'an as a *hadd*, thereby committing a grave injustice. In his juridical commentary on the Qur'an, the

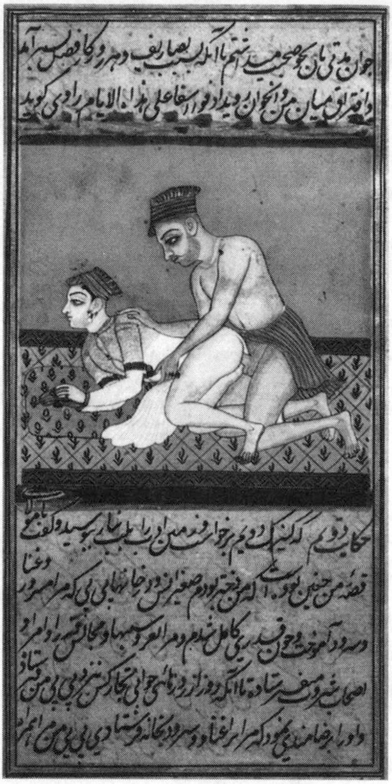

Miniature painting of two men engaged in anal sex, illustrating a story told by slave girls in Baghdad in an Indian text about erotic pleasure. Painted in Kashmir, India, in 1731. From Ḍiyāʾ al-Dīn Nakhshabī, *Ladhdhāt al-Nisāʾ*, ms. (Leiden: Library of the University of Leiden, Or. 14.650), fol. 55a.

Hanafi jurist al-Jassās argues that the Qurʾan specifies a *hadd* punishment of death for adultery and the punishment applies only to fornication between a man and a woman (not to anal sex between men or other types of sexual acts). He argues this position with two hadith reports attributed to the Prophet. "Whoever applies a *hadd* penalty to a crime that is not a *hadd* crime has committed injustice and oppression" and "The blood of a Muslim is not liable to be shed, except in these three cases: fornication (*zina*) after marriage, infidelity after adopting Islam, and murdering an innocent person."[65]

Despite this bold stand against the other legal schools, Indrapati notes that there have been differences of opinion within Hanafi ranks about male-to-male anal penetration. Indrapati's authoritative decision follows that of Abu Hanifa that male-to-male anal intercourse is not punishable by *hadd* because it is not *zina* by definition. There is a clear scriptural text (*naṣṣ*) about fornication between a man and woman but none about anal intercourse, so it falls under discretionary punishment. The fact that the Prophet's companions differed about suggested punishments for it (from burning, stoning, lashing, being thrown from a high place, buried alive, or imprisoned until death) shows that this act came under discretionary punishment and not *hadd* punishment. Indrapati notes that this disagreement among the early companions shows that they did not conceive of these suggestions as "independent legal reasoning (*ijtihād*) based on a clear scriptural reference" but rather as consensus based on their discretion. Therefore, anal intercourse between men cannot be considered *zina* or "fornication necessitating the *hadd* punishment," and the mandatory and inflexible punishment for *zina* should never be applied to an act that is not, by definition, *zina*.

In general, Abu Hanifa argued that *hadd* punishments should be tightly restricted, rather than defined broadly or applied widely. A bawdy story illustrates this important juridical principle: Once a man was walking through Baghdad carrying a wine flask until the police dragged him to court. The judge ruled that the *hadd* punishment for drinking wine should be applied, and that is lashing. Abu Hanifa, the founder of the Hafani legal method, heard of this and confronted the judge, demanding to know why the *hadd* penalty should be applied. The judge said, "Even if he did not actually drink, he was found carrying on his person the instruments for committing a crime punishable by the *hadd*, so the exemplary punishment should be applied and he should be lashed." Abu Hanifa retorted, "So stone him as well! Isn't he found carrying on his person the instruments for committing adultery also?" Indrapati follows the guidance of Abu Hanifa very closely in his authoritative decision for South Asian Muslims. So clearly, the threat of death against Shah Hussayn was not justified by reference to *hadd* punishment for adulterous penetrative intercourse.

If the threat against Shah Hussayn was not a *hadd* punishment, it may have been discretionary punishments (*taʿzir*). What is the discretionary punishment for anal intercourse between men? Is it applicable to other sexual acts between men, beyond the narrow definition of penetrative intercourse? *Taʿzir* punishments are set at the discretion of the Qadi but should never exceed in harshness the *hadd* penalty for analogous acts, according to Indrapati. However, impaling, as it was threatened against Shah Hussayn, is not a form of *taʿzir* punishment that is allowed by Hanafi jurists like Indrapati. He does not explicitly condone it and does not discuss it under "controversial topics" on which there is difference of juridical opinion. However, we find that medieval rulers in South Asia did apply impaling as punishment, beyond the bounds of the sharia and outside the jurisdiction of religious courts. They applied it to rebels and upstarts as a form of military punishment, meant to be public, horrifying, and deterrent to further rebellion.

However, impaling was never applied to interpersonal crimes, civil cases, or sexual indiscretions. So was the police chief, Malik ʿAli, threatening Shah Hussayn with punishment for sexual acts, for his countercultural sexuality, for creating public disorder, or for heresy? The issues are intermixed and hard to disaggregate. The hagiographic sources do not help us; they are less interested in the charges and more interested in the resolution of the drama. They picture Shah Hussayn confronting the police chief with a miracle: the chains kept falling from his ankles no matter how the police chief struggled to secure them. In the end, the police chief himself is impaled to death upon the command of the emperor for having failed him in some unrelated matter.

This violent end to one who threatens a saint was not the end of Shah Hussayn's trial. His further persecution, by authorities far more powerful than a mere police chief, might clarify for us how Shah Hussayn's society classified his trespasses. These inquisitions, by the chief jurist of the realm and then the emperor himself, show that Shah Hussayn's trespass was not "crime" defined by bodily or sexual comportment but rather was related more to belief (or heresy) and sincerity (or charlatanism). His case came before the Shaykh al-Islām, or chief religious scholar and jurist of the realm, ʿAbd al-Nabī Sulṭānpūrī. The judge approached Shah Hussayn as a "heretic" rather than for sexual improprieties and questioned him about the pillars of Islam. He escaped punishment by pointing out the moral flaws of the judge in a public ridicule of representatives of established religion. To test him, the judge asked him, "What are the five pillars of Islam?" Shah Hussayn replied, "The first is *tawhid* or belief in absolutely one God, to which both you and I comply. The second and third are prayer and fasting, which I ignore openly. The fourth and fifth and pilgrimage and alms, which you ignore in secret! Why are you more licensed to make an inquisition of me that I am to make an inquisition of you?"[66] To understand this bold retort, one must know more details about the political and theological controversy over the jurist's decisions.

The Shaykh al-Islam, ʿAbd al-Nabi Sultanpuri, was an avowedly sectarian Sunni who argued that the Shiʿa were not real Muslims. This was a very controversial position to take in his era. The Sunni Mughal empire was entering into intense political competition with the rival Safavid empire, which had come to rule in Iran as a Shiʿi state, even as the emperor Akbar tried to integrate Shiʿa nobles and military lords into his court. In this environment, the Shaykh al-Islam had made a very provocative ruling that the hajj to Mecca was no longer obligatory for all Muslims, since the Shiʿa had taken over Iran and the infidel Portuguese had taken over the Indian Ocean. It is to this decision that Shah Hussayn refers by pronouncing that the official jurist ignored the hajj, though it was part of the Muslim profession of faith. The Shaykh al-Islam, Sultanpuri, was also notorious for hoarding great wealth, which many suspected he had accumulated through graft and bribery; he was popularly alleged to avoid paying *zakāt*, obligatory alms, on the wealth that he accumulated. He persecuted other spiritual figures who accused him of graft and greed, like the communitarian Mawdawi leader Shaykh ʿAlāʾī, who said of him, "A fly which settles on shit is far better than a learned man who has made kings and emperors the object of his ambitions and flits about from door to door! Learning which exists for the sake of palace and garden is like a lamp for the night-loving thief."[67] A fly that lives on excrement is better than a scholar who lives on stolen or illegal money! Shah Hussayn mirrors such acidic critiques of the official jurist of the empire. This was the most damning of the allegations voiced by Shah Hussayn, for he claimed that the one who would judge him secretly avoided the most basic Islamic obligation for those who earn and save wealth.

With this public accusation of hypocrisy against the official, Shah Hussayn drove the Shaykh al-Islam to quiet his inquisition. However, rumor of Shah Hussayn's waywardness still circulated in the emperor Akbar's court. The emperor called him to court, upon accusations of trickery and rebellion. The royal inquisition centered on whether Shah Hussayn drank wine in public and whether he was miraculously able to turn wine into milk, water, tea, or punch. Sexuality or sex acts do not seem to have been foremost in this accusation. According to the hagiographic record of his life, Shah Hussayn was granted a miracle, which turned the emperor's goblet of wine into water and other beverages in his presence, convincing the emperor of the saint's authenticity despite his evident eccentricity.

Conclusion

When we look at these levels of persecution, we can conclude that the issue of sexual intimacy (whether perceived as sex acts that contravened religious law or sexuality that trespassed social norms) was foremost at the lowest level of authority—that of the police. Religious judges or rulers were more concerned with heresy or rebellion than with sexual order. And the police were not concerned with applying the sharia in theologically accurate and judicially subtle ways. Social order was perceived to reinforce religious morality, without nuanced discussion of the sharia. Most contemporary discussions of homosexuality or gender norms (most clearly in postrevolutionary Iran) refer immediately to the sharia. But in premodern times, this was not the modus operandi. Rather, sexual indiscretions were local concerns. They were policed by local authorities (perhaps often within households or neighborhoods without even involving the police) by means justified by patriarchal anxieties rather than sharia obligations.

In Shah Hussayn's story, as his case moves up the ladder of authority, the more protection he is granted and the more social authority he is able to command in Lahore. The admiration of Mughal nobles protects him from local censure, and reciprocally, he becomes a saint who protects Mughal rule. As Akbar acknowledged Hussayn as a great saint and one of the pillars of Lahore's spiritual well-being, protest against him in the circle of religious scholars quieted down. Nobles began to patronize him, seeking blessings for their various endeavors. As one of Akbar's chief nobles, ʿAbd al-Raḥīm Khān-i Khānān, was traveling with an army toward Sindh, he stopped in Lahore to receive the blessing of Shah Hussayn. The Mughal armies successfully conquered T͟hātta in Sindh, and Hussayn's reputation spread. To this day, Hussayn is seen as one of the patron saints of Lahore. His small tomb, shared with Madho, is the focus for a riotous celebration on the anniversary of his death, accompanied by frenzied drumming, ecstatic dance, and blazing fires. However, the contemporary residents of Lahore, even the custodians of his tomb, seem to have forgotten the erotic epic of his life story and the sexual nature of his love for Madho.

5

BODY REVIVED

The Heart of Ḥājji Imdādullah

Give the fullest when you measure and always weigh with fair balance,
for that is good and the most wholesome interpretation.
Do not imitate another in that of which you have no certain knowledge,
for surely he bears responsibility for all sensed
by the ear, the eye and the heart.
Do not walk over the earth with pride,
for you will never penetrate its depths
or reach the mountains in height.
—Qur'an 17:33–37

The Qur'an gives us moral guidance and advice: be fair, be honest, deal with others truthfully and generously. It uses marketplace imagery of weights and measures as standard themes to speak of justice, but it also links this moral advice to surprising images. Each individual bears absolute responsibility for everything sensed by ear, eye, and heart. Sensed by the heart? How is the heart a sense organ? Our common notion of five senses does not account for this; our sense of the heart as the seat of emotions does not account for the Qur'an's insistent centering of the heart as an indispensable organ of perception and moral judgment. If the heart cannot perceive clearly the human essence, then we might *walk over the earth with pride*, forgetting our humble origins and falling into the arrogance that we can penetrate its depths or reach the mountains in height. As Nakhshabi has said, "If you feel the heart is commander in chief / No no, one who takes heart gains the wisdom of true belief."[1]

In the previous chapter, we observed how Shah Hussayn abandoned the external constraints of the sharia to discover in this abandonment an expression of love and passion through the physicality of the body. Humility, for him, came from releasing all pretense to self-control, which is the root of hypocritical pride. Most Sufis, however, sought to gain intimacy to the presence of God through some sort of discipline. Most of them tempered emotive passion and erotic energy with a sense of internal control and civic rectitude. They saw the heart as the pivot of the balance of discernment in values more conducive to the public marketplace, rather than as the fountain of uncontrollable loving passion in values more conducive to secret intimacy.

One Sufi whose life story exemplifies the search of a balance between these seemingly incompatible values is Ḥājji Imdādullah Muhājir Makkī (1817–99). This chapter delves into his rich treatment of ritual to explore his anatomy of the heart as a moral organ. In Hajji Imdadullah's view, the heart is not just the font of vitality for the physical body. Rather, the dominant character of the heart is its constant motion; despite the appearance of its muscular mass, the heart is hollow, and that is the secret of its effectiveness. In his Sufi imagination, the heart is a *barzakh*, a place of meeting between two substances that contradict and yet relate. In the heart resides the spirit, and it acts as the interface between a person's body and personal presence. If the heart can be keep pure in intention and concentration, this interface between body and persona will be harmonious and tranquil, allowing the heart to reveal its deeper nature as the wellspring for God's presence in the world. Such profound ideas will become clearer as we explore Hajji Imdadullah's intriguing mixture of devotional meditation and imaginative anatomy.

This chapter on the heart not only explores Hajji Imdadullah's devotional manual and guide to the inner life, *Ḍiyā' al-Qulūb*, or "The Brilliance of Hearts." It also explores his life, for he lived at a historical *barzakh*, a boundary between two qualitatively different times for Muslims in South Asia: the early modern period, with continuity from medieval grandeur, and the modern period, with the humiliation of colonial European rule. The previous chapter, on Shah Hussayn's homoerotic play, suggested that the medieval and early modern periods were a time of flexibility and pluralism in Islamic communities, when understandings of gender were more fluid, norms of sexuality more flexible, and boundaries of communal allegiance more permeable. While this premodern fluidity should not be exaggerated (for Shah Hussayn ran up against boundaries that were usually enforced with violence, even as he transgressed them successfully), it is the sign of a strong polity governed by an optimistic elite and infused with self-confidence of its place in the political, economic, and moral order of the world. The Mughal empire was surely such a polity at its zenith and even through its decline. However, as European traders, especially the British East India Company, turned increasingly into colonial overlords in the nineteenth century, the Mughal polity seemed less sure, its Muslim nobility less confident, and its Sufis and saints less central to the moral order of the world. As the East India Company expanded from a trade network into a military force, it reduced the Mughal emperor to a vassal and reduced Muslims to a disempowered minority in a non-Islamic and rapidly modernizing state.

In this new colonial modern order, the fluidity of identities that we noted in the revious chapter evaporated. Categories became more fixed, and socio-religious boundaries became more reified. As the Mughal empire weakened, Muslims began to assert very different notions of "orthodoxy"; voices of theological rigidity that were minorities in the Mughal heyday amplified to define the majority belief. This trend accelerated in the aftermath of the Mughal revivalist uprising in 1857 (called the Sepoy Rebellion by the victorious British and called the First War of Independence by later Indian nationalists) as Muslims retreated into defensive theology, legal formalism, and critical anxiety over whether their ambiguity-embracing theology had been the secret cause of their political decline.

Hajji Imdadullah lived during the final collapse of the Mughal empire and the triumphant assertion of colonial modernity in South Asia. His life is emblematic of the *barzakh* between the early modern and modern eras. His discussion of the heart shows signs of substantial continuity with late medieval and early modern Sufi devotion but also indicates distinct changes in discursive framework; he was trying to recast Sufi devotion to allow it remain a force for social and moral meaning in the new era of modernity. As a Sufi leader and saint, he took on the role of a cardiologist surveying an ailing patient, the body politic of Islamic society in South Asia. His ritual manual presents meditations and contemplations for restoring the body through clearing its arteries and reviving its heart, as if he were presenting surgical techniques to avert the threat of massive cardiac arrest. In refashioning medieval Sufi discourse in a modern framework, he hoped not only to preserve his Sufi tradition but also to lead a Sufi revival in colonial South Asia.

This chapter examines his images of the heart in order to understand how he did this and assess in what ways he might have been successful. It looks inward for a deep reading of the text of the devotional manual for which he is famous, backward toward the long Sufi tradition of imagining the heart, and then, drawing on hagiographic accounts of his life, outward into the political arena in which Imdadullah was a religious authority as a Muslim saint in times of cataclysmic change.

The Heart of Ritual Is the Body

Hajji Imdadullah created a ritual that would discipline the body. Imdadullah's ritual manual focuses on the heart. As the Qur'an says, *Do not walk over the earth with pride, for you will never penetrate its depths or reach the mountains in height,* Imdadullah replies that, if one lives with humility rather than pride, one can reach the depths of the heart and rise above the mountains of the earth in spiritual ascension. If the body is the pivot point between moral order and cosmic order, the heart is the pivot point of the body. It is the very spot where God meets the world that is "other-than-God." It is the subtle point that gives creative energy to bring being forth from nonbeing; it is the moral criterion that separates light from darkness. In his manual, Imdadullah asserts that if one can concentrate on the heart, purify it, center it, and master it, then one can truly encounter God "face to face."

In this assertion, Imdadullah invokes a hadith in which God is reported to have said, "My earth and my heaven do not encompass me, but the heart of my faithful servant does encompass me." In saying that the heart is sacred because of its hollowness, rather than its muscular solidity, Imdadullah agrees with the assessment of our Sufi guide, Nakhshbi. "What is the heart? Arab anatomical manuals state that the heart is an oblong muscle, shaped like a pine cone, positioned in the center of the chest with its top tilted to the left side, red as a pomegranate. But what is the heart in reality? Leader of the Body! Friend of the Form! Ruler of the Organs! Proof of the Parts! Seed of the Flesh! . . . The Second Throne of God! The Cap of Light! Yes, ever since Adam was seated upon the dais on vice-regency, it is known that the Throne of God is within the human breast."[2] If the heart of a faithful servant (*'abd*) is the privileged place of manifestation of God, then religious ritual should concentrate on the heart. Accordingly, Imadadullah suggests meditations linked to physical movements to create a concentration that centers consciousness on the heart, specifically on rectifying the heart. The results are not merely spiritual or ethical but anatomically physical.

To achieve this spiritual awakening, ethical revival, and physical realignment, Imdadullah urges the ritual practitioner to "die to the self" before actual death. As Imdadullah mentions death, its methodical recollection and internalization, he asserts that the body itself can be transformed and the potential virtuous self within the body can be unleashed. "Repeat three times 'God give me light, bestow upon me light, increase for me the light, and make me myself light.' . . . As you allow your body to lighten and feel at ease, imagine you have died, and gather all your attention from head to foot, as you inhale and exhale, every hair on your body keeps expressing, that One is, One is, One alone is."[3] With such ritual advice, Imdadullah illustrates his mystical method. By advocating that one die to the self, mystics loosen the habitual bonds that bind the self to the socially constituted body, providing the space and freedom to rediscipline the body, to train it in a new set of stances, a new pattern of postures, a new repertoire of gestures. In short, mystics offer a method of acquiring a whole new bodily habitus, a new ground of being, driven not by selfish desires but rather by the embodiment of virtues. Such an enactment of death and the transformation of the body most clearly play out through ritual. His devotional manual, "The Brilliance of Hearts," gives instructions for the proper means of recitation, motion, and contemplation that can realign the heart, revive the body, and allow the practitioner to "imagine you have died" to the self.

Manuals of ritual devotion have received very little attention by scholars in Islamic and Sufi studies. However, in the context of Sufi imaginings of the human body, ritual manuals take on a new importance. Imdadullah's program for religious exercise involves invoking religious meaning through bodily actions. This is the realm of "ritual" as defined in the anthropology of religion. Talal Asad has keenly observed that ritual is an abused category in the anthropology of religion.[4] Western scholars of the late nineteenth century, with Victorian and Protestant biases, defined ritual as empty habitual action through which an objective observer could interpret the practitioner (as one would a text) in order to "read" the underlying reality of social institutions. They saw the acts of people as mere symbols for the reality of society, which was the more abstract, more comprehensive, and ultimately more important entity. This definition of ritual effectively effaces the practitioners and empties them of subjective authenticity. On the other hand, it authorizes and empowers the anthropological analyst who claims to understand the hidden meaning of ritual in order to decode the ritual acts and interpret the ritual actors.

In contrast, prior to the categorization of the modern science of anthropology, ritual was a script to be performed through rigor and discipline in order to enact or embody some virtue. In Talal Asad's words, ritual is the apt performance of what is prescribed, and it depends on intellectual and practical disciplines. In his 1935 essay "Techniques of the Body" the French sociologist Marcel Mauss attempted to specify how a person's body acts as the fulcrum between subjective consciousness and communal solidarity, as discussed in the introduction to this book. Asad has recovered Mauss's insights to reexamine religious ritual without the residue of Protestant theology that earlier anthropologists had enshrined in their basic assumptions. His theoretical sketch attempts to build on Mauss's assertion that there are body techniques that create religious experience. Asad's primary insight is that religious meaning does not usually manifest as a system external to those who venerate it through ritual, thus inviting analysis to decode it; rather, religious meaning is embodied as virtue, and virtue is enacted through the ritual of bodily performance, within the limits and training of authoritative disciplines.

Hajji Imdadullah's "The Brilliance of Hearts" illustrates Asad's theoretical critiques, for it is a true ritual manual in the premodern sense of the term. It lays out methods of training, scripts for proper recitation, and directories for the apt performance of actions that will transform the person who undergoes their rigor. It is a ritual manual that circulated widely in the nineteenth century and continues to find an active audience among South Asian Muslims today.[5] The first chapter, called "Exposition of Detailed Conditions of Recitations, Exercises and Contemplations of the Chishti Masters," shows how a spiritual guide (*murshid*) should embark on teaching a disciple (*murīd*) how to recite the names of God in meditation. "The spiritual guide should set his own heart facing [the disciple's] heart, and apply the rhythmic beat of the essential name of God to [the disciple's] heart. While doing this, he should imagine that 'the other is receiving the nature and disposition of the recitation at hand simply by facing me.' Imagine that his recitation is penetrating [the disciple's] heart and being conducted within it. Hurl one hundred and one such rhythmic beats, until desire and the heat of recitation affect the other's heart, and it begins to move with the rhythmic movement of recitation. After this, the disciple should be given a recitation appropriate to his or her level of experience, and the disciple will become occupied in the exercises that the guide instructs."[6] From the very first instance, Imdadullah focuses upon the heart. It is a physical organ that has shape, motion, volume, heat, and rhythm. It is a sensory organ, attuned to the intuitive transmission of information beyond the scope other sensory organs. It is a perceptive organ, receptive to the ideals, images, and archetypes that invest material forms with life and meaning.

After the disciple's heart becomes cleared of selfish concerns and routine anxieties, he or she can begin practicing basic meditation. Its ritual involves controlling and modulating the flow of blood in the arteries while reciting certain names of God. By starting with the extremities, one can work inward toward the core. One uses the tongue to recite the name of God while pushing that name inward toward the pith of conscience. One uses the eyes to visualize the appearance of the name of God while opening the vision of the heart to such a manifestation of God. One uses the pulse and arteries near the surface of the skin to reach deep within, to contact the heart as the source of intuitive knowledge and the locus of the spirit. "The disciple should shut the eyes, and lay both hands on both knees, keeping the fingers loosely unfolded, until the image of the name of God appears. With the big toe of the right foot, put pressure on the *kimas* artery, an artery that lies within the left knee and is connected to the inner heart, since its motion and heat affects the inner heart. After applying pressure, summon up humility, lowliness and presence of heart. Then say, 'O living One, O everlasting One, there is no divinity except you, I implore that you enliven my heart with the light of the knowledge of you, Allah, Allah, Allah.' After this, joy and delight will appear . . . from the deliciousness of *dhikr*, the disciple may go senseless."[7] The intense pursuit of such ritual meditations will initiate a paradoxical experience. As the disciple focuses concentration upon the heart to the exclusion of the wider world, ordinary sensory perception, and routine bodily experiences like pain and hunger, the heart itself seems to expand and engulf the body.

Other body parts begin to take on the special qualities of the heart, which might startle the disciple. Imdadullah warns his readers: "When the reciter achieves such perfection in recitation that the tongue can feel the movement of the inner heart, then the movement of the heart spreads throughout the whole body. The initial sensation of such spreading is when any limb starts to feel a throbbing motion that is normally particular only to the heart. Sometimes the hand will begin to move and throb without stimulation, sometimes the foot or sometimes the head. This throbbing will increase in intensity to the point that the reciter's entire world begins to appear to be in motion as well. Once this motion begins, the light of recitation spreads throughout the whole body, and an instant later encircles and encloses the whole body."[8] As a spiritual guide, Hajji Imdadullah cautions those who read and practice his devotional manual to beware of the side effects of such heart treatment. Intense focus upon the heart interrupts our normal reliance upon reason and calculation. It can also interfere with our routine engrossment in sensory perception. "On account of this recitation, various spiritual disclosures will come upon the disciple. Strange occurrences will be unveiled and presented themselves. He or she will sometimes cry or sometimes laugh, and sometimes be surprised or alarmed with perplexity.

The disciple should try to ignore these states and simply remain absorbed in recitation and cognition. If God's help surrounds and accompanies the disciple, sometimes the whole body will be found to be reciting holistically, and all the limbs and organs will consort in fellowship with the inner heart. This recitation is known as 'the recitation of combined and united limbs.'"[9] One might hear voices, one's own or those of others, while in this state of bewildering integration. But Hajji Imdadullah warns that the disciple should ignore these side effects as distraction and keep one's focus intently upon the heart.

This is the basic formula he provides for *dhikr*, or recitation. His manual continues to give variations of its practice, with different bodily postures and verbal formulas. Like a doctor, he prescribes different variations of recitation for different kinds of disease, which is spiritual "rust" that encases, stiffens, and ruins the heart, which, when healthy, is pliant and gently persistent. Before embarking on the details of different varieties of recitation, he offers this definition of the principle of recitation. "In the terminology of the Sufis, *dhikr* is that process through which humans recollect God by forgetting everything other than God. This is the process through which humans collect the intimate nearness of God and fellowship with God within the presence of the inner heart. This type of human recall and recollection is indicated when the Qur'an says, 'I am with my servant when he recalls me and his two lips are set in motion by me,' and 'I am seated in company with whoever recollects me' and *Glorify God in the early morning and in the evening* (Q 19:11). Become fully absorbed with the fullest concentration in the remembrance of God, so that you become completely unconscious of the self and enter into the company of *those who recall God while standing, sitting and laying down* (Q 3:191)."[10] In this definition of *dhikr*, the elements of ritual recitation come to stand in for the elements of the physical body. Its rhythm first imitates the beat of the heart, then becomes integrated with it, and finally replaces it such that the beating heart is actually conducting perpetual recitation. Likewise, recitation first taps the circulation of blood, then integrates with its flow through all the members and organs of the body, and finally replaces it, such that "*dhikr* will become the very substance of your life."

The most basic and universal variety of *dhikr* is the repetition of "No god but God" (*lā ilāha illā allāhu*). The Prophet Muhammad taught this meditative practice, with its inherently rhythmic rhyme, to his cousin and follower, ʿAli, and told him it was the most efficacious means of worship. All Sufi communities adopt it as a teaching of ʿAli, who figures prominently in their lineages of spiritual masters. It is repeated aloud or silently, with motion of the tongue or with motion of the head, along with drumming rhythm, instrumental melody, or in contemplative silence. Each variation of recitation has a different spiritual effect, and conscientious practice of them can act as a steed to carry the disciple in ascension from gross materiality to subtle spirituality and into the presence of God. "Recitation of the tongue is called body-centered recitation (*jismī*), while thinking is called self-centered recitation (*nafsī*), whereas contemplation is called heart-centered recitation (*qalbī*), and witnessing is called spirit-centered recitation (*rūḥī*). Finally clearly beholding divinity face to face is called the recitation of the inner secret (*sirrī*)." Though these levels seem to imply an ascending hierarchy of value and subtlety, in fact each variety of recitation at each level shares a common process and goal—"During this recitation, at the time of [saying] 'No god' the reciter should strive to negate all things, and at the time of [saying] 'but God' the reciter should strive to rectify all the organs and limbs of the body."[11]

Hajji Imdadullah turns to the detailed instruction of recitation according to the Chishti Sufi way in a chapter called "Exhaling and Inhaling and Recitation of God's Essential Name (Allah)." In it, we can observe the careful orchestration of bodily postures, rhythmic motions, and litanies of scriptural words. After completing the nightly canonical prayer,

> Raise your hands and with humility and lowliness recite the following three or five or six times: "O God, refine my heart from any other than you and illumine my heart with the light of the knowledge of you." . . . Then sit down [cross-legged] and take your right foot's big toe and those near it, and with these toes firmly compress the *kimas* artery [behind the left knee]. Keep both hands on your knees while facing in the direction of Mecca (*qibla*). . . . Bow your head so that your forehead comes very near your left knee. As you say "No god," move your forehead very near your right knee. Then in taking a single breath, imagine three rhythmic beats. Bowing your head toward the center [of your the belly] imagine that, "I ignore and leave behind me everything other than God." In releasing the breath, direct the rhythm of "but God" onto the heart with all your might, imagining, "My heart overflows with the passion and love of God."[12]

Just as the human body is a microcosmic mirror of the social world, it is also a mirror of the celestial world. In the human body are realms analogous to satanic, selfish, angelic, and divine forces. Imdadullah describes the path of the reciter's phrase as a spiral, starting in the left thigh, being drawn up to the right shoulder, and thrust forcefully down onto the heart within the left breast.

> In the beginning, at the time of saying "but God," you should imagine that there is no other object of worship (*lā maʿbūd*) but God, and in the middle imagine that there is no other object of desire (*lā maqṣūd*) but God, while at the end of completing the cycle, imagine that there is no other existence (*lā mawjūd*) but God—that God is all (*hama ūst*). . . . It should be understood that satanic thoughts reside in the left knee, and selfish thoughts reside in the right knee, while angelic thoughts reside in the right shoulder and finally, divinely compassionate thoughts dwell in the heart [nearer to the left shoulder]. Thus saying "No god" drives back satanic temptations of the left knee. Taking [this phrase] to the right knee repulses selfishness. Drawing it up to the right shoulder inhales angelic thought. And with saying "but God" you exhale divinely compassion thoughts [toward the heart].[13]

By circulating recited words in *dhikr* throughout these regions and rigorously "retaining" one's own breath (*ḥabs-i dam*), one can integrate the body and repulse the forces of darkness while invoking those of light, transforming the body from a biological organism into a moral vessel. Breath, speech, and motion all revolve around the heart in this ritual of purification and concentration.

Arteries of Temptation

Having looked deeply into Imdadullah's ritual manual, we can now look back from it into the past legacy that it creatively perpetuates. We can do this by focusing on the image of Shaytan, the tempter or Satan, dwelling within the body and threatening the purity of the heart. In Chapter 1, we encountered the Chishti Sufi Nizam al-Din Awliyaʾ, recounting a parable of how Shaytan's young son Khannas entered into the body of Adam and all this children. Imdadullah does not quote this story but does elaborate on the image in very dramatic ways as he describes the physiological changes engendered by active *dhikr*, or ritual recitation of God's names.

> Those arteries which are attached to the heart are rich in oily fats which block the arteries. Only through means of these oily deposits does Shaytan [Satan] pour whispers of doubt into the heart at that time when the blood is stalled in its flow. Therefore, through the movement and internal

> heat generated by recitation [when accompanied by retention of breath], the oily lubrication of the arteries is made soft, fluid and flexible; only then is the heart kept pure and Shaytan's attempts are in vain. Shaytan appears like a serpentine dragon, and its snakelike head is noxiously poisonous and has pain-inflicting barbs. When the disciple commits a misdeed or eats any forbidden thing, the serpent Shaytan's power increases and it slithers, coiling around in the outer limits of the disciples own heart, such that its venom seeps in, affecting the inner heart and giving rise to an obscuring darkness. However, if the disciple repents and engages effort in retention of breath, then Shaytan becomes weakened and illumination and purity are born in the inner-heart.[14]

Like the female Christian mystics discussed in Chapter 2, Hajji Imdadullah imagines the forces of temptation, seduction, and evil to be in the shape of a serpent. However, rather than asserting that the serpent is external to the human person, he pictures these forces to be internal to the human body. However, this is no reason to despise the body itself, for the serpent of temptation dwells in the arteries around the heart and is an integral part of the vital power of the body itself.

Rather than rejecting or denigrating the body itself, Imdadullah urges us to use the body under the care of self-control, for when engaged in ritual action, the body itself can keep the tempting serpent at bay, just as eating in moderation and daily exercise can keep disease at bay. Retaining the breath, by saying "No god but God" with every moment of inhale and exhale, is the means to care for the body and render harmless the serpent within. "Draw in breath through the navel, hold it in the inner heart, and extract the phrase 'no god' from the heart. Then envision that Shaytan is coiled around the heart like a dragon; envision that the scissors of 'no god' seize and capture Shaytan's breath. From up on the right shoulder, take up the negative exception of 'but God' and thrust it down on the heart. As you do this imagine that the beating blow [of *lā*, meaning "no," which is an integral part of *illā*, meaning "but"] has fallen on Shaytan's head. As you do this imagine that its head is retreating little by little, forced out of the environs of the heart. . . . Shaytan will be overwhelmed and the heart will be luminous with the lights of recollection."[15]

Imdadullah describes the coiled serpent within the blood stream as Shaytan, who is internal to human nature, since it is internal to the human body. To counter this serpent of delusion and temptation, he prescribes a coiled spiral of positive energy engendered by the passage of recitation's negation and affirmation as it circulated through the body's limbs, gaining momentum and force before hammering the invading Shaytan clear of the cardiac center. This is his spiritual medicine for ethical *atherosclerosis*, the clogging of the cardiac arteries with fiberofatty plaque, as the prime metaphor for spiritual murk.

Imdadullah's use of atherosclerosis indicates his surprising engagement with modernity.[16] However, his ritual manual also stands in continuity with a long tradition of Sufi ritual practice and is a creative effort to preserve the tradition. It is based upon a past model, the text of Shaykh Niẓām al-Dīn Awrangābādī (died 1729 C.E.), whose composition *Niẓām al-Qulūb*, "The Harmonic Order of Hearts," is the first Chishti work on how to perform recollection of God's names, with great ritual attention to bodily posture and motion. Before this, masters passed such instruction secretly and orally to their disciples, while written treatises were mainly intended to defend the practice of meditation as Islamic by showing its theoretical roots in the Qur'an and prophetic example (*sunna*). For this reason, the author goes to some pains to justify his setting these practices down in writing.[17] Imdadullah did not have to apologize, since the saint from Awrangabad had already cleared the way for such ritual manuals almost a century and a half before. Imdadullah named his ritual manual "The Brilliance of Hearts" in clear continuity with prior "The Harmonic Order of Hearts." If Nizam al-Din Awrangabadi collected the pearls of meditative practices and strung them together in harmonious order, it was left to Imdadullah to simple repolish them after some intervening years to restore the brilliance of their luster.

The textual tradition from which Imdadullah's ritual manual grows is not terribly old. However, as he invokes the serpent of evil within the blood stream, he participates in a tradition that is much, much older. His creative use of this image shows his inventive appropriation of a long tradition of Sufi imagination of evil within the human body. Probably the earliest and starkest of such images comes from al-Ḥakīm al-Tirmidhī (died 898 C.E.), the renowned early Sufi from Central Asia and the first Muslim mystic to composed a comprehensive spiritual autobiography.[18] It reveals a spiritual seeker of astounding audacity and loneliness as he abandoned worldly life to journey toward the center of his own heart. By his own account, al-Tirmidhi became a teacher in jurisprudence (*ʿilm al-raʾy*) and religious traditions (*ʿilm al-athār*) at the tender age of 8. At roughly 27, he set out from his hometown of Tirmidh (near Balkh in the Iranian highlands) for Mecca. Throughout the journey, he collected hadith reports, showing his commitment to worldly asceticism of being a religious scholar and jurist. However, his stay in Mecca marked a turning point in his life—he was overwhelmed by the desire to leave the world behind him and consecrate himself only to God.

Having returned home, he turned to the Sufi path, which was not yet codified or organized into systematic "brotherhoods" in his day. He began to search for a spiritual guide and heard of people who were called sages who knew God by intuitive understanding (*ahl al-maʿrifa*), and he read a book about training the self (*riyāḍat al-nafs*). His outer life played out between domestic retreat and excursions into the desert to rein in his lust impulses, but he never found companions or a spiritual guide.[19] In his apparent isolation, al-Tirmidhi unleashed the creative energy of his theological and mystical imagination. He wove a specifically Islamic form of mysticism from the strands of Gnostic tradition that were still vividly current in his home region of Balkh, which had been a vibrant center of Mahayana Buddhism and Manichaean thought before the population largely converted to Islam. He found the Qur'anic contrast between light and darkness to reinforce the older Gnostic tradition of seeing human life as a spiritual struggle between the ontological forces of darkness and light, forces that have the human body and soul as their battleground. In al-Tirmidhi's mystical theology, God's being is indescribable and indiscernible and can be indicated only by terms like quiddity (*hūwiyya*), inwardness (*bāṭin*), or unseen otherness (*ghayb*). In contrast, God has fixed attributes (*ṣifat*) that form the outer aspect of God's being, attributes that are realms of light. He thought of the light realms of the attributes as hierarchically ordered, which emerge one from the other in descending manifestations that suggest a Neoplatonic system of emanations that link the immaterial divinely real One to the material worldly multiplicity of otherness, the world in which we struggle to live. "God made man hollow and then placed within him the spirit, the carnal soul, life, power, knowledge and awareness (*maʿrifa*), understanding, memory, comprehensions and astuteness, reason, insight, intelligence, vision and lust, compassion, gentleness, kindness and love, joy, anger and indignation. Then God demanded that man make use of all this and bring it forth from his interior into the open by means of his bodily limbs."[20] These attributes of life and awareness are reflections of God's attributes; al-Tirmidhi calls them lights that have a source in God's unbounded being and a reflection in the human being bounded by a body. "Each of these things that is laudable and worthy of God, God brought into existence as one of [God's] own attributes. The attributes are lights. One light is for life, another is for compassion. One is for gentleness, one for joy, one for patience, one for contentment. One is for pride, one for cleverness, one for love and one for might and one for wealth. All of these are lights and each light is a separate realm. From each realm there came forth that thing which appeared at the creation. . . . God brought forth the attributes on behalf of His servants so that something of their lights would reach His servants, something which would be visible to their bodies and in their world."[21] By presenting the divine attributes as realms of light, al-Tirmidhi harks back to Gnostic models. The cosmos has originated through the interweaving work of the luminous realms of the attributes. Hence, the created world is an ever shifting series of manifestations of the divine attributes—it is not God in God's indescribably oneness but also cannot be said to be other-than-God.

This is the nature of the cosmos but also the nature of humanity, for the human being is a microcosmic reflection of the macrocosmic universe. The ultimate goal of the human being is to overcome the darkness of lustful delusion, which comes from the illusion of self-sufficiency and autonomy. Rather than thinking the self to be independent, we should come to realize our utter dependence on God's being. We need to see ourselves, like the wider universe, as a manifestation of God's names and qualities. With insightful knowledge, mystical intuition, and rigorous ascetic discipline, we can replace each selfish quality of our lower human nature with the divine qualities of God's luminous nature, raising ourselves in an ascension (*miʿraj*) of spiritual journeying back to our originally lofty and noble nature. Al-Tirmidhi records his own experience of such blissful ascension in his autobiography: "Along the way [to my house], my heart became open in a manner which I am unable to describe. It was as if something happened in my heart and I became happy and took delight in it . . . until the sky with its stars and its moon came down close to the earth. And while this was taking place, I invoked my Lord. I felt as if something was made upright in my heart, and when I experienced this sweetness, my interior twisted itself and contracted, and one part of it was twisted over the other because of the force of the pleasure and it was pressed together. This sweetness spread through my loins and through my veins. It seemed to me that I was close to the location of God's Throne. And this remained my practice every night until morning . . . meanwhile, my heart became strong through this."[22]

According to al-Tirmidhi, the higher nature, which should animate humankind, has its center in the heart (*qalb*). The lower nature with its representations, the impulse-soul or the self, has its seat in the belly. The lower nature originated from the earth's dust; it is the imprisonment of humanity in the soil of materiality (*turābiyya*) that must be left behind or tamed.

The higher faculties of humanity are light and originate from supersensory worlds. The light nature can come into effect only if humanity undertakes the deliberate trial to push back its dust nature, which would like to overwhelm the light nature.[23] The anxiety that humankind is a light nature hidden in matter is of ancient Gnostic origin, though al-Tirmidhi sees it as providing an ethical urgency for the moral life that is completely consistent with the Qur'an's message.

The human soul belongs to the earthly nature, whose outstanding quality is greedy craving (*shahwa*) and desire (*hawā'*). The soul and desire are empowered by Shaytan, whom he sees as a personified force of delusion and darkness that challenges the light-radiating power of God. In contrast to the rest of the body, especially the belly and genitalia, al-Tirmidhi sees the heart as the seat of the higher faculties: in the heart dwell the spirit (*rūḥ*) and reason (*ʿaql*), which are the seat of the awareness of God. Selfish desire, especially the lusts of the body, plunges the heart's higher nature down to the depths of imprisonment in the darkness of matter that is other-than-God. The pernicious effect of greedy desire is conditioned by the nature of materiality: it is Satan's nature and originates from hell. As al-Tirmidhi describes how the soul is incited to lust, we can see him evoke the image of the satanic serpent within the bloodstream in very vivid terms. "Desire raises itself from hell's fires and passes by the object of desire, which surrounds the fires of hell. It carries the glitter, the joy of the world, the pleasure and the delight of the lust object in the interior of the human being, in order to lead these things to the soul. When the soul takes them up, desire becomes its riding mount which is the breath of hellfire when it breathes. The soul rides then on the breath of hellfire, on the desire whose vanguard is the pleasure perception."[24] The soul itself, and the desire that it mounts to ride down into the hell of imprisonment in materiality, are the enemies of humanity's original light nature.

But there is a third enemy, Satan, who weaves in the middle between the soul and desire. Satan has personally invaded humanity: "God kneaded man's clay and formed him with His own hand. . . . Then God breathed into him of His spirit. And that was the spirit [breath] of life and of the good carnal soul. But the carnal soul slipped away and settled in the abdomen. . . . God gave him two nostrils to breathe and smell with, and a stomach which He made the house of nourishment. One door to this house is joined to the palate, and there are two doors in the lower part of the body. Of those two doors, one is the exit for man's progeny, and the other is the exit for waste and what is harmful. This is so because when Satan seduced man and made him eat of the tree, Satan found access to his stomach by means of the morsel man ate in obedience to him. So Satan settled in his stomach, and since that day what is in man's stomach stinks because of Satan's filth."[25]

From his seat in the belly and loins, the filth of Satan's presence spreads through the flow of humanity's blood and threatens the heart. The description of how the devil mixes with the blood in the arteries is drastic. "As a consequence of the violence of the flow (*shiddat as-sayr*) and the surge of the flow, the Shaytan in the straits of the blood vessels begins to sweat... its vileness leaves behind pollution in the arteries, the water and blood of the arteries is corrupted by its perspiration."[26] The pleasure perception of the soul, incited by desire, creates an impression that rises from the belly (the seat of the soul) upward and imprints its dark stain in the form of smoke and fire upon the originally clean and pure light nature (that is concentrated in the heart). In this way, al-Tirmidhi sees the reality of hellfire as completely immanent in the personality—it is a moral reality played out through the drama of human anatomy and the struggle for mastery between different organs of the body.

Al-Tirmidhi was an early exponent of the style of Sufism that became known as "Khurasani," which developed in northern Iran and Central Asia. It emphasized that Satan the tempter dwelled in the bloodstream and was energized by lusts and the adrenaline rush that accompanies lustful thoughts and actions. It nurtured a Manichaean urgency, preaching the need for absolute ascetic mastery of the body in order to control passions and the thoughts that fuel them. In contrast, the Sufism that developed in Iraq, which emphasized subtle intellectual theories and urbane civility, saw Satan as a mere pawn of God's master plan, for how could a second spiritual force of temptation and darkness ever challenge the absolute Oneness of God's power? The Khurasani Sufi masters were more rugged, more athletic in their ascetic exercises, and more pessimistic in their assessment of intellect and reason's power to temper the lusts of the body.

The Chishti community of Sufis emerged from the Khurasani tradition of Islamic mysticism and took its name from the Khwājagān-i Chisht, the spiritual masters of Chisht, a small town in Afghanistan that was part of the wider Khurasani cultural region. Their teachings were brought to South Asia by Shaykh Muʿīn al-Dīn Chishtī, who moved from Afghanistan to Rajasthan in the thirteenth century. Settling on the fringe of the Islamic Empire, he initiated a vibrant synthesis of rugged Khurasani Sufis and Indic forms of rapturous musical devotion. The resulting teachings, which characterize the Chishti Sufi community, are "to be stern with oneself" with rigorous austerities and bodily discipline "while being gentle with all others" in passionately gentle service to others, refinement through poetry and music, and uncritical love for humanity.

It is to Muʿin al-Din that the Sabiri branch of the Chishti community, to which Imdadullah belonged, traces its lineage of spiritual initiation. From his sayings and example Sabiris absorbed the ancient teaching that evil resided in the body, yet they also had a more optimistic assessment of the body's capacity for good. Spiritual cultivation was not just a matter of blocking the rise of Satan from the belly toward the heart but could actually open new gateways within the arteries to invite in-pourings of divine presence. Chishti Sufis attributed to Muʿin al-Din an epistle on the arteries, their anatomical place and spiritual function and how the meditative breath can energize the circulation of blood to enliven the heart and repel the darkness of habitual negligence. The epistle is entitled "On the Horizons and in the Selves," subtly referring to a Qurʾanic verse, *we will show them our signs on the horizons and in themselves* (Q 41:53), to explain how everything God created in the cosmos is mirrored in the human body; understanding the essential unity of these two realms is the key to seeing both as signs of God, which is the path to achieving union with God. "'This treatise explains the arteries that are in the human being. The prime artery is the artery of life. Then come two major arteries, known in Hindawi by the names *ingalā* and *pingalā*. After these branch into 360 arteries and after this branch into 16,000 arteries. Though we say there are three main arteries, they are in reality connected as one. This is called *sukhumnā* and it has its origin from the navel (*nāf*). A second artery extends inward from the navel but the origin of the *sukhumna* is [the umbilical connection of] the navel. It runs beneath the navel and is connection to the two main arteries."[27]

The reason to detail the path of these arteries is to follow them back to the source of life itself, the divine presence that sustains one. One's connection with God is like an embryo's connection with its mother's womb—life flows freely into it from another. But once the separation of birth happens, the umbilical connection falls away, the navel solidifies, and the infant begins to gain consciousness of being autonomous and alienated from its original source. "The goal is to [enliven these arteries] by drawing breath in from beneath the navel and pushing it up toward the heart by means of the *sukhumna* artery. Having reached the pinnacle [this breath] becomes spread and diffused through the flesh and skin. Having done this, gateways should open up, because there are nine gateways in the human body. . . . After the main gateway, which is the [umbilical connection] through which the mother's womb interpenetrates a person's body, there are six gateways in the folds of the navel, three to the right and three to the left. After that, these six gateways open. Then it [the navel] becomes solid."[28] As an adult, one needs to reopen these gateways, now found within the body and associated with the circulation of blood through the arteries. The goal of meditative practice is to find and open these gateways through a careful cultivation of breathing to cleanse the heart and imaginative pressure upon the arteries that connect the outside world to the heart and the heart to the rest of the body.

As one pushes the meditative breath upward from the navel and heart, according to Muʿin al-Din, the breath passes through twenty-eight resting places, each called a station (*manzil*). Passing through these stations, one moves not only through the tissues of the human body but through elements of the cosmos and varieties of sensation: for five stations are associated with the element of earth and the color ochre, five stations are associated with water and the color white, eight stations are associated with air and the color blue, five stations are associated with fire and the color red, and five stations are associated with light and the color black. Clearly the twenty-eight stations through which the meditative breath passes in reaching the heart mirror the passage of the moon through its cycle from fullness to fullness, which is the basis for the Islamic calendar. And the 360 arteries through which the breath is "spread and diffused" through the flesh of the body mirror passage of the sun through its cycle of 360 days.

According to this treatise, subduing the human ego through meditation will bring the body into harmony with the cosmos, allowing the ego to dissolve into union with God: "For from the distilled essence (*zubda*) of the cosmos arises the elements [that compose earthly matter], while from the essence of the earth arises the life of plant, and from the distilled essence of plant life arises the life of animals, and from the distilled life of animals arises humanity, and from the distilled essence of humanity, in every dimension, is the being of the true One (*ḥaqq*)."[29] Although the attribution of this epistle to Muʿin al-Din Chishti is most likely apocryphal, it is important that Chishti Sufis saw spiritualized anatomy as the core of their mystical devotion, taught by the saint who first established their community.

More than other branches of the Chishti community, the Sabiris maintained a more rigorous and physical emphasis on the body, between the extremes of ecstatic rapture and stern control. They take their name from a mysterious Sufi named ʿAlāʾ al-Dīn ʿAlī Ṣābir. He was a follower and nephew of Shaykh Farid al-Din "Ganj-i Shakar," the third axial saint after Shaykh Muʿin al-Din Chishti. Shaykh Farid al-Din lived far from the major urban areas where other Chishti masters were increasingly settling. In Punjabi jungles, he pursued strenuous devotional exercises. He perpetuated in South Asia the Central Asian Sufi practice of the "inverted prayer" (*ṣalāt-i maʿqūsī*). This consisted of a spiritual retreat for prayer by hanging by one's feet from a rafter or in a dry well, remaining in an inverted state of contemplation from daybreak to sunset, often continued as an isolated retreat (*chilla*) for forty days in succession. Though Farid al-Din never made this arduous exercise obligatory for his followers, it was integral to his own spiritual practice, and he saw it as crucial to forcefully dispel selfishness through such muscular ascetic practices. With them, he unleashed an inner spiritual heat and force that could either propel or singe others, depending upon the sincerity of their approach toward him.

Near the end of his life, Shaykh Farid al-Din delegated his authority to a young follower, Nizam al-Din Awliyaʾ. Farid al-Din charged him to become the embodiment of love, through whom the comforting shade of divine mercy would pour forth in the capital city of Delhi, infusing all corners of the Islamic empire in India. Upon his death in 1265, Farid al-Din sent his staff, sandals, and other tokens of his authority to Nizam al-Din in Delhi. During his long life in the capital, Nizam al-Din perfected the Chishti style of musical devotion, poetic interpretation of religion, and ardent love mysticism that spread throughout India, making the Chishti community the most popular style of Sufism in South Asia. However, not all Chishtis were followers of Nizam al-Din, even if the majority were, for Nizam al-Din was not the only follower of the passionate and ascetic Shaykh Farid al-Din. There was also the *shaykh*'s close follower and nephew, Shaykh Sabir, who continued his master's more reclusive and athletic style of devotion to oppose the bodily forces of lust and transform passion from fleshly lust into spiritual love.

Little is known of Shaykh Sabir's personality.[30] Followers of Nizam al-Din insist that Shaykh Sabir was passed over for succession in the Sufi order precisely because of his spiritual power. At a very young age, his rigorous devotional exercises, like the "inverted prayer" in which he followed Farid al-Din, gave rise to his fiercely powerful spiritual heat and power, akin to the Yogic concept of *tapas*, the inner force awakened by devotional penance. His ability to channel this force into performing miracles was so audacious that Shaykh Farid al-Din was wary of granting him leadership of the community and exposing the wider public to his spiritual heat. Instead, he sent the young Shaykh Sabir out to the wilderness to live in harmony with his own internal powers and cultivate closeness to God in isolation.

However, he was not quite isolated. A few rugged and passionately devoted followers of Shaykh Sabir regarded him as the true inheritor of Shaykh Farid al-Din's saintly authority and the only one of his followers to adhere closely to the saint's rigorous concentration on bodily control. While respecting Nizam al-Din and his amazing popularity, they insisted that Shaykh Sabir was an equally authentic branch of the Chishti masters. These Sabiri-Chishtis combined the Khurasani tradition of imagining the heart as the center of spiritual anatomy, as we have seen in al-Tirmidhi, with the rigorous Indic traditions of Yoga. It was as a Sabiri-Chishti that Hajji Imdadullah maintained a persistent concentration on the body and its internal discipline through ritual practices.

Yoga's Change of Heart and Islamic Conversion

We know very little about Shaykh Sabir's spiritual adventures in the wilderness north of Delhi. His immediate followers were few, as he lived outside the urban centers in which Sufism thrived under Nizam al-Din Awliya''s direction. The followers of Shaykh Sabir evidently spent their time in contemplation, athletic spiritual exercises of the type detailed above, and the hardship of wresting a simple living from wilderness. It appears that the Sabiri tradition had almost died out until an adventurous and unconventional Sufi, Shaykh Aḥmad ʿAbd al-Ḥaqq Rudawlī (died 1434), revived it. In his long wanderings in poverty, he consorted with Yogis and Qalandars while engaging in intensely athletic devotional exercises. He took initiation directly from the long-dead Shaykh Sabir in a visionary encounter and began to spread his teachings as the Sabiri branch of the Chishti community.[31] His teachings stressed absolute control over the body through concentrating on the breath and therefore formed an important bridge between the Central Asian teachings of Sufism brought to India by the Chishtis and indigenous Indic forms of Yogic contemplation.[32]

Shaykh ʿAbd al-Haqq Rudawli believed that the body itself could be transformed from a material prison of lust into a divinely empowered channel for God's manifestation in the created world. This transformation could be fueled by the very physical confrontation with death. The "inverted prayer" forced one to confront death and the limitations of the physical body while building up in oneself a very bodily stamina and spiritual self-control. While preserving this practice, Shaykh ʿAbd al-Haqq actually practiced a spiritual exercise of premature burial. He had his living body buried as if dead, and after practicing breath control, ecstatic contemplation, and severe bodily discipline for days on end, he would emerge from the earth still alive. This use of burial as devotional practice hints at important connections with Hatha Yoga as a form of ritual discipline of the body, for Yogis were adept at such practices of bodily stasis, surviving burial by consciously slowing down their breathing to the point of quieting the body into a stasis between life and death.

A hagiographic text entitled *Anwār al-ʿUyūn fī Asrār al-Maknūn* ("Perpetual Springs of Light about Secrets Hidden from Sight") records the life and teachings of Shaykh ʿAbd al-Haqq Rudawli. Even in the title of this hagiography, the author hints at the importance of the *shaykh*'s dramatic burial and rebirth to Sufi practice. The phrase "hidden from sight" usually describes pearls, whose luster is buried in the flesh of the oyster and whose beauty is hidden from sight by the ugly material of its shell. The author claims to "sing his praises by stringing together some reports of the Shaykh's spiritual states, sayings, miraculous gifts, and lofty desires, of which he had heard."[33] The author was uniquely qualified to do so, since he was the *shaykh*'s own grandson and major successor in the Sabiri-Chishti lineage. In the introduction he writes, "The author of these pages stayed at the devotional center and tomb of Shaykh ʿAbd al-Haqq for a long time. I pursued intense spiritual exercises and long struggles, crying and wailing in trial, burning with hunger and thirst, until he realized the steps of intimacy (*darrāj-i maʿīya*) and the station of oblivion (*maqām-i maḥwīya*). Then the nightingale of his soul raised its melody from within the garden of the beloved, and the beloved friend became united with him, in one voice and one conscience. Then he came to know the secret of the verse: *On that day [the convulsing earth] tells of her secrets, that your Lord had revealed to her* (Q 99: 4–5)." The author quotes one of the Qurʾan's most powerful short chapters, "The Earthquake," which describes how the earth and all things durable and stable will be upset and torn asunder on the day of judgment. By citing this verse, he claims that earth is a metaphor for the human body, for Adam was created of its clay and dust. Further, the body must be shaken from its routine through ascetic and meditative practices that prefigure death, just as the earth will be shaken on judgment day. And in overcoming the fear of death by confronting it directly, the body, like the earth, *tells of her secrets, that your Lord had revealed to her*. His hagiography tells a story about how the *shaykh* learned these inspired secrets from the body and from the earth, as each opened up to embrace the other.

After years of travel and learning from different Sufi masters (including a woman master named Bībī Fatima), Shaykh ʿAbd al-Haqq Rudawli headed back to his native region of Bihar, dissatisfied that any living person could fully explicate the secrets of Sufi teaching. Along the way, he encountered two strange men, both seemingly mad with love for God; by name, one (Sulṭān ʿAlāʾ al-Dīn) appears to have been a Muslim who became a Qalandar, while the other (Nīm Langūntī) was a Hindu who became a Yogi. After strange interactions, each grabs the *shaykh* and holds him close to his breast.[34] The encounter signaled to the *shaykh* that the secret knowledge he desired could be found only among the dead. He lived in a graveyard "to seek the meaning of the divine message he had received." There he spent day and night reciting a meditative formula, *yā hī hū, yā hī hū*. After a long time of such austerities, he said to himself, "O Ahmad, now die just like those who have already died, and lie in the grave and be buried like the dead." So he dug a grave with his own hands, laid down in it like a corpse, and had himself buried. "He remained buried underground for six months, passing through each realm of the inner worlds, seeking the presence of God in each, such that his eyes were lined with the beautiful mascara of *His gaze did not turn aside nor go too far* (Q 53:17). In each realm, he would say to himself, 'O Ahmad, this world is not worthy of worship, so wake up now and move on!'"[35] In this way he became separated from all worldly people, traversed spiritual realms, and absorbed himself with the real One (*al-haqq*). "He moved on until he came to a realm and a great expanse of water that was pure of any taint of how or how much. He heard the sound of *Then know that there is no god but I* (Q 16:2). Without voice and without pronunciation, without ear and without tongue he heard it. He passed out of himself, such that *if God manifests to any thing it passes away before God*. He lost consciousness of himself and came up out of the grave."[36]

The *shaykh*'s ascetic burial is an intensified form of the inverted prayer; in both, one goes down in order to prepare for rising up, in spiritual ascension. The hagiographic account specifies that "he stood out of the sweetness of oblivion and joy of intimacy, and attained completeness in the ascending steps of union (*miʿrāj-i wiṣāl*)."[37] In terms of his anatomical posture, vocal performance, and ritual process, he was adopting techniques of Yogic concentration; a later meditation manual provides us with crucial details about what Shaykh ʿAbd al-Haqq might actually have been doing in the graveyard. Burhān al-Dīn Shaṭṭārī calls it "meditation in the Hindawi langauage" and recorded how to do it in his "Shattari Treatise": "Sit cross-legged, just as the Yogis do. Raise your eyes and face to the heavens. Pronounce the following words of meditation (*dhikr*) one thousand times or more, and it will let you achieve in the end the realm of spiritual flight (*ʿalam-i ṭayr*). You must say just these syllables: *ū hī hī*, as is the initial training in the spiritual cultivation of the Yogis (*sulūk-i jōgiyya*) with these three things. After this, one can remain engrossed in meditation on these syllables with one's imagination (*wahm*). . . . This comprises the initial posture (*jalsa*) of their training. There are eighty-four types of meditation [postures], and in each one they say there is a different benefit. As for the author of this book, I have chosen to practice just one of these eighty-four different postures. In this single posture, I have found all the benefits of these various postures."[38]

It is difficult to interpret exactly what Shaykh ʿAbd al-Haqq, and later Burhan al-Din Shattari, were saying "in the Hindawi language."[39] Although the exact pronunciation is obscure, it is clear that ʿAbd al-Haqq revived early confrontation and cooperation between Chishti Sufis and Yogis. There are elliptical textual references to discussions between Shaykh Farid al-Din and some Hindu Yogis who visited his retreat in the Punjab. Despite these tantalizing fragments of evidence, the intriguing history of Sufi interactions with Yogis has received very little scholarly attention, though it appears on the margins of several studies about Islam in India. Fortunately, the American scholar Carl Ernst has recently taken up the challenge and is filling out the picture first mentioned by the Indian scholar Sayyid Athar Abbas Rizvi and explored in some depth by the British scholar Simon Digby.[40]

Their research reveals that in the sixteenth century there was a revival of interest in Yoga among Sufis in South Asia, or at least a new emphasis on recording in texts the techniques of practice that were passed on orally from master to disciple. We can observe this fluorescence of Islamic appropriations of Yoga in both the Sabiri-Chishti and the Shattari Sufi communities, and it left a textual trace in Imdadullah's imagery of the heart. The former community was Hajji Imdadullah's main allegiance, while the latter was a community into which he also had an initiation even if it was largely inactive in South Asia by the nineteenth century. In his ritual manual, Imdadullah subtly recast the figures of some past great masters of the South Asian Sufi tradition. The most crucial reference is to two in particular: his reference to the Sabiri-Chishti master named ʿAbd al-Quddūs Gangōhī (1456–1537 C.E.) is quite explicit, while reference to the Shattari master Muhammad Ghawth Gwāliyōrī, whom we met in the previous chapter, is implicit but nevertheless very strategic.

Shaykh ʿAbd al-Quddus from Gangoh was a pivotal figure in the spread and maturation of the Sabiri-Chishti community, for he was the primary successor of Shaykh ʿAbd al-Haqq Rudawli and is the author of the hagiographic work quoted above.[41] ʿAbd al-Quddus served as a revered prototype for Hajji Imdadullah. As Imdadullah asserted the necessity and Islamic authenticity of techniques of bodily discipline, he followed the example of the life efforts of ʿAbd al-Quddus in the early sixteenth century. ʿAbd al-Quddus strove to allegorize and refine the physiological exercises of the Yogic tradition and to give these exercises equivalent Sufi terms and an Islamic framework. He aimed to integrate Indic disciplinary techniques into Sufi devotional life and reframe them in an Islamic cosmology and moral narrative. Three centuries later, Imdadullah embarked on a parallel project by reintegrating ʿAbd al-Quddus's own techniques and terminology into a framework shaped more fully by the rhetoric of sharia and pietistic devotion to the person of the Prophet.

In explaining the complex textual and terminological reweaving by which ʿAbd al-Quddus reconfigured Yogic techniques as Islamic ones and linked them to Sufi practices, the scholar Simon Digby uses the term "allegorized." The British scholar explains that the Sufi master strove to allegorize Yogic disciplines and give them an Islamic character. Yet Digby's explanatory term "allegorize" needs to be sharpened and made more specific. The difference between Yogic and Sabiri-Chishti exercises is primarily a matter of narrative framework: ʿAbd al-Quddus distilled Yogic techniques into a narrative of personal love mysticism, whereas such references to union with a personal deity do not play a central role in Yogic teaching at all. Union with the essence of a beloved deity acted as bridge for transferring Yogic bodily disciplines into an Islamic moral framework. By looking into the details of how this was accomplished, we can achieve three things: appreciate how Yoga and Islam are compatible in the eyes of the medieval Indian Muslim, understand the particular force of Sabiri-Chishti love mysticism centered upon the heart, and comprehend how Hajji Imdadullah reinvented Sabiri images of the heart in his ritual manual.

Shaykh ʿAbd al-Quddus was renowned for teaching his students the Yogic text called the *Amrtakunda*, a text originally composed in Sanskrit and containing directions for the proper performance of Hatha Yogic exercises. The object of these exercises was to control the motion of bodily fluids and the passage of breath to preserve the health of the bodily and live in a state of perpetual bliss. In Digby's synopsis, "Yoga is largely conceived . . . as a physiological process toward the attainment of perfection, and many of their exercises are designed to reverse the processes of nature from which the human frame decays. The *bindu-rasa*, seminal fluid or vital juice [the water of life in the title of the *Amrtakunda*] drops down from a cavity in the skull above the throat to be consumed by the raging fire of *rajas* [carnal desire], situated close to the navel. When the loss of this and other vital fluids is prevented by the mastery of austerities, a dormant force, symbolized as a coiled serpent called *kundalini* and also *sakti*, is persuaded to rise through . . . the spine until it attains union with *siva*, the force responsible for the production of *bindu-rasa* in the skull."[42] At this point, the decay of the body is reversed, and a new bodily orifice opens up in the cranium, the gate of joy, through which the ascetic can find liberation from the dependence on the body and its senses. The key to this liberation is the knowledge of different types of breath and how they circulate in the body, for only by controlling these breaths and binding them together can the Yogic practitioner release the *kundalini* force and rejuvenate the body.

Although the Yogic text called the *Amrtakunda* mentions the heart in one chapter, the anatomical emphasis throughout is on other bodily locations: controlling the breath, regulating the flow of fluids like saliva and semen, and channeling vital energy up the spinal column against the gravity of sensual desire. Orchestrating these reversals of routine bodily processes is the path of spiritual perfection and bodily immortality in the view of the Yogic text. Consider the following key passages: "Now the mouth is the root that waters humanity to give it a basis in strength and motion. In it is the place of life, which is the saliva [analogous to the semen before it is wasted and consumed in sexual desire]. . . . Imagine that you are drawing in the semen, just as you draw water up a long tube . . . watering your body with the water of life at every time and moment."[43] As is clear in the *Amrtakunda*, Yogic teaching largely bypasses the heart as the locus of devotional exercise.

Although both Sufi techniques and Yogic techniques of bodily discipline emphasize the retention of breath, the effect of this breath retention manifests in different anatomical passages. In Yogic practice breath retention affects the passage of vital fluid through the spine, while in Sufi practice breath retention purifies the heart. Despite that difference, the actual technique of both is similar, to reverse the breathing process by holding the breath and turning it upside down and inside out. The *Amritakunda* explains, "The existence of the breath is in the microcosm from the great heat, and its dwelling place is the stomach. It is like a coiled rope in the shape of a circle, around the navel in the belly . . . and it appears in the form of a spiral. . . . In these breaths is the pivot of life."[44] This coiled life force, *kundalini*, is imagined in the form of a snake, which in Indic mythology has a positive role (as eternal life and perpetual renewal) if its dangerous power can be harnessed into protective force. ʿAbd al-Quddus cites this image when he directs the practitioner to stay engaged in "the activity of breath-control. In the language of the Jogis they call it *b<u>h</u>uvangam*, which means 'the snake' as it is breath-control for the snake."[45] Inverting the breath will invert the coiled life force, reverse the flow of semen, and open the powers of bodily and spiritual perfection.

ʿAbd al-Quddus did not just teach these techniques but also set them in a new framework—in a new religious narrative. He asserted that the goal of these bodily manipulations is not simply health, longevity, or spiritual prowess. Rather, these physiological changes are the foundation for spiritual union with God, metaphorically rendered by the opening of a new orifice in the body. ʿAbd al-Quddus uses the term *mula* in its standard Yogic valence, meaning the containing, binding, and redirection of the downward breath. Yet he also uses the same term, *mula*, to mean root, ground, or essence as a metaphor for the presence of the creator with and within creation. As Simon Digby explains, "If *mula* is understood in this sense, the *muladvara* is no longer the ordinary *muladvara* of Natha-panthi [Yogic] teaching. . . . It is the 'gate of the essence,' the door to liberation and, in this personalized mysticism, to union with God. In the interpretation of ʿAbd al-Quddus, the binding or closing of the wind there refers not to the beginning of the psycho-physical process of Hatha Yoga, but to the immediate prelude to its successful conclusion."[46] While God is immanent in creation, created beings need to undergo discipline and internal bodily transformation in order to realize this immanence. ʿAbd al-Quddus expresses the immanence of God in creation (or rather, the sustenance of creation in God's presence) in a Hindi couplet: "The bubble was formed from water, in water it disappears." These images, valorized under the label *wahdat al-wujud* (the unity of all being), circulated widely in South Asian Muslim circles in the century before ʿAbd al-Quddus lived and was embraced with particular warmth by the Chishti Sufis.

This metaphysical framework helped paved the way for Sufis to propose a more intricate engagement with Indic devotional techniques. ʿAbd al-Quddus has reframed these techniques of bodily discipline as integral stages in the narrative of monotheistic mysticism, expressed as personal love mysticism. On the potentially violent fault line between Islamic and Indic communities, ʿAbd al-Quddus tried to build a bridge by rendering homologous the bodily disciplines and ritual practices present in both religious traditions. In this way, he "converted" Yogic techniques into Islamic techniques and ensured that they could be taught among Muslim devotees as valuable methods for the internalization of Islamic teachings.

Scholars in South Asian Islamic history are very familiar with "narratives of conversion" to Islam; however, the case here is "conversion of narrative."

Hagiographic collections retelling the life stories of powerful Sufi saints in the medieval era are replete with references to Sufis moving to South Asia from Central Asian lands and "converting" powerful and feared Yogis to Islam. Hagiographies usually depict Yogis as losers in a struggle with a stalwart Sufi whose illuminated heart wins them over in the end. Such is the tale of the paradigmatic Chishti saint Muʿin al-Din. Upon his arrival in Rajasthan, he was challenged by a formidably ascetic Yogi who resided in the same locale. After a struggle of spiritual exercises and strenuous devotions, the Yogi was forced to submit to the more lofty authority of the personal love mysticism and radical monotheism of the Sufi and "converted to Islam."[47]

Many historians have seen such hagiographic conversion narratives as allegories of the political conquest of Muslim military rulers over an ever expanding stretch of South Asia. Yet none have yet considered them to refer figuratively to the "conversion of narrative." Sufis respected Yogis for their knowledge, techniques of bodily discipline, and occult craft. However, Sufis saw that these tools needed to be placed in the context of a different metanarrative to make them morally beneficial rather than manipulatively occult; that metanarrative was the personal path to union with the beloved creator, God. By this act of conversion, Sufis sought not only to enrich and intensify the bodily disciplines of their ritual tradition but also to build a bridge of communication between the religious elites of the Muslim community and those of other, non-Muslim Indic communities. This process is illustrated by how ʿAbd al-Quddus appropriated and reformulated Yogic terms and exercises.

A conversion narrative also exists to explain the translation of the actual *Amrtakunda* text, which played such an important role in the narrative conversion of Yogic practice into Sufi ritual, although the exact historical process is not clear. Supposedly, a Natha-panti Yogi who had trained under the regime of the *Amrtakunda* converted to Islam under the influence of a Sufi; with the new name of Ibrahim, he translated the useful Yogic text from Sanskrit into Arabic, with the title *Baḥr al-Ḥayyāt*, "The Reservoir of Life."[48] This process of borrowing, translating and "allegorizing" was long lived. Over time, Hindus interested in Yoga began to adopt and adapt the Arabic and Persian texts and even write their own texts in Persian. Traces of this process are revealed in a Persian text called *Muḥīṭ-i Maʿrifat* ("Ocean of Insight"), written in 1762 by a mystic and poet named Satīdāsa, son of Rām<u>bh</u>āī. His treatise is on divination and Yoga (in the various fields of Sankhya, Raja, Hatha, and Ashtanga Yoga). Although it is explicitly based on a Hindi work, the author is not simply translating; rather, he clarifies the work with his own poetic compositions in Persian, such as the following: "Come, my wine pourer, give my pitcher a fill / for none but your companionship can thrill. . . . Let me sip away and unselfconsciousness beget / make this heart of mine my own self forget."[49] This Hindu author even writes poetry under the Persian pen name ʿĀrif, or "Sage," revealing the intimate cooperation achieved by those pursing esoteric knowledge beyond confessional religious boundaries.

While ʿAbd al-Quddus gave Yogic techniques of bodily engagement and meditation a new narrative frame, Hajji Imdadullah three centuries later redeployed the body imagery altogether. He focused on the heart as the anatomical stage where the Sufi drama of union with the divine is played out. In this revision, Imdadullah sought to once again reaffirm these techniques of bodily discipline in the tradition of Sufi practice. Despite this new emphasis on the image of the heart, there is a basic continuity between ʿAbd al-Quddus and Imdadullah: both profess that the human body as a microcosm mirrors the ascending levels of the created cosmos and that the body is the starting point for ascending into the presence of the divine. In Imdadullah's ritual manual, this ascension arises out of meditative exercise. The devotee first controls the breathing process; this control generates internal heat, which clarifies the blood and melts the fatty plague that clogs the arteries; this exercise gives the heart a new flexibility and gentleness that dislodges the barbs of the serpent of temptation that coils around the heart, constricting it, hardening it, and darkening its moral vision. This clarity and purity allow the devotee to experience an inversion of the self, accompanied by sensations of rain, lightening, or thunder within the devotee's sensory perception. This is a sign that the body is subtly changing and realigning, leading to an obliteration of the egoself and union with God.

Imdadullah allegorized the body through the image of the heart while at the same time asserting the heart to be the place of indwelling of the immanent creator. This move was presaged by ʿAbd al-Quddus, who penned a Hindi couplet—"Within the flesh there is a heart, where my lord takes residence." This paraphrases a hadith *qudsi* in which Muhammad said that God says, "In the body of Adam there is a lump of flesh, and in that lump of flesh there is a secret, and in that secret am I."[50] ʿAbd al-Quddus asserts that this lump of flesh specifies the place where the breath is bound, inside the body near the navel. Imdadullah quotes the same hadith in a much more elaborate version that anatomically locates this fleshly seat of the indwelling presence of the creator as the human heart. This hadith, pinned to the heart, forms the narrative core that gives meaning to all of Imdadullah's devotional exercises. This hadith is crucial; it is an Islamic tradition that asserts that the human body is the microcosm of the harmonious cosmos. Thus disciplining the body is a way to purify the heart; and, as revealed in this hadith, purifying the heart creates a conduit for the divine presence immanent therein to radiate out into the created universe, sustaining it and urging it toward justice and selfless service. Imdadullah came to use this hadith to justify elevating the heart to be the potential seat of divine presence in the world.

Imdadullah arrived at this cardiac synthesis through the textual mediation of *Al-Jawāhir al-Khamsa*, "The Five Precious Essences," a ritual manual composed by Muhammad Ghawth Gwaliyori, the Shattari master who lived a generation after ʿAbd al-Quddus. The five precious essences are meditations (*adhkār*), practices (*ashghāl*), litanies (*awrād*), exercises (*riyāḍāt*) and contemplative disciplines (*murāqabāt*). The Shattari Sufi community was a relative newcomer in South Asia, arriving in the fifteenth century from the Central Asian region of Khurasan, but it quickly forged a radical synthesis with indigenous Indic symbols, techniques, and music, as we saw in Chapter 3.

In "The Five Precious Essences" the Shattari Sufi master recounts a moderately elaborate version of the hadith *qudsi* originally quoted by ʿAbd al-Quddus. This version of the hadith anatomically places the presence of God not simply in the human body but rather explicitly in the organ of the heart. "The human heart is like an endless treasury of divine secrets, or like a limitless storehouse of divine light. Yet it is a treasury covered over and concealed in obscuring veils, veils both exterior and interior. The existence of interior veils is revealed in these words of God as reported by the Prophet [Muhammad]: 'In the body of each human being there is a knot of flesh, and in this knot is a moral heart, and in this heart is a conscience, and in this conscience is a secret, and in this secret, there I am.'"[51] Thus God is present within every person, a presence dwelling in the innermost core of the human heart. But the light of God's presence is often obscured by veils both anatomical and spiritual or exterior and interior. "Exterior veils are suspended from the interior veils and are dependent on them. Meanwhile, the heart lies enclosed between the two sides of the chest, inclining toward the left side. A curtain of greasy fat has fallen hanging over the heart. In addition to these veils, three other veils obscure the heart as well, veils which cannot be agitated or shaken from their place, as has been tested by masters of the Sufi path who have experimented with this and verified it."[52] This spiritual potency of God's light that shines within the heart is veiled by greasy layers of fat,

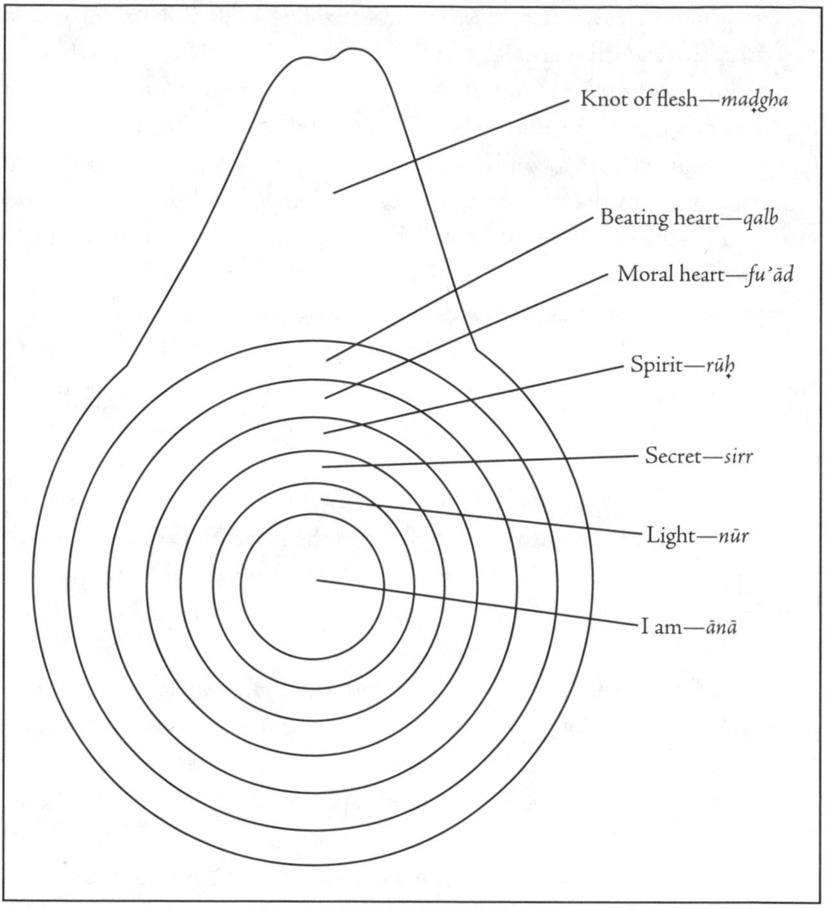

Subtle Layers of the Heart

Source: Adapted from Ḥājji Imdādullah, *Ḍiyā' al-Qulūb*, litho. (Lucknow: Matbaʿ Fakhr al-Maṭābiʿ, n.d.), 12.

which are both anatomical structures and spiritual murk, and clearing away these veils is arduous labor. "Any person who desires to observe and witness divine secrets and the manifestation of their illuminations must keep reciting, from the beginning of their days, during morning and night, at every moment and as far as possible, such that, from the multiplying abundance of recitations a fire might be ignited. Its heat will completely throw open each of the veils and melt away each one in turn, until dark obscurity thins and brilliant light beams from the heart."[53] These images of Muhamad Ghawth Gwaliyori are appropriated by Imdadullah, who integrates them into his ritual manual with an even more elaborate version of the same hadith. Imdadullah's version extends the description of the heart into seven nested levels of the heart, each more subtle than the previous.

Even though Imdadullah expands the image of the human heart and gives it a new centrality in comparison with the brief mention of the heart by ʿAbd al-Quddus, he does this to further the project that ʿAbd al-Quddus himself put forward: to draw equivalencies between Indic and Islamic devotional methods. Pursuing this goal, Imdadullah further juxtaposes two images, one from Indic sources and one from Khurasani sources, and unites the two in the heart. In juxtaposing these images, he draws equivalencies between them, thus continuing the conversion of narratives begun by ʿAbd al-Quddus and pressed forward by Muhammad Ghawth Gwaliyori. The first image comes from Indic devotional tradition. In the manuals of Hatha Yoga, the positive spiritual energy stored in each person with the potential to rise up and transform the body is called *kundalini*. Texts depict this potential transformative energy as a snake, coiled inside the body deep below the navel. The second image that Imdadullah skillful interweaves with the first comes from Khurasani tradition of Sufi devotion, as we have seen above: the image of Satan as a serpent coursing through the human bloodstream, whose poison must be repelled from the heart. With the arresting juxtaposition of these two images, Imdadullah tries to explain the necessity of *dhikr*, ritual recitation. With the same motion through which *dhikr* transforms the physical body, like the positive energy of the released *kundalini*, *dhikr* also creates the durable foundation for apt ethic actions by dispelling self-centeredness, which can be imagined metaphorically as repelling of the negative energy of Shaytan in the bloodstream.

The image of the *kundalini* as an awakening serpent of potential energy coiled beneath the navel is common to Hatha Yogic texts, as displayed by the *Amrtakunda*. ʿAbd al-Quddus transferred this use of serpent imagery intact in his devotions. However, Imdadullah did not reproduce this image verbatim but rather overlaid upon it the conception that Satan's misleading seduction infiltrates the heart through the coursing of blood in the arteries, as we have seen in the writings of al-Tirmidhi. In this Khurasani ascetic image, illicit desires and sensual excitements constrict the arteries, raise the temperature of the bloodstream, and thereby force the Shaytan in the bloodstream to secrete its poisonous sweat. Although the *Amrtakunda* does not present any heart imagery nearly as elaborate or anatomically detailed, this Yogic text does put forward an analogous proposal: that the "devil is inside of you" not just personally but bodily as well. This satanic force misleads the self through the common but impure processes of the body, if they are allowed to proceed unexamined and uncontrolled. In the words of the *Amrtakunda,*

> The microcosm is the secret of existent things and their meanings. . . . In the microcosm are the wonders of the heavens and the earth. It is forever put into motion, like the [celestial] spheres, by fortune good and ill. . . . Therefore the microcosm is called the heart (*qalb*), because it is always in transformation (*taqallub*) and this is its form. . . . The blameworthy characteristics that are in the heart's zodiacal signs are from the property of the black blood that is found in its left hollow; this is the army of the devil who causes the bloodstream to run in the limbs, the veins, and the joints. The praiseworthy characteristics that are in its zodiacal signs are from the property of the purity that is found in its right hollow; this is the army of the angel who causes the bloodstream to run in the limbs, the veins, and the joints. . . . Do not be with the companion on the left, for he is the devil who is inside you.[54]

Imdadullah draws these two images together for the goal of illustrating the drama of the ritual practitioner's *dhikr* as it intensifies the rhythm of the heart, amplifies this rhythm, to the point where it clarifies the body and the spirit, obliterates self-interest, and opens the door to union with God and thus allows the selfless performance of duties in the social world.

The Heart That Gives the Sharia Life

In his ritual manual, Imdadullah creatively reworked the figures and texts of past devotional masters in both these Sufi communities in order to assert the necessity of *dhikr* and the centrality of bodily discipline in the transformative power of this ritual. Imdadullah insists that *dhikr* at once transforms the physical body and creates a durable foundation for external ethical acts without crippling exertions or hypocritical display. Imdadullah avows that bodily discipline is the foundation for overtly Islamic moral acts. To drive home this claim, he gives instructions about how to perform these techniques of discipline, focusing each exercise on the organ of the heart, the image of which figures prominently in Qur'anic discourse, prophetic hadith, and early Islamic devotional literature. Even though he gave a crucial role to bodily discipline, Imdadullah moderated the emphasis on athletic ascetic discipline as found in prior devotional masters. The purpose of this moderation was to highlight the second part of the intent of *dhikr*: to facilitate the apt performance of outwardly ethical actions.

In Imdadullah's metaphor, the heart is the center of the body, and without a sincere heart the body will fall into corruption. But the heart cannot stand alone and needs an encasing body to enliven it, if it is to live up to its potential, or to live at all. It is as if Sufism is the heart while the sharia is the outer body. *Dhikr* is medicine to keep the heart pure and harmonious, to enliven the body's outward performance of legal and ethical acts. Like later generations Shattari Sufis, after the persecution of Muhammad Ghawth, the Sabiri-Chishti Sufis of ʿAbd al-Quddus Gangohi's community emphasized that ecstatic inner experience must be enclosed by an outer casing of social and religious behavior conforming to the sharia. This is the Sabiri tradition that Imdadullah inherited.

Hajji Imdadullah lived on the cusp of great and accelerating changes encompassing the wielding of power, the organization of society, and the hegemony of concepts. From this vantage point, he is a transitional figure in the religious history of Muslims in South Asia, and in transition, he embodies contradictions. In one sense, his writing marks substantial continuity with the earlier traditions of Sabiri-Chishti devotion. However, within this continuity, Imdadullah also engaged the accelerating changes that surrounded him and his community throughout the nineteenth century. The continuity of expression with prior devotional tradition does not mean that Imdadullah's works simply repeat earlier theories and formulations. To assume this would be to accept modernist condemnations of ritual as empty gestures and ritual practitioners as traditionalists alienated from the true meaning of their actions.[55] Imdadullah linked his Sufi devotion to new ascendant discourses, such as medical anatomy, growing sharia-mindedness, and emphasis on rigorous outward upholding of the legal injunctions of the Qurʾan. As the political and economic superstructure of the Mughal empire shrank and, by 1859, crumbled under British domination, Imdadullah explored alternative styles of devotion and rhetoric of leadership.

Imdadullah's primary concern was to maintain the validity of *wilaya*, or sainthood; this meant asserting that the Sufis were still the vanguard of Islamic piety, the cornerstone of community life, and the pivot of cosmic order. Toward this goal, Imdadullah recast earlier Sufi masters in an attempt to unite Qurʾanic ethics with spiritualized anatomy. Imdadullah's Urdu translator places special emphasis on this unstated foundation of Imdadullah's project: "The intention of contemplation is to extend into the social order [the Qurʾanic exhortation] to *encourage the accepted good and discourage the rejected evil* (Q 3:104). Contemplations in a more specific sense are just this: to conceive of Allah's essence in such an intensity that one becomes unthinking and unconscious of one's own [thinking and conscious] self."[56]

The central goal of Imdadullah's teachings is to present a method by which Muslims can embody the aspirations and exhortations of the sacred words of the Qur'an. These scriptural words are to be embodied in the human personality, and thus extended into the social world, through various exercises of contemplation. Only through rigorous contemplation can one lay aside oneself and fully take on the burden of becoming a pillar for the surrounding Muslim society. Once a Sufi disciple has undertaken these exercises and achieved the goal of self-transformation, then the disciple can return to society in a position of ethical and even political leadership. Thus no matter how respectful Imdadullah is to past Sufi figures, and no matter how faithfully he transmits the details of their practice, his theoretical superstructure is responsive to wider religious and political concerns of his contemporary community. In its most distilled form, the ultimate cure for heart disease is the internalization of the Qur'an itself and the emulation of its bearer, the Prophet Muhammad.

Imdadullah presents the complex regimen of "The Brilliance of Hearts" as simple methods of self-disciplinary, devotional action, followed by their resulting moral benefits. The author only alludes to an underpinning metaphysical system rather than systematically displaying it. The text itself is not about metaphysics but rather about metaphysiology: that is, how the human body and especially the heart can be trained to adopt postures and motions that have transcendent ethical effects so that the body itself can become a mirror for a just cosmic order.

Despite this apparent unconcern for explicit metaphysics, Imdadullah frames the discrete methods of devotion between two metaphysical anchors. The first is a Delphic maxim: those persons who know their selves know God.[57] And the second is a Qur'anic maxim: those who surrender their selves serve God. Hajji Imdadullah bases the bodily training and spiritual discipline resulting in ecstasy, illumination, and inspiration upon the former maxim; yet he aims these same ritual techniques toward achieving the latter, activist maxim. Retraining one's body techniques can unite knowledge and service.

At the point when actions are emptied of selfish intent and devotions are cleared of hypocrisy, the ritual performer has entered the state called *wilaya*, or sainthood. Nullifying the self, remembering God's presence in order to invert the self, turning it inside out, and sparking the state of *wilaya* have constituted the goal of Sufi communities since they were instituted as formal organizations in the twelfth century. Although definitions and demarcations of *wilaya* changed over time between regional Sufi communities, and between contemporary authors, *wilaya* itself remained the highest level of authority among Sufis and the stage at which the divine will acts within the human realm. This is what Sufis call "achieving union" with God. But this elevated state does not grant a saint special dispensation or excuse from social obligations and legal responsibility. "After [achieving this state of sainthood], the seeker should remain occupied with worship as it should justly be done, and preserve the dignity and commandments of the sharia properly. Having become supported on the seat of guidance, pointing out the path for fellow seekers of the Truth, his *wilaya* and *mushaykha* will stay sound and valid."[58]

Imdadullah and his followers, however, advocated a subtle but important shift in terms. The final sentence of this passage introduces a new term just after mentioning *wilaya*: that is *mushaykha*, or mastery. The fact that this stage comes after *wilaya* indicates that selfless sanctity is not complete in and of itself but only when further refined by mastery. The editor of the Urdu translation of "The Brilliance of Hearts" penned an insightful marginal note to clarify this passage. "What is known as *wilaya* is really finding one's being, through obliterating oneself in God's presence, and sustaining oneself only through God's sustenance, and gaining purification through God's own purity. In this world and the next, extending the commands of God and exerting one's whole power of will in this extension is called *mushaykha*, being a master. The level of *mushaykha* is more lofty than the level of *wilaya*."[59] The previous goal of devotion, unification with the beloved divine, has become sublimated into a more refined goal: service to the community on behalf of the absorbed and permeating divine. The phrase "extending the commands of God" is a wide reference to any human activity that supports the sharia and extends its edges. Such activity could include juridical decisions based on Islamic law, teaching prophetic traditions to a new generation, or addressing the material and political needs of the Muslim community in general. This paradigm shift in imagining selflessness, from *wilaya* to *mushaykha*, is subtle; yet it had become pervasive by the nineteenth century.

Hajji Imdadullah composed his ritual manual to ensure the transmission of devotional rituals (and the bodily disciplines that were their underlying foundation) to a new generation. Such disciplinary practices can change only slowly and incrementally; however, they do change over time. The slow pace of change in these disciplines is due in part to the bodily focus of the practices and in part due to the intended aim of these practices to embody virtues; neither these means nor these goals are very contingent on the vicissitudes of historical time. Talal Asad points out that the modernist preoccupation with interpretation and representation not just inhibits understanding of the moral force of ritual but actually inhibits the embodiment of the virtues sought through ritual. Asad has cautioned those who analyze ritual to distinguish between the modern intellectual's engagement in interpretation and representation and the ritual practitioner's engagement with moral transformation. "Symbols call for interpretation, and even as interpretative criteria are extended, so interpretations can be multiplied. Disciplinary practices, on the other hand, cannot be varied so easily, because learning to develop moral capabilities is not the same thing as learning to invent representations."[60] The goal of these disciplinary exercises is not to invent something new or to represent a given subject in revolutionary manner. It is rather to tear down one's bodily habitus that had been silently learned since childhood and reconstruct in its place a new moral body with heightened symbolic significance. In accord with this ideology of continuity, Imdadullah carefully concealed the subtle reworking of tradition that is evident in a close intertextual analysis of his ritual manual. He did this to heighten his own claim to authority, not as an innovative author but as a doctor prescribing time-honored remedies for spiritual disease and social decay. Despite this appearance of continuity with tradition, Imdadullah fully engaged modern changes.

Imdadullah presents "The Brilliance of Hearts" as a medical manual to avert diseases of the heart. Despite his intense scrutiny of past Sufi masters and his mobilizing their resources, Imdadullah was undoubtedly a spiritual surgeon in a body politic that was on the verge of collapse under the forces of European colonization. He displays a deep concern for his contemporary fellows even as the Mughal empire fell to the British forces. This concern forced him to put himself forward as a spiritual guide with ritual tools that could reshape society and shore up political collapse. This concern underlies his authorship of this text and his bid for authority among discredited or rival leaders in Islamic South Asia.

In the devotee's passage from selfhood through self-inversion into sainthood and ultimately into self-mastery, Imdadullah notes that the behaviors that characterize the saint are an effortless enactment of the duties, prescriptions, and recommendations of the sharia. Even though Imdadullah may quote past masters like Muhammad Ghawth Gwaliyori, his increasing emphasis on sharia behaviors sets him apart from them. For Imdadullah, the goal of the devotee is to perform effortlessly and sincerely the duties prescribed by God through the sharia; the most efficacious way of doing this is to adopt the techniques of bodily discipline gathered from past masters in the Shattari and Sabiri-Chishti communities, among other Sufi communities. Commensurate with this new emphasis on the sharia, Imdadullah moderates or suppresses the more extreme athletic-ascetic qualities of these techniques, although he carefully preserves the bodily rigor associated with them.

An example of moderation can be found in the how Imdadullah justifies the importance of breath retention. Although both writers advocate breath retention as the physically necessary exercise to make recitation effective and transformative, they advocate this exercise with different goals. ʿAbd al-Quddus presents his exercises with the goal of binding the breath, thereby opening a new gateway to union with Allah from within the body itself. In contrast, Imdadullah frames the retention of breath as fueling the devotee's *bāṭinī miʿrāj*, "internal ascension" from the world toward God.[61] In this process, the devotee ascends through the layers of the self that are analogous to the layers of the heart's organ, just as the Prophet Muhammad had ascended physically through the layers of heaven on his night journey to the divine throne. In describing the effects of these exercises not just as liberation (*najāt*) but as ascension, Imdadullah opted for a metaphor focused on the person of the Prophet and supported by hadith traditions in order to advocate the ritual exercises first put forward by ʿAbd al-Quddus. However, his discussion of ascension is also dramatically different from that of Muhammad Ghawth's, which we observed in detail in Chapter 3. Hajji Imdadullah calls the Sufi's passage through selflessness into self-mastery an "internal ascension" in order to clarify that no Sufi, no matter how spiritually adept, can ascend in an "outward ascension" through the cosmic layers of heaven with the body intact and the sense organs operative, as Muhammad Ghawth had claimed to do. Hajji Imdadullah was heir to the sharia-mindedness of ʿAli Muttaqi in his outward expression, even as he tried to perpetuate Shattari and Yogic ideals of body engagement through ritual as the internal practice of his Sufi community.

Imdadullah's treatment of ascension provides an example of moderation of past Sufi rhetoric. His ritual manual also provides an example of suppression of past Sufi practices, as seen in how he treats the *salat-i maʿqusi*, or inverted prayer, the most athletically dramatic exercise that typified ʿAbd al-Quddus's disciplinary regime. Imdadullah does not present the inverted prayer as a technique in itself. Rather, he mentions it as an allegory for the beneficial moral results of less extreme forms of physical exercise through recitation. He pronounces that any prayer or recitation that overturns the ego's pretension to self-sufficiency and reaffirms dependence on God is a manifestation of this dramatic "inverted prayer." It is "inverted" not because of any athletic physical accomplishment but is rather "inverting" in that it overturns our habitual delusions of self-reliance. In Imdadullah's expositions, the "inverted prayer" is negating the profitable use of the world and affirming dependence on God's presence in the world, rather than being a distinct physical technique. It is any skillful means by which one imagines oneself constantly at the moment of death, thereby absorbing those virtuous qualities that sprout up from this foundation of willing the death of the self before actually dying.

These concrete ritual examples illustrate how, although Imdadullah takes the content of his ritual program from the teachings of medieval Sufis, he fits them into a new rhetorical framework. Earlier Sufis had advocated these techniques as means to achieve purity through bodily rigor and spiritual ecstasy, while Imdadullah advocates them as means to achieve to purity through anatomical knowledge and spiritual insight. Imdadullah discusses these bodily techniques as physical means of interiorizing the recitation of "no god but God." In contrast, medieval Sufis saw no reason to justify or explain them at all. They assumed that the ecstasy caused was justification enough for their performance and transmission. In Imdadullah's exposition, he is careful to argue repeatedly that such techniques of bodily discipline lead to the ethical state of "death before death"; they accelerate the spiritual disintegration of the self to erase the will and achieve union with God, allowing the apt performance of *sunna*.

This increasing emphasis on performance of the *sunna* leads us to acknowledge Imdadullah's own bid for authority among his contemporary Islamic leaders and his surprising engagement with modernity as it overtook colonial South Asia. Hajji Imdadullah claimed that self-mastery, rather than just sainthood, was the highest level of sanctity. Those who achieved self-mastery could exercise social and political authority in a selfless and virtuous manner. He therefore ranked those Sufis who upheld the sharia, the criterion for self-mastery, above those who were absorbed in ecstatic music or poetry (and certainly above those who had simply inherited Sufi positions from their forefathers). He promotes a type of activist social ethics in which the Muslim saint should be not just a paragon of virtue but a political leader in his community. His rhetoric of self-mastery presents the fully realized saint not as reclusive or emotive but rather as embodying the life of the political body of his community. He would do this by becoming involved in building institutions for education or charity, being a mediator in social crises, and upholding fairness in market practices and equality in wealth.

This rhetoric of social activism led Hajji Imdadullah to take on roles not normally associated with quietist Sufis, such as the majority in his Chishti community. During the uprising of 1857, many of his colleagues from his devotional institute at Thāna Bhawan joined the military insurgency against British colonial forces. One hagiographer asserts that he preached jihad against the British and learned to fire a rifle in order to participate in the battle of Shāmilī in the district of Muẓaffarnagar.[62] The record is deliberately obscure, as his followers tried to protect him from the aftermath of the failed uprising, when the British publicly hung anyone they could find associated with "the mutiny." They closed his center at Thana as a suspected site of insurgency, and Imdadullah was driven into hiding. After closely missing arrest, Imdadullah fled through the Punjab and Sindh, visiting Sufi shrines and eventually sailing from Karachi into exile in Mecca.

In the midst of this political chaos that initiated the "imperial" phase of British colonialism, Imdadullah advocated a moderate reform of Sufi institutions in order to proclaim Sufi saints as leaders of the Muslim community in South Asia. It is as if the Mughal emperor could no longer represent the axis of Muslim public order in South Asia, so that Muslim saints had to step in and assert authority as social and even political leaders in a decentralized network rooted in diverse places that could not be easily eliminated or coopted. The mood was urgent, for the British had blinded the last Mughal emperor and banished him to Burma after hanging for treason most of the men of his royal family. In response, Imdadullah urged that Muslim saints desist from boasting about their particular lineage of masters, for these were forms that divided them. Through his devotional ritual, Imdadullah aimed to unite the various Sufi lineages and their distinct techniques. He regretted "the fact that the various modes and behaviors of the Path have become innumerable" by his own generation and stressed the common core of devotional exercises from various sources.

In "The Brilliance of Hearts" he tried to broadly define contemplation or recitation in order to show the student the core unity of the disparate forms of devotion. He redeployed the heritage of the *tariqa* into new forms in order to meet the challenge of accelerating social change and the breakdown of the Mughal polity. Encroachments of the British colonial project and the sense that the Islamic political order was in danger of collapsing fueled their efforts at reform. Although the British colonial administration claimed legitimacy by justly administering Islamic law to Muslims and Hindu law to Hindus, many Muslims were not convinced that the sharia could maintain its authentic form and its loyal following under the suzerainty of the British.[63] Even after their spiritual guide had been exiled, Hajji Imdadullah's students in South Asia organized the Deoband Academy. This academy was an innovative school, started after the British sacked Delhi in 1857; its purpose was to revive the teaching of the Islamic disciplines, especially jurisprudence, to give the Muslim community a new foundation after the last vestiges of the Mughal polity were destroyed. The scholars who founded it were disciples of Hajji Imdadullah.[64] In this way, Imdadullah's discourse about the heart as the center of ritual devotion was to place the saint at the heart of the body politic. This was a bid not only for his personal authority as an activist saint but also for the authority of the Islamic reassertion that his followers were conducting in the middle of colonized South Asia.

Imdadullah was a figure living on the cusp of modernity even while he was fully immersed in the Islamic heritage of the late medieval and early modern periods. From this vulnerable position he maneuvered through the issues of Islamic authority and Sufi practice with a rich attention to detail and nuance, from which we (on the other side of modernity) can learn much. Earlier in this chapter, we observed how the early Khurasani Sufi tradition, as epitomized in the dramatic serpent imagery of al-Tirmidhi, depicts the very basic operations of the body as the root of evil in an almost Manichaean way. As long as the body lives and the heart beats, *Shaytan* in the bloodstream will be agitated and threaten moral pollution. The Shattari and Chishti Sufis of South Asia, on the other hand, recast this image in a far more optimistic framework, recommending techniques that can not only discipline the body but also actually transform its physiology. Imdadullah, going one step further in these transformations, retains this optimism that the body can be fully transformed but couches this optimism in the socially conscious rhetoric and sharia-mindedness that was gaining ascendance during his age. Rather than urge the complete transformation of the body, as Yogis and many medieval Sufis did, Imdadullah focused upon the "rectified heart" as the locus for mystical experience, religious authority and social reform.

During their heyday in the medieval period, Sufis in South Asia extolled the mystical, anatomical, and almost magical effects of meditative discipline. Their surrounding society accorded great social authority and political power to adepts who could master such effects. However, by Imdadullah's era, this robust self-confidence had eroded, along with the umbrella of Islamic kingship under which these practices had thrived. Therefore, Imdadullah felt the need to remind his followers and readers of the necessity of the deep practice of these bodily disciplines. He did this by turning to sharia-oriented activity that Sufis before him took so much for granted that they hardly felt the need to mention it—building a mosque.

Imdadullah uses the metaphor of architectural space to merge the pursuit of illumination through bodily discipline with the urge to embody socially active ethics that are more explicitly Qur'anic. In his metaphor, building a disciplined body is like building a congregational mosque: if the building is firm and beautiful, then virtues, like worshipers, will come on their own volition and inhabit such a space, endowing it with sanctity. If worshipers are corralled into the mosque by harangues or threat, the mosque will be a house of hypocrisy and dissimulation rather than one of sincere worship. Likewise, one cannot entrust the acquisition of virtues to self-will or intellectual capacity; rather, it is the more basic postures of bodily discipline that can subvert self-will and harness intellection, creating a space for sincerity to alight. "Every seeker should safeguard the self through obedience to the Shaykh from all damaging moral behavior that is the very essence and necessary ingredient for substantial material existence. Every seeker should build for the self [in the heart] a congregational mosque in order to gather together of virtues and perfections. Do not allow any space in the heart for imagining anything other than God."[65] The heart, like a mosque, must be a space cleared of all otherness in competition with the presence of divinity. This image again suggests the heart of a resurrected body, which is upright only through the operations of divine power, rather than through the body's own habitual motions.

By imagining virtuous conduct as building a mosque or "house of God" in the heart, Imdadullah evokes potent images from the Sufi tradition. The heart of the true believer is the real, internal Kaʿba, of which the stone shrine in Mecca is a reminder. The human heart is also the worldly site of the throne of God, the physical place that is the locus for God's manifestation. Sufis imagine an ascending axis of three symbolic sites that reflect each other in different planes of the cosmos: the heart in the center of the human body, the Kaʿba in the center of the world, and the throne of God in the center of the cosmos.

In this metaphor of building a mosque or shrine in the heart, Imdadullah also stresses emphatically that the devotee should start gathering virtues through harnessing the material body, as the Shattari and Sabiri-Chishti masters had done in the past. The practitioner should begin this ritual by reciting with the tongue, aloud in the presence of the egoself. Only when practitioners habituate to audible *dhikr* should they move on to the more potent form of silent *dhikr* and breath retentions, for bodily habits form the basic foundation for achieving union with God. Yet Imdadullah is careful to point out that this materiality can be transcended, for its necessary ingredient is internal heedlessness of the ever present God and external bad moral behavior. Through remembering God's presence by harnessing the foundation of the body, these material limitations, which he calls "veils," can be breached. In this way, the heart can be rectified and transformed into a vessel to "contain" God, just as a mosque or shrine is imagined to be a "house of God" in which divinity dwells, despite the immateriality of God.

These instructions on how to perform ritual meditation and the intertextual references woven into them are very subtle, yet through them Imdadullah constructs his claim to authority as an Islamic leader and Sufi master. By the mid-nineteenth century, even the most nostalgic Muslim of post-Mughal South Asia had to face irreversible disintegration in the surrounding society. In reaction, reformers concentrated on reviving sharia disciplines and fashioning more hadith-centered devotional life. Although Hajji Imdadullah participated in this sharia-minded revival, he was careful to also preserve an intense interior focus on those moments in Islamic scripture that urge faithful believers to search for God's presence within their own hearts.

Conclusion

Despite this reformist activism, Imdadullah was not an ideologue. His devotional manual is multidimensional and works on four levels. It is conservative in preserving the lessons and images, some verbatim, from past masters, especially in passing on to new generations the explicitly body-centered devotion of ʿAbd al-Quddus Gangohi and Muhammad Ghawth Gwaliyori. The manual is also creative in subtly expanding the centuries-long conversion of Yogic body techniques into Islamic Sufi practices. His manual is also transformative as it operates on the individual reader, urging her or him to reimagine the body-in-ritual in ways that open new horizons of experience, specifically mystical experience. However, even though this alone is its stated aim, Imdadullah's manual works at a fourth level as well—it is "reformist" in struggling to reassert for modern times that mystical experience and sainthood are central pillars in social welfare and political cohesion. This forward-thinking and critical concern marks his very modern dimension, and it, too, was expressed through body metaphors. Imdadullah was aware that too much emphasis on the external elements of worship could lead the Muslim elite toward the empty exhortation of virtues, rather than toward sincere means to practice and internalize these virtues—that is, toward an overemphasis on the limbs of the body and a neglect of the vital center in the heart. According to Imdadullah, there could be no revival of the external topography of religion (for the purpose of political autonomy or social cohesion) without an intrepid and far more frightening exploration of the interior of religion as spiritual anatomy.

These four levels work in almost seamless harmony in his ritual manual, but the balance that he advocated did not become actualized in obvious form. Although his students remained firmly committed to Imdadullah as their spiritual father figure and regularly consulted him on important decisions in their life passage, their religious activities verged toward institution building in the colonial state. These institutions, preeminently the Deoband Academy and its branch academies, stressed the importance of studying hadith and issuing fatwas in shaping the devotional life of their adherents. Although many of the early Deobandis displayed the self-surrender and fellow service advocated by Imdadullah as the highest level of sanctity, few of them publicly referred to Imdadullah's ritual manual as the foundation of such virtuous behavior.

Rather, they adopted an increasingly oppositional stance toward the colonial state and its manipulation of Islamic legal institutions and rhetoric. This public opposition began to justify their self-sacrifice and civic duty, marginalizing Sufi devotional rituals to the realm of private belief. In this private realm, Imdadullah's writings may have retained a loyal following. However, a vivid connection between personal sanctity and social authority, which combined in the figure of Muslim saints, a connection that so pervasively shaped religious life among premodern Muslims, was increasingly displaced in the public rhetoric of colonial South Asia. Under the twentieth-century forces of colonialism, nationalism, and continuing or increasing poverty in South Asia (and most other regions of the Islamic world), the situation has deteriorated markedly. So much so, in fact, that "Deobandi" has transformed completely. It no longer stands for the name of an educational and legal academy founded under Hajji Imdadullah's inspiration. Instead, it is used to label a group of Sunni fundamentalists who, under guidance from the Wahhabi movement, helped give rise to the Taliban

(Madrassa Students' Movement) in Afghanistan and other militant groups, like the Sipah-i Sahaba (Cavalry of the Prophet's Companions) in Pakistan and the Lashkar-i Tayyiba (Army of Medina) in Indian-held Kashmir.

To assess this startling transformation, the conclusion to this book now turns to the contrast between Wahhabis and Sufis. This will allow us to assess the continuing importance of images of the human body in the crises currently challenging the interregional and international networks of Muslim communities.

CONCLUSION
Corporeality and Sacred Power in Islam

Let the human perish, how thankless you find him!
From what did [God] *create him?*
From a sperm God created and empowered him
Then along a smooth path guided him
Then brought him to death and entombed him.
Then, if God wills, from the dead God raises him.
—Qur'an 80:17–22

The Qur'an returns insistently to the human body to remind us of our frailty yet also reminds us of its resilience. The body that we take for granted and hold autonomously upright was once not so strong—it was just a spermazoid, requiring many further acts of empowerment to even grow into anything approaching a powerful human body. After a short time, the body itself, after coursing its smooth path, will again revert to the microscopic life forms that gave rise to its complex organization as it passes through death and is entombed. But this very fragility gives the Qur'an a stage on which to illustrate the potential of life after the grave: *then, if God wills, from the dead God raises him.* This concluding chapter focuses on tombs and graves as the site of intra-Muslim debate over the nature of the body. It highlights both grave threats and the hope of renewed life, which are the twin poles between which Sufis chart their course in our modern period.

The verses above come from one of the most amazing chapters of the Qur'an, entitled "He Frowned." The Prophet Muhammad's wife, 'A'isha, said that if any chapter of the Qur'an could be wiped out, Muhammad had wished that it would be this short chapter, which addresses him as the one who frowned and chastises him for his behavior with a blind man. The old and feeble man came seeking some knowledge about the new religion of Islam, but his arrival interrupted an important gathering of Arab tribal elders, powerful and rich men who, if they had embraced the religion, would have greatly strengthened the community, as it was under dire threat. Muhammad had done what almost anyone would do to look out for the welfare of his community through practical means: he ignored the blind old man and continued to engage with the tribal strongmen. *He frowned and turned away when a blind man came his way. How do you know if* [his heart] *might be purified or recall* [God] *and by recollection be rectified? For those who are called wealthy, you attend to them closely and don't bother if they are purified! Yet from one who comes to you hopeful, fearful and clearly humble, you let your attention be shunted aside!* (Q 80: 1–12).

In these, the harshest words directed toward the Prophet, the Qur'an admonished him with a reminder (*dhikrā*), the revelation itself. It reminded him not only of his own error but of the fragility of the body, the imminence of death, and the inevitable moral recompense at resurrection. The body and the grave are closely associated in this moral discourse. What one does in this world with the body generates a kind of moral energy that is stored up in potential, to be released as kinetic motion only once the body unravels and one passes beyond the grave into another realm. To keep one's deeds positive takes a persistent consciousness of the next world as already present, even though this world has not yet been left behind. The Qur'an chides the Prophet for being momentarily distracted from the insight of such consciousness. Sufis understand that the warning is not just to the Prophet but to all human beings; the revelation moves quickly from addressing him, as one who *frowned and turned away*, to addressing each of us in *let the human perish, how thankless you find him!* Between letting the human being perish and cultivating the insight to perceive the innate potential for goodness in each, Sufi teaching both embraces death and hopes for renewed life in each breath.

The goal of the Sufi tradition is to encourage Muslims to confront death at the individual level and to build exemplary communities that promote selflessness and concern for others at the communal level. The Sufi tradition was also crucial in perpetuating the common life of Muslims by passing on ideals of virtue and the means to reach them at the social level, so that Islamic societies might find their spiritual vigor ever renewed, despite the vicissitudes of war or the fall of political dynasties. At the heart of this many-leveled structure of aims and ideals are the Muslim saints. As we have seen in these chapters, stories about saints are the arteries that run through all these levels, and virtue is the nutrient that they strive to provide to each part of the structure.

This was the ideal picture of premodern Islamic societies in the view of a vast majority of Muslims. Few took exception to it: the small minority of rationalist theologians who could not accept the phenomenon of mystical experience, the vocal party jurists who were skeptical of the propriety of some Sufi practices to cultivate such experiences, and the rare ruler who suspected that the popularity of saints might threaten his power. Despite the shrillness of the naysayers, this Sufi-infused ideal vision thrived while Islamic societies were strong. It was an expression of that strength, in its acceptance of diversity, practical flexibility, and powerful union of aristocratic and popular cultures. The idea that saints act as the pillars of society allowed for massive public building of tomb shrines and encouraged the inclusive cultic activity that maintained their sacredness. It also served as an umbrella for the activities of otherwise marginalized people, such as women, ethnic minorities, the rare individuals whose expression of sexuality differed from the norm, or the fringe individuals who altered gender roles. Their difference from the numerical majority of Muslims could be transformed from a threatening difference into a difference that marked the presence of the sacred. The saints' stories presented here illustrate the wide variety of experiences that channeled into the institution of sainthood. They were chosen to descriptively celebrate that diversity rather than to prescriptively argue what is the true pattern of Islamic sainthood.

These stories span the wide chronological terrain of the "early modern period" (from the mid-fifteenth to the mid-nineteenth century). Over these centuries, the weakness of Islamic polities compared against the emerging powers of Europe became clear. The story of Mawlay Idris reveals the first hints of internal weakness in the mid-fifteenth century, as Morocco confronted European conquest of trade routes, port entrepôts, and later continental heartlands. By the time of Hajji Imdadullah in the mid-nineteenth century, the cracks in Islamic polities had split wide open; the final chapter of Hajji Imdadullah's story shows an empire collapsing before direct European colonization. In reaction to these slow developments that wreaked dramatic results, the Wahhabi movement spread and fueled related puritanical reform movements. Yet Sufi communities still exist today and in fact constitute an Islamic global network; however, they are seemingly quiet and hard to detect, in contrast to their dominant and vivid social roles in early modern Islamic societies. This concluding chapter ventures to explain this partial retreat by Sufis from public life as well as their persistence by exploring the Wahhabi movement and its conception of the body that is basically the image of the body buried and gone. This will reveal to us in greater relief the Sufis' approach to the human body, relief granted by their stark contrast to the Wahhbis. After having visited some very lively and vivacious saints, we now return to the subject of graves.

Grave Threats as Sufis and Wahhabis Meet

Although Portugal and Spain waged war against Moroccan and other North African rulers in the fifteenth century, it was their arrival in the Americas and rapid exploitation of gold and silver there that really shattered the Old World order that Muslims dominated. New trade routes destroyed economic markets and commercial networks in the Indian Ocean, the Red Sea, and the Mediterranean. At the same time, new monetary flow into Europe, combined with technical specialization, capitalist markets, and internal cultural change, sparked modernization processes in Europe, which the historian Hodgson has termed "the Great Western Transmutation."[1] Napoleon invaded Egypt in 1798, followed by the French occupation of Algeria in 1832, displacing provincial Muslim rulers nominally vassal to the Ottoman Empire. The British transformed their trading colony in Calcutta into an army to seize political rule of Bengal in 1757 and steadily expanded their rule in India until they toppled the Mughal empire by 1857. The Dutch eagerly followed suit, turning their spice trade in the Indonesian archipelago into colonial occupation of the formerly Islamic polities there. Inland empires were less vulnerable to European naval prowess, but they, too, depended directly or indirectly on trade routes that were fast disintegrating. The czarist Russian Empire opened a colonial advance across Central Asia, displacing provincial Islamic rulers and threatening the Qajar dynasty in Persia, which also saw its maritime opportunities curtailed by British forces that occupied Hormuz on the Persian Gulf. The Austro-Hungarians and Russians slowly and steadily rolled the Ottoman Empire, which had once threatened the gates of continental Europe, back to its Anatolian core.

These radical changes in geopolitical power necessarily changed relationships between Muslims themselves: between rulers and subjects, between scholars and reformers, between established tradition and emergent practice, in short between stable past and the precarious present. These changes deeply affected Sufi communities at the same time that they fostered the growth of the Wahhabi movement. In the previous chapter, we observed how Hajji Imdadullah increasingly adopted sharia rhetoric and opposed British colonial expansion. Some scholars claim this increasing attention to the sharia combined with military opposition to colonial European domination as the signs of a paradigm shift in Sufi communities, and they label such movements in the nineteenth century as "Neo-Sufism." Neo-Sufi movements supposedly shared many characteristics with the Wahhabi reform movement: a exoteric focus on enforcing the sharia, adoption of jihad rhetoric, and concern for renewing juridical independence (*ijtihad*).[2] Yet this label may be misleading even as it points to important changes. Even as he advocated the qualities listed above, Hajji Imdadullah promoted ritual engagement with the body that was almost Yogic in its athletic and imaginative regime, which different radically from the prescriptions of Wahhabi movement.

Lest this be blamed solely on his Indian origins or his allegiance to the Chishti Sufi community, we can fruitfully compare Imdadullah with another influential nineteenth-century Sufi leader who is often labeled "Neo-Sufi," Ahmad Ibn Idris. Both Sufi figures differed from the Wahhabis in their theology and their ritual engagement with the body even if, on the surface, they seemed to increasingly resemble the Wahhabis. Ibn Idris (1760–1837) hailed from northern Morocco and studied Islamic law and scripture at al-Qarawiyyin madrassa in Fes, just around the corner from the tomb shrine of Mawlay Idris, who was his genealogical ancestor. In 1800, only a few years after Napoleon's invasion of Egypt, Ibn Idris traveled through Egypt to Mecca. He lived in Arabia as it fell increasingly under Wahhabi control, and near the end of his life his many disciples back in North Africa fought against the French invasion of Algeria.

Ibn Idris stayed in an uneasy truce with the Wahhabis, who occupied the holy cities for a decade. He challenged the Wahhabis in a famous debate (*munāẓara*), even as he shared some ethical urges with their movement. Like them, he rejected the necessity of following the established juridical schools and felt that Muslims needed to refer to the original sources of the Qur'an and hadith to revive the sharia. This intellectual similarity with the Wahhabis has caused some scholars to conclude that Ibn Idris himself was "a pseudo Wahhabi" or was uniquely sympathetic to their movement.[3] However, Ibn Idris was, beneath the surface, very different from the Wahhabis, especially in his view of ritual, ethics, and scriptural interpretation. He criticized the Wahhabi excesses, narrowness, and violence against other Muslims. He called them "miserable wretches who are bound inflexibly to the externalities of the law. They know the details of knowledge and use them to accuse of heresy those who oppose them."[4] He also differed from them in their suspicion of the human body as a locus of sacredness.

The research of Rex O'Fahey and Berndt Radtke gives us a clear picture of Ibn Idris's mystical practices. He did not write out an explicit ritual manual, yet evidence of his ritual practices are clear in his disciples' records. The most characteristic prayer of their community was: There is no God but God and Muhammad is the Prophet of God in every glance and breath, to the number only comprehended by God.[5] The mention of reciting in each glance and each breath hints at how the prayer should pervade the physical body. The conjunction of specific words of prayer, bodily movements, and techniques of breathing and visualization hints at a rich conception of ritual, which Ibn Idris told his disciplies would carry one "beyond the bounds of nature." From engaging the tongue, eyes, and limbs, this practice moves inward, through one's breathing. Eventually, its effects will lodge in one's heart. Ibn Idris's primary disciple, Muhammad ibn ʿAli al-Sanūsī (1787–1859), defines their *ṭarīqa*: "when you busy your tongue with saying the *taṣliya* [blessing the Prophet] . . . it overwhelms your heart and permeates your deepest self, so that you quiver when you hear him mentioned and the vision of him takes hold of your heart and you see his form before your inner eye."[6] In this ritual practice, the Prophet Muhammad is important not just as the vehicle for revelation, as if he were an inert megaphone through which God speaks and people obey, a caricature of the Wahhabi understanding of the Prophet, but an accurate one.

Rather, contemplating his form and keeping it in one's vision can transform the practitioner's body. In a letter, Ibn Idris counseled another major disciple to recite each day special litanies that he provided "to purify and illuminate the heart and to attract the divine influences, and as for the great universal revelation (*fatḥ*) which is the self-displaying of the most sublime power and the overflowing of the manifestation of the greatest glory on all parts of the body, including the hair, the skin, the bones and the flesh, it will, before long if God wills, reach you and all your brethren like an all-embracing torrent *which spares not nor leaves alone* (Q 74:28)."[7] Clearly, Hajji Imdadullah was not alone in upholding a ritual engagement with the body and advocating a meditative transformation of the body from the inside out. Such a theological and mystical optimism cannot be attributed to Imdadullah's South Asian background or allegiance to the Chishti Sufi community. Ibn Idris, from Morocco and in the Shadhili Sufi community, upheld the same principles even as he lived in the midst of the Wahhabi movement and came under great pressure to conform to its reformist innovations.

To understand this essential difference between Sufi and Wahhabi understandings of the human body, we must turn now to a close investigation of the Wahhabi movement in Arabia. It is commonly understood as a puritan theological movement, but it was equally a political rebellion against Ottoman rule in Arabia. The Ottoman emperor in Istanbul ruled his polity not just as sultan but also as vice-regent of God (*khalīfat allah*) and the Shadow of God on Earth. After Selim I conquered Egypt and Arabia, he took the title Protector of the Holy Cities (*khādim al-ḥaramayn*). The Ottomans' control over the holy cities, Mecca and Medina, gave them popular religious justification for their rule. Their control over Mecca and Medina was mediated by a local vassal, the *sharif* of Mecca (who, like the Moroccan rulers, claimed the right to rule as descendants of the Prophet through ʿAli and his son, Imam Hasan). As a political movement, the Wahhabis rebelled against both the local sharifian rulers of Mecca and their Ottoman overlords. As a theological means to wage their political rebellion, Wahhabis attacked Sufism and saints' tombs. The political instability of the advent of the modern period was not resolved by finding saints' bodies and building shrines over them but rather by denouncing saints' bodies and destroying their shrines and tombs. This iconoclastic Wahhabi urge contrasts starkly with the Sufi approach to the human body.

The Wahhabi movement saw tombs as idols, in diametric opposition to the Sufi-informed assessment of tombs as holy places where the sacred radiated into the world. Wahhabis decried devotional ritual at tombs of saints and prophets as idolatry, rather than patronizing them as communication with spiritual powers and ultimately communion with God. The Wahhabi claim that tombs are idols is rooted in a different understanding of the body, one that can be seen as disenchantment with the past; it is rooted in a bitter denial that the human body is invested with sacred power and acts as the vessel for God's spirit. Therefore, this conclusion will now analyze the Wahhabi view of spirituality and the body and juxtapose it with its Sufi rival.

Assessing the Wahhabi movement is difficult, for it has many dimensions while its goals and means have changed over time. The movement has a reformist theological core, a radical political purpose, a purist devotional agenda, an antirational philosophical stance, and an ascetic aura; all the dimensions fused together to justify open rebellion against Islamic authorities of the past and wage violent conflict with Muslims who disagreed with them. To understand its direction and force, we will examine the writings of the movement's founder, Muhammad ibn ʿAbd al-Wahhāb, as amplified by his family and followers. He lived in the Arabian Peninsula, in the interior oasis region of Najd, far from urban areas or centers of cosmopolitan Islamic civilization. There he confronted the local practice of Islam, denounced its authorities (among them jurists, Sufis, and adepts at folk customs and magic), and asserted that he could return to a purified form of "original Islam" as practiced by the Prophet Muhammad's companions. To do that, he stripped off the historically sedimentary layers of discursive interpretation, legal reasoning, and mystical allegory that had become the corpus of Islamic tradition. Although Ibn ʿAbd al-Wahhab claimed to uphold Sunni orthodoxy, his theology was far too radical to be called conservatively orthodox. Astute contemporary observers note that the movement's dynamics and ideals most resemble the Khariji movement in the seventh century, which was seen as heretical by all Sunni and Shiʿi versions of orthodoxy.[8] He denounced the traditions of Islamic law as religious innovation, dismissed discursive theology as rationalist heresy, and discredited Sufi leaders as satanic hypocrites.

His theological puritanism and utopian audacity emboldened political upstarts, and he formed an intimate alliance with al-Saʿūd tribal leaders. They cooperated closely, with one providing the theological ideology and the other providing the military might, and proceeded to rebel against the sharifian rulers of Mecca and their Ottoman sovereign. Their most powerful weapon was not military but ideological. More effective than rifles and cavalry were religious labels and critical ideas. Ibn ʿAbd al-Wahhab charged that his definition of radical monotheism (*tawhid*) was the only one possible, even though it contradicted accepted definitions of consensual practice of Muslims over the previous twelve hundred years. The brutal consequence of this assertion was that any Muslim who did not agree with him was not actually a Muslim but rather an infidel (*mushrik*) guilty of associating other gods with the one God. By denouncing other Muslims as infidels (*takfīr*), Ibn ʿAbd al-Wahhab declared that their lives were forfeit and their property liable to destruction. If they argued with him theologically or resisted him culturally, this only made them more vulnerable to physical attack, since it showed that they were heretical Muslims, more dangerous to the purity of the faith than outside rejecters or adherents to rival religions: he called jurists the "Jews" hiding within Islam and called Sufis the "Christians" in Islamic garb.[9] He did allow that those he labeled "heretical hypocrites" could repent and declare allegiance to his creed; then they could live in safety, but only after confirming their repentance with action and joining in the violent jihad against nonconforming Muslims beyond the bounds of their pure and righteous community.

Such a radical theology proved very powerful. In a time of rapid change as European domination altered the globe and impinged on Muslim polities, it offered the reassurance that this collapse was a good sign. If Islamic empires fell, Islamic traditions died, and Islamic worldviews collapsed, this was good because they were not really Islamic. For Ibn ʿAbd al-Wahhab and his followers, Islam did not exist in the actual past of lived communities but only in the utopian future. Past forms of Islam were a threat to be discarded, dismantled, or dismembered in order to make way for the utopian advent of pure Islam. It is as if no Muslim had ever lived out the religion of Islam since the Prophet's immediate followers passed away, until Ibn ʿAbd al-Wahhab came upon the scene. So powerful has this ideology been that even some insightful Western scholars have accepted it as the essential form of Islam that defines the religion.[10]

Just as the Wahhabis despised history, they distrusted reason. Although his Wahhabi followers, upon coming to power in Arabia, claimed to uphold the Ḥanbalī school of Islamic law, in fact Ibn ʿAbd al-Wahhab rejected all the schools of Islamic law and all the processes of juridical reasoning and community consensus upon which they were based. Although the Wahabbis claimed to champion Sunni orthodoxy, in fact they rejected the theological schools upon which the Sunni consensus had been built. In its place, they claimed to simply obey the Qurʾan in a literal reading of its meaning, without exerting rational interpretation. Of course, this is impossible. All reading requires reason and interpretation, even one that disavows rational interpretation. Like all other Muslims, the Wahhabis were forced to use tools of interpretation; they solved this problem by rhetorically accepting only one tool—hadith, traditional reports about what the Prophet Muhammad is alleged to have said or done.[11] Ibn ʿAbd al-Wahhab ignored the fact that writing down hadith was just as much an innovation in religion as legal reasoning, discursive theology, or mystical allegory (in fact, all these interpretive traditions took form in roughly the same era, the two or three centuries after the Prophet Muhammad's death). Outside of the textual tool of hadith, the Wahhabi version of Islam was greatly informed by other interpretive strategies. Tribal chauvinism, Arab nationalism, and patriarchy were all pre-rational and informal sources for their ideals and to a great extent shaped the results of their rhetorically "purist" interpretation.

Body Image and Idolatry

Muhammad Ibn ʿAbd al-Wahhab, the architect of this ideology, was a genius as a reductionist. He reduced complexity into simplicity and reduced subtle shades of difference into polar binaries. Such is the power of ideology. He reduced Muslim Sufis into non-Islamic pagans, reduced their complex devotion into "worship of tombs," and reduced their mystical path, their way of finding signs of God in the created world and the human body, to simple idolatry. Such operations are apparent in the central text of the Wahhabi movement, Ibn ʿAbd al-Wahhab's *Kitāb al-Tawḥīd* ("Book of Monotheist

Belief"), to which we turn for illustration and example. In this text, Ibn ʿAbd al-Wahhab sets out his doctrinal core. It is exemplary of his thinking, and in it he even reduced writing from discursive prose into a list of statements.[12]

He first defines Islamic belief and then moves quickly to discuss everything that threatens it. In his first chapter, "The Benefit of Pure Monotheistic Belief and What Sins Invalidate It by Infidelity," he asserts that the only important thing in life is to get to heaven when life is over.[13] Getting there depends on rigid monotheistic belief, allegiance to Islam, and conformity to the narrowest interpretation of Islamic rituals and customs. In his view, neither followers of other monotheistic traditions, like Jews and Christians, nor Muslims of other interpretations or sectarian communities are granted access to heaven. They are beyond the bounds of his group, called "the one saved community" (*al-firqa al-nājiya*). He combines this definition of belief with a deeply pessimistic assessment of human nature, for any action outside of immediate conformity is "perversion" (*itbāʿ al-hawāʾ*). He dismisses historical reality, for any change in Islamic practice or thought is "deviation" (*bidʿa*). He denounces humanist free will, for any trust in human conscience or the human body is "hypocrisy" (*zandaqa*). This pessimism is compounded with a puritanical attitude characteristic of the Khariji movement, in which any fault, error, or admission of ambiguity is a sign of personal damnation and requires that one be branded an infidel and expelled from the one saved community. Professing faith that God is one and that Muhammad is a prophet is not enough, for it allows pluralism, both within the Islamic religion and among monotheistic religions. Rather, Ibn ʿAbd al-Wahhab argues, one enters heaven by one's faith and actions, which must conform to the norms of the one saved group, whom he asserts "will have access to heaven without divine judgment."[14] Although he does not state so explicitly, Ibn ʿAbd al-Wahhab's vision of belief, action, and judgment pictures a very limited role for God, for his is a God who understands no ambiguity, admits no subtlety, allows no intercession, judges without allowing purgation, and acts without mercy.

From the perspective of the Wahhabi movement, Muslims who do not agree with this vision of God's nature, human nature, and zealous belief are infidels. Any deference or respect accorded to another person, whether political ruler, religious authority or family elder, is idolatry. Ibn ʿAbd al-Wahhab even criticizes Muslims' respect for, insight into, and veneration of the Prophet Muhammad. He confines Muhammad's role to the limits of safely bearing God's message to humanity but denies him any role in the cosmic order beyond that. Ibn ʿAbd al-Wahhab's rejection of every human authority other than himself is the root of his conflict with Sufis, who hold that interior states of faith and belief are primary over outer actions, such that restraining from judging others is the best way to avoid being judged. "O Nakhshabi, do not accuse others of your own faults / Do not expect copper to have the same value as gold / People who have many faults and lack a good character / should not blame others for the shortcomings they themselves hold."[15] To achieve the wise insight and humble restraint necessary to withhold egoist judgment of others, Sufis extol the cultivation of prophetic virtues. They attest that the Prophet brought not just outer rules to obey but inner states of purity, sincerity, love, and compassion to embody. They claim that the Prophet continues to be present in the world. The Prophet's essence is light that is eternal within and beyond the body, his presence is felt closely at his tomb, and his charismatic intuition is continually perpetuated in his followers, in those *shurafa'* who emulate his character and in those saints who exemplify his virtues. Of course, opposing idolatry is central to Islamic belief and practice. Sufis also demean the worshiping of idols, but they have a radically different understanding of what constitutes an "idol." Our Sufi guide has said, "O Nakhshabi, worshiping idols is a waste of time / One who prays to lifeless forms will not obtain his desires / If he prostrates himself before objects deprived of life / He is as worthless as the false images he admires."[16] Despite his contempt for the worship of objects as idols, Nakhshabi and other Sufis assert that the tombs of prophets and saints are not at all lifeless and therefore undermine the Wahhabi critique. Further, Sufis (along with all orthodox Sunnis) affirm that the Prophet will be present with them on the day of judgment, empowered by God to intercede for them, as a manifestation of God's quality of subtle wisdom, inexhaustible grace, and undeserved compassion. For Sufis, to follow one's egoistic urges is to worship an idol—in their mystical and psychologically penetrating view, the only real idolatry is selfishness.

With these contrasts so deep and fundamental, it is not surprising that Ibn ʿAbd al-Wahhab confronts the Sufis early on in his doctrinal text. He does so at first through wrestling with terminology and does so later through direct confrontation. At first, he appropriates the term *awliya' allah*, "the Friends of God." The term is found in the Qur'an, so in fairness all Muslims can refer to it and must take account of its use. However, by the time of Ibn ʿAbd al-Wahhab, the term had become, for the majority of Muslims, saturated with the meaning that Sufi activities generate. Sufis use "the Friends of God" to denote the special status of saints who have achieved a level of firm sincerity, absolute trust, selfless concern, and unbounded love. Ibn ʿAbd al-

Wahhab tried to reclaim the term, emptying it of this popular understanding and filling it in with his own definition: "people are the lordly friends [of God] due to their keeping free of associating anything with God."[17] If this subtle redefinition was too oblique, the Wahhabi editor adds an explanatory note of brutal clarity: "Each of those who believe in God, who warily avoid associating anything with God, is in fact a friend of God (*walī*). However, the degrees of status of the friends differ according to the degrees of their struggle to stay warily conscious of God. Whoever is more wary of God is in closer friendship (*wilaya*) with God. But adherents to Sufi orders make deviations in religion and cause divisions among the Muslims, who call people to worship themselves and worship created objects or beings other than them and lure people away with their magical trickery. These people [the Sufis] are actually the friends of the tempter (*awliya' shaytan*) and his partisan supporters. Woe be to them and their followers on the day of judgment!"[18] These words of the editor are clearly intended by Ibn ʿAbd al-Wahhab himself, as we will see, and all Wahhabi commentators on "The Book of Monotheistic Belief" (the most prominent of them come from Ibn ʿAbd al-Wahhab's direct descendants) make similar explicit attacks against Sufis and accuse them of being satanic agents. However, in his text, Ibn ʿAbd al-Wahhab avoids making statements like this that smack of opinion and builds his argument more gradually through a pastiche of hadith and Qur'an citations.

Ibn ʿAbd al-Wahhab's argument begins to circle obsessively around the human body. First, he praises the prophet Abraham for rejecting the worship of idols, *Abraham was a model (umma), humble with God, upright and was not one of the idolaters* (Q 16:120), and exhorts Muslims to cleave to Abraham's example by dismissing all idols, whether conceived of as material statues, heavenly bodies, or inherited traditions. Second, he condemns the Jews and Christians for *taking their rabbis and monks as Lords in place of God* (Q 9:31) and exhorts Muslims to similarly reject all human authority or conception of divinity commingled with human agency. Third, he despises pre-Islamic Arabs for idolatrous practices, *those who take associates in place of God and love them as the love of God* (Q 2:165), accusing most Muslims of continuing pre-Islamic practices in gross or subtle form despite their claim to be Muslims. Ibn ʿAbd al-Wahhab crafts his argument from these three elements, praise for Abraham, suspicion of Jews and Christians, and spite for pagans.[19] It is a tantalizing argument, since these three elements are shared by many Muslims and have been around since the time of Muhammad himself. However, Ibn ʿAbd al-Wahhab derives conclusions from these three points that no Muslim theologian had drawn before, with absolutism and virulence that justified violence.

Having warned his audience against taking bodies as God, whether they are material forms in the shape of bodies, celestial bodies, the corpus of tradition, or the bodies of religious authorities, he begins to detail the bodily practices that perpetrate the sin of associating others with God. Ibn ʿAbd al-Wahhab begins with folk practices of protection and divination: wearing a brass ring to ward off disease, wearing a thread amulet to ward off calamity, wearing charms on the body to gain specific benefits, visiting sacred trees and stones to gain blessing, or sacrificing an animal to any power other than God.[20] Ibn ʿAbd al-Wahhab uses these clear condemnations to mount a case against other, more ambiguous practices. He argues that it is equally *shirk* to consecrate or dedicate anything to other than God, to take a vow with any power other than God, to seek protection (*istiʿādha*) or sustenance (*istighātha*) with anyone other than God. This gross associationism (*shirk akbar*) amounts to blatant infidelity (*kufr*).[21] These practices are far more closely linked to Sufism, for Islamic mysticism is based upon the goal of experiencing God's presence directly, a goal only attainable through the guidance, mediation, and help of a holy person. By placing trust in such persons, one's *shaykh* or spiritual guide, and turning to them with deference and respect as channels through which God's protection and nurture come, one can hope to internalize virtues, overcome selfishness, and render one's heart open to experiences of God's compassionate presence. Turning to spiritual authorities through such practices is quite ambiguous and difficult to judge, since the practices depend upon the practitioner's intent (*niyya*). Ibn ʿAbd al-Wahhab ignores this and reduces people's intentions to the crassest level: in his view, people seek protection or sustenance from God through another person only to gain material benefit or avoid harm, rather than to cultivate values like humility, respect, and honor or to venerate God by not appealing for help with arrogant directness.

In some cases, positive models for such practices exist in the Islamic community of the Prophet's earlier followers. Take the example of calling upon someone other than God to ask for sustenance (*istighatha*), which means to appoint someone as the mediator between those in need and God, who provides sustenance, usually in the form of rain during drought or food during famine. Members of the early Islamic community called upon the Prophet to pray to God for rain to sustain them during drought, and the vice-regents of the Prophet directed the people to call upon his cousin, Ibn ʿAbbās, who excelled in wisdom, knowledge, and piety, to play that role of mediator and intermediary after the death of the Prophet. Such examples of early companions being singled out as holy people reveal how Muslim saints are an integral part of the Islamic religion and perpetuate the Prophet's charisma in his community, despite Ibn ʿAbd al-Wahhab's accusation that this is *shirk* that invalidates one's Islam.

The continuing spiritual authority of living holy people, who mediate between the devoted public and God's presence, is a topic linked to the continuing spiritual authority of the Prophet Muhammad himself. Ibn ʿAbd al-Wahhab accused most Muslims, and Sufis in particular, of "deifying" the Prophet by upholding the doctrine that the Prophet can intercede for believers facing God's judgment (*shafāʿa*), such that their love for the Prophet might mitigate their lack of merit in God's eyes. In Ibn ʿAbd al-Wahhab's jaundiced evaluation, faith in the Prophet's intercession limits God's transcendence, exaggerates the Prophet's supernatural being, and offers an easy backdoor entry to heaven for those who do not really deserve it.[22] For the majority of Sunnis, including Sufis, faith in the Prophet's intercession was part of faith in God's mercy and is based on the hadith that report him to have told believers that "my intercession (*shafāʿa*) is made available on the day of reckoning to whoever petitions God [to bless and sanctify my name] so that I might be granted the means (*waṣīla*) to reach intimacy with God."[23] God granted the prophets intercessory power as an expression of God's quality of compassion and as a vehicle for forgiveness, which nobody, not even ascetic virtuosos or rampaging reformers, could deserve by their actions in the world. Believers cannot earn such compassion or forgiveness, but they can implore it through their love for others, especially for the Prophet and his delegates, who embody his qualities, from among his descendants and the saints. For this reason, Sufis as well as ordinary Sunnis and Shiʿa flock to the tomb in Medina where the Prophet's body is buried as the natural conclusion to their pilgrimage to the shine at Mecca or compensate for their inability to travel there with visitation to the local tombs of saints. And for this reason, the Wahhabis demolished the tomb of Imam Hasan and threatened to do the same to the Prophet Muhammad's tomb, which had been enlarged and adorned by Ottoman rulers.

In Ibn ʿAbd al-Wahhab's assessment, the power of living saints to mediate the sacred realm and the power of the Prophet to intercede with God are two integrally related issues. Both exaggerate the status of holy people. Ibn ʿAbd al-Wahhạb argues, "The reason that the children of Adam have become infidels and have left the true religion is their exaggeration of the status of righteous people (*al-ghuluw fī al-ṣāliḥīn*)." By exaggeration, he means devotion in which the righteous holy people are believed to be so powerful that their presence exceeds the bounds of their bodies so that their blessing transmits to people close to them or objects they have touched, their personalities can be present in places far beyond their physical limitations in space, and their presence can persist long after the mortal duration of their bodies.

In his "Book of Monotheistic Belief," Ibn ʿAbd al-Wahhab did not directly confront the fact that early Muslims saw some of their members as especially holy and able to mediate with God on their behalf, nor did he deal plainly with the Qurʾan's affirming of the practice of praying over tombs (Q 9:83–84). Instead, he deflects attention onto Christians to illustrate how "the children of Adam have become infidels and have left the true religion [because of] their exaggeration of the status of righteous people." To critique this exaggeration, he quotes a hadith: "The Prophet Muhammad said, 'Do not transgress in praising me as the Christians transgressed in praising the son of Mary; I am indeed a human servant, so just say [I bear witness that Muhammad is] God's servant and messenger.'"[24] The editor of "The Book of Monotheistic Belief" makes the critique inherent in this line clearer, honing in upon the Sufis as guilty of such heretical exaggeration. "Some of the Sufis go beyond the bounds of insolence in claiming that the Prophet is present in their assemblies of uproar and hand clapping, and is present in all gatherings of those who follow them in their devotional path. In these assemblies of noise and nonsense that they call remembrance of God (*dhikr*), they spread a white cloth in the center of their circle for the Prophet and his vice-regents to sit upon. . . . Some of them even claim that the Prophet pervades the entire universe. . . . They waste their lives in isolated retreats, muttering and droning babble, and spend all their wealth on the Satanic deceivers who swindle them (*al-dajjāl īn al-mushʿawidhīn*), who beguile them with all this out of greed. For it is impossible to see the Prophet with one's own eyes filling up heaven and earth and the universe between them!"[25] It is almost as if the editor's anger were directed against Ibn Idris and his Sufi followers, whom we encountered earlier. Their practice of *dhikr*, invoking the remembrance of God and calling down blessings upon the Prophet as their connection to God, is in their own words, "accompanied by a visible manifestation when you see the Prophet himself . . . and the vision of him takes hold of your heart."

As Ibn ʿAbd al-Wahhab attacks the theoretical structure of Sufism and the later Wahhabi commentators on his work attack Sufis in a more personal way, we must question the judgment of some Western scholars who suggest that Ibn ʿAbd al-Wahhab may not have been hostile to Sufis. The most nuanced argument of this kind is offered by Esther Peskes, who argues that Ibn ʿAbd al-Wahhab should not be seen as particularly anti-Sufi because fundamentally he was against everything associated with the Islamic status quo of his day, including Sufis, folk practices, legal structures, and governments. She argues that "the impact and continuity of Muhammad ibn ʿAbd al-Wahhab's doctrinal position underlying his categorical rejection of saints, shrines and practice of veneration, is more significant than the physical destruction of shrines which he inspired or engaged in personally."[26] Why the theory that inspired such destruction should be decoupled from the actual destruction is not clear; this study's focus on the human body should make it clear that these two dimensions of Wahhabi activity are fundamentally unified. One cannot separate an ideology's image of the body from its practices regulating the body, especially when the ideology advocates revolutionary change and violence against its opponents. Nor is it clear in Peskes's article why this analytical operation exonerates Ibn ʿAbd al-Wahhab from being labeled as anti-Sufi when his movement, from its earliest inception in the oases in central Arabia, destroyed the tomb shrines that were the central meeting places of Sufis and the architectural focus of their spiritual geography.

From its advent, Ibn ʿAbd al-Wahhab's rebellious movement has sparked critique and rebuttal from jurists, theologians, and Sufis.[27] So divisive was his preaching that even Ibn ʿAbd al-Wahhab's own brother, Sulayman (died approximately 1792), wrote a learned refutation of his claims. In this text, "Divine Thunderbolt in Refutation of the Wahhabi Cult," his brother repudiates Ibn ʿAbd al-Wahhab and his followers' calling other Muslims infidels, especially those who visit the graves of ancestors or holy people, who circumambulate the graves, who wipe themselves with dirt from the graves, or take blessing from objects associated with graves.[28] He protests that the Wahhabis' intent in perpetrating such irresponsible *takfir* is not purification of religion as they state but is actually the breaking of consensus (*kharq al-ijmāʿ*) in order for Wahhabis to claim that their leaders have the right to rule authoritatively. Such early insight into the movement by a family member, who would be assumed to support his brother or at least keep a decorous silence, reveals the integral connection between body practices, opposition to Sufism, and the authority to rule in rebellion against established norms. This integral connection continues today as the movement's contemporary manifestation in kingdom of Saudi Arabia bans Sufi literature, forbids visitors from lingering near the tombs they have not razed, and arrests people on charges of "practicing Sufism."

Contrary to Peskes, this study maintains that the Wahhabi movement is anti-Sufi in its ideological marrow. Of course the movement has changed over time in reaction to historical contingencies, especially in morphing from a local rebellion into a durable militant minority into a ruling regime. However, the bare bones of its ideology have remained remarkably constant, and its virulent opposition to Sufi ideas and practices is one of the main forces that animate it. Ibn ʿAbd al-Wahhab's interpretation of the prophet Noah especially reveals this ideological bias.

Holy People and Sacred Power

We have seen above how those who believe that prophets and saints act as channels for sacred power to permeate the world perceive in them an image that exceeds the body. Upon their death, this devoted public creates a likeness of the body, or a substitute for it, in a material replica of the image it held dear. This, Ibn ʿAbd al-Wahhab asserts, is the origin of idolatry. To prove this point, he makes reference to an obscure interpretation of the story of Noah and his people's idolatrous rejection of his prophetic message (the same story with which Chapter 3 began). He quotes the verse in which Noah, in his despair at how his people reject him, petitions God to destroy them utterly. *Noah said, "Lord, they have disobeyed me and . . . they take recourse to terrible devious plots, saying, 'Do not forsake your gods, Wadd, Suwāʿ, Yagūth, Yaʿūq or Nasr.' They have led many astray and only increase the wrongdoers in misguidance." Because of their sins they were drowned and hurled into the fire, from which they found none to help them apart from God. Noah said, "Lord, do not leave any of the infidels on the earth for if you do they will mislead your servants and will beget only corrupt ones and disbelievers"* (Q 71:21–27).

Most Sunni interpreters accept the apparent meaning of this verse and understand the wealthy elite of Noah's time to have defended the idolatrous worship of their indigenous gods, referred to by the proper names Wadd, Suwaʿ, Yaguth, Yaʿuq and Nasr. The earliest commentators describe these as pagan gods of the pre-Islamic Arabs and their Semitic ancestors.[29] Ibn ʿAbd al-Wahhab interprets these verses with a more complex scenario that makes them a pivot point of his ideology, claiming that these five names signify holy men whose status had been "exaggerated" until they were worshiped as gods. He complicates the apparent simplicity of the verses by citing a report about Ibn ʿAbbas (whom Muslims respect as the earliest commentator on the Qur'an), who allegedly commented on these proper names: "These are the names of holy men of the people of Noah. Once they were destroyed, Satan inspired in the minds of the people of Noah, 'Erect in their places of assembly where they used to gather some constructions and call them by their names.' So they did this, but without worshiping [them]. Then after those [people] perished and the knowledge was forgotten, they [the constructions] were worshiped."[30]

In this way, Ibn ʿAbd al-Wahhab revives a tradition that asserts not only that these names are of pre-Islamic gods but that the gods are deified holy men in whose image statues were carved. The early Muslim philosopher and historian Hishām ibn al-Kalbī (died 822), recorded this tradition in "The Book of Idols."[31] "One of the children of Cain addressed their relatives saying, 'O ye who are bereaved! Shall I make unto you statues after the image of your departed relatives? I can readily do that, although I cannot impart life to them.'"[32] With this pious warning, he carved five statues depicting the images of their departed relatives and erected them over their graves. The relatives would visit the graves marked by these images, paying respect to them by walking around the statues. "Another century followed during which people venerated and respected those statues . . . [then] the people said, 'Our forefathers venerated these statutes for no other reason than the desire to enjoy their intercession before God.' Consequently they worshipped them, and became far gone in disbelief."[33] Although Ibn al-Kalbi relates this tradition as the origin of idolatry and calls such idolatrous worship of images "disbelief," he does so in a very neutral way, as if he were an early anthropologist of religion noting the evolution of a ritual practice. He envisions idols as funerary images, much like the startling images in the Archeological Museum in Amman, Jordan, which are claimed to be the oldest-known statuary created by human hands: skulls of the dead plastered over with fired clay, as if pottery could restore the flesh to bone and symbolically house the presence of the dead.

Ibn al-Kalbi hints that degeneration into idolatry is inherent in human nature, as the natural consequence of our drive to memorialize the dead and represent in material form our hope for transcendent continuity beyond the mortal body. For the philosophical Ibn al-Kalbi, the first human body provided the raw material for the first grave, the first graven image, and the first gravel path of pilgrimage and circumambulation; Adam's children made his grave in a cave on the mountain on which he had alighted on earth, on the island of Sarandīp (Sri Lanka), and made a rite out of walking around it out of veneration.[34] Ibn al-Kalbi even claimed that the origin of idol worship at the Kaʿba was respect for the shrine itself, the Islamic center of monotheistic worship. "No one left Mecca without carrying away with him a stone from the stones of the Sacred House as a token of reverence to it and as a sign of deep affection to Mecca. Wherever he settled, he would erect that stone and circumambulate it in the same manner that he used to circumambulate the Kaʿba [before his departure from Mecca], seeking thereby its blessing and affirming his deep affection for the Sacred House."[35] Clearly, Ibn al-Kalbi relates these traditions about idolatry with affection, as a part of the Arab and Semitic past that reveals deep human yearnings and frailties.

In contrast, Ibn ʿAbd al-Wahhab cites the same tradition about the idols of Noah's people but with none of the warmth and affection of the folkloric philosopher Ibn al-Kalbi. Rather, Ibn ʿAbd al-Wahhab's list of points is as stark as the conclusions he extracts from this story.

> 1. the estrangement of Islam and the power of God to change hearts in strange ways. 2. knowledge that the first instance of *shirk* in the world was in the form of righteous people. 3. the first thing that altered the religion of the Prophets and what caused this alteration despite the fact that people knew God had sent the Prophets. 4. the acceptance of deviations in religion (*bidaʿ*) even though systems of religion based on Prophetic teaching (*sharāʾiʿ*) and original human nature (*fiṭar*) reject them. 5. that the cause of all this was intermixing the truth with falsehood, the truth being love of the righteous people and the falsehood being that people of religious knowledge create something from which they desired good, but from which others after them think they desired something else. 6. that this explains the Qur'an's verse [about Noah]. 7. that the human instinctual penchant (*jibillat al-ādamī*) for truth lessens in the heart while falsehood increases. 8. testimony to what the early Muslims (*salaf*) have been reported to say, that religious deviation is the cause of infidelity (*kufr*). 9. proof that the tempter (*shayṭan*) knows what will lead eventually to religious deviation, even if those who invent a practice aim at righteousness. 10. knowledge of a universal principle forbidding all exaggeration and knowledge of that to which it leads. 11. the harm brought by gathering at a tomb (*al-ʿakūf ʿalā al-qabr*) even for a righteous action. 12. the prohibition against idols and likenesses (*tamāthīl*) and the wisdom of eradicating them. 13. the importance of this story and the intensity of our need for it despite the fact that it is forgotten or neglected.[36]

As Ibn ʿAbd al-Wahhab extracts his list of points from the story, he dispenses even with verbs: the story is not "analyzed" or "interpreted" so that it "reveals" information or "conveys" knowledge. Verbs would imply human agency in the interpreter, so Ibn ʿAbd al-Wahhab elides them, allowing his list of points to stand, in starkly self-revelatory reality, as a literal and incontrovertible reading of the text. The list of points continues, so that those who think Ibn ʿAbd al-Wahhab is only conveying theory can understand its very practical, political, and even violent implications.

> 14. wonder upon wonder that people read this story in their books of Qurʾan interpretation and Prophetic tradition and know the meaning of its discourse, but still God shapes a spiritual state between them and their hearts such that they believe that the action of Noah's people was the best of worshipful action! This they believe, despite the fact that God and God's Prophet have prohibited it, for it is explicit infidelity that makes licit killing them and confiscating their property. 15. clarification that such people [who worshiped idols] intended intercession (*shafāʿa*). 16. their opinion that the religious scholars who shaped the images (*ṣuwar*) had intended them for this purpose. 17. clarification of the meaning of [the hadith], "Do not transgress in praising me as the Christians transgressed in praising the son of Mary," may blessings and peace be upon the one who preaches the true message clearly. 18. advice to us to destroy those people who are pig-headedly obstinate (*mutanṭiʿīn*).[37]

Even though Sufis are not named explicitly, the points in the end of this list constitute a judgment that Sufis are idolators, are like Christians, are not Muslims, and are therefore apostates who can be legally killed.

When he says that the idolaters worshiped images for intercession, he means that any Sufi who believes in the intercession of the Prophet Muhammad or the mediation of the saints in his spiritual lineage is actually an idolater. When he says this list gives a great clarification of the hadith "Do not transgress in praising me as the Christians transgressed in praising the son of Mary," he means that Sufis who exaggerate the spiritual status of the Prophet Muhammad are guilty of idolatry, just as the Christians are guilty for elevating Jesus into the Son of God. His fundamental intention is clear: these scriptural verses and prophetic traditions advise us "to destroy those people who are pig-headedly obstinate" in maintaining any practice that the Wahhabis deem to be *shirk*.

Such a justification of violence against fellow Muslims constitutes the most radical type of fatwa imaginable, made even more radical by its eschewing any dependence on Islamic law or established norms of juridical reasoning. At his most explicit, Ibn ʿAbd al-Wahhab maintains, "The spiritual state of some Muslims changes to such an extent that they think the worship of monks to be the most lofty of action—this is called 'sainthood.' And the worship of Rabbis is called 'jurisprudence and theology.' Then their spiritual state changes even further, such that these human authorities, who are not even righteous holy people, are worshiped instead of God. This progresses to the point that the worshipers take on a new identity, and in their worship become purely un-Islamic pagans (*jāhilīn*)."[38]

Later Wahhabi commentators systematically decode the meaning of these lists of points in a more explicit way. A great-grandson of Ibn ʿAbd al-Wahhab, named ʿAbd al-Rahman ibn Hasan ibn Āl al-Shaykh (died 1842), makes plain that this list of points constitutes an ideological attack on Sufis. His commentary "Conquest of the Mighty in Explanation of the Book of Monotheistic Belief" preserves and expands earlier partial commentaries, like that of the Wahhabi ideologue Sulayman ibn ʿAbdullah.[39] He explains in detail Ibn ʿAbd al-Wahhab's citation of the story of how Noah's people came to worship as gods statues originally created to memorialize holy people: "Satan inspired in the minds of the people of Noah, 'Erect in their places of assembly where they used to gather some constructions and call them by their names.'" The command to "erect" (*anṣibū*) leads him to explain that these statues were constructions erected (*anṣāb*) on the holy people's tombs, which are justifiably called idols rather than markers or memorials. "The word idol (*wathn*) includes comprehensively every object of worship (*maʿbūd*) that is not God, whether that object of worship is a tomb (*qabr*) or memorial (*mashhad*) or image (*ṣūra*) or anything else."[40] Here, the commentator reveals the elasticity of Wahhabi interpretations of idols. They are not just the statues of gods or deities. Any image can become an idol, especially those images that reflect the body, whether in a lifelike manner, a symbolically abstract manner, or in an architecturally monumental manner.

ʿAbd al-Rahman condemns Sufis in this vague and infinitely expandable "definition" of an idol. He comments, "These images fashioned in the likeness of the forms of these holy men became the means through which to worship them. Everything that is worshiped which is not God, whether grave or memorial or image or pagan idol (*ṭāghūt*) has its origin (*aṣl*) in extreme exaggeration."[41] In this commentary, Sufi devotion is explicitly reduced to mere saint worship, and rituals at a tomb become idolatry. He condemns the Sufis of Egypt who venerate the long-dead saint Ahmad Badawī, who he says is a person of no known repute or virtue or knowledge or piety but who is nevertheless their greatest deity (*āliha*). "Satan made worshiping him seem beautiful to their eyes, and they believed that he had power over destiny in the universe, to extinguish fires and rescue the drowning; so they treat him as if he had divinity and lordship and knowledge of the unseen. They believed that he could hear them and answer them from distant locations. Among them are some who prostrated on the threshold of his presence [at his tomb]. The people of Iraq . . . believe in ʿAbd al-Qadir al-Jilani the same way people in Egypt believe in Ahmad Badawi. . . . The people of Syria worship Ibn ʿArabi [who is buried in Damascus]; he is the leader (*imām*) of the people of unity (*waḥda*), who are the most infidel (*akfar*) of any people on earth and most people who believe in him have no virtue and no moral worth, like many people in Egypt and other places."[42] The commentator's choice of regions to criticize is crucial. He singles out Egypt, Iraq, and Syria and reduces their regional cultures to heretical cults of saint worship. These three regions were key areas where Arabs were loyal to Ottoman rule. This theological rant not only questions their political loyalty and resistance to the Wahhabi political revolt but also judges them as infidels who cannot be granted the status of real Muslims and whose blood and property are therefore forfeit. They do not worship God but rather Satan. The commentator ʿAbd al-Rahman explains that Satan beguiles people, "making the worship of constructed images (*aṣnām*) seem beautiful and ordering them to do it. So Satan became, in reality, the object of their worship. . . . Satan causes them to start practicing *shirk* through exaggeration in these holy men and going beyond all bounds (*ifrāṭ*) in loving them. Such has happened to some in this [Islamic] community. [Satan] shows them exaggeration and deviation (*bidʿa*) in the bodily form (*qālib*) of holy men and inordinate love for them, then they get overtaken by something much worse than that by their worshiping them instead of God."[43]

In this commentary, the Wahhabi distrust of the human body becomes clearer. Infidelity comes through revering the bodily form of holy people, for as Ibn ʿAbd al-Wahhab himself said, the human instinctual penchant is "for truth to lessen in the heart while falsehood increases." To expand on the idea that the body in its grave constitutes the basis of idolatry, he condemns all the elements of a sacred space that we saw present at the tomb of Mawlay Idris in Chapter 1: "It is especially the praise of their [holy people's] graves that causes this exaggeration that leads to worshiping them, like building domes over them, covering them with cloths, lighting lamps nearby, and the establishing of custodians. Satan stays close by them to call the people to worship them with all types of dedicated offerings and the money accrues to them. . . . Those people who imagine that they go to the graves for moral admonition or to recall the afterlife, those graves upon which are erected those constructions (*anṣāb*) and around which are built those enclosures (*maqāṣīr*), are among the most ignorant of people and the most distant from the guidance of Islam."[44] In this condemnation, the commentator charges that any grave marked as a body is not Islamic, writing that Islam acknowledges only those graves over which is built nothing, upon which is written nothing, which are not covered with cloths of silk or other substances. He concludes this description and juridical judgment with a prayer that God help the Wahhabi movement destroy all such places and the people who revere them. "We beseech you, O God, to hasten the razing of these idols and purify the earth of them all . . . to preserve belief in one God from the pollution of *shirk*, the greatest cause of which are these graves."[45] In this impassioned prose, which builds an impressive edifice of vitriol upon the bare bones of Ibn ʿAbd al-Wahhab's list of points, the commentator reveals an ascetic urge. It is the ascetic denial of spiritual value to the human body that informs the whole Wahhabi movement and explains its vehement opposition to Sufism, Shiʿism, and the folk practices of Islam.[46]

Wahhabis' ascetic extremism comes down to an obsession with dirt. Wahhabi ideologues, like these commentators and Ibn ʿAbd al-Wahhab in his text upon which they elaborate, want to reduce the body to mere dirt. They want to bury the body with no marker or memorial. Yet at the same time they are horrified by dirt in the form of filth and pollution. This reveals a fundamental discomfort with the body, which was created from dirt, continually defiles itself, and will inevitably revert to putrefaction. It is an ascetic vigilance that cannot admit that the human body, like the human personality that arises from it, is a transient but overwhelming reality that persistently confounds the efforts of reason, especially moralistic reason, to control it and assimilate its bewildering otherness into the moral order imposed upon it. It is an ascetic horror that cannot accept that this defiling construction of mere dirt is the consummate creation of God and the dwelling place of God's "breath of the merciful One" (*nafas al-raḥman*). Just as the Wahhabis deny that the Prophet Muhammad was anything more than mere megaphone for God's Speech, they cannot see the human body as an assembly of the signs of God. In this sense, their approach to the body approximates that of Cartesian modernism. The way that Descartes described the human body, "first as a statue and then as a machine, undermines its biblical status as a vessel that is animated by the breath of God."[47] Descartes attempted to gain distance from the body in order to achieve intellectual certainty (and along the way to find clarity about religious quandaries like the nature of the soul); in contrast, the Wahhabis' quest is for religious certainty while, along the way, they abdicate intellectual clarity. However, both are united in the drive for certainty and commit ideological violence against the body to banish it as a source of moral doubt and ontological ambiguity.

In the end, however, Wahhabis cannot erase the body and its image. The more rigidly they try to prescribe it through law, morality, and asceticism, the more it looms up within, provoking horror at oneself and violence against others. Al-Zahi comments insightfully on the inevitable failure of prohibiting the making of images of the body, for "the image of the body becomes present in the rigidity of the juridical position against it, beyond the margins that it demarcates for itself . . . exceeding, to a great extent, the possibility of burying (*iqbār*) the proofs of its presence."[48] In their obsession with denying the sacredness of concupiscent bodies, Wahhabis must cover living bodies with regulations and limitations while demolishing the covering of buried bodies. Yet images of the body rear up beyond the boundaries of their ability to bury, cover, and demolish. The Wahhabi ideology can sustain itself only by pushing the body toward death, by enjoining continual martial jihad against all outsiders, with whom it has no ability to compromise and no desire to live in concord.

Embodiment between Vitality and Disenchantment

Ibn ʿAbd al-Wahhab's primary text, as amplified and applied by his commentators, demonstrates that Wahhabi doctrine is one of disenchantment. It bitterly denounces the places and people in whom the majority of Muslims find access to the sacred canopy that makes the routine world a cosmos saturated with the signs of God's presence; those are holy people, whether prophets or saints, and the burial sites of their bones, through which materiality becomes suffused with spirituality.

What causes this fundamental disenchantment that gives the Wahhabi ideology its vehemence? Wahhabis' writings have the tenor of vengeful reproach of one who feels betrayed. The commentator ʿAbd al-Rahman admits that he joined the Sufis but tasted only disappointment and failure before turning in compensation to the Wahhabi movement.[49] This is one man's perspective, but we cannot attribute a dynamic movement to just a personal grudge, for people have joined the Wahhabis with differing motivations. Undeniable, however, is the fact that the movement was inspired and colored by a jaded reformer's grudge against a whole civilization, as Ibn ʿAbd al-Wahhab felt Islam had betrayed its origins and fallen into decay, such that it became dominated by European Christians and the Jews who have assimilated into European modernism. Therefore, his attack on the sacred bones of the buried body is an attack on the *imaginairé* of medieval and early modern Islamic societies. This *imaginairé* was the pattern of thought through which Muslims imagined the cosmos to consist of hierarchal levels of value linking the material world to the sacred realm beyond, as mediated and connected through the human image.[50] Thus the material world, the society that inhabits it, the political system that orders it, the religious specialists who maintain it, and the Prophet who began it are linked like rungs in a rising ladder of being. The Prophet Muhammad is thus seen as primordial light and the complete human being, upon whose pattern and through whose radiance the first body of Adam was formed, according to the hadith that reports Muhammad to have said, "I was a Prophet while Adam was still between water and dust." Thus the Prophet Muhammad was not just a historical person or a megaphone for God's Speech. In this Islamic *imaginairé*, he plays a cosmic role of the lens of the human image through which microcosm and macrocosm mirror each other; in later times and diverse locales, the saints and their very fallible bodies reflect this role and take on the aura of sacredness.

This Islamic *imaginairé* that dominated the medieval and early modern period is expressed most profoundly by Sufis and is articulated most lastingly by Islamic art and architecture. This Islamic *imaginairé* still persists among Muslims who have not given in to the disenchantment imposed by colonial modernism from without and wrought by Wahhabi critique from within. In notions of how the body must be buried and the belief that the buried body manifests sacred power even as it disappears from direct view, we see deeply into Islamic ideas of the human body, its worth, and its function as a sign of the unseen power of God.

We can understand the power of this Islamic *imaginairé* through the phenomenological scheme of embodiment outlined in the Introduction, with Farid al-Zahi as our guide. Indeed, the Islamic *imaginairé* described above is embedded in Muslims' notion of corporeality, the symbolic dimension in which the physical reality of the body conditions and is conditioned by the furthest horizon of how we imagine embodied human beings. Without using the technical term "*imaginairé*," al-Zahi describes its nested harmony of images that begin with the body and expand outward and upward through society and religion to give form to a meaningful universe. "Our endeavor here is to expand the understanding of the image (*ṣura*) to include the mental image (*ṣura dhihniyya*) rather than just the rhetorical image (*ṣura balāghiyya*). This is in order for us to express in its fullest the issue [of the importance and limitations of the Islamic prohibition of making images, which al-Zahi calls "one of the greatest difficulties known to the cultural history of the Arabs"]. For the physical body and its visual image also exist in the image of writing, in the calligraphic script (*khaṭṭ*) in art and the mystical image of being (*ṣurat al-wujūd*) among the Sufis. From our perspective, this issue entails a further examination into the separation between the human and nonhuman (*al-marʾī waʾl-lā marʾī*)."[51] Indeed, the image forms the link between the body, as the material reality of the human being, and the sacred, which is imagined both to infuse the body with its life and to be necessarily beyond the body, even inaccessible with the body, in order to secure for the sacred realm a power, duration, and scope that is beyond decay, corruption, and alteration. Only in this form can the sacred realm give meaning to the inhabited world as a foundation to the lived experience of changeable states, material limitations, and temporal mortality. The relation of human consciousness with the human body takes the form of the relations of human to nonhuman. The material dimension of being inevitably becomes a corpse, transformed rapidly into a mark in the soil, whether reduced to ash in cremation, stripped to bone in exposure, or covered over by burial.

To conclude this comparison between Sufi images of the body and those of their Wahhabi rivals, we can note succinctly that Sufis embrace the ambiguity of embodiment and channel it to achieve access to the sacred realm that is beyond the limit of materiality. In contrast, Wahhabis denounce the ambiguity of embodiment and strive to achieve radical purity by banishing or burying images of the body as well as actual bodies of opponents. Serving the needs of the Saudi monarchy and its oil economy has moderated the radical core of Wahhabi ideology; however, in contemporary times after the Cold War world order has broken down, the radical core of Wahhabi ideology has resurfaced with a vengeance. Al-Qaeda, the Taliban, and other splinter groups of Wahhabi-inspired militants express this ideology's most violent inner drive. Those radicals who cannot or will not engage in military jihad engage in cultural jihad by prohibiting body images in other ways: suppressing women, denouncing Sufis, or reviling as idolatry technologies of visual communication (like photography, cinema, and television).[52]

In view of their nihilistic desperation, it is no surprise that Wahhabis cling to the story of Noah to justify their despair and convey their blanket condemnation of the present order. Noah gave up all hope in his people. He petitioned God to destroy them and erase all trace of their constructions, to bury them in water and mud so that history might have a clean slate to start anew. Not surprisingly, Sufis have a different assessment of Noah. The Sufi intellectual Ibn ʿArabi chastised Noah for his lack of patience and insight, as if these were personality failings despite his status as a prophet. He charges that Noah did not look upon his people with the eye of spiritual insight to know that, even if they worshiped idols, they could not help but worship God because nothing exists apart from God, not even idols.[53] Of course, such an outspoken position was controversial and provoked Wahhabis to single out Ibn ʿArabi for particularly hostile attacks.[54] While Ibn ʿArabi's writing raises the ambiguous issue of whether saints can have insight and spiritual prowess greater than prophets, it also has the merit of demonstrating, in the most dynamic and subtle terms, how God pervades the cosmos and interacts with material existence through the mediating image of the embodied human being.[55] His critique of Noah shifts our attention from the despair at the beginning of his story to the hope at its end. "O Nakhshabi, hope is a rare and wonderful blessing / how much grief and sadness it cleanses from the troubled mind / Even though one's aims and desires are not attainable / still unceasing hope is the consolation of humankind."[56] Noah's most enduring sign is the arc of the rainbow that signifies the hope of reenchanting the world that would sprout anew. From his family that survived came the messenger, Abraham, and the plurality of religious communities that take him as their founder, as varied as the spectrum of light refracted through the moisture of rain. The wooden dwelling of his ark could, in later times, give rise to the ark of the covenant, the temple sanctuary, and the tomb shrines of saints as buildings of hope where death becomes transmuted into a promise of renewed life.

The Wahhabis preach a religious ideology of disenchantment that, in their view, gives them Noah-like authority to declare their civilization corrupt and its spirituality dead. However, they offer no rainbow—their ideology buries the body, offering no explanation of how the light of sacred presence refracts through the materiality of our worldly atmosphere. Their vision is in black and white, admitting neither the colorful spectrum of diversity nor the gray shades of ambiguity. Rather than the rainbow, their sign is the sword. Their vision of the future is a continuous battle against those they have excised from their own faith community and whose blood they declare licit. They can only preach the razing of domes that, like the rainbow, arc over dry bones as if to connect earth to heaven. They can only advocate the demolition of shrines that, like the ark, are built to house the remains of the righteous body and carry it from the valley of death to the further shores of new life.

Conclusion: The Heart of the Matter

As Muslims confront the violence of extremist groups like the Wahhabis, it is clear that fostering engagement with the body in an Islamic context is crucial. Although many contemporary Muslims may view Sufism as sorely antiquated, overly traditionalist, too authoritarian, or suspiciously heterodox, this study asserts that the Sufi tradition offers a valuable archive of experiences, practices, and worldviews that value the human body, defend its integrity, and strive to comprehend human embodiment in an integral way. Sufism contains crucial resources in the struggle of conscientious Muslims to assert basic human dignity, humane values, and humanitarian rights in the face of the rapid growth of fundamentalist and Wahhabi-inspired movements.

This study illustrates how such resources can be found within Sufism. Sufis insist that religious values cannot be imposed upon others but only inspired within them; moral order cannot result from swift coercion of threat and force but rather from the slow persuasion of wisdom and example. Outer actions are conditioned by the inner state of intention and conscience, which must be clean if actions are to be effective and wholesome. Our Sufi guide, Nakhshabi, has said, "A problem which can be settled by consultation cannot be handled by the use of force. The task of clearing the house of litter can be performed with a broom—not a stick, and the chore of taking rubbish out of the home can be accomplished by means of a basket—not with a sword or an arrow."[57]

Increasingly, Muslims are confronted with fundamentalist violence that denies the integrity of the human body. Such violence reduces the body's biological complexity, social value, and spiritual worth to instrumental uses as ideological tools, seen at its extreme in suicide bombings. In contrast, Sufism embraces the complexity of the human body as the vehicle that nurtures the heart. Sufis call their tradition the "discipline of hearts" (*ʿilm al-qulūb*). As the heart that animates the human body never finds itself in the same situation for long, we are challenged to always strive anew to hear the voice of conscience that arises from the heart. Let us draw to a close this conclusion, then, by listening one last time to the voice of our Sufi guide to the human body, Nakhshabi. "The power of every person comes totally from the heart. One should never let the heart grow weak! One should spend one's every moment keeping engaged by forging an ever new contract with the heart. . . . That which works in you / Is the part alone called heart / All else besides the heart / Is just clay and dust."[58] Nakhshabi's discourse on the heart, from "The Parts of the Wholes," reminds us how easy it is to forget the whole: to forget the whole body distracted by its parts, to neglect the integral person diverted by the body, to subsume personal dignity in exigencies of social conformity or ideological purity. How easy it is to neglect the heart amid the anxieties of confronting new situations and the clamor of finding routines and institutions to cope with new circumstances! How easily we are lulled into treating others in heartless ways. We criticize their actions without gaining insight into their intentions and without being introspective ourselves. We exploit others or allow them to be exploited for our own benefit, as if their bodies were only a matter of matter. We dismiss others by allowing ideologies based on religion, politics, or ethnic chauvinism to reduce them to cogs in a system rather than listening to the beat of their hearts in rhyme and rhythm with our own.

Listen to Nakhshabi as he explains the paradox of the fullness of the hollow human body in his praise for the heart. "Iblis the Tempter opened the mouth of Adam, which was the passage through which his life [as breath] arose. Iblis rushed quickly down this passageway. He made his way to every body part and each organ and declared, 'This is simple!' When Iblis arrived at the heart, every secret that was visible from the vast cosmic Throne of God was visible there within that small, pinecone-shaped lump of flesh. The Throne of God is the place of God's sitting firmly and ruling in the macrocosmic world, and can be described as merciful intentionality (*raḥmāniyya*). Similarly, in the microcosmic world, the heart is like the Throne, the place where God's presence abides, and can be described as subtle spirituality (*rūḥāniyya*). However, the heart only lives up to this description once its potential has been actualized through purifying refinement and progressive development (*taraqqī*)."[59]

Nakhshabi explains that the body of Adam was hollow but its very hollowness contained and harbored a great spiritual treasure—the potential to become God's vice-regent. Our Sufi guide to the body affrims, "The sages confirm that when Iblis entered the mouth of Adam, that is, when he entered into the microcosmic universe [of the human body], he saw openly displayed there all the parts and organs except for the heart. For the heart is the second Throne of God, and was therefore veiled from Iblis's apprehension. Hey now, pay attention! Iblis was a bandit and Adam's heart was a rich treasure of wise knowledge (*maʿrifa*). Of course, caretakers take pains to shield valuable treasures from thieving bandits. So when Iblis emerged from

Adam's body, he announced, 'This person has no heart! Anything without an animating heart is just dust and clay!' Though Adam was totally permeated with heart, Iblis saw him as simply clay."

Our Sufi guide to the human body then turns to address his audience directly, and we conclude this study with his words. "My dear brothers and sisters, do you know why Iblis failed to grasp the heart of Adam on that fateful day? It was because, from the eternity before time, Iblis was destined to be rejected by all hearts. From this first moment when one heart, that of Adam, rejected him and repulsed him, until the day of judgment, no true heart will accept the tempter. Talking about the acceptance of hearts is a discourse that should transpire from one heart directly to another heart. Although I am helpless in mastering my own heart, I still cannot be separated, even for a moment, from the innate nature that runs through my blood. So let me speak from the heart about the heart! If you have a heart, listen well, and take heart."

NOTES

Introduction

1 For a discussion of the benefits and dangers of using the term "saint" to describe Sufi exemplars in Islam, see Kugle, *Rebel between Spirit and Law,* 31–33.

2 All translations of quotations from the Qur'an are by the author, with gratitude to other translators for their guidance: N. J. Dawood, M. H. Shakir, ʿA'isha and ʿAbd al-Haqq Bewley, and Michael Sells.

3 Simsar, *Ṭūṭī-Nāma,* 131.

4 This builds on Schimmel, "I Take Off the Dress of the Body," in Coakley, *Religion and the Body,* which is insightful about Sufi literature but does not engage social theory.

5 Strathern, *Body Thoughts,* 198.

6 See Margaret Lock, "Cultivating the Body: Anthropology and Epistemology of Bodily Practices and Knowledge," *Annual Reviews in Anthropology* 22 (1993): 133–55, and Synnott, *Body Social,* 7–39.

7 Mauss, "Body Techniques," in *Sociology and Psychology,* 122.

8 Ibid., 101.

9 Judovitz, *Culture of the Body,* 22, discusses Montaigne's theory of embodiment and the importance of habit (*coutume*) in ways that parallel Mauss.

10 Quoted in Talal Asad, "Remarks on the Anthropology of the Body" in Coakley, *Religion and the Body,* 46.

11 Mauss, "Body Techniques," 104.

12 Douglas, *Natural Symbols,* 93.

13 O'Neill, *Five Bodies.*

14 Langer, *Merleau-Ponty's Phenomenology of Perception,* 25. For a Sufi approach, see Shaykh Fadhlalla Haeri, "The Model—on Body-Mind Intellect," *Al-Muntaqa* 3, no. 1 (1986): 70–88.

15 Bourdieu, *Outline of the Theory of Practice,* 89.

16 Langer, *Merleau-Ponty's Phenomenology of Perception,* 47.

17 Asad, "Remarks on the Anthropology of the Body," 42. See also Synnott, *Body Social,* 241–45.

18 Feher, Naddaff, and Tazi, *Fragments for a History of the Human Body,* 1:13.

19 Asad, *Genealogies of Religion*; Bell, *Ritual Theory, Ritual Practice.*

20 Khuri, *Body in Islamic Culture.*

21 Katz, *Body of Text.*

22 Werbner and Basu, *Embodying Charisma,* 1–27.

23 Chebel, "Vision du corps en Islam."

24 Al-Zahī, *Al-Jasad al-Ṣūra wa'l-Muqaddas,* 27.

25 Ibid., 27–28.
26 Ibid., 28.
27 Ibid.
28 Chebel, "Vision du corps en Islam," 207, as quoted in ibid., 29.
29 Al-Zahī, *Al-Jasad al-Ṣūra wa'l -Muqaddas*, 29.
30 Such a dialogue between Sufism and the reform of Islamic law was begun by Taha, *Second Message of Islam*, and Naim, *Toward an Islamic Reformation*.
31 Simsar, *Ṭūṭī-Nāma*, 242.
32 Mauss, "The Physical Effect of the Idea of Death," in *Sociology and Psychology*.
33 Sex is not included as a core activity for the continuity of the body because sexual activity is not explicitly necessary for the continuity of bodily existence. We are not speaking here of bodies as bearers of genetic material that has its own will toward perpetuation and continuity beyond the life of the individual body.
34 Nakhshabī's biography is preserved in ʿAbd al-Ḥaqq Muḥaddith Dihlawī's hagiographic record of Indian Sufis, *Akhbār al-Akhyār*, or "News of the Pious and Secrets of the Generous." From an Iranian family, he hailed from the city of Nakhshab (known as Nasaf in Arabic sources) and lived in Badāyūn near Delhi.
35 Simsar, *Ṭūṭī-Nāma*, 100–101.
36 Nakhshabī, *Juzʾiyāt o Kulliyāt* (ms.), 3–14.
37 Ibid., 14–15.
38 Kugle, *Rebel between Spirit and Law*, 112.
39 Nakhshabī, *Juzʾiyāt o Kulliyāt*, 9–10.
40 Here Nakhshabī quotes the famous definition of *tawḥīd* by al-Junayd, an early Sufi of Baghdad: "Sifting the eternal from the temporal, the essential from the subsidiary, the unchanging from the ephemeral is truly the way to declare the unity of God." Al-Junayd argued that Sufis, as masters of the "knowledge of hearts," complemented and completed the monotheism as defined by rational theologians and legal jurists.
41 Nakhshabī, *Juzʾiyāt o Kulliyāt*, 9–10.
42 Eliade, *Sacred and the Profane*.
43 See Austin, *Ibn ʿArabī*, 56, and Ibn ʿArabī, *Whoso Knows Himself*.
44 Less optimistic Muslim theologians, including most modernists and Wahhabis, take a dimmer view of Adam and speculate that he was taught only the names of things, or perhaps the names of the angels, which he then told to them in order to prove his superiority. Why angels would need to know their own names is left unanswered by such pessimistic body-denigrating theological stances. See Brinner, *ʿArāʾis al-Majālis*, 48.
45 Gēsū-Darāz, *Muḥabbat-Nāma* (ms.), 1.
46 Iblīs was among the angels most ardent in worshiping God. Like the angels, he radiated light, but unlike them, he was created from fire, which is light and also heat.
47 Maaike de Haardt, "Transience, Finitude and Identity: Reflections on the Body Dying," in Bekkenkamp and de Haardt, *Begin with the Body*, 18–19.
48 Brinner, *ʿArāʾis al-Majālis*, 45.
49 Lawrence, *Morals for the Heart*, 164–65.

50 I am grateful to Stephen Hopkins for many enlivening comparisons between Sufi love poetry and Hindu literature; see Hopkins, *Singing the Body of God*, chap. 5, and "Extravagant Beholding."

51 Nakhshabī, *Juz'iyāt o Kulliyāt*, 10–12.

52 Al-Zahī, *Al-Jasad al-Ṣūra wa'l -Muqaddas*, 76. Narrated by ʿĀ'isha and attributed to the Prophet Muḥammad.

53 Nakhshabī, *Juz'iyāt o Kulliyāt*, 12–13.

54 Ibid., 15.

55 Dihlawī, *Akhbār al-Akhyār*, 87th biography, as translated by Bruce Lawrence (unpublished manuscript). Many thanks to Bruce Lawrence for sharing with me this work in progress.

Chapter One

1 Indo-Aryan myth is rich in such legends, from Scandinavia to India. In Hindu myth Prajapati, the supreme creator, was a manifestation of Purusha, the cosmic human, who embodies sacrifice to endow the material universe with being emitted by his sacrificed and divided body. See Charles Malamud, "Indian Speculations about the Sex of the Sacrifice," in Feher, Naddaff, and Tazi, *Fragments for a History of the Human Body*, 91–99.

2 Chishtī, *Risāla-yi Afāq o Anfus* (ms.).

3 Jean Lévi, "The Body: The Daoists' Coat of Arms," in Feher, Naddaff, and Tazi, *Fragments for a History of the Human Body*, 105. Many thanks to Julius Tsai for originally teaching me about Daoist ritual.

4 Al-Zahī, *Al-Jasad al-Ṣūra wa'l -Muqaddas*, 101, cites Eliade, *Sacred and the Profane*.

5 Peter Brown, response to a lecture during a colloquium entitled "Sufis, Shrines and South Asia: A Colloquium in Honor of Simon Digby" at the Center for South Asian Studies, University of Pennsylvania (October 2003).

6 Brown, *Cult of the Saints*, is an inspiring study whose insights into saints' bones in Latin Christianity this chapter will transpose onto Islamic evidence.

7 Nakhshabī, *Juz'iyāt o Kulliyāt*, 12–13.

8 Brinner, *ʿArā'is al-Majālis*, 449. Moses's staff is the object that characterizes the first part of his prophetic mission—to lead the Tribes of Israel out of Pharaoh's Egypt. Moses's stone tables are emblematic of the second part of his mission, after he speaks with God on Mount Sinai and leads the Tribes to the threshold of Canaan.

9 Berquist, *Controlling Corporeality*, 11.

10 Al-Fāsī, *Al-Durr al-Nafīs*, 149. Mawlay Idrīs also left a daughter by a different mother, but she is rarely counted as his child because she could not inherit his reign.

11 Ibid., 7–8.

12 Ibid., 162.

13 Ibid., 163. For a discussion of architecture as reflecting God's relation to the universe, see Clinton Bennett, "Islam," in Holm, *Picturing God*, 132–33.

14 Al-Fāsī, *Al-Durr al-Nafīs*, 4.

15 Ibid.
16 Ibid., 7–8.
17 Ibid.
18 Samuel Landell Mills, "The Hardware of Sanctity: Anthropomorphic Objects in Bangladeshi Sufism," in Werbner and Basu, *Embodying Charisma*, 39.
19 Al-Fāsī, *Al-Durr al-Nafīs*, 7–8.
20 Nakhshabī, *Juz'iyāt o Kulliyāt*, 10–12.
21 Al-Fāsī, *Anīs al-Muṭrib*, 50.
22 Al-Jaznā'ī, *Janā Zahrat al-Ās*, 26.
23 Al-Nāṣirī, *Kitāb al-Istiṣqā'*, 3:90, 111. Sultan Yusūf ibn Ya'qūb ibn 'Abd al-Ḥaqq al-Marīnī seems to have adopted the practice, which had begun in Egypt roughly a century earlier.
24 Cornell, *Realm of the Saint*, 341–42, discusses this celebration's importance in the construction of "sharifian Sufism," which depicts Muḥammad as the primordial human being and champions his descendants as the rightful rulers of Islamic polities.
25 Al-Nāṣirī, *Kitāb al-Istiṣqā*, 4:114. The 'Imrānī clan descended from Yaḥyā al-Jūṭī, a descendant of Mawlay Idrīs—see al-Sharrāṭ, *Al-Rawḍ al-'Aṭir*, 224. From him, four major clans take their name, "al-Jūṭī": the clans are known as at-Ṭālibī, al-Farjī, at-Ṭāhirī, and al-'Imrānī. This last branch was the dominant group in Fes during later Marinid times, as discussed by al-Qādirī, *Nashr al-Mathānī*, 2:341.
26 *Nubdha min Tārīkh al-Maghrib* (ms.), 220, which was probably written in 1648 during the Sa'dian era in Fes.
27 Ibid. His father, Muḥammad ibn Muḥammad ibn al-'Imrānī, had been the first assigned leader of the *shurafā'* by order of Abū Sālim ibn Abī al-Ḥasan al-Marīnī.
28 *Nubdha min Tārīkh al-Maghrib*, 221.
29 See Kugle, *Rebel between Spirit and Law*, 50–64, for more information on juridical Sufis like this prayer leader at al-Qarawiyyin, al-'Abdūsī.
30 Al-Fāsī, *Al-Durr al-Nafīs*, 309.
31 D. Eustache, "Idris II," in *Encyclopedia of Islam*, new ed. (Leiden: E. J. Brill, 2000).
32 Al-Kattānī, *Salwat*, 1:82.
33 Al-Fāsī, *Al-Durr al-Nafīs*, 308–10.
34 Ibid. The subject of this poem is called "al-Ṭalḥāt (of the women of the al-Ṭalḥa)" because his mother was Ṣafiya, daughter of al-Ḥārith, the son of Ṭalḥa, son of Ṭalḥa, son of 'Abd al-Manāf.
35 Berquist, *Controlling Corporeality*, 19–20. For the whole body as male, see 35–40.
36 *Nubdha min Tārīkh al-Maghrib*, 220.
37 The neighborhood was called al-Ṣirāwiyyīn, now known as al-Qalī'a.
38 Al-Kattānī, *Salwat*, 2:17, cites fatwas of Aḥmad al-Wansharīsī in *al-Mi'yār* about whether Islamic law sanctioned healing through soil of Abū Ghālib's tomb.
39 Ibid., 22. The poet is Muḥammad ibn Idrīs al-'Imrānī, apparently the father of the poet who adorned the wall of al-Khalwa al-Qādiriyya with his verses.

40 Ibid., 20.

41 Al- Jīlānī, *Al-Safīna al-Qādiriyya*, 166–67.

42 Al-Kattānī, *Salwat*, 2:20–21, preserves the text of these fatwas.

43 Davies, *Island of the Animals*, x.

44 Radtke and O'Kane, *Concept of Sainthood*, 228.

45 Al-Kattānī, *Salwat*, 2:19.

46 Ibn al-Qāḍī, *Jadhwat*, 241. In Moroccan, *illī kayuḥibb sīdī Bū Ghālib yuḥibbū bi-quṭūṭū*.

47 Al-Fāsī, *Al-Durr al-Nafīs*, 309–12, 322–29, discusses the perfumed fragrance of Mawlay Idrīs's body that permeates everything near his tomb.

48 Ibid., 298.

49 Ibid.

50 Waghorne, *Raja's Magic Clothes*, 258.

51 Mills, "Hardware of Sanctity," 51.

Chapter Two

1 Nakhshabī, *Juzʾiyāt o Kulliyāt*, 10–12.

2 Simsar, *Ṭūṭī-Nāma*, 139. In contrast, most of Nakhshabī's narratives cast women as weak, undependable, or inherently wicked. Even as he notes exceptions, Nakhshabī is almost completely constrained by the patriarchal presuppositions of his society, as revealed in this quatrain from page 80, "O Nakhshabī, friendship with women causes suffering / because of them men endure sorrow and anxiety / Happy is the man who can abandon them entirely / and still keep his dignity and act with propriety," or one from page 66, "O Nakhshabī, treachery in some women is innate / a base woman even with her curls is full of pretense / the nature of deceitful women, everyone agrees / is inherited for which there is ample evidence."

3 Bryan Turner, "The Body in Western Society," in Coakley, *Religion and the Body*, 26.

4 See the scholarship of Ahmed, *Women and Gender in Islam*, and Mernissi, "Women, Saints and Sanctuaries."

5 Judovitz, *Culture of the Body*, 92, quotes Descartes' *Meditations*, HR 1:151.

6 Ibid., 81, esp. n. 48.

7 Kundera, *Laughable Loves*, 81–82.

8 Wadud, *Qur'an and Woman*, 16–23.

9 Sells, *Approaching in the Qurʾan*, 202.

10 Gemeʿah, *Stories of the Prophets*, 17; see also Brinner, *ʿArāʾis al-Majālis*, 48–49.

11 Al-Bukhārī judged this report to be genuine and included it in his *Saḥīḥ* collection.

12 Al-Kisāʾī, *Badʿ al-Khalq*, 120–121.

13 Brinner, *ʿArāʾis al-Majālis*, 55–56. These are only the major punishments from among ten, which also include lesser inheritance than men, more restricted divorce rights than men, and exclusion from Friday congregational prayers.

14 Fedwa Malti-Douglas, "Faces of Sin: Corporal Geographies in Contemporary Islamist Discourse," in Law, *Religious Reflections*, 69.

15 Caroline Walker Bynum, "The Female Body and Religious Practice in the Later

Middle Ages," in Feher, Naddaff, and Tazi, *Fragments for a History of the Human Body*, 182.

16 Sandnes, *Belly and Body in Pauline Epistles*, 9.

17 Ibid., 57.

18 Ibid., 110.

19 Petroff, *Body and Soul*, 98. Many thanks to Ellen Ross for her insights into Christian women saints.

20 Ibid., 102.

21 Ibid., 106.

22 Ibid., 205.

23 Bynum, "Female Body," 162.

24 Ibid., 165. Saint Francis was the first man to experience bleeding stigmata; in many ways Francis did not conform to masculine norms in his society.

25 Bakhtin, *Rabelais and His World*, 26.

26 Al-Sharrāṭ, *Al-Rawḍ al-ʿAṭir*, 86–87. She was married to her cousin, Yahya, and died around 1553 at the age of 78.

27 Zarrūq, *Al-Kunnāsh fī ʿIlm Āsh* (ms.), 57. Āmina's lineage of spiritual authority led back to Aḥmad Zarrūq, a Maliki jurist, leading Sufi, and social critic of the late fifteenth century; see Kugle, *Rebel between Spirit and Law*.

28 Al-Sharrāṭ, *Al-Rawḍ al-ʿAṭir*, 76. ʿAlī al-Ṣanhājī died approximately 1540–41 and is buried outside Bab Futūḥ in Fes, and Āmina is buried just behind his tomb.

29 Ibn ʿAskar, *Dawḥat al-Nāshir*, 81.

30 Al-Sharrāṭ, *Al-Rawḍ al-ʿAṭir*, 77.

31 Ibid., 75–76. ʿAlī al-Ṣanhājī had other "female servants" who were devoted to caring for him, and this suggests that the sexual accusation against them may have been due to the opposition of Āmina's family. He routinely subdued their outraged husbands with miracles, such as inflicting on them temporary paralysis.

32 Ibid., 75.

33 Simsar, *Ṭūṭī-Nāma*, 17.

34 Al-Fāsī, *Mumtiʿ al-Asmāʾ*, 132.

35 Petroff, *Body and Soul*, 161.

36 Al-Kattānī, *Salwat*, 3:144.

37 Al-Fāsī, *Mumtiʿ al-Asmāʾ*, 130.

38 Al-Sharrāṭ, *Al-Rawḍ al-ʿAṭir*, 87.

39 Al-Fāsī, *Mumtiʿ al-Asmāʾ*, 129.

40 Cornell, *Realm of the Saint*, 173–76.

41 Al-Fāsī, *Mumtiʿ al-Asmāʾ*, 135.

42 Ibid., 130.

43 Ibn ʿAskar, *Dawḥat al-Nāshir*, 133.

44 Cornell, *Realm of the Saint*, 396. Both ruling families were descended from the saint Ibn Mashīsh and were sharifian in genealogy, descended from Imām Ḥasan.

45 Elizabeth Robertson, "The Corporeality of Female Sanctity in *The Life of Saint Margaret*," in Blumenfeld-Kosinski and Szell, *Images of Sainthood*, 268–88.

46 An example is Mirabai (1516–46) in the Hindu Bhakti tradition; see Mukta, *Upholding the Common Life.*

47 Al-Kattānī, *Salwat,* 3:209.

48 Mariëtte van Beek, "Images of Lālla ʿAwīsh: A Holy Woman from Marrakesh," in Marin and Deguilhem, *Writing the Feminine,* 199–220.

49 For historical approaches, see the scholarship of Pierre Bonie and Nelly Salameh-Amri. For sociological approaches, see Sossie Andezian, "Le mysticisme extatique maghrebin: Une forme religiouse populaire?," presentation delivered at the Second International Conference on Popular Culture in North Africa and the Middle East, Hammamet, Tunisia, April 3–6, 2002.

50 Ibn Ṣabbāgh, *Manāqib al-Walīya al-Ṣāliḥa Sayyida ʿĀʾisha* (ms.). Researchers should compare this with two copies of a seemingly later text with similar titles by an anonymous author housed in the same archive in Tunis. For biographical details about the hagiographer, see Douglas, *Mystical Teachings of al-Shadhili.*

51 Ibn Ṣabbāgh, *Manāqib al-Walīya al-Ṣāliḥa Sayyida ʿĀʾisha,* 148.

52 Ibid., 147. Khiḍr is associated with both the servant of Moses (Mūsā) who baffles the Prophet with his intuitive wisdom and the servant of Alexander (Dhūʾl-Qarnayn) who finds the font of the water of life; see Qurʾan 18:60–82.

53 Ibn Ṣabbāgh, *Manāqib al-Walīya al-Ṣāliḥa Sayyida ʿĀʾisha,* 150.

54 Ibid., 150. Sayyida ʿĀʾisha also compares herself to the female saint of the past Mīmūna, who says to her, "I am your serving girl and will sweep your home."

55 Ibid., 149.

56 Ibid., 151.

57 Ibid., 150.

58 Ibid., 148.

59 Al-Kattānī, *Salwat,* 2:293.

60 See Gellner, *Saints of the Atlas,* 5–12, and Geertz, *Islam Observed,* 9.

61 Al-Fāsī, *Mumtiʿ al-Asmāʾ,* 138–45. His full name was ʿAbd al-Raḥmān ibn ʿAyyāḍ al-Ṣanhājī.

62 Al-Qādirī, *Al-Maqṣad al-Aḥmad,* 294.

63 Al-Kattānī, *Salwat,* 2:221.

64 This erasure of a woman as a pivotal anchor in a patriarchal genealogy mirrors the operation of sharifian families, whose genealogy back to the Prophet Muḥammad runs through his daughter, Fāṭima, even as it is imagined as a male-to-male inheritance of patriarchal authority.

65 Al-Majdhūb, *Al-Qawl al-Maʾthūr,* 93. These couplets initiate ʿAbd al-Raḥmān's *Diwan.*

66 Ibn ʿAskar, *Dawḥat al-Nāshir,* 81.

67 Al-Fāsī, *Mumtiʿ al-Asmāʾ,* 131–35.

68 Al-Kattānī, *Salwat,* 2:223. See for more detail Al-Fāsī, *Mirʾat al-Maḥāsin.*

69 Al-Kattānī, *Salwat,* 2:31.

70 Munson, *Religion and Power in Morocco,* 87–88.

71 Mernissi, "Women, Saints and Sanctuaries." See also Kugle, "Dancing with Khusro."

Chapter Three

1 Synnott, *Body Social*, 208.
2 Al-Zahī, *Al-Jasad al-Ṣūra wa'l -Muqaddas*, 65.
3 In Sells, *Approaching the Qur'an*, 181–207.
4 For Ibn Sina's fascinating discussion of whether the Prophet's ascension was bodily or spiritual, see Heath, *Allegory and Philosophy in Avicenna*.
5 Lawrence, *Morals for the Heart*, 70.
6 Ibid.
7 Ibid., 313–14.
8 Al-Sulamī, *The Subtleties of the Ascension*.
9 Shāh ʿAbdullah Shaṭṭār settled in Mandu, but the order spread through his delegated disciple in Jawnpūr, Shaykh Ḥafiẓ Jawnpūrī. Muḥammad Ghawth hailed from a small town near Jawnpūr, and by his era the Shaṭṭārī lineage had become powerful in urban centers from Gujarat to Bengal; see Rizvi, *History of Sufism in India*, 2:151–73, and K. A. Nizami, "Shattariyya," in *Encyclopedia of Islam*, 11:369–70.
10 It was assumed that the seven heavens mentioned in the Qur'an corresponded with the seven orbits of the planets, including the moon as the closest "planet" to the earth. In Muḥammad Ghawth's time, the farther planets in our system had not yet been observed.
11 The belief that the human being is a compound of primal elements and therefore a microcosm for the totality is common after Ibn ʿArabī; see Jackson, *Sharafuddin Maneri*, 331–32.
12 Al-Zahī, *Al-Jasad al-Ṣūra wa'l -Muqaddas*, 104, quotes Y. Fekkar, "La femme, son corps et l'Islam," in *Le Maghreb musulman en 1979* (Paris: CNRS, 1983), 139.
13 Ernst, *Shambhala Guide to Sufism*, 110; Haq, "Ghawth Gwaliori," 57.
14 Rizvi, *History of Sufism in India*, 1:333–47.
15 Ghawth, *Awrād-i Ghawthiyya*, 109–16. This printed version has been compared against several manuscript versions of the same narrative and has in several places been corrected in favor of expressions found in the manuscripts: Chishtī, *Mukhbir al-Awliyā'* (ms.), 630–35; two copies of Ghawth, *Awrād-i Ghawthiyya* (ms.); Ghawth, *Miʿrāj Nāma* (ms.).
16 Shaṭṭārī, *Manāqib-i Ghawthiyya* (ms.), composed in 1534–35 C.E..
17 Shaykh Qāzan of Bengal, a member of the Shaṭṭārī community, was the master of Shaykh Ḥamīd Ẓuhūr al-Ḥaqq, who was the spiritual master of Muḥammad Ghawth and adopted him as a spiritual son.
18 Shaṭṭārī, *Manāqib-i Ghawthiyya*, 28.
19 Ghawth, *Awrād-i Ghawthiyya*, 103.
20 Shaṭṭārī, *Manāqib-i Ghawthiyya*, 29–30.
21 ʿAlawī, *Malfūẓāt-i Wajīh al-Dīn Gujarātī* (ms.), 10–11.
22 Ibid., 11.
23 Shaṭṭārī, *Manāqib-i Ghawthiyya*, 60.
24 Muḥammad Ghawth does not mention the year of the experience; however, in the introduction to his text, *Kalīd al-Makhāzin* (ms.), he alludes to the year

932 Hijri, when he had a tremendous spiritual experience, which likely was his *miʿrāj*.

25 Brinner, *ʿArāʾis al-Majālis*, 87.

26 Ibid., 88. The Queen's name was al-Zuhra, like the planet Venus, who ascended into heaven using the beneficial knowledge she extracted from the angels through passionate love, becoming the celestial body in the heavens known as Venus.

27 Al-Qazwīnī, *ʿAjāʾib al-Makhlūqāt* (ms.), 106.

28 Dihlawī, *Takmīla-yi Madārij al-Nubuwwa* (ms.), clarifies that when al-Jīlī writes that "the manifestation of God is in him in his essence," he means both in God's essence and in Muḥammad's essence. ʿAbd al-Ḥaqq Dihlawī was one of the major followers of ʿAlī Muttaqī, introduced later in this chapter.

29 Muḥammad Ghawth relates this saying, *al-nisāʾ jubāʾil al-shayṭān*, as if it were a hadith attributed to the Prophet. However, it does not appear in any of the six authoritative Sunni hadith collections. It may come from a rare source or could be an aphorism popularly attributed to the Prophet. It resembles a hadith in *Ṣaḥīḥ al-Bukhārī*, Kitāb al-Nikāḥ number 22: "When I look into the fire [of hell] most of the people in it are women."

30 Ibn ʿArabī, quoted in Chodkiewitz, *Ocean without Shore*, 45.

31 Cenkner, *Evil and the Response of World Religion*, 89.

32 This elaborates on a hadith *qudsī*, or a saying attributed to the Prophet, who interprets in his own words a meaning given by God; on the relations between Muḥammad, Aḥmad, and Aḥad, see Schimmel, *Deciphering the Signs of God*, 190–91.

33 Ghawth, *Kalīd al-Makhāzin*, 30–31.

34 Shaṭṭārī, *Manāqib-i Ghawthiyya*, 75, and the discussion of his follower, Wajīh al-Dīn, in Chishtī, *Mukhbir al-Awliyāʾ*, 648 b. Such sayings circulated among Sufis in South Asia, like "Take care, O brother, since we ourselves are sin, it is now necessary to become something else! Have you not heard this? When asked what sin I had committed, Love replied, 'Your very existence is a sin! No other could be greater than that!'" See Jackson, *Sharafuddin Maneri*, 255 and 17.

35 Al-Zahī, *Al-Jasad al-Ṣūra waʾl -Muqaddas*, 65.

36 Muḥammad Ghawth claims that he learned these invocatory techniques directly from the great Shaykh al-Suhrawardī in a visionary encounter. Many Shaṭṭārīs in the generations following Muḥammad Ghawth wrote treatises on such invocations.

37 Shaṭṭārī, *Manāqib-i Ghawthiyya*, 109–10.

38 See Kugle, "Heaven's Witness," 24–31.

39 Muḥammad Ghawth must have left Gwalior some time between 1540 and 1542, between when the Afghan Sūrī dynasty took Delhi and when they finally conquered Gwalior.

40 Chishtī, *Mukhbir al-Awliyaʾ*, 629 *b.

41 See Kugle, *Rebel between Spirit and Law*, 36–52, for descriptions of the juridical Sufism adopted by ʿAlī Muttaqī.

42 For a fuller biography of ʿAlī Muttaqī, see Kugle, *In Search of the Center*.

43 Dihlawī, *Zād al-Muttaqīn* (ms.). A shorter biography is found in his *Akhbār al-Akhyār*.
44 Ernst, *Eternal Garden*, 118–32, 147–54.
45 Muttaqī, *Asrār al-ʿĀrifīn wa Sayr al-Ṭālibīn* (ms.).
46 Muttaqī, *Ghāyat al-Maʿmūl fīʾl -Sulūk waʾl -Wuṣūl* (ms.).
47 Chishtī, *Mukhbir al-Awliyaʾ*, 635 *a.
48 Carl Ernst, "Persecution and Circumspection in the Shattari Sufi Order," in De Jong and Radtke, *Islamic Mysticism Contested*, 3–7.
49 ʿAlawī, *Miṣbāḥ al-ʿĀlam* (ms.), 50. Thanks to Dr. Muḥammad Zubayr Qurayshi for facilitating access to the B.J. Institute of Learning and Research in Aḥmadābād.
50 Fārūqī, *Khulāṣat al-Wajīh* (ms.), 2.
51 Ibid.
52 ʿAlawī, *Miṣbāḥ al-ʿĀlam*, 63. A daughter of Wajīh al-Dīn married a grandson of Muḥammad Ghawth.
53 Ibid., 69.
54 Chishtī, *Mukhbir al-Awliyāʾ*, 628 *b.
55 Ernst, "Persecution and Circumspection," 4, and Ghawthī, *Gulzār-i Abrār*, 288.
56 Chishtī, *Mukhbir al-Awliyāʾ*, 634 *b.
57 Ibid.
58 Ibid., 638 *a.
59 Ibid., 635 *a.
60 Ibid.
61 Ibid., 636 *a.
62 Ibid., 637 *b.
63 Ibid.
64 Ibid., 637 *a–644 *a. There is no other copy of this letter, to the extent of my knowledge.
65 Ibid., 638 *a.
66 Ibid., 637 *a. Sultan Maḥmūd, his ministers, and the scholars of Ahmadabad used to say that if not for the secret protection of Shaykh Muḥammad (Sīdī Wajdī), Wajīh al-Dīn's efforts to speak on behalf of Muḥammad Ghawth would have come to nothing.
67 Ibid., 641 *a. Wajīh al-Dīn authored a commentary on *Kalīd al-Makhāzin* that tried to rectify Ghawth's cosmic claims to the Prophet's experience in his ascension.
68 Chishtī, *Mukhbir al-Awliyāʾ*, 638 *a.
69 Ibid., 641 *a.
70 Ibid., 636 *a–637 *a.
71 Ibid., 645 *a; Ernst, "Persecution and Circumspection," 6. Muḥammad Ghawth remained in Ahmadabad until after Humayun reconquered Delhi in 1555–56 C.E.
72 Ernst, "Persecution and Circumspection," 11.
73 Muttaqī, *Tanbīh al-Ghāfilīn* (ms.), folio 50 *a–b.
74 Ulūghkhānī, *Ẓafar al-Wālih*, 315.

75 Ibid., 315.
76 Dihlawī, *Zād al-Muttaqīn*, 32 *a.
77 Brinner, *ʿArāʾis al-Majālis*, 46.

Chapter Four

1 Nakhshabī, *Juzʾiyāt o Kulliyāt*, 10–12.
2 Ernst, "Persecution and Circumspection," notes that this circumspection was the real result of the persecution among later generations of Shaṭṭārī Sufis.
3 Maḥmūd ibn Muḥammad Pīr, *Haqīqat al-Fuqarāʾ (ms.)*, 72–73. See note 6 below for bibliographic details. Portions of the biography of Shāh Ḥussayn were previously published in Kugle, "*Haqiqat al-Fuqara*: Poetic Biography of 'Madho Lal' Hussayn," in Vanita and Kidwai, *Same Sex Love in India*, 145–56. Smaller excerpts have been translated in Christopher Shackle, "Beyond Hindu and Turk: Crossing the Boundaries in Indo-Muslim Romance," in Gilmartin and Lawrence, *Beyond Hindu and Turk*, 55–73.
4 The debate between constructivist and essentialist assessments of homosexuality is ongoing, partly because the debate has to do with the nature of human beings and "cause" of sexual desire in general. For review of Western scholars, see John Boswell, "Concepts, Experience and Sexuality," in Comstock and Henking, *Que(e)rying Religion*, 116–29, who presents and defends the fundamental assumption of the essentialists: "that humans are differentiated at an individual level in terms of erotic attraction, so that some are more attracted sexually to their own gender, some to the opposite gender, and some to both, in all cultures."
5 Bahār Khān reportedly stayed with Shāh Ḥussayn to record the saint's daily actions and speeches, compiling a text known as *Tadhkira-yi Bahāriyya*, which would make it a contemporary source from Shāh Ḥussayn's own lifetime. However, this book no longer exists, even in manuscript form. Ḥussayn was also held in high esteem by other Mughal nobles, including Dārā Shikōh, who mentions Shāh Ḥussayn in his book on spiritual boasts of the saints, *Shaṭḥiyāt*, and in his memorial to the saints, *Ḥasanāt al-ʿĀrifīn*, published in an Urdu translation (Lahore: Islamia Steam Press, n.d.), 46.
6 Maḥmūd ibn Muḥammad Pīr, *Haqīqat al-Fuqarāʾ*, fol. 30. This hagiographic poem was composed about 1662, just sixty-two years after Shāh Ḥussayn's death. The author's father had been a companion of Shāh Ḥussayn's, while the author himself was a close attendant of his successor, Ma<u>dh</u>ō.
7 Shaykh Bahlūl Daryāʾī initiated Ḥussayn into the Qādirī lineage in Chiniot, a village outside Lahore, when he was about 10 years old. The Qādirīs have a reputation for being "orthodox" in their orientation, but in Shāh Ḥussayn's day, the Qādirīs also consisted of freethinking and antinomian characters. In Lahore today, the Qalandars (who completely abandon legal norms and social conventions and even gender distinctions) are still associated with the great Qādirī saints of the city, like Shāh Ḥussayn, Shāh Jamāl, and Miyān Mīr.
8 Simsar, *Ṭūṭī-Nāma*, 17–18.
9 Subhan, *Sufism*, 277–78.

10 Simsar, *Ṭūṭī-Nāma*, 107.
11 Maḥmūd ibn Muḥammad Pīr, *Haqīqat al-Fuqarā'*, 38.
12 Ibid., 39.
13 Turner, *From Ritual to Theatre*.
14 Maḥmūd ibn Muḥammad Pīr, *Haqīqat al-Fuqarā'*, 42.
15 Ibid., 44.
16 Ibid., 49.
17 Simsar, *Ṭūṭī-Nāma*, 246.
18 Both couplets translated by the author. The couplet by Dard comes from the *ghazal* in his Urdu *dīwān*, which begins: "*Tuhmatēn chand apnē dhimmē d͟har chalē / kis liyē āē t͟hē ham kya kar chalē*." The couplet by Ḥāfiẓ comes from his *ghazal*, which begins: "*Dil mī-rawad ze dast-am ṣāḥib-dilān khudā-rā / dardā keh rāz-i pinhān khwāhad shud āshkārā*."
19 Maḥmūd ibn Muḥammad Pīr, *Haqīqat al-Fuqarā'*, 50, 52.
20 Knysh, *Ibn Arabi in the Later Islamic Tradition*, 83.
21 Jalal al-Din Rumi, *Mathnawi*, 1:1989.
22 Maḥmūd ibn Muḥammad Pīr, *Haqīqat al-Fuqarā'*, 50. Modern Urdu sources have filtered out vivid erotic information from this Persian source that they supposedly translate and transmit. Chishtī, *Taḥqīqāt-i Chishtī*, 307–61, describes Shāh Ḥussayn and Mad͟hō, claiming to quote *Haqīqat al-Fuqarā'*. Yet when he describes this intimate scene between them at Bābūpūr, he writes in one line only, "So the saint, while drinking wine, embraced Mad͟hō and made him arrive at the truth (*wasl bi-ḥaqq*), making Mad͟hō into a complete and perfected saint himself without any rigors or strenuous labors." The erotic encounter of kissing and embracing is erased; the only trace of a sexual element is the term "arriving" (*wasl*), which can mean arriving at a place, arriving into the loving intimacy of a lover, or engaging in a sexual union until arriving at a climax. Most contemporary Urdu sources are based on *Taḥqīqāt-i Chishtī* and repeat his erasure; see Mālik, *Awliyā'-yi Lāhōr*, 145–74. Other Urdu sources mention nothing of Mad͟hō at all and also neglect Ḥussayn's poetic output, as in Qudūsī, *Tadhkira-yi Ṣūfiya-yi Punjāb*. See also Fārūqī and Diwāna, *Ḥālāt o Kāfiyān Madhō Lāl Ḥussayn*, and Mirzā, *Shāh Ḥussayn*. This erasure began early, for even in the Persian collection of saints' stories composed in 1865, Lāhōrī, *Khazīnat al-Asfiyā'*, 141–46, Mad͟hō is mentioned only once, in an accusation against Ḥussayn that is never confirmed.
23 Maḥmūd ibn Muḥammad Pīr, *Haqīqat al-Fuqarā'*, 22.
24 This nickname has led some writers to falsely conclude that Mad͟hō's full name was "Mad͟hō Lāl." In fact, Ḥussayn's nickname was "Lāl Ḥussayn" alluding to his penchant for wearing only red clothing. After he fell in love, his lover's name was added to his own, resulting in "Mad͟hō Lāl Ḥussayn."
25 An example of such distortion is the biography of Shaykh Mak͟hū, a Gujarati Sufi of the Shaṭṭārī lineage who was a contemporary of Shāh Ḥussayn's. *Gulzār-i Abrār*, or "Blooming Garden of the Righteous," in its original and unpublished Persian states that the saint, at the age of 40, fell in love with a handsome young man named Hansu. Yet the Urdu translation that is published and widely quoted records that Hansu was a beautiful young woman; see Ghawthī, *Adhkār-i Abrār*,

458. For a brief biography of Shaykh Makhū in English, see Rizvi, *History of Sufism in India*, 2:164.

26 In one of his poems, Ḥussayn recalls his own biography, saying, "O Friend, Ḥussayn is a weaver, no profit accrues to him / Neither was he betrothed nor married / Nor was any matrimony ceremony held for him / He was neither a householder nor a traveler / He was neither a believer nor an infidel / He is now just as he was." Alhaq, *Forgotten Vision*, 2:230.

27 Alhaq, in ibid., 247 n. 72, claims that this hagiographic poem had once been published, in Lahore in 1966. I not found any evidence of this publication in libraries in Lahore and doubt the assertion that *Haqīqat al-Fuqarā'* has ever been published, since no author writing after 1966 has quoted the text.

28 Ramakrishna, *Punjabi Sufi Poets*, 32–46. "Un-natural" is Ramakrishna's term; it smacks of Victorian British morality and has no analytic value. She acknowledges that, to these two medieval Punjabis at least, their sexual relation seemed natural enough. Other studies that focus on Shāh Ḥussayn as a poet include Ramakrishna and Luther, *Madho Lal Hussayn*, along with writings by Syed and Waqar.

29 It is clear that Ramakrishna knew of the existence of *Haqīqat al-Fuqarā'* but chose not to consult it, although she did consult other manuscripts at the same archive. This provides an example of how "queer themes" in Islamic culture are suppressed and marginalized by the mentality and intention of researchers. Ramakrishna limited her references to the poetry itself in order to claim that, "as far as poetry can help us, we can find no immoral flaw in Lal Hussayn's love for Madho," imposing her own morality by suppressing material that contradicted her views about sex and sexuality.

30 Alhaq, *Forgotten Vision*, 2:219–34. In addition, Rizvi, *History of Sufism in India*, 2:64–65, 437–38, cites the love of these two men without analyzing it.

31 Maḥmūd ibn Muḥammad Pīr, *Haqīqat al-Fuqarā'*, 102.

32 Scott Kugle, "Sultan Mahmud's Make-Over: Colonial Homophobia and Persian-Urdu Poetics," in Vanita, *Queering India*.

33 Suvorova, *Muslim Saints of South Asia*, 194–98.

34 Yogi Sikand, "Martyr for Gay Love," *Trikone: Lesbian, Gay and Bisexual South Asians* 13, no. 1 (January 1998).

35 Karamustafa, *God's Unruly Friends*, 25–31.

36 Ewing, *Arguing Sainthood*, 217–18.

37 Anwar, *Paths Unknown*, 68, on whose translations from Punjabi I rely, adapting them slightly in English.

38 Ibid., 1–2.

39 Simsar, *Ṭūṭī-Nāma*, 16.

40 Anwar, *Paths Unknown*, 35.

41 Ibid., 36.

42 Ibid., 75.

43 Simsar, *Ṭūṭī-Nāma*, 148.

44 See Kinsley, *Divine Player*, 124–25.

45 Huizinga, *Homo Ludens*, 17–18.

46 Kinsley, *Divine Player*, 237.

47 Haberman, *Journey through the Twelve Forests*.

48 Haberman, "Enraptured by the Sound of Krishna's Flute: The Life and Poetry of Ras Khan," presented at the symposium "Performing Ecstasy: The Politics and Poetics of Religion in South Asia," Swarthmore College, October 23, 2004.

49 Dihlawī, *Kitāb Taḥṣīl al-Ta'arruf* (ms.), end of Sufism section.

50 In another poem, Shāh Ḥussayn refers to his red tattered clothes as the dress of a bride, like the heroine Hīr, who longs for her ideal bridegroom, Rānjhā. "To hell with your white garb/ better is the rag of the faqir / only she is wedded who stands up/ to dance in his courtyard with abandon." In yet another poem, his identity with Hīr is more explicit, "Crying for my beloved, I myself became Rānjhā / May all the people call me Rānjhā and not Hīr anymore / I have finally found the beloved I sought for so long / It was after meeting the sadhus, says Ḥussayn/ that the uncertainty has vanished." Alhaqq, *Forgotten Vision*, 2:234.

51 In his assertion that there were more commonalities than differences between Islamic and Hindu devotion, Shāh Ḥussayn belongs to the tradition of Kabir and Guru Nanak. Like them, he found vernacular and folk poetry to be the best vehicle to expression this fusion of Sufi and bhakti ideals of mystical and passionate love.

52 New Muslims (*naw-musalmān*) from weaver castes converted to join the Islamic community in Punjab slightly later than in Hindustan, where the mystic poet Kabir displays the same kind of Sufi-bhakti synthesis a century earlier. The castes of weavers who converted to Islam in the medieval centuries had most likely been Shudras. Biographers like Ramakrishna have asserted that Shāh Ḥussayn came from a Rajput or Kayasth clan than had converted to Islam, and this assertion is based on some later Urdu sources that claim that his family belonged to the Dahda Rajput clan. However, these castes did not engage in weaving, and conversion rarely affected a caste's means of livelihood. The stories of Ḥussayn's "noble" lineage are later accretions to make his image more acceptable to society, as are the stories of Madhō's "conversion" to Islam.

53 Hammoudi, *Master and Disciple*, 89.

54 Kugle, "Dancing with Khurso."

55 They include Shams-i Tabrēzī, who inspired Mawlana Rumi; Aḥmad Ghazālī, the master of Persian love poetry; Awḥad al-Dīn Kirmānī; and Fakhr al-Dīn 'Irāqī, the interpreter of Ibn 'Arabī in Persian poetry, despite the reticence of modern scholars to acknowledge their homoerotic expression. See Nasrollah Pourjawady, "The Witness Play of Ahmad Ghazali in Tabriz," in Lawson, *Reason and Inspiration in Islam*, 200–220.

56 Muttaqī, *Tanbīh al-Aḥibba fī 'Alāmāt al-Muḥabba* (ms.).

57 Maḥmūd ibn Muḥammad Pīr, *Haqīqat al-Fuqarā'*, 72. In an Urdu translation of this list of offenses in Chishtī, *Taḥqīqāt-i Chishtī*, 322, the allegation about dancing with handsome young men has been elided entirely. It reflects the liberality of Shāh Ḥussayn's era that mention of his homosexuality is not given much im-

portance, in contrast to Victorian mannerisms of the nineteenth- and twentieth-century Urdu reports that suppress mentioning his sexuality at all.

58 Maḥmūd ibn Muḥammad Pīr, *Haqīqat al-Fuqarā'*, 72–73, and Chishtī, *Taḥqīqāt-i Chishtī*, 327. In the accusation that Ḥussayn always stares at beautiful young people, the police chief uses a term that is not gender-specific: *but-i sāda*, simple innocent young people as beautiful as carved idols. This poetic term "idol" is applied to ravishing beautiful beloveds of either gender. In the earlier couplet, the accusation of debauchery, *fisq*, also uses an ambiguous term: it could mean adultery, sexual lasciviousness, or moral corruption and disobeying religious law in general.

59 For a critical assessment of this tradition, see Scott Kugle, "Sexuality and Sexual Ethics in the Agenda of Progressive Muslims," in Safi, *Progressive Muslims*, 190–234.

60 Robb, *Strangers*, 46.

61 Indrāpatī, *Fatāwa-yi Tātār-Khāniyya*, was written before Mughal rule but remained the classical Hanafi legal manual for centuries. It was replaced only in Emperor Aurangzeb's rule by a new collection, *Fatāwa-yi ʿĀlamgīrī*.

62 Indrāpatī, *Fatāwa-yi Tātār-Khāniyya*, 5:81. *Zinā* is often translated into English as "adultery," although it means more exactly "fornication" between a man and a woman outside legally prescribed boundaries.

63 Imām al-Shāfiʿī's judgment makes this explicit when he is reported to have said, "He should be punished with the *ḥadd* penalty for fornication by reason of juridical analogy." Imām Mālik leaves the process of making this juridical analogy invisible, declaring only that a man who penetrates another man or is penetrated should be punished by the *ḥadd* penalty for *zinā*.

64 Hanafi decisions were cited by the Mālikī jurist al-Qurṭubī, *Tafsīr al-Jāmiʿ*, 7:244.

65 Al-Jassās, *Aḥkām al-Qur'ān*, 2:363, under the discussion of adulterers in *Surat al-Nur*.

66 Mirzā, *Shāh Ḥussayn*, 111.

67 Badāyunī, *Muntakhab al-Tawārikh*, as discussed in Kugle, "Maulana Azad," 97.

Chapter Five

1 Nakhshabī, *Juz'iyāt o Kulliyāt*, 11–12.

2 Ibid., 156.

3 Imdādullah, *Ḍiyā' al-Qulūb*, chap. 1, sec. 2, "Exercise of Dominating Power of Recitation."

4 Asad, *Genealogies of Religion*, 62.

5 It has been translated into Arabic for Imdādullah's disciples in Turkey, Egypt, Morocco, and Syria; see the bibliographic study in Fārūqī, *Nawādir-i Imdādiyya*, consisting of his rare and previously unpublished letters.

6 Imdādullah, *Ḍiyā' al-Qulūb*, chap. 1, sec. 1, "On the Instruction of Recitation."

7 Ibid. The *kimas* artery most likely refers to the popiteal artery that runs behind the knee.

8 Ibid., chap. 1, sec. 1, "Beneficial Moral Results of Recitation."

9 Ibid.

10 Imdādullah, *Ḍiyā' al-Qulūb*, chap. 1, sec. 1, "On the Exposition of Recitation." The two citations in single quotation marks are not from the Qur'an but come from hadith *qudsī*.

11 Ibid.

12 Ibid., chap. 1, sec. 1, "Exposition of Pronounced Recitation by Exhaling and Inhaling."

13 Ibid.

14 Ibid., chap. 1, sec. 2, "Discourse on Recitation for Warding Off Disturbing Thoughts."

15 Ibid., chap. 1, sec. 2, "On Exercises and Recitations" and "Discourse on Recitation for Warding Off Disturbing Thoughts." In Arabic script, the word "no" (*lā*) looks like a pair of scissors, with two blades attached at the bottom and opening upward. Sufis often compare "No god but God" to scissors or a broom, based on its calligraphic appearance; see Annemarie Schimmel, "Sufis and the Shahada," in Hovannisian and Vyronis, *Islam's Understanding of Itself*.

16 Arterial clogging begins at around age 5 and eventually develops into the leading cause of death in adults, especially in the modern situations of overconsumption.

17 Awrangābādī, *Niẓām al-Qulūb*, intro. He almost apologizes for writing down the Chishtī methods of meditative recollection, explaining that it was in response to sincere requests from friends and reflects accurately the teachings of his pious ancestors, "and in the end, God knows best."

18 For his autobiography, see Radtke and O'Kane, *Concept of Sainthood*, 15–36.

19 The following on al-Tirmidhī paraphrases the German of Radtke, *Al-Hakim al-Tirmidhi*.

20 Radtke and O'Kane, *Concept of Sainthood*, 226–27.

21 Ibid., 227–28.

22 Ibid., 22.

23 Radtke, *Al-Hakim al-Tirmidhi*, 63.

24 Radtke, *Al-Hakim al-Tirmidhi*, 64–65. On the first line of this quotation, see also Radtke and O'Kane, *Concept of Sainthood*, 219.

25 Radtke and O'Kane, *Concept of Sainthood*, 218–19.

26 Radtke, *Al-Hakim al-Tirmidhi*, 65. See Radtke and O'Kane, *Concept of Sainthood*, 226.

27 Chishtī, *Risāla-yi Afāq o Anfus*, fols. 272–74; also known as *Risāla dar Sulūk dar Shān-i Rag-hā-yi Adamī* (ms.). There is considerable difference between the two manuscripts of the same text, and Carl Ernst has undertaken a comparative translation of them both. See Ernst, "Two Versions of a Persian Text."

28 Chishtī, *Risāla-yi Afāq o Anfus*, fols. 272–74.

29 Ibid., 274a.

30 Shaykh Ṣābir's cave retreat is preserved near the place where Farīd al-Dīn died (in Pakpattan in Pakistan); his tomb is in the town of Kalyar, north of Delhi, where he lived.

31 He claimed a conventional initiation from Jalāl Panipatī via Shams al-Dīn Turk Panipatī from Shaykh Ṣābir.
32 Rizvi, *History of Sufism in India*, 1:270–71.
33 Gangōhī, *Anwār al-ʿUyūn*, 9.
34 Ibid., 35–36.
35 Ibid.
36 Ibid., 36–37. The phrase in italics is in Arabic but is not from the Qurʾan, yet it paraphrases Q 7:143.
37 Ibid., 37.
38 Shaṭṭārī, *Risāla-yi Shaṭṭāriyya* (ms.), 46, is the first systematic treatise on Shattari principles and practices, after Shāh ʿAbdullah Shaṭṭār's *Laṭāʾif-i Ghaybiyya*.
39 The syllables when written in Persian script are open to various pronunciations in Hindi, and they have been recorded with different variations in texts of different eras. The description in the "Shattari Treatise" was recorded almost verbatim in "The Harmonic Order of Hearts," which in turn was the source for Hajji Imdadullah's "The Brilliance of Hearts." It may even be that the syllables did not make semantic sense but were purely sound mantras to provide rhythmic control of the breath.
40 See Rizvi, "Sufis and Natha Yogis," and Carl Ernst, "Chishti Meditation Practices," in Lewisohn and Morgan, *Late Classical Persianate Sufism*, 344–59; "Situating Sufism and Yoga"; and "Islamization of Yoga." In addition, see contributions on Bengali Sufi-Yogic interactions in the scholarship of Muhammad Enamul Haq and Tarafdar.
41 This spiritual guide was a grandson of Shaykh ʿAbd al-Ḥaqq, though ʿAbd al-Quddūs was devoted to spirit of the *shaykh* himself directly, without human intermediary.
42 Digby, "Abd al-Quddus Gangohi." 45.
43 Carl Ernst, trans., "The Arabic Version of 'The Pool of the Water of Life' (Amrtakunda)" (ms.), chaps. 2 and 6. Many thanks to Professor Ernst for generously sharing of his scholarship.
44 Ibid., chap. 5.
45 Digby, "Abd al-Quddus Gangohi," 48.
46 Ibid., 50.
47 Suvorova, *Muslims Saints of South Asia*, 59–80.
48 On the translation of the *Amrtakunda* from Sanskrit into Arabic and Persian, see Ernst, "Sufism and Yoga according to Muhammad Ghawth."
49 Satīdāsa, *Muḥīṭ-i Maʿrifat* (ms.).
50 Digby, "Abd al-Quddus Gangohi," 84.
51 Ghawth, *Al-Jawāhir al-Khamsa*, 343.
52 Ibid.
53 Ibid.
54 Ernst, "Arabic Version of 'The Pool of the Water of Life,'" chap. 3.
55 Douglas, *Natural Symbols*, 20.
56 Imdādullah, *Ḍiyāʾ al-Qulūb*, chap. 1, sec. 3, "On Illuminations That Manifest in Recitation."

57 The "Delphic" reference of this maxim had long ago been absorbed in Islamic culture and is repeatedly attributed to ʿAlī, the son-in-law and cousin of Muḥammad, the heroic leader of the early Muslim community, and the focal point for much of Islamic spirituality; see Gēsū-darāz, *Asmār al-Asrār*, 30–32.
58 Imdādullah, *Ḍiyāʾ al-Qulūb*, chap. 1, sec. 1, "Other Ways of Recitation during Inhaling and Exhaling."
59 Ḥājji Imdādullah, *Ḍiyāʾ al-Qulūb*, Urdu translation, edited by Shāhid (Deoband: Kutub-Khāna Rāshid Company, n.d.).
60 Asad, *Genealogies of Religion*, 77.
61 Imdādullah, *Ḍiyāʾ al-Qulūb*, chap. 1, sec. 1, "The Exercise of the Spread Carpet."
62 Fārūqī, *Nawādir-i Imdādiyya*, 34. For hagiographies, see Thānwī, *Imdād al-Mushtāq ilā Ashraf al-Akhlāq*; Zaydī, *Ḥājji Imdādullah Muhājir Makkī: sīrat o ṣawāniḥ*; and al-Ḥasa, *Ḥayyāt-i Imdād*.
63 See Kugle, "Framed, Blamed and Renamed."
64 Other disciples founded the leading religious academy of Hyderābād, the Madrassa Niẓāmiyya. On the importance of the Deoband Academy to the communal consciousness of Indian Muslims under colonial rule, see Metcalf, "Nationalism, Modernity, and Muslim Identity"; Kucukcan, "Analytical Comparison"; and Mansurnoor, "ʿUlamaʾ in Changing Society."
65 Imdādullah, *Ḍiyāʾ al-Qulūb*, intro. and benediction.

Conclusion

1 Hodgson, *Venture of Islam*, 3:187–96.
2 Rex O'Fahey and Bernd Radtke, "Neo-Sufism Reconsidered," *Der Islam* 70, no. 1 (1993): 52–87.
3 Esther Peskes, "The Wahhabiyya and Sufism," in De Jong and Radtke, *Islamic Mysticism Contested*, 146.
4 O'Fahey, *Enigmatic Saint*, 74.
5 *Lā ilāha illā allāh, Muhammad rasul allah fi kulli lamha wa nafas ʿadada ma wasaʿahu ʿilm allah.*
6 O'Fahey, *Enigmatic Saint*, 3–4. Al-Sanūsī cites al-Ajimi.
7 Thomassen and Radtke, *Letters of Ahmad Ibn Idris*, 65.
8 Sulaymān Ibn ʿAbd al-Wahhāb, *Al-Ṣawāʿiq al-Ilāhiyya*, demonstrates that Sunni opponents accused the Wahhabi movement of returning to Khārijī ideology. Insightful Western scholars have also identified the Wahhabis as such, rather than as "puritans" or Islamic "protestants."
9 Muḥammad Ibn ʿAbd al-Wahhāb, *Kitāb al-Tawḥīd*, 61.
10 Hawting, *Idea of Idolatry*, 78–85; his argument about the origins of Islam valorizes the Wahhabi position as the only essentially Islamic position possible.
11 Their reliance upon hadith had great emotional appeal among literalist Sunnis and had been a rallying cry for jurists in the Ḥanbalī legal school, though none of them before Ibn ʿAbd al-Wahhāb made the claims he did.
12 The writing style is sparse, quoting Qurʾanic verses in short excerpts and often out of context, supported by citing hadith with little or no discussion of their

authenticity or reliability. His position is that to say more, in his own words, would be allow rational analysis to creep in, tainting his argument and engaging in interpretation (*ta'wīl*) at a distance from the scriptural text.

13 Muḥammad Ibn ʿAbd al-Wahhāb, *Kitāb al-Tawḥīd*, 5.

14 Ibid., 7.

15 Simsar, *Ṭūṭī-Nāma*, 26.

16 Ibid., 25.

17 Muḥammad Ibn ʿAbd al-Wahhāb, *Kitāb al-Tawḥīd*, 9.

18 Ibid., n. 1. Footnotes were written by the editor of this edition, Muḥammad ibn ʿAbd al-Qādir al-Hilālī, who depends upon the earlier commentary of ʿAbd al-Raḥmān ibn Ḥasan ibn Āl al-Shaykh (mistakenly named "Ḥasan ibn ʿAbd al-Raḥmān").

19 Ibid., 13–14.

20 Ibid., 15–20.

21 Ibid., 24–25.

22 Ibid., 30. Ibn ʿAbd al-Wahhāb has difficulty reconciling his critique of intercession with the Qur'anic verses and hadith that he quotes, which state that God can and does grant power of intercession to people of pure sincerity.

23 Muḥammad Ibn ʿAbd al-Wahhāb, *Thalāthat al-Uṣūl*, 153, 164–66, struggles to limit the application of such hadith that justify intercession by picturing the Prophet's existential intimacy with God, his ability to mediate God's judgment of believers, and their capacity to draw close to his presence even after his death through rituals of remembrance.

24 Muḥammad Ibn ʿAbd al-Wahhāb, *Kitāb al-Tawḥīd*, 33–34, 36–38.

25 Ibid.

26 Peskes, "Wahhabiyya and Sufism," 154.

27 Muḥammad Ibn ʿAbd al-Wahhāb, *Kitāb al-Tawḥīd*, 61–62, justified political rebellion by claiming that "whoever obeys religious scholars or worldly leaders in forbidding what God allowed or allowing what God forbid has taken these human beings to be their gods."

28 Sulaymān Ibn ʿAbd al-Wahhāb, *Al-Ṣawāʿiq al-Ilāhiyya*, 39–40. Many thanks to Omid Safi for bringing this text to my attention.

29 Early commentators described these idols as gods of various Arab tribes, as did most authoritative lexicographers—see Lane, *Arabic-English Lexicon*, 2:2306 *b.

30 Muḥammad Ibn ʿAbd al-Wahhāb, *Kitāb al-Tawḥīd*, 33.

31 Ibn al-Kalbī was a philosophical Arab interested in pre-Islamic traditions of the Arabs and their folklore to an extent that more "orthodox" Islamic scholars found suspicious. They shunned his book as an attempt to preserve pre-Islamic Arab lore based on questionable sources, information that should rightly be forgotten in the Islamic dispensation. Ibn al-Kalbī claims that this information about Noah is based on traditions related by Ibn ʿAbbās. While citing the traditions, Ibn ʿAbd al-Wahhāb rather predictably neglects to mention that they are preserved in Ibn al-Kalbī's works, preferring simply to say that they were related by Ibn ʿAbbās. Hawting, *Idea of Idolatry*, 89–110, treats al-Kalbī, anachronistically,

as an Islamizing source even though Islamic-oriented traditionists saw him as a "secular" source championing Arab chauvinism above Islamic loyalty.

32 Faris, *Book of Idols*, 44–45. Al-Kalbī relates the same story as Genesis 5:24.

33 Ibid., 44–45.

34 Ibid., 43–44.

35 Ibid., 4.

36 Muḥammad Ibn ʿAbd al-Wahhāb, *Kitāb al-Tawḥīd*, 34–35. He also alleges that the pagan goddesses Allāt and ʿUzza were similarly holy women who had set up charitable institutions in Mecca to feed and care for pilgrims to the Kaʿba before they were deified: see pp. 38–39. Such a claim is not supported by early Islamic traditions of Ibn al-Kalbī, who refers to them as goddesses and idols but never as holy women who were deified.

37 Ibid., 35.

38 Ibid., 61–62. See his treatise on visiting tombs: Muḥammad Ibn ʿAbd al-Wahhāb, *Thalāthat al-Uṣūl*, 152.

39 Ibn Āl al-Shaykh, *Fatḥ al-Majīd*, 214–18.

40 Ibid., 215. See also Muḥammad Ibn ʿAbd al-Wahhāb, *Thalāthat al-Uṣūl*, 161.

41 Ibn Āl al-Shaykh, *Fatḥ al-Majīd*, 215–16, quoting here an earlier Wahhabi text, *Qurrat al-ʿUyūn*.

42 Ibid.

43 Ibid., 216.

44 Ibid., 216–17, quoting from the earlier commentary, *Qurrat al-ʿUyūn*.

45 Ibid.

46 Muḥammad Ibn ʿAbd al-Wahhāb, *Kitāb al-Tawḥīd*, 38, blames the Shiʿa for the "deviation" of turning tombs into mosques and excludes them altogether from the community of Muslims.

47 Judowitz, *Culture of the Body*, 74.

48 Al-Zahī, *Al-Jasad al-Ṣūra wa'l -Muqaddas*, 116. Wahhabis' literalist reading of scripture and refusal to interpret through reason, analogy, or metaphor forces them (like their Ḥanbalī predecessors) to insist that God has body parts: the hands, feet, face, and seat that are mentioned in the Qur'an. Sufi and traditionalist Sunni opponents who oppose the Wahhabis criticize their "theological anthropomorphism" even as Wahhabis attack their opponents for idolatry and incarnationism.

49 Muḥammad Ibn ʿAbd al-Wahhāb, *Kitāb al-Tawḥīd*, 33–34 n. 1.

50 Castoriadis, *Imaginary Institution*, 131. He theorizes the *imaginairé*, or "social imaginary," as the network of images through which a society institutes itself, bridging the gap between the reality of material conditions and the symbolic order that gives them meaning.

51 Al-Zahī, *Al-Jasad al-Ṣūra wa'l -Muqaddas*, 116.

52 Such reactions can be seen in the Taliban movement and are theologically justified by publications like al-Ṭībī, *ʿIbādat al-Awthān*, which denounces photography, cinema, and television as "worship of idols."

53 Austin, *Bezels of Wisdom*, 75–81.

54 Ibn Āl al-Shaykh, *Fatḥ al-Majīd*, 215–16.
55 Austin, *Bezels of Wisdom*, 50–57.
56 Simsar, *Ṭūṭī-Nāma*, 159.
57 Ibid., 109.
58 Nakhshabī, *Juz'iyāt o Kulliyāt*, 150.
59 Ibid., 157–58.

BIBLIOGRAPHY

Unpublished Manuscripts in Arabic or Persian

ʿAlawī, Wajīh al-Dīn Gujarātī. *Malfūẓāt-i Wajīh al-Dīn Gujarātī*. Hyderabad: Oriental Manuscript Library and Research Institute, Farsi Tasawwuf 547.

ʿAlawī Ḥussaynī, Sayyid ʿAbd al-Mālik. *Miṣbāḥ al-ʿĀlam*. Ahmadabad: B.J. Institute of Learning and Research, 293.

Chishtī, Muʿīn al-Dīn Ajmērī. *Risāla dar Sulūk dar Shān-i Rag-hā-yi Adamī*. Ahmadabad: Pir Mohammedshah Dargah, 152, fols. 1–15.

——— *Risāla-yi Afāq o Anfus*. London: British Library, India Office Collection, Islamic 1754.

Chishtī, Rashīd al-Dīn Lālā. *Mukhbir al-Awliyā'*. Ahmadabad: Nasir Bagh Dargah.

Dihlawī, ʿAbd al-Ḥaqq Muḥaddith. *Kitāb Taḥsīl al-Taʿarruf bayn al-Fiqh wa'l-Taṣawwuf*. Rampur: Reza Library, 1347 Arabic.

——— *Takmīla-yi Madārij al-Nubuwwa*. Calcutta: Asiatic Society of Bengal, Curzon Collection, 352 Persian.

——— *Zād al-Muttaqīn*, London: British Library, India Office Collection, 217.

Fārūqī Aḥmad ibn Muḥammad. *Khulāṣat al-Wajīh*. Ahmadabad: B.J. Institute of Learning and Research, 291.

Gēsū-Darāz, Muḥammad Ḥusaynī. *Muḥabbat-Nāma* London: British Library, India Office Collection, Islamic 1754, pt. 2.

Ghawth, Muḥammad Gwāliyōrī. *Awrād-i Ghawthiyya*. Hyderabad: Oriental Manuscript Library and Research Institute, Farsi Tasawwuf 487, and Calcutta: Asiatic Society Collection, 1252 and 446 Farsi.

——— *Kalīd al-Makhāzin*. Patna: Khuda Bakhsh Library, 1376 and 1376A.

——— *Miʿrāj Nāma*. Ahmadabad: Pir Mohammadshah Dargah, 1503, 1216, and 1217.

Ibn Ṣabbāgh, Muḥammad Abū ʿAbdullah. *Manāqib al-Walīya al-Ṣāliḥa Sayyida ʿĀ'isha*. Tunis: Khizānat al-Zaytūna, 6556, fols. 147–76.

Khweshgī, ʿAbdullah. *Maʿārij al-Wilāya*. Lahore: Punjab University Library, H-25/7765 Farsi.

al-Kisā'ī, Abū Jaʿfar Muḥammad. *Kitāb ʿAjā'ib al-Makhlūqāt wa Ṣanʿat al-Ḥayy al-ladhī lā yamūtu*. Leiden: 538 Warn.

Maḥmūd ibn Muḥammad Pīr. *Haqīqat al-Fuqarā'*. Lahore: Punjab University Library, 3253/248 Farsi.

Manāqib al-Walīya al-Ṣāliḥa Sayyida ʿĀ'isha. Tunis: Khizānat al-Zaytūna, 16577, fols. 1–46, and 9500, fols. 1–26.

Muttaqī, ʿAlī. *Asrār al-ʿĀrifīn wa Sayr al-Ṭālibīn*. Patna: Khudabakhsh Library, catalog vol. 13, no. 957.

——— *Ghāyat al-Maʿmūl fī'l -Sulūk wa'l -Wuṣūl*. Lahore: Punjab University Library, 4862/1842, fols. 9–11.
——— *Tanbīh al-Aḥibba fī ʿAlāmāt al-Muḥabba*. Delhi: Shah Abul Khayr Dargah, 21 Tasawwuf, fols. 1–9.
———*Tanbīh al-Ghāfilīn*. Rampur: Reza Library, 1975 Tasawwuf Farsi.
Nakhshabī, Ḍiyā' al-Dīn. *Juz'iyāt o Kulliyāt*. London: British Library, India Office Collection, Islamic 905.
Nubdha min Tārīkh al-Maghrib al-Aqṣā. Rabat: al-Khizāna al-ʿAmma, 2152 d.
Al-Qazwīnī. *ʿAjā'ib al-Makhlūqāt wa Gharā'ib al-Mawjūdāt*. London: British Library, India Office Collection, Islamic 3243.
Satīdāsa, *Muḥīṭ-i Maʿrifat*. London: British Library, India Office Collection, William Jones College, 142 Persian (occult sciences).
Shaṭṭārī, Burhān al-Dīn Ibrāhīm ʿAṭā' Anṣārī. *Risāla-yi Shaṭṭāriyya*. Hyderabad: Oriental Manuscript Library and Research Archive, Farsi Tasawwuf 745.
Shaṭṭārī, Faḍlullah. *Manāqib-i Ghawthiyya*. Ahmadabad: B.J. Institute of Learning and Research, 294.
Zarrūq, Aḥmad. *Al-Kunnāsh fī ʿIlm Āsh*. Rabat: al-Khizāna al-ʿAmma, 1385 k.

Published Studies in Arabic, Persian, or Urdu
Awrangābādī, Niẓām al-Dīn. *Niẓām al-Qulūb*. Litho. Delhi: Matbaʿ Mujtabā'ī, n.d.
Chishtī, Nūr Aḥmad. *Taḥqīqāt-i Chishtī*. Lahore: Koh-i Nur Press, 1993.
Dārā Shikōh. *Ḥasanāt al-ʿĀrifīn*. Urdu translation. Lahore: Islamia Steam Press, n.d.
Dihlawī, ʿAbd al-Ḥaqq Muḥaddith. *Akhbār al-Akhyār fī Asrār al-Abrār*. Litho. Delhi: n.p., 1308 Hijri.
Fārūqī, M. Ḥabībullah, and Mohan Singh Diwāna. *Ḥālāt o Kāfiyān Madhō Lāl Ḥussayn*. Lahore: Mālik Aḥmad Tāj Book Depot, n.d.
Fārūqī, Nisār Aḥmad, ed. *Nawādir-i Imdādiyya*. Gulbarga: Gesudaraz Tahqiqati Akademi, 1996.
al-Fāsī, Aḥmad ibn ʿAbd al-Ḥayy al-Ḥalabī. *Al-Durr al-Nafīs wa'l -Nūr al-Anīs fī Manāqib al-Imām Idrīs ibn Idrīs*. Litho. Fes: n.p., 1314 Hijri.
al-Fāsī, ʿAlī ibn Abī Zarʿ. *Anīs al-Muṭrib bi-Rawḍat al-Qirtās*. Rabat: Dār al-Manṣūr, 1972.
al-Fāsī, Muḥammad al-ʿArabī. *Mir'at al-Maḥāsin fī Akhbār al-Shaykh Abī al-Maḥāsin*. Litho. Fes: n.p., n.d.
al-Fāsī, Muḥammad al-Mahdī. *Mumtiʿ al-Asmā' fī Dhikr al-Jazūlī wa'l -Tabbāʿ wa mā lahumā min al-Atbāʿ*. Casablanca: Maṭbaʿat Dār al-Najāḥ al-Jadīda, 1994.
Gangōhī, ʿAbd al-Quddūs. *Anwār al-ʿUyūn fī Asrār al-Maknūn*. Litho. Lucknow: Maṭbaʿ Gulzār-i Muḥammad, 1295 Hijri.
Gēsū-darāz, Muḥammad Ḥussaynī. *Asmār al-Asrār*. Edited by Mawlvī Sayyid ʿAṭā Ḥussayn. Hyderabad: Aʿẓam Steam Press, n.d.
Ghawth, Muḥammad Gwāliyōrī. *Awrād-i Ghawthiyya*. Litho. Raichur: Maṭbaʿ-yi Sibghatullahī, 1313 Hijri.
——— *Al-Jawāhir al-Khamsa*. Urdu translation. Delhi: Naz Publishing House, n.d.
Ghawthī Shaṭṭārī, Muḥammad. *Adhkār-i Abrār: Urdu Translation of Gulzār-i Abrār*. Translated by Faḍl Aḥmad Jiyūrī. Lahore: Islamic Book Foundation, 1975.

——— *Gulzār-i Abrār*. Agra: Maṭbaʿ-yi Mufīd-i ʿĀmm, 1326 Hijri.
al-Ḥasa, Muḥammad Anwar. *Ḥayyāt-i Imdād*. Karachi: Sherkoti Press, 1965.
Ibn ʿAbd al-Wahhāb, Muḥammad al-Najdī. *Kitāb al-Tawḥīd*. Bombay: al-Maktab al-Qayyim, 1344 Hijri.
——— *Thalāthat al-Uṣūl wa Adillat-uhā*. Cairo: Maṭbaʿ al-Minār, 1340 Hijri.
Ibn ʿAbd al-Wahhāb, Sulaymān al-Najdī. *Al-Ṣawāʿiq al-Ilāhiyya fī Radd ʿalā al-Wahhābiyya*. Cairo: Dār al-Insān, 1987.
Ibn Āl al-Shaykh, ʿAbd al-Raḥmān ibn Ḥasan. *Fatḥ al-Majīd Sharḥ Kitāb al-Tawḥīd*. Edited by Muḥammad Ḥāmid al-Faqī. Cairo: Maṭbaʿ Anṣār al-Sunna al-Muḥammadiyya, 1362 Hijri.
Ibn ʿAskar, Muḥammad al-Ḥasanī al-Shafshāwī. *Dawḥat al-Nāshir li-Maḥāsin man kāna bi'l -Maghrib min Mashā'ikh al-Qarn al-ʿĀshir*. Rabat: Dār al-Maghrib, 1976.
Ibn al-Qāḍī, Aḥmad al-Miknāsī. *Jadhwat al-Iqtibās fī dhikr man ḥalla min Aʿlām Madīnat Fās*. Rabat: Dār al-Manṣūr, 1973.
Imdādullah, Ḥājji. *Ḍiyā' al-Qulūb*. In *Kulliyāt-i Imdādiyya*. Lucknow: Fakhr al-Matābiʿ, n.d.
——— *Jihād-i Akbar*. Deoband, India: Rashid Publishing Co., n.d.
——— *Kulliyāt-i Imdādiyya*. Persian original. Edited by Muḥammad Fakhr al-Dīn Mālik. Kanpur: Maṭbaʿ-i Aḥmadī, n.d.
——— *Kulliyāt-i Imdādiyya*. Urdu translation. Deoband, India: Rashid Publishing Co., n.d.
Indrāpatī, ʿAlīm ibn al-ʿAlā' al-Anṣārī. *Fatāwa-yi Tātār-Khāniyya*. Karachi: Idārat al-Qur'ān wa'l -ʿUlūm al-Islāmiyya, n.d.
al-Jassās, Abū Bakr Aḥmad al-Rāzī. *Aḥkām al-Qur'ān*. Beirut: Dār al-Kitāb al-ʿArabī, 1978.
al-Jaznā'ī. *Janā Zahrat al-Ās fī Binā' Madīnat Fās*. Rabat: al-Maṭbaʿa al-Malakiyya, 1991.
al-Jīlānī, ʿAbd al-Qādir. *Al-Safina al-Qādiriyya*. Tripoli, Libya: Maktabat al-Najāḥ, n.d.
al-Kattānī, Muḥammad ibn Jaʿfar. *Salwat al-Anfās wa Muḥādithat al-Akyās bi-man uqbira min al-ʿUlamā' wa'l -Ṣulaḥā' bi-Fās*. 3 vols. Litho. Fes: n.d.
al-Kisā'ī, ʿAlī ibn Hamza. *Bad' al-Khalq wa Qiṣaṣ al-Anbiyā'*. Edited by Al-Tahir ibn Salama. Tunis: Dār Nuqūsh ʿArabiyya, 1998.
Lāhōrī, Ghulām Sarwār. *Khazīnat al-Aṣfiyā'*. Lucknow: Nawal Kishore, n.d.
Lāhōrī, Muḥammad Ṣāḥib. *Ḥadā'iq al-Ḥanafiyya*. Lucknow: Nawal Kishore, n.d.
al-Majdhūb, ʿAbd al-Raḥmān. *Al-Qawl al-Ma'thūr min Kalām Sayyidī ʿAbd al-Raḥmān al-Majdhūb*. Casablanca: Maktabat al-Waḥda al-ʿArabiyya, 1995.
Mālik, Muḥammad Laṭīf. *Awliyā'-yi Lāhōr*. Lahore: Sang-i Meel, n.d.
Mirzā, Shafqat Tanwīr. *Shāh Ḥussayn*. Islamabad: Lōk Wirsa Ishaʿat G͟har, 1989.
al-Nāṣirī al-Slawī, Aḥmad. *Kitāb al-Istiṣqā' li-Akhbār Duwwal al-Maghrib al-Aqṣā'*. 6 vols. Casablanca: Dār al-Kitāb, 1955.
al-Qādirī, ʿAbd al-Salām ibn al-Ṭayyib. *Al-Maqṣad al-Aḥmad bi-Taʿrīf Sayyidina ʿAbdullah Aḥmad*. Litho. Fes: n.p., n.d.
al-Qādirī, Muḥammad ibn al-Ṭayyib. *Nashr al-Mathānī li-Ahl al-Qarn al-Ḥādī ʿAshar wa'l-Thānī*. Rabat: Dār al-Maghrib, 1977.

Qudūsī, ʿIjāz al-Ḥaqq. *Tadhkira-yi Ṣūfiya-yi Punjāb*. Lahore: Salmān Akademi, 1962.
al-Qurṭubī, Muḥammad ibn Aḥmad. *Tafsīr al-Jāmiʿ fī Aḥkām al-Qurʾān*. Cairo: Dār al-Qalam, 1967.
al-Sharrāṭ, Muḥammad ibn ʿĀshūn. *Al-Rawḍ al-ʿAṭir al-Anfās bi-Akhbār al-Ṣulaḥāʾ min Ahl Fās*. Casablanca: Maṭbaʿat al-Najāḥ al-Jadīda, 1997.
Shaṭṭārī, Faḍlullah. *Manāqib-i Ghawthiyya*. Urdu translation by Muḥammad Ẓāhir al-Ḥaqq. Litho. Agra: Abū Maʿāl ī, 1933.
Thānwī, ʿAlī Ashraf. *Imdād al-Mushtāq ilā Ashraf al-Akhlāq*. N.p.: Maktaba-yi Burhān, 1981.
al-Ṭībī, ʿUkāsa ʿAbd al-Mannān. *ʿIbādat al-Awthān: al-Aṣnām, al-Tamāthīl, al-Taṣwīr, al-Sīnīmā, al-Tilifiziyūn*. Cairo: Maktabat al-Turāth al-Islāmī, 1990.
Ulūghkhānī, Muḥammad "Ḥājji al-Dabīr." *Ẓafar al-Wālih bi-Muẓaffar wa Ālihi*. Edited by E. Denison Ross. London: John Murray Publishers, 1910.
al-Zahī, Farīd. *Al-Jasad al-Ṣūra wa'l-Muqaddas fī'l-Islām*. Beirut: Ifrīqiyā al-Sharq, 1999.
Zaydī, Sayyid Nazar. *Ḥājji Imdādullah Muhājir Makkī: sīrat o ṣawāniḥ*. Ahmadabad: Maktaba-yi Ẓafar, 1978.

Published Studies in English and Other European Languages

Ahmed, Leila. *Women and Gender in Islam: Historical Roots of a Modern Debate*. New Haven, Conn.: Yale University Press, 1992.
Alhaq, Shuja. *Forgotten Vision: A Study of Human Spirituality in the Light of the Islamic Tradition*. London: Minerva, 1996.
Andezian, Sossie. *Expériences du divin dans l'Algérie contemporaine: Adeptes des saints de la région de Tlemcen*. Paris: CNRS Editions, 2001.
Ansari, Z. *Life, Times and Works of Amir Khusrau*. Delhi: National Amir Khusro Society, 1975.
Anwar, Ghulam Yaqoob, trans. *The Paths Unknown: Kafiyan Shah Hussain*. Lahore: Majlis Shah Hussain, 1966.
Asad, Talal. *Genealogies of Religion: Discipline and Reasons of Power in Christianity and Islam*. Baltimore: Johns Hopkins University Press, 1993.
Austin, R. W. J., trans. *Ibn ʿArabī : Bezels of Wisdom*. Mahwah, N.J.: Paulist Press, 1980.
Bakhtin, M. M. *Rabelais and His World*. Translated by H. Iswolsky. Cambridge, Mass.: MIT Press, 1968.
Bekkenkamp, Jonneke, and Maaike de Haardt, eds. *Begin with the Body: Corporeality, Religion and Gender*. Leuven, Netherlands: Peeters, 1998.
Bell, Catherine. *Ritual Theory, Ritual Practice*. New York: Oxford University Press, 1994.
Berquist, Jon. *Controlling Corporeality: The Body and the Household in Ancient Israel*. New Brunswick, N.J.: Rutgers University Press, 2002.
Blumenfeld-Kosinski, Renate, and Timea Szell, eds. *Images of Sainthood in Medieval Europe*. Ithaca, N.Y.: Cornell University Press, 1991.
Bonie, Pierre. "Figures historique de la saintete dans la Societe Maure." *Annuaire de l'Afrique du Nord* (1994): 284–90.

Bouhdiba, Abdelwahhab. *Sexuality in Islam*. London: Routledge and Kegan Paul, 1985.
Bourdieu, Pierre. *Outline of the Theory of Practice*. Translated by Richard Nice. Cambridge: Cambridge University Press, 1977.
Brinner, William, trans. *ʿArāʾis al-Majālis fi Qiṣaṣ al-Anbiyāʾ or Lives of the Prophets as Recounted by al-Thaʿlabī*. Leiden: Brill, 2002.
Brown, Peter. *The Cult of the Saints: Its Rise and Function in Latin Christianity*. Chicago: University of Chicago Press, 1980.
Bulliet, Richard. *Islam: The View from the Edge*. New York: Columbia University Press, 1994.
Castoriadis, Cornelius. *The Imaginary Institution of Society*. Cambridge,Mass.: MIT Press, 1987.
Chebel, Malik. "Vision du corps en Islam." *Les cahiers de l'orient* 8–9 (1988).
Chodkiewicz, Michel. *An Ocean without Shore : Ibn Arabi, The Book, and the Law*. Albany: SUNY Press, 1993.
Coakley Sarah, ed. *Religion and the Body*. Cambridge: Cambridge University Press, 1997.
Comstock, Gary David, and Susan Henking, eds. *Que(e)rying Religion: A Critical Anthology*. New York: Continuum Publishing, 1997.
Cornell, Vincent. *The Realm of the Saint: Power and Authority in Moroccan Sufism*. Austin: University of Texas Press, 1996.
Dabashi, Hamid. *Authority in Islam: From the Death of Muhammad to the Establishment of the Ummayads* New Brunswick, N.J.: Transaction Publishers, 1993.
De Jong, Fred, and Berndt Radtke, eds. *Islamic Mysticism Contested: Thirteen Centuries of Controversies and Polemics*. Leiden: Brill, 1999.
Digby, Simon. "Abd al-Quddus Gangohi: The Personality and Attitudes of a Medieval Indian Sufi." In *Medieval India: A Miscellany*, vol. 3. Delhi: Asia Publishing House, 1975.
Douglas, Elmer, trans. *The Mystical Teachings of al-Shadhili*. Albany: State University of New York Press, 1993.
Douglas, Mary. *Natural Symbols: Explorations in Cosmology*. London: Barrie and Jenkins, 1970.
Eliade, Mircea. *The Sacred and the Profane: The Nature of Religion*. New York: Harcourt, 1959.
Ernst, Carl. *Eternal Garden: Mysticism, History, and Politics in a South Asian Sufi Center*. Albany: State University of New York Press, 1992.
———"Islamization of Yoga in the *Amrtakunda* Translations." *Journal of the Royal Asiatic Society*, ser. 3, 13, no. 2 (2003): 199–226.
——— *Shambhala Guide to Sufism*. Boston: Shambhala Press, 1997.
———"Situating Sufism and Yoga." *Journal of the Royal Asiatic Society*, ser. 3, 15, no. 1 (2005): 15–43.
———"Sufism and Yoga according to Muhammad Ghawth." *Sufi* 29 (1996): 9–13.
———"Two Versions of a Persian Text on Yoga and Cosmology Attributed to Shaykh Muʿin al-Din Chishti." *Elixir* 2 (2006): 69–125.

Ewing, Katherine. *Arguing Sainthood: Modernity, Psychoanalysis and Islam*. Durham, N.C.: Duke University Press, 1997.
Faris, Nabih Amin, trans. *The Book of Idols: Kitāb al-Aṣnām by Hishām Ibn al-KalbI*. Princeton, N.J.: Princeton University Press, 1952.
Feher, Michel, Ramona Naddaff, and Nadia Tazi, eds. *Fragments for a History of the Human Body*. 3 vols. New York: Zone, 1989.
Geertz, Clifford. *Islam Observed: Religious Development in Morocco and Indonesia*. Chicago: University of Chicago Press, 1968.
Gellner, Ernest. *Saints of the Atlas*. London: Weidenfeld and Nicolson, 1969.
Gemeʿah, Muhammad Mustafa, trans. *Stories of the Prophets by Ibn Kathīr*. New Delhi: Islamic Book Service, 2000.
Gilmartin, David, and Bruce Lawrence, eds. *Beyond Hindu and Turk: Rethinking Religious Identities in Islamic South Asia*. Gainsville: University of Florida Press, 2000.
Haberman, David. *Journey through the Twelve Forests: An Encounter with Krishna*. New York: Oxford University Press, 1994.
Hammoudi, Abdellah. *Master and Disciple: The Cultural Foundations of Moroccan Authoritarianism*. Chicago: University of Chicago Press, 1997.
Haq, Muhammad Enamul. *A History of Sufi-ism in Bengal*. Dacca: Asiatic Society of Bengal, 1975.
Haq, Muhammad Muzammil. "Ghawth Gwaliori: A Sixteenth Century Shattari Saint of India, His Works and Disciples." *Dacca University Studies* 36/A (1982).
Hassan, Riffat. "Feminist Theology as a Means of Combating Injustice toward Women in Muslim Communities and Culture." In William Cenkner, ed., *Evil and the Response of World Religion*. St. Paul, Minn.: Paragon House, 1997.
Hawting, G. R. *The Idea of Idolatry and the Emergence of Islam: from Polemic to History*. Cambridge: Cambridge University Press, 1999.
Heath, Peter. *Allegory and Philosophy in Avicenna Ibn Sina with a Translation of the Book of the Prophet Muhammad's Ascent to Heaven*. Philadelphia: University of Pennsylvania Press, 1992.
Hodgson, Marshall. *The Venture of Islam: History and Conscience in the World Civilization*. 3 vols. Chicago: University of Chicago Press, 1974.
Holm, Jean, ed. *Picturing God*. London: Pinter Publishers, 1994.
Hopkins, Stephen. "Extravagant Beholding: The Love of Two Bodies and the Language of Excess in *The Song of Songs* and South Indian Devotion." *Journal of the American Academy of Religion*, forthcoming.
——— *Singing the Body of God*. New York: Oxford University Press, 2002.
Hovannisian, Richard, and Speros Vyronis Jr., eds. *Islam's Understanding of Itself*. Malibu: Undena Publications, 1983.
Huizinga, J. *Homo Ludens: A Study of the Play Element in Culture*. 1938. Boston: Beacon Press, 1955.
Ibn ʿArabī, *Whoso Knows Himself . . . from the Treatise on Being*. Oxford: Beshara Publications, 1976.
Jackson, Paul, trans. *Sharafuddin Maneri: The Hundred Letters*. New York: Paulist Press, 1980.

Johnson-Davies, Denys, trans. *The Island of the Animals*. Austin: University of Texas Press, 1994.
Judovitz, Dalia. *The Culture of the Body: Genealogies of Modernity*. Ann Arbor: University of Michigan Press, 2001.
Karamustafa, Ahmet. *God's Unruly Friends: Deviant Renunciation in the Islamic Later Middle Period*. Salt Lake City: University of Utah Press, 1994.
Katz, Marion. *Body of Text: The Emergence of the Sunni Law of Ritual Purity*. Albany: State University of New York Press, 2002.
Khuri, Fuad. *The Body in Islamic Culture*. London: Saqi Books, 2001.
Kinsley, David. *The Divine Player: A Study of Krsna Lila*. Delhi: Motilal Banarsidass, 1979.
Knysh, Alexander. *Ibn Arabi in the Later Islamic Tradition: The Making of a Polemic Image in Medieval Islam*. Albany: State University of New York Press, 1999.
Kucukcan, Talip. "An Analytical Comparison of the Aligarh and Deobandi Schools." *Islamic-Quarterly* 38, no. 1 (1994): 48–58.
Kugle, Scott. *The Book of Illumination: An English Translation of Kitab al-Tanwir fi Isqat al-Tadbir by Shaykh Ibn 'Ata' Allah al-Iskandari*. Louisville, Ky.: Fons Vitae Press, 2005.
———"The Brilliance of Hearts by Hajji Imdadullah." In Barbara Metcalf, ed., *Islam in South Asia in Practice*. Forthcoming.
———"Dancing with Khusro: Gender Ambiguity and Spiritual Power at a Chishti Dargah." In Richard Martin and Carl Ernst, eds., *Islam in Theory and Practice: Essays in Comparative Religious Studies*. Forthcoming.
———"Framed, Blamed and Renamed: The Reshaping of Islamic Law in Colonial South Asia." *Modern Asian Studies* 35, no. 2 (2001): 257–313.
———"Heaven's Witness: The Uses and Abuses of Muhammad Ghawth Gwaliori's Ascension." *Journal of Islamic Studies* 14, no. 1 (2003): 24–31.
———"In Search of the Center: Authenticity, Reform and Critique in Early Modern Islamic Sainthood." Ph.D. diss., Duke University, 2000.
———"Maulana Azad Resurrects a 'Mahdi' between Ethical Vision and Historical Revision." *Islamic Culture* 72, no. 3 (1999): 79–114.
——— *Rebel between Spirit and Law: Ahmad Zarruq and Juridical Sainthood in North Africa*. Bloomington: Indiana University Press, 2006.
Kundera, Milan. *Laughable Loves*. New York: HarperCollins, 1999.
Lane, Edward. *Arabic-English Lexicon*. 1863. Reprint, Cambridge, England: Islamic Texts Society, 1984.
Langer, Monika. *Merleau-Ponty's Phenomenology of Perception: A Guide and Commentary*. Tallahassee: Florida State University Press, 1989.
Law, Jane Marie, ed. *Religious Reflections on the Human Body*. Bloomington: Indiana University Press, 1995.
Lawrence, Bruce, trans. *Morals for the Heart: Conversations of Shaykh Nizam al-Din Awlia Recorded by Amir Hasan Sijzi*. Mahwah, N.J.: Paulist Press, 1992.
Lawson, Todd, ed. *Reason and Inspiration in Islam: Essays in Honour of Hermann Landolt*. London: I. B. Tauris, 2005.

Lewisohn, Leonard, and David Morgan, eds. *Late Classical Persianate Sufism, 1501–1750: The Safavid and Maghal Periods*. Oxford: Oneworld, 1999.
Luther, A. R., and Ramakrishna. *Madho Lal Hussayn: Sufi Poet of the Punjab*. Lahore: Shaykh Mubarak Ali, 1982.
Mahmoud, Ibrahim. *Geography of Pleasures: Sex in Paradise*. Beirut: Riad el-Rayyes, 1998.
Mansurnoor. "'Ulama' in Changing Society: A Re-Examination of the Deoband Movement, 1867–1924." *Hamdard Islamicus* 16 (1993): 97–114.
Marin, Manuela, and Randi Deguilhem, eds. *Writing the Feminine: Women in Arab Sources*. London: I. B. Tauris, 2002.
Mauss, Marcel. *Sociology and Psychology: Essays*. 1950. London: Routledge and Kegan Paul, 1979.
Mernissi, Fatima. "Women, Saints and Sanctuaries." *Signs* 3, no. 1 (1977): 101–12.
Metcalf, Barbara Daly. *Islamic Revival in British India: Deoband, 1860–1900*. Princeton, N.J.: Princeton University Press, 1982.
——— "Nationalism, Modernity, and Muslim Identity in India before 1947." In *Nation and Religion*. Princeton, N.J.: Princeton University Press, 1999.
Mukta, Parita. *Upholding the Common Life: The Community of Mirabai*. Delhi: Oxford University Press, 1997.
Munson, Henry. *Religion and Power in Morocco*. New Haven, Conn.: Yale University Press, 1993.
An-Naim, Abdullahi Ahmed. *Toward an Islamic Reformation: Civil Liberties, Human Rights, and International Law*. Syracuse: Syracuse University Press, 1996.
O'Fahey, Rex. *The Enigmatic Saint: Ahmad ibn Idris and the Idrisi Tradition*. Evanston, Ill.: Northwestern University Press, 1990.
O'Neill, John. *Five Bodies: The Human Shape of Modern Society*. Ithaca, N.J.: Cornell University Press, 1985.
Petroff, Elizabeth Alvilda. *Body and Soul: Essays on Medieval Women and Mysticism*. New York: Oxford University Press, 1994.
Radtke, Bernd. *Al-Hakim al-Tirmidhi, ein islamisher theosoph des 3/9 jahrhunderts*. Freiburg: Klaus Schwarz Verlag, 1980.
Radtke, Bernd, and John O'Kane. *The Concept of Sainthood in Early Islamic Mysticism*. Surrey: Curzon Press, 1996.
Ramakrishna. *Punjabi Sufi Poets: A.D. 1460–1900*. New Delhi: Ashajanak Publications, 1973.
Rizvi, S. A. A. *History of Sufism in India*. 2 vols. Delhi: Munshiram Manoharlal, 1989.
——— "Sufis and Natha Yogis in Medieval North India." *Journal of the Oriental Society of Australia* 7 (1970): 119–33.
Robb, Graham. *Strangers: Homosexual Love in the 19th Century*. London: Picador, 2003.
Rumi, Jala al-Din. *The Mathnawi of Jalaluddin Rumi*. Edited and translated by Reynold Nicholson. 8 vols. London: Messrs Luzac & Co., 1925–40.
Safi, Omid, ed. *Progressive Muslims: On Gender, Justice and Pluralism*. Oxford: Oneworld, 2003.

Salameh-Amri, Nelly. "Écriture hagiographique et modèles de sainteté dans l'Ifrikiye Hafside 8–9th siècles / 14–15th C.E." *Cotures de Tunisie* 173, no. 2 (1996): 13–31.
Sandnes, Karl Olav. *Belly and Body in Pauline Epistles*. Cambridge: Cambridge University Press, 2002.
Schimmel, Annemarie. *Deciphering the Signs of God: A Phenomenological Approach to Islam*. Albany: State University of New York Press, 1994.
Sells, Michael. *Approaching in the Qur'an: The Early Revelations*. Ashland, Ore.: White Cloud Press, 1999.
Shaikh, Sa'diyya. *Spiritual Cartographies of Gender: Ibn Arabi and Sufi Discourses of Gender, Sexuality and Marriage*. Ph.D. diss., Temple University, 2004.
Simsar, Muhammed, trans. *Ṭūṭī-Nāma: Tales of a Parrot by Ziya' u'd-Din Nakhshabi*. Cleveland: Cleveland Museum of Art, 1978.
Strathern, Andrew. *Body Thoughts*. Ann Arbor: University of Michigan Press, 1996.
Subhan, John. *Sufism: Its Saints and Shrines*. Lucknow: Lucknow Publishing House, 1960.
Al-Sulamī, Abu Abd al-Rahman. *The Subtleties of the Ascension*. Translated and edited by Frederick Colby. Louisville, Ky.: Fons Vitae, 2006.
Suvorova, Anna. *Muslim Saints of South Asia: The Eleventh to Fifteenth Centuries*. London: Routledge Curzon, 1999.
Syed, Najm Hosain. *Recurrent Patterns in Punjabi Poetry*. Lahore: Majlis Shah Husain, 1968.
Synnott, Anthony. *The Body Social: Symbolism, Self and Society*. New York: Routledge, 1993.
Taha, Mahmoud. *The Second Message of Islam*. Syracuse: Syracuse University Press, 1996.
Tarafdar, M. R. "An Indigenous Source for Bengali Sufism." In Anna Libera Dallapiccola and Stephanie Lallemant, eds., *Islam and Indian Regions*. Stuttgart: Franz Steiner Verlag, 1993.
Thomassen, Einar, and Bernd Radtke, trans. *The Letters of Ahmad Ibn Idris*. Evanston, Ill.: Northwestern University Press, 1993.
Turner, Bryan. *The Body and Society*. Oxford: Basil Blackwell, 1984.
Turner, Victor. *From Ritual to Theatre: The Human Seriousness of Play*. New York: Performing Arts Journal Publications, 1982.
Vanita, Ruth, ed. *Queering India: Same-Sex Love and Eroticism in Indian Culture and Society*. New York: Routledge, 2001.
Vanita, Ruth, and Saleem Kidwai, eds. *Same Sex Love in India: Readings from Literature and History*. New York: St. Martin's Press, 2000.
Wadud, Amina. *Qur'an and Woman*. Kuala Lumpur: Penerbit Fajar Bakti, 1992.
Waghorne, Joanne. *The Raja's Magic Clothes: Revisioning Kingship and Divinity in England's India*. Philadelphia: University of Pennsylvania Press, 1994.
Waqar, Azra. "Devotional Songs of Shah Hussain Lahori." *Pakistan Journal of History and Culture* 17, no. 1 (1996): 143–57.
Werbner, Pnina, and Helene Basu, eds. *Embodying Charisma: Modernity, Locality and the Performance of Emotion in Sufi Cults*. London: Routledge, 1998.

INDEX

Note: Arabic (Ar.), Persian (Pr.), and Urdu (Ur.) terms are listed when different words are used for the same term, but terms that are common to all three languages are given without specification. When gender difference is important, both feminine (fem.) and masculine (masc.) forms are given. Names of prophets are spelled as they are commonly spelled in English, and the Arabic equivalent as found in the Qur'ān is provided in parentheses.

Baghdād, 69–70, 72, 216–17, 296 (n. 40)
Bahādur Shāh Ẓafar (emperor of Gujarāt), 163–64
Bahār Khān (Mughal minister), 185, 305 (n. 5)
Bahlūl, Shaykh (brother of Muḥammad Ghawth, also known as Shaykh Phūl), 161
Bakhtin, Mikhail, 97–98
Balkh, 232–33
Banaras, 134
Basant. *See* Spring season
Baṣra, 109, 111
Bāyazīd Bisṭāmī, 134–35, 138
Beauty (*jamāl*), 16, 29, 30, 40, 45, 77, 110, 111, 113, 124, 138, 149, 151, 158, 162, 186, 188, 190, 195, 198, 206, 209–12, 241, 261, 285, 309 (n. 58)
Being (*wujūd*), 131, 134–35, 137, 147, 153, 155–58, 161, 169, 170, 174–75, 211, 224, 230, 233, 234, 255, 287, 289–90, 297 (n. 1), 303 (n. 34)
Being, oneness of (*waḥdat al-wujūd*), 73, 134–35, 147–48, 153, 156–59, 161, 166, 167, 170–71, 173, 174–75, 179, 209–10, 230, 237–38, 246, 286, 291
Bel, Alfred, 116
Belly, 41, 81, 82, 84, 88, 93, 94, 95, 96, 109, 110, 117, 118, 234–37, 245
Berbers (Amazīgh), 13, 54, 55, 61, 63
Berquist, John, 51, 67
Bhakti. *See* Hindu beliefs and writings
Bharōch, 173–74
Bible, 30, 33, 43, 52, 56, 71, 87, 94–95, 287, 314 (n. 32)
Bihār, 241
Biology, 19–20, 22, 24–26, 90, 93, 124, 230, 292, 296 (n. 33)
Birth. *See* Reproduction
Blessing (*baraka*), 60, 70, 99, 110, 112, 126, 161, 178, 195, 211, 220, 277, 279–83, 291
Blood, 32, 44, 53, 60, 61, 69, 71, 72, 74, 93, 94, 97, 105, 107, 108, 144, 178, 182, 186, 226, 228, 230, 232, 235–38, 248, 251–52, 260, 291, 294, 300 (n. 24)
Body: burial of, 46–49, 57, 65–69, 76, 79, 220, 240–42, 267, 271, 286–91; death of, 6, 8, 20, 24–25, 34–35, 41–44, 47, 67, 71, 74–75, 83–84, 98, 111, 123, 138, 176, 183, 193, 203, 213, 216, 224–25, 240–42, 258, 265–67, 279, 282, 288, 290, 292; denigration of, 8, 10, 14–15, 19, 20–21, 25, 35, 41, 82, 86–87, 93, 96, 231, 244, 271, 287–88, 290, 296 (n. 44); discipline of, 13, 15, 23, 24, 73, 76, 94–95, 177, 221, 224–26, 231, 234, 236–40, 244–45, 247–49, 252, 255–58, 261, 270; dualism with mind, 12, 21–22, 26, 35, 86–87, 96, 287, 295 (n. 14); engagement with, 22–23, 25–26, 248, 269–70, 292; holistic view of, 16–21, 26, 28, 41, 51, 67, 73, 75, 91, 97, 123, 127, 131, 224, 227–30, 270, 292–94, 298 (n. 35); human, xi–xii, 1–40 passim, 44, 48, 50–53, 56, 63, 67, 79, 81, 87–89, 94–97, 101–7, 123–41 passim, 148–50, 155, 158, 163, 164, 167, 170, 176, 177, 179, 182, 186, 188, 202–4, 215, 221–48 passim, 253, 254, 257, 261–81 passim, 285–94, 295 (n. 9), 296 (n. 33), 297 (n. 1), 302 (n. 4), 314 (n. 48); Islamic discourse about, 8–9, 15–17, 30, 45, 92, 94, 100, 132, 147, 184, 186, 215, 265, 314 (n. 48); movement of , 17–22, 24, 40, 127, 136, 141, 182, 188, 206, 208–9, 218, 222, 224–32, 245, 254, 261, 270; regeneration of, 25, 41, 71; release into, 22–25; restraint of, 22–23, 25–26, 200, 221; techniques of, 10–11, 19, 225–26, 244, 258, 280. *See also* Dance; Embodiment; Rapture; Resurrection
Body politic and polity, 13, 19, 50–52, 55, 60, 67, 75–77, 132–33, 222, 256, 258, 260, 262, 267, 270, 289, 298 (n. 24)
Bones, 41–50, 52, 60–68, 74–79, 83, 86, 201, 270, 281, 287–91, 297 (n. 6); marrow, 9, 61
Bordieu, Pierre, 13
Bouhdiba, Abdelwahhab, 16

Gender, grammatical, xv, 89, 111, 113, 157
Genealogy (*nasab*), 5, 48–50, 55–58, 61, 70–72, 75, 83, 90, 119, 148, 215, 241, 258, 276, 300 (n. 44), 301 (n. 64), 308 (n. 52)
Generosity (*karam*), 5, 69, 106, 131, 176, 221; institutionalized in alms (*zakāt*), 218–19
Genitalia, 40–41, 82, 94–96, 98, 213, 215, 234–36; circumcision, 70
Gēsū-Darāz, Muḥammad Ḥussaynī, 33
Ghawth (the Succor), 121, 125, 132–33, 134, 142, 161, 167, 173–74, 277
Ghawth, Muḥammad Gwāliyōrī, 123, 130–36, 141–51 passim, 156, 158–77, 182, 249–57 passim, 262, 302 (nn. 10, 17, 24), 303 (nn. 29, 36, 39), 304 (nn. 52, 66, 67, 71)
Ghiyāth al-Dīn, Shaykh, 167–69
Gibraltar, 76
Gnostic, 15, 144, 233–35
God: aid from, 125, 133, 161; compassion and mercy of, 82, 140, 143, 145, 149, 151, 160, 162, 169, 230, 233, 239, 274–78, 287; creative activity of, 2, 27–34, 39, 41, 44–45, 57, 73, 81–82, 87–89, 93, 95, 124, 134, 144, 147, 153, 156, 158, 172, 174, 180–81, 194, 224, 233, 235, 237, 246, 248, 265, 287, 289; essential name of, 135, 145, 179, 201, 226–27, 229, 303 (n. 26); grace and care of, 33, 60, 65, 72, 82, 86, 90, 112, 121, 176, 181, 194, 233, 274–75; image of, 30, 33–34, 39, 167, 206, 227, 229, 233–34, 297 (n. 13); immanence of, 4, 30, 32, 39–40, 47–52, 79, 89, 105, 112, 126–27, 134, 167, 170, 174–77, 209, 218, 224, 228, 234, 246, 248–49, 262, 273, 276–77, 291; judgment of, 3, 44, 49, 72, 89, 92, 200, 211, 255, 274–75, 278, 291, 313 (n. 23); love of, 4, 5, 33, 55–58, 84, 100, 101, 109–11, 117, 136, 138, 158–59, 165, 186, 192, 194–95, 205–11, 228–29, 244, 247, 255, 276; manifestation of (theophany), 29, 30, 39, 49, 51, 79, 151, 209, 222, 224, 227, 234, 240, 242, 270, 273, 293, 303 (n. 28); might and wrath of, 140, 142, 145, 149–53, 155, 158, 162, 274, 281, 283; names (*asmā*ʾ) of and attributes and qualities (*ṣifāt*) of, 4, 29, 32–34, 39–40, 73, 82, 126, 130–31, 135, 148, 151–58, 162, 201, 209, 226–27, 233–34, 270, 274; omniscience of, 27, 29, 32–33, 35, 43, 112, 123, 143, 150, 159, 269, 274; presence of, 49–50, 73, 136, 137, 150, 155–57, 167, 181, 222, 229, 234, 237, 238, 242, 248–49, 254–55, 258, 262, 270–71, 277–78, 288, 293; signs and messages of, 2, 123–24, 126, 138, 140, 149, 152, 237, 241–42, 270, 273, 274, 281, 283, 287–88, 297 (n. 8); transcendence of, 4, 30, 39, 51, 89–90, 151, 156, 209, 228, 230, 233–34, 262, 269, 278; understanding of, 6, 39, 134, 157, 186, 192, 227–29, 233, 235, 253–54; will of, 5, 32–33, 48, 52, 59, 64, 76, 81, 106, 107, 110–12, 135, 141, 161, 176, 178, 193, 236, 254, 261, 265, 270
Goliath of the Philistines or Canaanites, 48–50
Gospel. *See* Bible
Granada, 69
Greece. *See* Hellenic culture
Greed, 94–95, 201, 219, 235, 279
Guide, spiritual (*murshid* or *shaykh*), 26–28, 47, 82–83, 102, 116, 133, 138, 140, 162, 177–78, 185–87, 191–92, 202, 204, 208–9, 224, 226, 233, 256, 261, 263, 275, 277, 292–94, 311 (n. 41)
Gujarāt, 162–66, 168, 173, 177, 206, 302 (n. 9), 306 (n. 25)
Gulbarga, 33
Gwāliyōr, 124, 174–75, 303 (n. 39)

Habitus, 10, 13, 241
Ḥadīth (sayings of Muḥammad), 36, 40, 56, 90, 91, 127, 130, 151, 152, 164–66, 171, 176–77, 216, 232, 252, 257, 262,

Qaṣr Kutāma, 106
Queer theory, 13, 121, 183–84, 195–96, 199, 208–9
Qur'an or God's Speech, xii, xv, 1–9, 26–38 passim, 43–46, 48–50, 52, 56, 58, 63, 73, 81, 82, 87–93, 112, 113, 124–27, 130, 141, 144, 164, 171, 173–76, 181, 184–86, 195, 200, 211, 214–17, 221, 224, 228, 232, 233, 235, 237, 241, 242, 252–54, 261–89 passim, 295 (n. 1), 301 (n. 52), 302 (nn. 9, 10), 309 (n. 65), 310 (n. 10), 311 (n. 36), 312 (n. 12), 313 (n. 22), 314 (n. 48)

Rābiʿa al-ʿAdawiyya, 109–12
Rā<u>dh</u>a, 206–7
Radtke, Bernt, 269, 310 (n. 19)
Rainbow, 147, 291
Ramakrishna, Lajwanti, 197, 199, 307 (nn. 28, 29), 308 (n. 52)
Rān<u>jh</u>ā and Hīr, 207, 308 (n. 50)
Rapture, 7, 22–27, 69, 71–76, 100, 115, 165–68, 175, 181, 186, 188, 191–94, 203, 206, 210, 220, 221, 227, 234, 236, 238, 244, 254, 258
Rāsa (vital fluid), 244–45
Rāshid (vice-regent to Mawlay Idrīs al-Azhar), 54–55
Rās Khān, 206
Rās-līlā, 189–90, 205–7, 210
Reason (*ʿaql*), ix, 4–5, 9–14, 33, 35, 73, 84, 86–87, 91–95, 100–111 passim, 119, 127, 130, 142, 155, 172, 185, 189, 205–6, 215, 217, 227, 233, 235, 266, 271–73, 284, 287, 296 (n. 40), 313 (n. 12), 314 (n. 48)
Recitation, 22, 27, 32, 54, 112, 124, 135, 226, 270; of God's names (*dhikr*), 135, 179, 201, 226–32, 242, 250–53, 257–59, 262, 279
Refinement, spiritual (*taraqqī*), 34, 56, 127, 141–42, 156, 179, 185, 194, 205, 229–30, 243, 293
Reform, 84, 86, 223, 259–60, 262, 268, 270, 278, 288, 296 (n. 30)
Relic, 46, 48–51, 239, 291, 297 (n. 8)
Religious studies, 8–9, 12, 16, 19, 53, 204–5
Renunciation, 3, 5, 83–84, 95, 131, 138, 162, 199–200, 203, 233, 299 (n. 2)
Reproduction, 23, 34, 54, 64, 81–83, 88–95, 98, 116, 120–21, 200, 235, 237. *See also* Womb
Responsibility (*khilāfa*), 32–33, 88, 91, 92, 105, 200, 211, 221
Resurrection (*qiyāma*), 4, 34, 43–45, 97, 265–66
Retreat, devotional (Ar. *khalwa*, Pr. and Ur. *chilla*), 28, 47, 136, 137, 139, 142, 159, 167–69, 198, 233, 239, 243, 279, 298 (n. 39)
Revolt, rebellion, and revolution, 4, 48–49, 52, 60, 68, 76, 104, 120, 140, 141, 151, 181–84, 202, 208, 211, 218–20, 259, 270–72, 280–81, 286, 313 (n. 23)
Rhetoric. *See* Metaphor and analogy
Ritual, 15, 24, 26, 29, 46–47, 51, 63, 72, 75, 79, 99, 101, 102, 105, 107, 135, 161, 177–79, 195, 198–99, 204–6, 222, 224–31, 240, 242, 246, 249, 253, 256, 262, 263, 269, 271, 274, 282, 313 (n. 23)
Rivers, 38, 44, 142, 147, 191, 200, 207
Rizvi, Sayyid Athar Abbas, 243
Robertson, Elizabeth, 107
Roman, 62–63, 94
Rudawlī, Aḥmad ʿAbd al-Ḥaqq, 240–43, 311 (n. 41); tomb of, 241
Rūmī, Mawlānā Jalāl al-Dīn, 194, 308 (n. 55)

Al-Sabʿ, Saʿīd, 115
Ṣābir, ʿAlāʾ al-Dīn ʿAlī, 238–40, 310 (n. 30), 311 (n. 31). *See also* Chishtī Sufi way: Ṣābirī community
Sacred (quality of being), 8–9, 21, 29, 46, 50–53, 56, 61, 64, 66, 68, 74–79, 99, 106, 107, 177, 182, 194, 204–5, 211, 224, 265, 267, 271, 277, 279, 281, 288–91
Sacrifice, 25, 44, 52, 53, 148, 277, 297 (n. 1)

Saʿdian dynasty, 76, 77, 105, 106, 107, 108, 116–17, 298 (n. 24)
Saʿdullah, 185–86, 211
Safavid dynasty, 218–19
Safi, Omid, xiii, 313 (n. 28)
Saint, axial (masc. *quṭb*, fem. *quṭba*, plural *aqṭāb*), 110–11, 113–14, 117, 125, 161, 238
Saints, Muslim, xii, 1, 5–8, 15, 45–47, 52–54, 57–58, 66–79 passim, 83, 85, 101, 110, 113, 115, 118, 120, 134, 142, 143, 148–51, 155–61, 165, 166, 179, 183, 185, 187, 208–9, 220, 223, 247, 259, 266, 271, 275, 278, 280–84, 288, 289, 305 (n. 5), 306 (n. 22); sainthood, 253–56, 258, 262–63, 267, 275–76, 281, 285–86, 291, 295 (n. 1)
Saliva, 110, 182, 189, 195, 245
Salvation (*najāt*) and liberation, 50, 56, 72, 112, 161, 192, 206, 245–46, 274, 278
Samarqand, 131
Samuel, 48–49
Sanskrit, 27, 133, 244, 247, 311 (n. 48)
Al-Sanūsī, Muḥammad ibn ʿAlī, 270
Sarandīp (Sri Lanka), 282
Satīdāsa Rām<u>bh</u>āī, "ʿArif," 247–48
Al-Saʿūd tribe, 272
Saul (Tālūt), 48–50, 63
Secret (*sirr*), 40, 58, 71, 101, 132, 138, 152, 161, 166, 169, 172, 179, 182, 188, 192, 203, 204, 219, 222, 229, 232, 241–42, 248–50, 293, 304 (n. 66)
Self-recognition, xi, 28–29
Self-righteousness, 5, 200, 204
Selim I (Ottoman emperor), 270–71
Sells, Michael, 89, 124, 295 (n. 2)
Semen, 244–46, 265. *See also* Orgasm
Sensory perception, 13, 21, 25, 35, 40, 52, 75, 79, 99, 123–25, 132, 137, 144, 160, 181, 182, 189, 221, 226, 227, 235, 245, 248, 257; sensory deprivation, 22
Sexuality, 5–27 passim, 35, 39, 40, 58, 84, 88–101 passim, 144–45, 158, 181–87, 191–201, 205–6, 209–10, 218–19, 221–22, 233, 234–36, 239, 244–45, 267, 296 (n. 33), 299 (n. 2), 303 (n. 26), 305 (n. 4), 309 (n. 58); opposite-sex orientation, 8, 19, 88, 183–84, 196–97, 210, 213, 215–16, 309 (n. 62); same-sex orientation, 8, 14, 183–84, 187, 191–99, 205–10, 212–16, 218–20, 267, 305 (n. 4), 306 (nn. 22, 24, 25), 307 (nn. 28–30), 308 (n. 55), 309 (n. 63); sexual penetration, 213–19, 309 (n. 63)
Shackle, Christopher, 199, 305 (n. 3)
Al-Shādhilī, Abū'l-Ḥasan, 99, 110, 113–14
Shādhilī Sufi way, xiii, 99, 110, 113, 114, 270, 300 (nn. 27, 44)
Shāhid-bāzī (playing the witness), 209–10
Sharīʿa. *See* Law, Islamic
Sharīf (plural *shurafāʾ*) (descendent of Muḥammad), 53–76 passim, 83, 104, 106, 113, 148, 269, 271, 275, 278, 298 (nn. 24, 25, 27), 300 (n. 44), 301 (n. 64)
Shaṭṭār, Shāh ʿAbdullah, 130, 302 (n. 9), 311 (n. 38)
Shaṭṭārī, Burhān al-Dīn, 242–43, 311 (n. 38)
Shaṭṭārī Sufi way, 125, 130–31, 134–35, 141, 143, 157–67 passim, 172–73, 176, 182, 242–43, 249, 253, 257, 260, 262, 302 (nn. 9, 17), 303 (n. 36), 305 (n. 2), 306 (n. 25), 311 (nn. 38, 48)
Shayṭān (plural *shayāṭīn*). *See* Iblīs
Shiʿa, 3, 55, 143, 148, 218–19, 272, 278, 287, 314 (n. 46)
Al-Shiblī, 72, 73
Shrine, 43–53 passim, 57, 59–60, 64, 69, 78–79, 83, 115, 174, 185, 259, 261–62, 267, 269, 271, 278, 280, 283, 291, 297 (n. 5)
Sickness, 20, 25, 70, 71, 104, 277
Sight, 1, 28, 29, 52, 79, 123–27, 131–37, 139, 142, 145, 147, 149, 155–57, 177, 179, 182, 188–89, 191, 198, 203, 209, 212–13, 227, 233–34, 241, 242, 265–66, 269–70,

ISLAMIC CIVILIZATION

& MUSLIM NETWORKS

Scott Kugle

Sufis and Saints' Bodies:
Mysticism, Corporeality, and Sacred Power in Islam
2007

Roxani Eleni Margariti

Aden and the Indian Ocean Trade:
150 Years in the Life of a Medieval Arabian Port
2006

Sufia M. Uddin

Constructing Bangladesh:
Religion, Ethnicity, and Language in an Islamic Nation
2006

Omid Safi

The Politics of Knowledge in Premodern Islam:
Negotiating Ideology and Religious Inquiry
2006

Ebrahim Moosa

Ghazālī and the Poetics of Imagination
2005

miriam cooke and Bruce B. Lawrence, eds.

Muslim Networks from Hajj to Hip Hop
2005

Carl W. Ernst

Following Muhammad:
Rethinking Islam in the Contemporary World
2003